Character Begins at Home:

Family Tools for Teaching Character and Values

by Karen D. Olsen and Sue Pearson

Illustrated by Gwendolyn Pribble

Character Begins at Home:
Family Tools for Teaching Character and Values

by Karen D. Olsen and Sue Pearson

© 2000 Susan J. Kovalik
Printed in the United States of America
ISBN 1-878631-61-6

Copy Editor: Kathleen Wolgemuth
Graphics: Gwendolyn Pribble
Cover Design: Marni Erwin
Layout and Design: Kristina Roe

Published by: Susan Kovalik & Associates, Inc.
Distributed by: Books For Educators, Inc.
17051 SE 272nd Street, Suite 18
Kent, Washington 98042
Phone: 888/777-9827
Fax: 253/630-7215
www.books4educ.com

All rights reserved. No part of this publication may be reproduced, stored in a retrieval system, or transmitted in any form or by any means, electronic, mechanical, photocopying, recording or otherwise, without the prior permission of the publisher.

Dedication

To all the children and their families

who have taught us how much they want and appreciate

learning character, values, and attitudes

through the ITI Lifelong Guidelines and LIFESKILLS.

~ ~ ~

To my mother, Dulcie Brown, whose great wisdom and unfailing love

for children—those in her classroom and at home—

shine through these pages.

Thank you for your presence in my life.

It is a privilege to share your wisdom and love with

the readers of this book. May their lives and the lives of their children

be enriched as mine has been.

Karen D. Olsen

Acknowledgements

To all who helped give birth to the precursor of this book, *Tools for Citizenship and Life: Using the ITI Lifelong Guidelines & LIFESKILLS in Your Classroom*, we again gratefully acknowledge your wisdom and support. We especially wish to thank the tens of thousands of ITI students around the world for their overwhelming endorsement of the Lifelong Guidelines and LIFESKILLS. From preschool age to high school seniors, they remind us that we all yearn for a sense of community, a place in which we are free of unpleasantness and threat, a place in which we can safely become the people we were meant to be. They recognized the power of the Lifelong Guidelines and LIFESKILLS to create just such an environment in their classrooms and carried the message home.

We thank, too, the hundreds of parents who have shared their experiences with us as they worked with the ITI Lifelong Guidelines and LIFESKILLS at home. Their joys and triumphs convinced us that this book—just for parents and families—must be written.

Thank you one and all.

Karen D. Olsen
Sue Pearson

Table of Contents

Dedication i

Acknowledgements ii

Table of Contents iii

Foreword v

Introduction vii

Chapter 1— Welcome to the ITI Lifelong Guidelines and LIFESKILLS 1.1-1.4

Chapter 2—Trustworthiness 2.1-2.12

Chapter 3—Truthfulness 3.1-3.10

Chapter 4—Active Listening 4.1-4.14

Chapter 5—No Put-Downs 5.1-5.10

Chapter 6—Personal Best 6.1-6.12

Chapter 7—Caring 7.1-7.12

Chapter 8—Common Sense 8.1-8.12

Chapter 9—Cooperation 9.1-9.14

Chapter 10—Courage 10.1-10.12

Chapter 11—Curiosity 11.1-11.12

Chapter 12—Effort 12.1-12.12

Chapter 13—Flexibility 13.1-13.12

Chapter 14—Friendship 14.1-14.16

Chapter 15—Initiative 15.1-15.12

Chapter 16—Integrity 16.1-16.12

Chapter 17—Organization 17.1-17.18

Chapter 18—Patience 18.1-18.14

Chapter 19—Perseverance 19.1-19.14

Chapter 20—Pride 20.1-20.10

Chapter 21—Problem Solving 21.1-21.12

Chapter 22—Resourcefulness 22.1-22.12

Chapter 23—Responsibility 23.1-23.12

Chapter 24—Sense of Humor 24.1-24.12

Chapter 25—Parents As Teachers: Tips of the Trade 25.1-25.12

Chapter 26—Getting Started 26.1-26.10

Appendix A A.1-A.4

Appendix B A.5-A.8

Book Lists— L.1-L.8

Bibliography— B.1-B.2

Index— I.1

Order Form

Foreword

Parents are their children's first teachers. They are the early teachers of habits of mind—character, values, attitudes, and behaviors—that last throughout one's lifetime. Because these habits are so powerful in setting the course of a young person's life, parents and other family members should carefully examine and rethink what they want to pass on to the next generation. This book is designed to help you do just that. You'll find a chapter for each Lifelong Guideline and LIFESKILL. Each describes what that Lifelong Guideline/LIFESKILL is, why it is important, how to implement it, what it looks like in and outside the home, and specific activities to practice it at home. Also included are recommended books, literature for your child, and resources for you in your role as teacher.

The aspects of character, values, and attitudes addressed in this book come not from a religious context but rather from considering the qualities citizens must possess to fully and effectively participate in nurturing our democratic society. They are universally admired characteristics. Without them, a democratic society cannot long survive nor can family life provide the supportive, nurturing environment children need and deserve. The five Lifelong Guidelines are: Trustworthiness, Truthfulness, Active Listening, No Put-Downs, and Personal Best. Personal Best is defined by 18 LIFESKILLS: Integrity, Responsibility, Common Sense, Problem Solving, Organization, Resourcefulness, Effort, Perseverance, Sense of Humor, Initiative, Curiosity, Courage, Flexibility, Patience, Friendship, Caring, Cooperation, and Pride.

This book is designed to assist you and your family in teaching these skills and values to your child. It provides a menu of resources that can be added to what you are already using to teach your child important lessons about life.

If your child attends a school currently implementing the Kovalik ITI* model schoolwide, these same Lifelong Guidelines and LIFESKILLS are being used in your child's classroom. This book will assist you in understanding your child's experiences at school and thus help you form a strong partnership with your child's teacher. You will discover that these Lifelong Guidelines and LIFESKILLS are the basis for interaction among students, between students and adults, and among adults. They are also used instead of "discipline" programs because, except in extreme cases, misbehavior is usually the result of children not knowing enough appropriate behaviors (or when to use them) and/or knowing too many inappropriate behaviors. In the ITI model, misbehavior is viewed first as a teaching opportunity rather than as a "discipline" event. This perspective results in high expectations and accelerated student performance in both behavior and academic achievement.

---

* The ITI model (Integrated Thematic Instruction) was developed by Susan Kovalik more than 20 years ago and is annually updated to align with emerging brain research. See Appendix A to identify the ITI text for your grade level. Each text describes the brain research concepts that constitute the core of the model as well as how to implement these concepts in common sense, powerful ways.

This view of misbehavior does not mean, however, that there shouldn't be consequences for such behavior. Disrupting class, disrespectful acts or harming another person (physically or verbally) should never be allowed. Children must learn behaviors that will work in adult life. We all need the opportunity to learn from our mistakes and choose more appropriate strategies to handle similar situations in the future. I believe that the Lifelong Guidelines and LIFESKILLS help young people grow in wisdom and spirit.

Welcome to the Lifelong Guidelines and LIFESKILLS.

Susan Kovalik

Introduction

When trying to put something together, do you always read the directions first, even before you take anything out of the box? Or, like members of the authors' families, do you first dump the contents of the box on the ground and look for logical connections, only reading the directions when all else fails? Whatever your approach, compare this book to a carpenter's toolbox filled with a variety of tools. Use whichever ones will support your job as a family member helping your child build character and develop values.

HOW TO USE THIS BOOK

Jump right in! If you want to look ahead to the LIFESKILL of Sense of Humor before reading about the Lifelong Guideline of Active Listening, jump to that chapter. Start with what you think will be most beneficial for you and your child now. Do *not* treat this book like a textbook to be read mechanically, page by page. You are in charge here. You are doing this for your child. Shape it to fit his/her needs and the current activities of your family.

Browse First

By glancing through each section, you'll notice the same pattern of presentation for every Lifelong Guideline and LIFESKILL topic. This is by design, intended to make the book "user-friendly." These headings include:

- The name of the Lifelong Guideline or LIFESKILL

- An appropriate quotation

- A definition from *Webster's Ninth New Collegiate Dictionary*

- The "kid friendly" definition from the Kovalik ITI model

- What is_____? (what that Lifelong Guideline or LIFESKILL is)

- Why practice_____? (why that Lifelong Guideline or LIFESKILL is important in life)

- How do you practice_____?

- What does_____look like in the real world?

- How does _____look at home? (for children and adults)

- Opportunities to practice_____?

- Signs of success (for adults and children)
- Literature links to____(books to read to your child and resources for you as his/her most influential teacher)

A Word About Opportunities to Practice

The Opportunities to Practice, or activities, in each chapter are written with your child as audience. In other words, they are written as directions to the child to guide him/her through an opportunity to practice using the Lifelong Guideline or LIFESKILL discussed in that chapter. You can read the activities to your child or have him/her read them. We expect that there are some inquiries that you will use as written, others you will want to modify, and still others that will be replaced by activities of your own design. Our hope is that you and your child will begin to write your own Opportunities to Practice so that living the Lifelong Guidelines and LIFESKILLS will become an everyday habit of mind.

IT IS NOT WHAT WE SAY

We teach from who they are. It is not what we say that changes the lives of our children, it is what we do, what we model. As parents and family members, we must "walk our talk"—match our behavior with our words. How we choose to live our lives minute-by-minute is how we teach character, values, and attitudes.

Co-author Karen Olsen remembers walking into her mother's house one day and hearing peels of laughter coming from her mother and her mother's sister. They were laughing about how they were "becoming their mother" as they aged—despite the fact that my grandmother was a very difficult woman to be around at times. What had been modeled during their impressionable, growing-up years had slept just below the surface for 40 years. In little ways, here and there, it had begun to seep through—little mannerisms, turns of phrase, a reaction to this or that. After laughing along with them, it suddenly struck Karen that this wasn't funny at all! How much of her grandmother's not-so-nice qualities would seep through to her along with the good ones? Yikes! Lucky are those whose parents modeled the character, values, and attitudes that helped guide us to take the higher road in life.

Parents on Center Stage

Given today's pressures and hectic pace, it's harder than ever for us to model character, values, and attitudes. It's also harder to compete with outside influences that cut across the grain of what we're trying to model for our children.

In this book, we stress the invaluable contribution you make to the future success and well-being of your child as you consciously model the character attributes, values, and attitudes you want your children to emulate. Use the information to keep yourself on center stage modeling what you want to pass on to your children.

Welcome to the ITI Lifelong Guidelines and LIFESKILLS

Chapter 1

WHAT ARE THE ITI LIFELONG GUIDELINES AND LIFESKILLS?

Emotions play a critical role in learning. According to Dr. Robert Sylwester of the University of Oregon, "Emotions drive attention and attention drives learning and memory."* Therefore, the quality and nature of the relationships between parent and child and among siblings are vital factors for all learning, including development of character, values, and attitudes. The behavior guidelines of the ITI model are based upon a common-sense respect for self and others. They provide consistent boundaries and expectations for one's behavior and performance—now and as an adult. They are thus referred to as "lifelong" guidelines.

LIFELONG GUIDELINES

TRUSTWORTHINESS: To act in a manner that makes one worthy of trust and confidence

TRUTHFULNESS: To act with personal responsibility and mental accountability

ACTIVE LISTENING: To listen with the intention of understanding what the speaker means to communicate

NO PUT-DOWNS: To never use words, actions, and/or body language that degrade, humiliate, or dishonor others

PERSONAL BEST: To do one's best given the circumstances and available resources

---

* See *A Celebration of Neurons: An Educator's Guide to the Human Brain* by Dr. Robert Sylwester (Alexandria, VA: ASCD Publications, 1995), p. 86.

Just imagine what a better place the world would be if each family member, neighbor, co-worker and boss—everyone—would practice and live by these guidelines! It would be so easy if we could be like Jack in the Beanstalk and give each child five magic pills every morning—one for each Lifelong Guideline—and then watch the character traits grow. However, there is no magic here—just consistency and perseverance. It begins first in the home and then, hopefully, is carried on in our schools.

WHAT ARE THE LIFESKILLS?

The LIFESKILLS define the Lifelong Guideline of Personal Best. According to Susan Kovalik, in her book, *ITI: The Model*, the purpose of the LIFESKILLS is to guide children to an understanding of the personal and social behaviors that will enable them to do their personal best and thus enhance the likelihood that they will succeed in attaining their goals in life and in becoming contributing members to society.* The 18 LIFESKILLS, described on the next page, paint a rich and concrete picture of what it means to do one's personal best. If children want to succeed at something, the LIFESKILLS give them a blueprint for how to proceed, how to give something their best shot.

DO THEY LOOK FAMILIAR?

As you read through the list of Lifelong Guidelines and LIFESKILLS, you may have thought, "These are the things my mom and dad were always reminding me to follow when I was growing up." Your parents were right: These skills are definitely the building blocks for success in life.

The Lifelong Guidelines and LIFESKILLS also answer the question, "Who are the heroes in your life and what are the qualities about them that you admire?" Today, more than ever, children need heroes that demonstrate the qualities necessary for living a full and successful life, personally and as a contributing citizen. What better heroes than parents!

Also, as noted in the Foreword by Susan Kovalik, the aspects of character, values, and attitudes addressed in this book come not from a religious context but rather from the qualities citizens must possess to fully and effectively participate in nurturing our democratic society. They are universally admired characteristics. Without them, a democratic society cannot long survive nor can family life provide the supportive, nurturing environment children need and deserve. This book provides you, the parent, with a handbook to help students grow and become the kinds of people we would like for our next-door neighbor, friend, spouse, co-worker, and fellow citizen.

---

* See *ITI: The Model, Integrated Thematic Instruction, Third Edition* by Susan Kovalik with Karen Olsen (Kent, WA: Susan Kovalik & Associates, Inc., 1997), p. 29. For more information about the Kovalik ITI model used in public, private, and parochial schools across the U.S. and many countries around the world, see www.kovalik.com

LIFESKILLS

CARING: To feel and show concern for others

COMMON SENSE: To use good judgment

COOPERATION: To work together toward a common goal or purpose

COURAGE: To act according to one's beliefs despite fear of adverse consequences

CURIOSITY: A desire to investigate and seek understanding of one's world

EFFORT: To do your best

FLEXIBILITY: To be willing to alter plans when necessary

FRIENDSHIP: To make and keep a friend through mutual trust and caring

INITIATIVE: To do something, of one's own free will, because it needs to be done

INTEGRITY: To act according to a sense of what's right and wrong

ORGANIZATION: To plan, arrange, and implement in an orderly way; to keep things orderly and ready to use

PATIENCE: To wait calmly for someone or something

PERSEVERANCE: To keep at it

PRIDE: Satisfaction from doing one's personal best

PROBLEM SOLVING: To create solutions to difficult situations and everyday problems

RESOURCEFULNESS: To respond to challenges and opportunities in innovative and creative ways

RESPONSIBILITY: To respond when appropriate; to be accountable for one's actions

SENSE OF HUMOR: To laugh and be playful without harming others

TOOLS FOR TEACHING AND USING THE LIFELONG GUIDELINES AND LIFESKILLS

Tools and tips for teaching and using the Lifelong Guidelines and LIFESKILLS are discussed in Chapters 25 and 26. Before you begin, however, take time to assess your own personal understanding of the Lifelong Guidelines and LIFESKILLS. Which ones are you strong in? Are you not as strong as you could be in some? Remember, these behavior guidelines are something you must live and model, not just "teach" about.

The Importance of Self-Evaluation

Evaluate yourself in relation to each of the Lifelong Guidelines and the LIFESKILLS. Where do your strengths lie? Which skills need work? If you're like the authors of this book, some of the Lifelong Guidelines and LIFESKILLS made us squirm. Organization? Egad! When working on the chapter about the LIFESKILL of Organization, both of us had to jump up from our computers and start organizing and cleaning our office areas (both of us write at home) and, eventually, the entire house. You can't just talk about these; you have to do them!

And, there is no vacation. Once you embark on using the Lifelong Guidelines and LIFESKILLS, do not stop. Don't expect to teach them once and be done. As children grow and mature, application of the Lifelong Guidelines/LIFESKILLS should deepen. All of us are a work in progress—development of character, values, and attitudes is a lifelong journey full of daily challenges and delights.

Trustworthiness

Chapter 2

"OTHERS HAVE CONFIDENCE IN ME."

trustworthiness *n* **1a:** worthy of confidence: dependable
trust *n* **1a:** assured reliance on the character, ability, strength, or truth of someone or something **b:** one in whom confidence is placed

Trustworthiness: To act in a manner that makes one worthy of confidence and trust

WHAT IS TRUSTWORTHINESS?

If we were artists commissioned to paint a piece representing the Lifelong Guideline of Trustworthiness, we would choose for our model a mother rocking her infant child, the baby's eyes intently studying her mother's face, a tiny hand reaching up to touch her mother's cheek. The purest form of trust in life is child to mother. The mother provides food when the child is hungry, warmth when cold, and comfort when hurt. This relationship between mother and baby is a child's first experience with trustworthiness.

Yet we know there are other pictures in which food is late or lacking, comfort is in short supply, and warmth is missing. What do such babies begin to learn about trustworthiness? They learn that "people in my world are not reliable." Such early experiences with family and caretakers can impair a child's ability to have confidence in other people.

Trustworthiness: An Umbrella in Stormy Weather

Trustworthiness, identified by specific attributes such as reliability and dependability, is vital because it is an umbrella under which we protect ourselves from stormy weather. Each one of us needs at least one such umbrella for protection—a parent or close family member with whom we can talk and know that our words will go no further. We need to trust that those close to us will adhere to the principles represented in the Lifelong Guidelines and LIFESKILLS. Likewise, we need to be an umbrella of protection for other people by providing confidentiality, steadiness, and support during those occasional drizzles, steady rains, and torrential downpours that life presents.

Trustworthiness Is a Double-Sided Coin

But trustworthiness is more than an umbrella that we use as we seek out those who are trustworthy, safe, and comfortable to be with. Trustworthiness is a double-sided coin, a two-way street. It isn't just what we receive; we in turn must be trustworthy for others. Children must be taught that they can't expect the gift of trustworthiness from others if they are not trustworthy in return.

Parents, as their child's first teacher, must teach both sides of the Lifelong Guideline of Trustworthiness—how to give it as well as how to receive it. Implicit in this is teaching the child the sign posts for recognizing this characteristic in others. Who really deserves their trust and won't take advantage? How do they extend their trust so that relationships of all levels can deepen and enrich their lives?

WHY PRACTICE TRUSTWORTHINESS?

The Lifelong Guideline of Trustworthiness forms the basis of relationships—effective working partnerships, close friendships, healthy family bonds, and the long-lasting intimate relationship of husband and wife. Simply put, if people can't trust us, they don't want to be around us—it's too risky. The lower the level of our trustworthiness, the more distant people remain from us. Yet, because few pursuits in life are solitary and most goals require the participation of others, if we are to succeed in our goals, we must become a trustworthy person.

At Work

The higher the stakes, the more crucial trustworthiness becomes. Consider these examples of everyday work environments in which our trustworthiness and ability to work as a team can have life-and-death or life-changing impact: designing seal rings for the space shuttle booster rocket, solving safety design problems on a Boeing aircraft assembly line, and doing customer service in a small business into which its owner has invested his/her entire life savings. Trustworthiness makes a difference in the lives of all of us.

Are our co-workers confident that we are dependable (the job gets done), consistent (high quality of work), and reliable (follow directions and meet deadlines)? Does our supervisor feel confident and secure when assigning tasks to us, working on projects with us, or discussing confidential information with us?

As our trustworthiness grows, we are more likely to be included in upper-level planning and decision making, a key element in worker satisfaction in the workplace, and the more likely we are to be promoted to better-paying, more satisfying positions.

At Home

Close relationships of any kind, but particularly the intimacy of marriage and the primacy of parent-child bonds, cannot exist without trustworthiness. It is the cornerstone of respect and liking. One can love someone without liking and respecting them—a common burden of children abused by their parents. It is also the source of one's sense of security, safety, and confidence.

A key ingredient of trustworthiness in the home is emotional consistency—that the child knows the parent loves him/her and that the parent's emotional and physical behaviors are consistent with that love, that no matter what else happens, the child knows he/she will be safe with the parent.

For Children

When children feel safe and secure, they are free to learn and grow emotionally because the bodybrain* can focus on learning. There is no need to act out, clamor for attention, or be stuck with regrets or bad feelings. They are free to explore, fully, thoughtfully, and responsibly.

It is important to recognize that trustworthiness develops in stages. Expectations of trustworthiness for five-year olds should differ from expectations for fifteen-year olds.**

HOW DO YOU PRACTICE TRUSTWORTHINESS?

Trustworthiness begins with how we treat ourselves. Do we do what we promise ourself we will do? Are we developing the skills and knowledge necessary to accomplish what we say we want to do? Are we honest with ourselves? Do our actions match our words?

Children practice being trustworthy with others by not abusing others' trust; they don't tell secrets, ignore deadlines, spread rumors, talk behind backs, lie, cheat, steal, or exhibit any of the other behaviors that would abuse trust.

Making Wise Choices

Trustworthiness is the result of making wise choices over time. The ability to do so, however, isn't automatic. It takes practice, in the midst of which we make mistakes—lots of them! Do you remember some of these situations from your own childhood experiences? One friend shares a

---

* Technology has led today's brain researchers to the same conclusion the Greeks surmised 2,000 years ago: the body and brain are connected, in fact, inseparable. For a riveting discussion of the bodybrain partnership, see *Molecules of Emotion: Why We Feel the Way We Feel* by Candace Pert, Ph.D. For practical applications, see *ITI: The Model* by Susan Kovalik and Karen D. Olsen.

** Common sense and experience with children over time make this a rather obvious point and recent research backs up such observations. See *Thinking and Learning: Matching Developmental Stages with Curriculum and Instruction* by Dr. Lawrence F. Lowery (Kent, WA: Books for Educators, 1989).

secret with another, who promises not to tell. The two are part of a trust-building pact. Did the secret emerge as soon as another warm body was in sight or did it remain private? Or, remember going to a friend's house and *promising* to return home by dinner time? Were you at your place at the dinner table or nowhere to be seen? Remember finding money around the house or at school? Did you search for the owner or pocket the cash? These are all examples of early opportunities to build trustworthiness. The major lesson to be learned is that each time trust is broken, it takes longer to be restored; sometimes it can be irrevocably broken.

As adults, every action we take, every deed we accomplish, and every word we utter creates the person others see us to be. People either believe us or they don't. Building trust is a definitive example of actions speaking louder than words; all the good intentions and promises in the world can't compensate for jobs not done, deadlines ignored, secrets revealed, and promises broken. So, tell the truth, keep your word, work to your personal best—be a person viewed as reliable, dependable, and believable.

Building a Reputation Takes Time

A reputation of trustworthiness is slowly earned. It is based on a collection of positive experiences among people over time. Consistency, reliability, and honest actions all typify a person who is worthy of our trust. The same is true for each of us. Our actions and reactions will be watched for awhile, before we are known to be trustworthy.

WHAT DOES TRUSTWORTHINESS LOOK LIKE IN THE REAL WORLD?

We

- Honor promises made to family, friends, customers, and clients
- Obey the traffic laws at all times, not just when we see a police car
- Provide accurate insurance information after being involved in an accident
- Respect the privacy of others and any information shared in confidence
- Adhere to written and verbal contracts and agreements
- Research political candidates' platforms and voting records to verify honest fulfillment of campaign promises
- Behave in an open and friendly way to all people, regardless of race, religion, or ethnicity
- Say what we mean and mean what we say
- Share honest emotions with family members and friends
- Pay bills in a timely way

WHAT DOES TRUSTWORTHINESS LOOK LIKE AT HOME?

Adults

- Model the Lifelong Guidelines and LIFESKILLS at all times not just when in a "good" mood or things are going well; remain emotionally consistent with family and friends
- Rely on one another to work together to create a successful working/living team
- Remain faithful to our spouses
- Keep agreements about finances and live within a budget
- Honor privacy and information shared in confidence
- Expect others to be trustworthy; trust them until we have reason not to
- Understand that trust, once lost, takes time to rebuild and, in fact, may be lost forever
- Share the work of maintaining house and family
- Confront the person responsible for our concern rather than whining to an audience
- Live within our income and plan for our family's future needs

Children

- Follow the Lifelong Guidelines and LIFESKILLS at home with family, friends, visitors, and babysitters; also follow them when a guest at others' homes
- Respect parental decisions for their safety, such as curfews, off-limit sites, and friends
- Follow family rules and expectations without complaining about what other parents do and don't allow
- Complete all chores/tasks without reminders and do so using the Lifelong Guideline of Personal Best
- Listen to parents' stories and apply the lessons learned to their own lives
- Support their brothers and sisters during difficult situations
- Honor privacy and information shared in confidence
- Respect public and private property
- Promise only what they can deliver
- Follow family safety Internet guidelines

OPPORTUNITIES TO PRACTICE TRUSTWORTHINESS

AGES 4-8

- Listen to a family member read the story *Stellaluna* by Janell Cannon. Share a time when Stellaluna was being a trustworthy friend. Draw a picture illustrating that part of the story and hang it in your room.

- Listen to a family member read *Little Red Riding Hood*. Identify and describe two strategies that the wolf used to convince Little Red Riding Hood to trust him. Design a "WANTED" poster to educate the public about the dangerous "big, bad wolf." Include a drawing of him, his description, and two sentences explaining why no one should trust him.

- Brainstorm three different ways to ask permission to borrow from a family member something you need to use. Include words such as: "May I . . .?" "Please, may I use . . . ?" "Would you please lend me . . . ?" Add information explaining how it will be used and cared for and when you will return it to its owner.

- Construct a chart labeling two or more chores that are yours to do around the house; list these along the left side of the page from top to bottom and add the days of the week across the top of the page. Put an "X" next to each job after you complete it. At the end of one week, review your marks to determine if you have been a trustworthy worker.

- Design a chart with three pictures that illustrate the Lifelong Guideline of Trustworthiness. Include polite and helpful behaviors that you will use when a grandparent or babysitter is taking care of you. Show this to your family. Hang the chart up and share it with your caretaker when he/she comes to take care of you.

- Read the daily newspaper. Find one article about a community helper whom someone trusted for help. Explain to a family member the ways this community helper develops trust with the people he/she is serving.

- Find a cardboard box larger than two pairs of boots. Cut off the cover (ask an adult for help if the cardboard is too strong). Paint the sides of the box a favorite color. Add some designs and create a sign that reads, "Lost and Found Box." Put it in a convenient place in your house. Use it to hold lost and misplaced items that belong to family members and guests.

- Develop a plan for your family members to use if ever there is an emergency in the house. Choose an emergency situation (e.g., tornado, fire, flood,). Write/list/draw four or more procedures for family members to follow. Include a place for everyone to meet for a safety check. Practice the plan at least three times to make sure that it works. If there are problems, find a way to correct them for everyone's safety. Practice the newly revised plan. Post the procedures in a convenient place.

- Ask a parent to take you along to the polling place on Election Day. Enter the voting booth and watch the procedures that he/she follows. Ask your parent how he/she studied the issues to decide who/what to vote for. Keep your parent's choices private.

AGES 9-12

- Compile an address book listing the names, addresses, and phone numbers for ten or more of your closest friends. Make a special cover for the book; include your name and photograph. Offer it to your family so they can easily contact you when you are visiting one of your friends.

- Brainstorm at least two responses—one showing the Lifelong Guideline of Trustworthiness and one showing lack of trustworthiness—for each of the following situations. Invite a brother, sister, or friend to help act out each situation and possible ways to respond to them. Present the skits to the adults in your house. After each problem, invite your guests to offer other ways to respond to the problem.

    ~ Your best friend takes out a bag of M&M's, offers you some candy, and then tells you that he/she shoplifted this item from a neighborhood store. What do you do?

    ~ You tell your parents that you are going to play basketball at the corner playground and will be home in time for dinner. When it is time for you to leave, the other kids beg you to stay to finish the game. How do you react?

    ~ While walking through the kitchen, you find a ten-dollar bill on the floor. No one is around to watch you pick the bill up off the floor. Later that afternoon, your older brother is looking for money he has lost. How do you respond?

- Read the "Lost and Found" section of your local newspaper for a week or longer. Organize the ads in the following way: pets, jewelry, money, and "other." Tally the number of ads for each group. Determine which category has the most ads for that week. Then tally the ads a second time using these categories: Reward/No Reward. Discuss with an adult or friend the idea of offering/accepting a reward for lost and found items.

- Produce a list of 10 or more websites that you would like to use/visit. Offer the list to your parents and invite them to visit the websites to view their content. Every day for a week, record which of these websites you visit and the amount of time spent viewing the material. Share your findings with your parents and what you have learned about the Lifelong Guideline of Trustworthiness.

- Choose a board game (Candyland, Checkers, Monopoly, etc.). Teach a younger brother/sister/friend how to play the game. Play along and read the rules aloud as needed. Stress having fun playing together and not competing to be the winner. Reflect on how playing to have fun with others might make you more trustworthy to be around rather than when you play to win. Make a list of games that you want to play for the fun of it and those which you want to play to win. Show the list to an adult family member. Ask him/her to share childhood experiences with playing for fun using the Lifelong Guideline of Trustworthiness versus playing to win. After thinking about what he/she said, review your list of games. Would you now choose to play one (or more) of the play-to-win games for fun rather than to win? If so, why? Share with a parent what you have learned about yourself and the Lifelong Guideline of Trustworthiness.

Character Begins at Home: Family Tools for Teaching Character and Values

- Plan a birthday party for yourself or a sibling. Include the following items on your planning sheet: time schedule, guest list, party procedures, menu, and safe group activities that will entertain the guests. Discuss the plan with your parents. Address any concerns they may have and make changes (if necessary). Request their permission to actually have the party. Recruit volunteers to help you organize and carry out the party. After the party, evaluate the effectiveness of your organizational and planning skills.

- Set up safety procedures to follow while shopping at the mall. Include information such as: number of people in group, best times to visit, precautions to follow with strangers, and steps to follow if you feel uneasy about a situation. Share these procedures with your parents and friends. Check with mall security to determine if you have left out any important rules. Add any procedures that they suggest. Share your final product with a parent. Use these safety procedures each time you visit the mall.

- Experiment with being trustworthy on a "Trust Walk." Take turns leading a blindfolded family member through an obstacle course using only verbal directions. Discuss how it feels to have to rely on someone else to move around the house or yard.

- Listen to a family member read a book with the theme of trustworthiness (for example, *Charlotte's Web* or *My Side of the Mountain*). Identify two characters (one trustworthy and one not) and write their names at the top of a piece of paper. Identify and list six or more actions by each character that explain why one is trustworthy and the other is not. Share your results with a family member.

- Identify three people in your neighborhood who are trustworthy citizens. Create the front page of a newspaper to honor these people. Write a short article explaining what each one has accomplished. Use real photographs if they are available to you.

- Interview a family member or neighbor about how people use or don't use the Lifelong Guideline of Trustworthiness where he/she works. Ask which trustworthy behaviors he/she values the most and which behaviors showing lack of trustworthiness bother him/her the most. Share your information with a family member.

- Ask a parent to take you along to the polling place on Election Day. Enter the voting booth and watch the procedures that he/she follows. Keep your parent's choices confidential.

AGES 13+

- Create action plans that demonstrate the Lifelong Guideline of Trustworthiness for the following scenarios:

    ~ A friend tells you that he/she has brought a gun to school

    ~ You go to a friend's party only to discover that there are no adults in attendance

    ~ Your best friend did not have time to study for a social studies test and signals you to slide your answer sheet over where he/she can read it

    ~ While walking through the mall with some friends, one of them finds a wallet with a significant amount of cash and decides to keep the money

- On the way to a school dance, your date pulls out a six-pack of beer and offers some to you

- While at a friend's house, you are offered some drugs

- While working as a clerk in a neighborhood store, an underage friend requests a pack of cigarettes from behind the counter

• Set up safety procedures to follow while shopping at the mall. Include information such as: number of people in group, best times to visit, precautions to follow with strangers, and steps to follow if you feel uneasy about a situation. Share these procedures with your parents and friends. Check with mall security to determine if you have left out any important rules. Add any procedures that they suggest. Share your final product with a parent. Use these safety procedures each time you visit the mall.

• Attend and complete the requirements for a babysitter's course offered by a local hospital, 4-H, Girl Scouts, or Boy Scouts organization. Design business cards that contain all the necessary information for prospective customers. Include a name for the business, phone number, qualifications, and any additional information that you feel will help clients choose your services. Add a "catchy" graphic. Visit prospective clients to introduce yourself, answer any questions they might have about your service, ask any questions you need answered about expectations, working conditions, hours; also, leave a business card with them.

• Identify (with a caring adult) the kinds of "safe" personal information you will give out in e-mail, instant messages, or in chat rooms. Learn the procedures for blocking unwanted e-mail from your mailbox. Research the procedures for reporting any aggressive, sexual, or harassing e-mail messages to your server. Consult an adult concerning any e-mail that appears to be aggressive, scary, or that makes you feel uncomfortable.

• Obtain a learner's permit for driving when you reach the legal age or older. Ask a responsible driver to teach you driving skills and to provide supervised practice time. Decide when you are ready for the driver's test and set-up an appointment. When you are awarded a license, discuss safety procedures with your parents in regard to borrowing the car for personal use. Determine consequences if these procedures are not followed.

• Research the candidates for a local election to assist you in determining if they "practice what they preach." Study any previous voting records, organization memberships/affiliations, and their actions while on the campaign trail. Explain to your parents which candidate you would vote for and why.

• Choose a book from the literature list at the end of this chapter. Read the story and share two or more instances where a character builds or breaks down others' trust in them. Share with a friend or family member the book and segments you chose. Explain the actions you would have chosen under similar circumstances.

• Keep a journal for a month or longer. Note three times or more when you feel your actions have contributed to improving your trustworthiness with your parents. Also, list one or more times when your actions led to a loss of trust with a family member or friend. Create an action plan to rebuild your trustworthiness in his/her eyes.

SIGNS OF SUCCESS

Congratulations! Children are showing signs of Trustworthiness when they

- Keep a secret or a confidence
- Choose to follow the Lifelong Guideline and LIFESKILLS both in and outside the home
- Identify and eliminate behaviors, words, and actions that destroy a relationship built on the Lifelong Guideline of Trustworthiness
- Complete all age-appropriate chores and tasks to the best of their ability when or before expected
- Return tools and materials in the same, or better, condition than when they were first borrowed or offer to replace them if they were damaged or lost
- Meet agreed upon expectations and keep promises to others
- Try to locate the owner(s) of "found" items
- Return home on or before the expected curfew time
- Follow the original plans for the evening and notify parents of any changes
- Handle safety concerns regarding drugs, weapons, and dangerous actions; ask for help when the situation moves beyond their control
- Consistently tell the truth and honor their word

Keep trying! Children need more practice when they

- Tell lies to excuse culpability
- Constantly offer excuses for shortcomings
- Make numerous promises but keep few of them
- Ignore chores/jobs
- Can't be relied on to carry out tasks and assignments in an accurate and timely fashion
- Take or use family members' belongings without asking permission
- Find items and do not attempt to locate the owner(s)
- Shoplift/steal things from stores, homes, school
- Cheat on tests

Literature Link ~ Trustworthiness

Ages 4-8

Blue and the Gray, The (AFA)	Eve Bunting (New York: Scholastic Books, 1996)
Boy on the Beach, The (AFA)	Niki Daly (New York: Simon & Schuster, 1999)
Home to Medicine Mountain (NA)	Chiori Santiago (San Francisco: Childrens Book Press, 1998)
Horton Hatches the Egg	Dr. Seuss (New York: Random Library, 1987)

Ages 9-12

Abel's Island (TE)	William Steig (New York: Farrar, Strauss & Giroux, 1988)
Last of the Really Great Whangdoodles	Julie Andrews Edwards (New York: HarperTrophy Books, 1989)
On My Honor	Marion Dane Bauer (New York: Yearling Books, 1987)
Strider (TE)	Beverly Cleary (New York: William Morrow & Company, 1991)

Ages 13+

Behind the Secret Window: A Memoir of a Hidden Childhood During World War II	Nelly S. Troll (New York: Dial Books, 1993)
Bless Me, Ultima (HA)	Rudolfo A. Anaya (New York: Warner Books, 1999)
Canyons	Gary Paulson (New York: Laureleaf, Random House Publishers, 1991)
Dicey's Song	Cynthia Voigt (New York: Fawcett Books, 1995)
I Am the Cheese	Robert Cormier (New York: Laureleaf, Random House Publishers, 1991)

Multicultural books: **(AFA)**=African American, **(ASA)**=Asian American, **(HA)**=Hispanic American, **(ME)**=Multi-Ethnic, **(NA)**=Native American, **(TE)**=listed in the teacher edition of this book, *Tools for Citizenship and Life: Using the ITI Lifelong Guidelines and LIFESKILLS in the Classroom,* **(BFE)**=available through Books for Educators

Family Resources

Raising Children With Character: Parents, Trust, and the Development of Personal Integrity   Elizabeth Berger, M.D. (Northvale, NJ: Jason Aronson, 2000)

10-Minute Life Lessons for Kids: 52 Fun and Simple Activities to Teach Your Child Honesty, Trust, Love, and Other Important Values   Jamie C. Miller (New York: HarperTrade, 1998)

Truthfulness

Chapter 3

"Families deserve the truth."

truthfulness *n* telling or disposed to tell the truth
truth *n* **1a:** constancy **b:** sincerity in action, character, and utterance
2a: (1) the state of being the case: fact   (2) the body of real things, events, and facts

Truthfulness: To be honest about things and feelings with oneself and others

WHAT IS TRUTHFULNESS?

Truthfulness has many aspects; its complexity unfolds as children mature. It is a difficult Lifelong Guideline to practice. Its attributes are complex and often dependent upon circumstances. The definition of truthfulness that follows is the result of brainstorming by a class of teachers and administrators at U.C. Davis, California.

"To be truthful means being honest about things and feelings . . . being honest with ourselves and with others. Being truthful is not always easy because truth is not absolute (black and white) and two seemingly contradictory statements could both be the truth depending upon the perspectives of the observers (for example, the blind men discovering an elephant). It takes courage to be truthful because others may disagree.

"Being truthful requires good judgment about:

- What to say (possible risk to our source of information)

- When to say it (in private or before others)

- To whom to say it (to the person responsible for the problem/situation or as a complaint to anyone who will listen)

- How (with sensitivity and tact or intended to hurt)

"Truthfulness is a critical building block for human relationships and therefore has significant consequences for each of us, both short-term and long-term."*

---

* Karen D. Olsen, instructor, extension course in brain-compatible learning at the University of California, Davis, 1993.

Preserving the Truth

Preserving the truth depends on each of us refusing to exaggerate, change, or vary the facts we are sharing. This requires careful observation and clear thinking as we perceive and analyze a situation; it also requires precise communication when sharing the information.

Whether it's the policeman asking, "What happened here? Which driver caused the accident and how?" or the parent asking, "How did this happen? Who started this?" the situation calls for the truth. How well did we observe the incident? Do we stick to the facts or make inferences that may or may not be true? Are we committed to telling the truth despite consequences?

WHY PRACTICE TRUTHFULNESS?

Most people will believe what they hear *unless* the information is proven to be inaccurate. After that, the informant's word is not as good as it used to be; people then listen with a sense of disbelief or the feeling that they should check another source. Recall the story from *Aesop's Fables* about the boy who cried wolf. The boy lied so many times about the wolf being after the sheep that when the wolf really did attack, none of the villagers responded to his cries for help. If we aren't truthful at all times, people—especially family and friends—will be suspicious when we share stories; they'll want proof or verification from other sources. The greater the number of lies and careless statements that pass through our lips, the more corroboration our listeners will need.

It is important, sometimes even a matter of life or death, that people believe us. Nothing is as precious as our reputation that we say what we mean and mean what we say. Truthfulness is the bedrock of trustworthiness.

Effective Relationships Rely on Truthfulness

Based on a survey of more than 15,000 people, 88 percent chose honesty as the key trait of effective leadership.* Honest people have credibility; credible leaders gain the trust and confidence of their followers. They keep their promises and follow through on their commitments. In contrast, people who consistently lie are shunned, have few friends, and have fewer options for well-paying employment.

In personal relationships, if we can't be trusted to tell the truth even with insignificant information, how can anyone believe that our important ideas are true? By always telling the truth, friends, family, and co-workers will believe what we say. We become respected and valued members of our families and communities.

When the Lifelong Guidelines of Truthfulness and Trustworthiness are present, a sense of community develops. Then, all family members are less likely to be dishonest because each is genuinely cherished for who he/she is. When we belong, we have something to lose if we break the norms of our group and we have no need to pretend or create some persona bigger and better than in real life.

* See *The Leadership Challenge* by James M. Kouzes and Barry Z. Posner, Jossey-Bass, Inc., San Francisco, CA, pp. 21-22.

Benefits to Telling the Truth

According to Dr. Abraham Kryger, D.M.D., M.D., there are real physical and psychological benefits from telling the truth. Among them are: greater success/personal expertise, an increased sense of grounding/confidence, less anxiety/worry/guilt, increased ability to deal with crises/breakdowns, improved problem-solving abilities, improved interpersonal relationships, greater emotional health/control of one's emotions, increased ability to influence others, better sleep, better health, increased ability to think well/reason soundly, less need to control, good humor, and greater self-expression and self-satisfaction.* Do those sound like qualities you'd like in your life? Truth—and its dark twin, lies—drive world events, nudge the fall of civilizations, and sculpt our lives like no other character trait.

Consequences of Not Telling the Truth

There are also consequences of not telling the truth. Some of these consequences according to Dr. Kryger are: more frequent failures/frustrations in life, being distrusted by others, lack of self-esteem/self-confidence, dysfunctional interpersonal relationships, inability to self-correct, and stress of many kinds. Virtually all types of human stress can be traced to not telling the truth at one level or another.**

HOW DO YOU PRACTICE TRUTHFULNESS?

Always tell the truth! It was Mark Twain who said, "If you tell the truth, you don't have to remember anything."*** It is easier to remember what really happened, what words were really spoken, than to try to recall a made-up story or a distorted version. You also practice the Lifelong Guideline of Truthfulness by telling the entire truth immediately rather than telling the story a little bit at a time until finally the whole truth emerges. Credibility is easy to destroy with just some simple untruths told in a moment to either create a better impression, deny involvement, or refuse to acknowledge that an incident has occurred. As a parent, you're on stage 24-hours a day. Remember, what you *do* is more important than what you *say* you do!

Recognize That There are Barriers to Telling the Truth

When teaching children about the Lifelong Guideline of Truthfulness, we must admit to ourselves and to them that there are formidable barriers to telling the truth in our society. Perhaps the biggest is refusing to accept that it is possible to tell the truth. A widespread but false belief is that it simply isn't humanly possible to tell the truth. That is just a handy excuse that absolves us of the need to question our lack of truthfulness.

---

*   *Benefits of Telling the Truth* by Abraham Kryger, D.M.D., M.D. http://www.wellnessmd.com/tellingtruth.html
** The lie detector test is based on physiological evidence of the body's reaction to lying—more rapid pulse and rise in blood pressure. Also see *The Orman Health Letter* published monthly by TRO Productions, Inc., Baltimore, MD, and Kruger, ibid.
*** Mark Twain, *Notebook,* 1984 edition.

A second powerful barrier is fearing the consequences of being truthful. For example, fear that the boss will fire us, that someone close to us will lose respect for us, or that people will retaliate for our having challenged their belief system.* However, telling a lie almost always has far-reaching consequences, too often of greater severity than if we simply spoke the truth up-front and accepted the consequences, as unpleasant as they might be.

Practice, Practice

Have your child practice sharing personal stories and repeating information as accurately as possible. Teach him/her to write terms and facts on paper so he/she can refer to them if needed. Show your child the importance of being willing to recheck any data that seem to lack credibility by going back to the source of the information. Teach him/her many problem-solving strategies; when logical, reasonable choices are available, a child is less likely to lie. Avoid setting a trap for your child, such as when you already know the answer but ask the question anyway. All you accomplish is "catching" him/her in a falsehood.

Whenever possible, support your child's willingness to tell the truth however difficult the consequences.

WHAT DOES TRUTHFULNESS LOOK LIKE IN THE REAL WORLD?
We

- Use accurate figures when computing our yearly federal/state income tax
- Report accurate losses to insurance companies
- Abide by contractual agreements
- Say "No!" when we have no time to add anything more to our calendar
- Return/insist on paying for extra items from the grocery bag that we weren't charged for
- Keep our word; say what we mean and mean what we say
- Ignore rumors and search for the truth; avoid gossip and half truths
- Offer genuine feelings and sincere opinions with tact and without being judgmental
- Observe carefully and stick to accurate information when sharing about incidents
- Provide accurate reasons for being late or not showing up
- Eliminate back-stabbing and put-downs

---

* Kryger, ibid.

What Does Truthfulness Look Like at Home?

Adults

- Share with family members our feelings and thoughts accurately yet tactfully and without burdening them

- Don't make promises to spouse and children that they don't keep

- Don't misrepresent who, what, or why to buttress our statements or beliefs, such as "So-and-so said we had to do this" rather than saying "I think this is important and want you to do it today"; or "That's silly. Why would you want to buy that?" rather than saying "That's not in our family budget this month"

- Say "No" to more responsibilities when we don't have the necessary time

- Accurately and fairly explain and apply consequences rather than trying to scare children into behaving, for example, "The mad hatchet man will get you for doing this."

- Share financial information with our spouse

- Give children accurate parameters and expectations of what family resources can provide

Children

- Tell the truth about behavior especially when there may be consequences

- Say "I forgot . . . " or "I didn't . . . " rather than make up a story to divert responsibility

- Share their thoughts and feelings openly but tactfully

- Verify information about other people and don't spread rumors or hurtful stories

- Go where they say they will be

- Respect promises

- Repeat stories without exaggeration

- Share information that relates to safety (e.g., friend with a gun, drugs/alcohol at a party)

OPPORTUNITIES TO PRACTICE TRUTHFULNESS

AGES 4-8

- Listen to/read the book *Sam, Bangs and Moonshine* by Evaline Ness. In your own words, explain what you think "moonshine" is in the story. Brainstorm three or more examples of moonshine you have heard somewhere and share them with an adult in your family.

- Choose a tune that you know (e.g., "Twinkle, Twinkle, Little Star" or "Row, Row, Row Your Boat") and write new lyrics for two or more verses about the importance of telling the truth. Sing the song for your family at dinner time.

- Listen to the story, *The Boy Who Cried Wolf*. Choose three or more positive ways the boy could have received attention when he was lonely. Create a puppet for each of the main characters and practice retelling the story at least five times until you remember the words with ease. Perform the story for family or friends. Invite the audience to share what they think the moral (lesson) of the story is.

- Create a chart with the title of "Truthfulness." Make three columns with these headers: Looks Like, Sounds Like, and Feels Like. Brainstorm with family members words and phrases for each category.

- Draw pictures of three or more people that tell the truth to you. At the bottom of the picture, write a sentence sharing how their truthfulness with you makes you feel. Hang these pictures up in your room.

- Watch three or more TV toy commercials. Write/draw what you learned about each toy. Visit a toy store to check out the three products. Decide whether or not the ads tell the truth about the toys and share your information with a brother/sister or parent.

- Think about the following actions. Discuss with Mom/Dad which actions show the Lifelong Guideline of Truthfulness and which ones don't.

    ~ You take a quarter from your mom's purse without asking her permission and lie about it.

    ~ You choose a pack of your favorite gum at the checkout counter and pay the clerk.

    ~ On the way to school you find a wallet on the sidewalk. You turn it in to the office as soon as you arrive.

    ~ On the way to school, you find a wallet, pocket the money, and then toss the wallet into a trash can. At lunchtime, you offer to buy all of your friends ice cream.

    ~ Your friend has some Pokemon cards. When he/she isn't looking, you take them and put them in your backpack.

    ~ The teacher is giving a spelling test. Even though you have studied the words, there are three that you can't spell. During the test, you keep peeking at a neighbor's paper and copy those words.

Chapter 3—LIFELONG GUIDELINE #2: **Truthfulness**

- Draw a picture that shows a time when someone told you a lie. Include yourself, the other person, and objects that will help someone else understand what happened. Share this story with an adult. Tell how you felt when you found out about the lie.

- Read/listen to the story *The Berenstain Bears and the Truth* by Janice and Stan Berenstain. Explain what you would have done if you were the bears.

- Write two or more sentences about a lie you told. Also tell what happened when the lie was found out. Share your story with your parents/grandparents.

- Ask someone in your family to share a "life" story about when he/she told a lie, got into trouble, and learned a lesson. Find out what lesson he/she learned.

AGES 9-12

- Keep a journal for one month by writing a daily experience with truth vs. lying. Describe times when you have lied and when you have told the truth. Record your feelings when lying and when telling the truth. Share with a parent what you are learning about the impact of truthfulness on your life and the life of others.

- Search the local newspaper for a story that emphasizes the importance of being truthful. Carefully cut it out and glue it on a piece of colored paper, share it with your family during dinner and then post where visitors can see it.

- Choose and read a book from the literature list at the end of this chapter. In three or more sentences, write how you think the plot of the story connects to the Lifelong Guideline of Truthfulness. Share your reflections with an adult.

- Observe two different school friends who often argue. Determine if there are times when either one or the other is not telling the truth. If so, why do you think this person tells lies? Share your thoughts with a parent.

- Read a biography about either George Washington, Abraham Lincoln, or another president of your choice. Share at least one incident that the author uses to demonstrate that this president was a truthful, trustworthy person.

- Design a card for someone you trust to tell the truth. Share your feelings about his/her truthful ways. Use colored paper and markers to make a drawing and write your sentiments. Mail/deliver the card when done.

- Locate three or more quotations using any of the following words: truth, truthful, truthfulness, and honesty. Choose the statement that you find most interesting and memorize it. Recite the quotation to yourself whenever you are tempted to lie.

- Watch a minimum of three TV programs and/or movies. List any examples of body language you observe that demonstrate that the character is not telling the truth.

- Discuss the following questions with a parent:
    ~ Are there situations in which lies are acceptable? Is there such a thing as a "good" lie? Does the truth ever change?

- ~ How do you get people to believe you after you lied to them?
- ~ What should you do when someone tells you a lie?

AGES 13+

- Watch the nightly news broadcast for one week. Record the number/type of stories related to the Lifelong Guideline of Truthfulness or lack of. Choose the one you find most offensive and discuss, with a parent or grandparent, the content of the event and the other choices the person(s) had.

- Interview an owner of a video or video game store. Ask him/her what impact lack of the Lifelong Guideline of Truthfulness has upon the business. What procedures are in place to handle shoplifting and lying? What does shoplifting and lying cost the business? How much does that cost other customers? What do employees do if they suspect someone of ripping them off? Share the information with your parents/grandparent/math teacher.

- Ask a friend to role-play the following situations with you. Practice answers that promote honesty and a sincere effort to do your personal best.

  - ~ A classmate/good friend/date offers you drugs at a party.

  - ~ Put-downs are passing around school showing blatant disrespect for your best friend's family members, area of residence, income, and/or physical looks.

  - ~ Your parents think you are attending a party at your best friend's home. Instead, you are drinking beer and driving around town looking for fun things to do. Unfortunately, there is a minor traffic accident and the police have been called.

- Interview an adult in a leadership position (e.g., boss, CEO, administrator). Invite him/her to share the quality traits most valued in employees and why. Research the company policy on stealing and deceitful practices. Prepare an essay/explanation as to whether or not you would want to work for this person/company some time in the future.

- Design a collage that represents your interpretation of the Lifelong Guideline of Truthfulness. Include photos and personal items that will help to convey your feelings. Send it to an aunt/uncle or grandparent with a letter of explanation.

- Research a political issue (e.g., bribery, corruption, kickbacks, white collar theft) in your community. Research and discover the facts of the story. Write and submit an article for your school or local newspaper offering your perspective on the issue.

- Identify programs that your local police department uses to prevent minors from purchasing tobacco products and alcoholic beverages. Verify the consequences for anyone found to be aiding and abetting a minor in obtaining these products.

- Investigate two or more famous people or leaders from businesses who have lied to the public and only admitted wrongdoing after they were caught. Research two or more famous people or company executives who told the truth even when they knew it might damage their image/business. Write a news report comparing and contrasting the reactions of the public to the two different situations. Tape record your discussion and play the tape for your family at dinner time.

- Research the tobacco industry's relationship with the public about the dangers of smoking. Investigate both sides of the story, that of cigarette makers and of cigarette smokers. Take the position, either that of a tobacco industry representative or of a smoker with serious medical problems caused by smoking such as cancer or emphysema. Debate your position with a friend or family member representing the opposite view.

SIGNS OF SUCCESS

Congratulations! Children are showing signs of Truthfulness when they

- Tell the truth even when the consequences may be harsh or the outcome embarrassing
- Accept responsibility for lies they have told and do their best to make amends
- Report situations/events/conversations with accuracy
- Recognize negative physical symptoms (e.g., upset stomach, heart rate increase) as their body's response to lying
- Listen to their conscience telling them what is truthful and what is not
- Correct misinformation and stop gossip from spreading
- Tell the truth with tact

Keep trying! Children need more practice when they

- Lie to avoid getting in trouble
- Make up stories and pretend they are the truth; exaggerate beyond the truth
- Bend the facts or exaggerate to make themselves sound "bigger and better" than life
- Tell the truth only when it is of benefit to them
- Routinely lie about the family's income, religion, race, and/or ethnic background
- Change the basic "facts" of an incident every time it is told
- Refuse to acknowledge that they have been caught in a lie
- Realize they can't remember what version of a story they have told before
- Tell lies that hurt their family or friends

Character Begins at Home: Family Tools for Teaching Character and Values

Literature Link ~ Truthfulness

Ages 4-8

Big, Fat, Enormous Lie, A	Marjorie Sharmat (New York: E.P. Dutton, 1993)
Day's Work, A (HA) (TE)	Eve Bunting (Boston: Clarion Books, A Division of Houghton Mifflin, 1997)
Honest-to-Goodness Truth, The (AFA)	Patricia C. McKissack (London: Athenium, 2000)
Honest Tulio (HA)	John Himmelman (Mahway, NJ: Bridgewater Books, A Division of Troll, 1997)

Ages 9-12

Dog Years	Sally Warner. New York: Knopf, 1995.
Don't Tell a Whopper on Fridays: The Children's Truth-Control Book	Adolph Moser (Kansas City: Landmark Edition, 1999)
Jeremy; The Tale of an Honest Bunny	Jan Karon (New York: Viking Press, 2000)
Spider Boy	Ralph Fletcher (Boston, MA: Clarion Books, Houghton Mifflin, 1997)

Ages 13+

Black Water	Eve Bunting (New York: HarperCollins Publishers, 1999)
First Honest Book About Lies, The	Jonni Kincher (Minneapolis: Free Spirit Publishing, 1992)
Nothing But the Truth	Avi (New York: Orchard Books, 1991)
Speak	Laurie Halse Anderson (New York: Farrar, Strauss & Giroux, 1999)

Family Resources

Dealing With Lying	Lisa K. Adams (New York: Power Kids Press, 1998)
Raising Good Children from Birth Through the Teen Years: How to Help Your Child Develop a Lifelong Sense of Honesty, Decency, and Respect for Others	Dr. Thomas Likona (New York: Bantam Doubleday Dell Press, 1994)

Multicultural books: **(AFA)**=African American, **(ASA)**=Asian American, **(HA)**=Hispanic American, **(ME)**=Multi-Ethnic, **(NA)**=Native American, **(TE)**=listed in the teacher edition of this book, *Tools for Citizenship and Life: Using the ITI Lifelong Guidelines and LIFESKILLS in the Classroom*, **(BFE)**=available through Books for Educators

Active Listening

Chapter 4

"LISTEN WITH YOUR HEAD AND HEART, THEN TALK."

active *adj* **1:** characterized by action rather than by contemplation or speculation
listening *v* **1:** to hear something with thoughtful attention: give consideration

Active Listening: To listen with the intention of understanding what the speaker intends to communicate

WHAT IS ACTIVE LISTENING?

Hearing is an inactive, involuntary process that occurs when the ears pick up sound waves and forward them to the brain. Listening, however, is an active, voluntary process which includes recognizing, understanding, and correctly interpreting messages received. Listening requires participation, patience, energy, and the intention to "get it"—not just what the speaker said but what he/she intended to communicate.

To actively listen, the brain must be physiologically active. Not only must it perceive the sounds correctly but it must also compare words to emotional nuances for consistency, convert words into images that can be analyzed, compared, and used to create new understandings, and then store them for future reference. This is an extremely active process.

Most people, however, listen passively. That means the sound acts on them—enters their ears—but they don't actively and consciously participate in the process; they don't exert effort to listen and attend to what they are hearing. For example listening to music while driving, TV while cleaning house, or daydreaming during class. In contrast, active listening is more complex than passive listening because it demands that we "listen" with our eyes, ears, heart, and undivided attention as illustrated in the *tang*,* a Chinese character for "to listen." An active listener not only hears but also pays close attention, focusing on the words, ideas, and emotions of the speaker. (See the tang symbol on the next page.)

---

* For a wonderful discussion of the meaning of the Chinese symbol for "to listen," see *TRIBES: A New Way of Learning and Being Together* by Jeanne Gibbs (Sausalito, CA: CenterSource Publications, 1999), pp. 93-94. The book also provides many ready-to-go activities—for home and parties and family get-togethers as well as the classroom—that provide opportunities to practice the Lifelong Guideline of Active Listening. See also *ITI: The Model* by Susan Kovalik, 1997, pp. 26-27.

Character Begins at Home: Family Tools for Teaching Character and Values

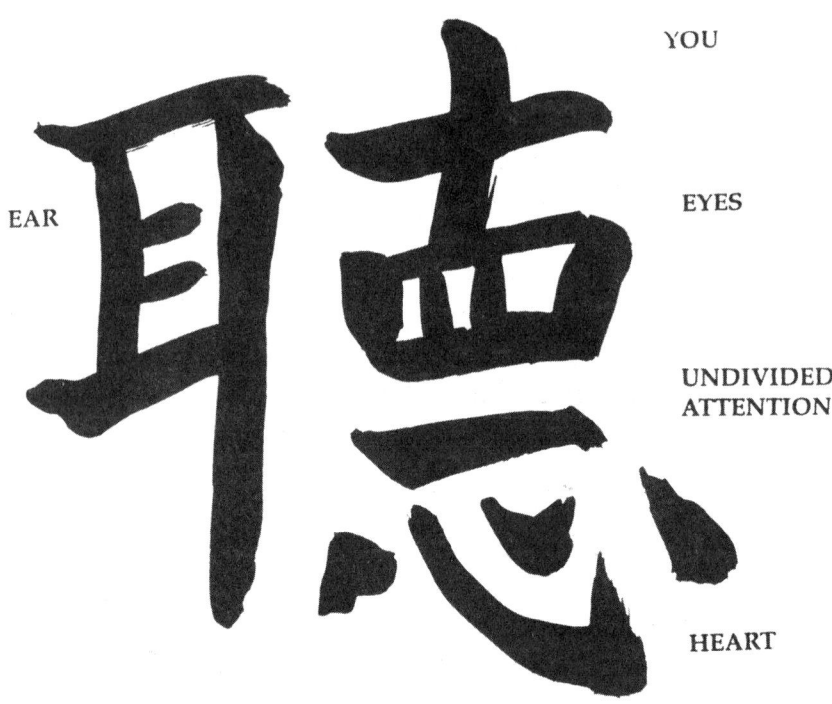

TRIBES: *A New Way of Learning and Being Together* by Jeanne Gibbs, p. 93

The active listener is more than a receiver. In many ways, he assists the speaker to deliver his message by providing encouragement, such as attentive body posture, full eye contact, positive body signals, and multi-tiered acknowledgements, such as "Mmm; uhuh; yes; I understand; I agree; yes, interesting; I heard something about that yesterday . . . tell me more." The listener is saying to the speaker, "I understand. Your ideas and message are important to me and to others in the room. I will listen while you communicate with me and then I will ask questions if I disagree or don't understand. Above all, I respect your opinions and your right to speak."

WHY PRACTICE ACTIVE LISTENING?

Active listening is critical because it is the doorway to understanding. Whether in social settings, at work, or with family and friends, not "getting it" can cause serious problems. At best, it is embarrassing and makes us feel like outsiders. All too often, lack of understanding is also costly in terms of our relationships with others and expensive for our employers when we misinterpret instructions. It is difficult to be successful in life if we are not taking in accurate information about the world and how it works.

On a daily basis, our sense of hearing collects a wide range of information that we need to protect ourselves and to enhance our problem solving. What might happen, for instance, if a jogger, wearing head phones and listening to music, is crossing the street against the walk sign and can't hear a persistent honking horn? Or, if a worried parent is unable to focus on the doctor's directions for the baby's medicine and care? Wouldn't you feel sad if you missed your plane to

Disney World because you didn't hear the final boarding call? Since one of the ways we stay safe and make informed decisions includes listening to sounds collected from the real world, isn't it common sense to concentrate on what we hear?

Unlike the process of reading, we can't regulate the pace of someone else's speech, replaying it again to check an unfamiliar word. Thus, we may miss important information reported to us and respond in a peculiar way. To immediately understand what we hear, it's crucial that we perfect the skill of listening well. We can only talk intelligently about a topic when we can grasp what is said to us. To be able to listen well gives us confidence when communicating with others. Listening in the real world is a critical everyday skill.

Spotlight on Brain Research

What happens in our heads when we listen and learn? Fortunately, the technology now available to brain researchers lets us see our brain in action. And what goes on is quite amazing.

Most of us, parents and educators alike, don't realize that active listening—turning words into mental images that can be processed and stored in short- and long-term memory—requires neural wiring (pathways from brain cell to brain cell) that over 25 percent of the population haven't sufficiently developed by the time they start school to succeed academically.* The good news, however, is that such mental wiring can easily be developed. If your child has difficulty with comprehension (listening and/or reading), contact Lindamood-Bell Learning Processes Center, San Luis Obispo, California, 800/233-1819. They have centers throughout the country for working with children one-on-one with both comprehension and decoding/spelling difficulties. They also work with whole schools as well as train individual teachers. For an introduction to their work to develop comprehension, which is also a do-it-yourself manual, see *Visualizing and Verbalizing for Improved Language Comprehension*. This book describes typical symptoms of those who have difficulty listening, any one of which makes it difficult and frustrating to learn as well as get along in life. If a child (or adult) has difficulty listening and processing what they hear, he/she:**

1. *Will often fail to understand jokes.* Language humor depends on imagery, whereas sight humor (pie in face) does not and is more easily understood. Almost everyone gets sight gags but not everyone gets language-based humor.

2. *May not understand concepts of cause and effect.* To process cause and effect relationships the listener must be able to process a gestalt (whole picture) from which to judge an effect or result.

3. *May not respond to verbal explanations.* If a child's behavior needs correcting, a "talking to" may be only partially understood or not understood at all because he/she is connecting to only a part of the oral explanation.

4. *May ask and re-ask questions that have already been answered.* The child may hear the answer but can't connect it to our question so he/she asks again, only phrasing it differently. Often the child is not aware that he/she is asking the same question over and over, only with modified language.

---

* Not surprisingly, the more hours spent in front of a television, the less time spent developing language. See *Visualizing and Verbalizing for Improved Language Comprehension* by Nanci Bell (Palo Alto, CA: Gander Publishing, Inc., 1991), p. 21.

** ibid, p. 21.

5. *May not grasp the main idea or inferences from television shows or movies.* Although the child may get a few details, he/she seems to miss concepts or nuances from movies and has trouble interpreting the story sequence.

6. *May lose attention quickly in conversation or lectures.* If unable to connect to the gestalt (whole picture of what's going on), the child gets "lost" in just a few minutes and drifts away mentally and/or physically.

7. *May have weakness in auditory memory and following directions.* These symptoms may be severe or subtle weaknesses that cause others to suspect the child lacks intelligence or lacks motivation.

Sound familiar? Every adult can list friends or children who have exhibited these frustrating symptoms. There is more to being an active listener than most people realize.

The Brain Wires Itself to Do What It Is Asked to Do. As Jane Healy points out in her book *Endangered Minds: Why Our Child Don't Think,* the human brain wires itself to handle what we ask it to do.* And that wiring doesn't always lend itself to handling other tasks. For example, the mental wiring developed for endless hours of watching television, playing video games, or using the computer (except for Internet and other academic pursuits) does *not* translate into the mental wiring needed for academic success. Why? Because during all three pursuits, your child is a passive receiver of language—language comes in with lots of visuals and therefore the child doesn't need to make his/her own mental images nor give a verbal response. In other words, a full language loop is simply not needed (words perceived, images made, content thought about/analyzed, and a verbal response made). The more time a child spends watching TV and playing video/computer games, the less time they spend developing their listening/speaking/thinking skills.

Here is just a sampling of research conclusions about the impact of TV and video games.**

- The average American—child and adult—watches four hours of television per day (more than any other single activity but sleep)

- Action video games tend to stimulate the brain's visual cortex but to leave unstimulated, or actually depress, activity of the prefontal cortex with its role in practically all thinking, reading, planning, and organizing

- A child's kinesthetic ability is a facet of his or her intelligence and the physical passivity inherent in TV viewing is clearly detrimental to exercising kinesthetic intelligence . . . perhaps television's most pernicious quality is the tendency for even its best shows to encourage *mental* passivity—to dull the imagination and stifle active thought. Two weeks of the most culturally approved shows on network television, such as *Mister Rogers* and nature films, resulted in promoting a mild degree of creative play in children with the least active imaginations but depressed creative play in all the other kids who had livelier imaginations to start with

- There is an insidious link between diet, obesity, sedentary habits, and television. Those who watch an average of one hour per day were half as likely to be obese as those who watched three to four hours daily

---

* *Endangered Minds: Why Our Children Don't Think* by Jane Healy (New York: A Touchstone Book, a division of Simon & Schuster)

** *Magic Trees of the Mind: How to Nurture Your Child's Intelligence, Creativity, and Healthy Emotions from Birth Through Adolescence* by Dr. Marian Diamond and Janet Hopson (New York: A Plume Book/Penguin Books), pp. 216-222.

- Television erodes the sense of community (the more television a child or adult watches, the less they trust other people, the less they vote, and the less likely they are to take part in organized activities outside the home)

Although we're not trying to alarm you, you need to know that time spent watching television and playing video games does negatively impact a child's preparation for and success in academic pursuits. The California State Department of Education conducted an extensive study of the impact of watching television 3-4 hours a day and concluded that there was an undeniable, and negative, impact and that one could even predict, with a high degree of success, individual student achievement levels.

HOW DO YOU PRACTICE ACTIVE LISTENING?

If the listening difficulties described on pages 4.3 and 4.4 sound familiar, take heart. Developing the necessary neural wiring and social-based listening techniques is easier than you might guess. The first two steps are limiting the time your child spends on activities that don't promote developing active listening. Then, increase their time on activities that actively enhance development of the needed mental wiring and that provide lots of opportunities to practice active listening and processing language.

Restrict TV, Video Game, and Computer Use

Limit your child's electronic input (TV, video, and non-academic computer use) to a maximum of one hour per day. For school age children, even academic use of computers should be restricted. Consider a one-hour limit for elementary students, two hours for middle schoolers, and no more than three for high school students. For preschoolers, limit the electronic input of all kinds to not more than one hour per day.

Work Directly on Developing Needed Neural Wiring

If you believe your child needs help developing the neural wiring needed for listening and processing language, you owe it to yourself and your child to read Nanci Bell's book, *Visualizing and Verbalizing for Improved Language Comprehension*.* Use it as a teacher's manual and work with your child every day for 30 minutes for at least six weeks. You'll be astounded at the transformation in academic capability and confidence in social interaction.

Once the necessary neural wiring is in place, more traditional ways to teach children to pay closer attention, try harder, focus more, and so forth, can be used with greater success.

---

* You'll be pleasantly surprised to discover how user-friendly this book is. It provides both theory and practical lessons and activities to use.

Use the Chinese Symbol for Listening

The Chinese symbol which depicts "to listen" as an act involving ears, eyes, heart, and undivided attention is a good place to start. It offers a handy visual and expands the meaning of the verb "to listen." Teach your child that a big part of communication is *intention*—the listener *intends* to "get" what the speaker *intends* to communicate. Listening with intention helps the listener "hear" with an open mind and rid him/herself of any prejudicial notions that would interfere with or corrupt the speaker's message. Or, they are so busy thinking up a retort that they miss what is actually being said. Or, they get so involved in the speaker's style of delivery, or status, or how hip he/she appears that they miss the message.

Listening with heart and undivided attention is difficult in our Western, "hurry-up, gotta go" culture. The best ways to teach it are consistent modeling by adult family members and by having your child reflect daily on how good it makes him/her feel when others listen to him/her with undivided attention.

Social Expectations

In Western culture, certain behaviors are expected of a good listener, including "attending skills" and "follow-up skills." Attending skills include not interrupting the speaker, listening for what he/she intends to say rather than what we want or think he/she will say, holding eye contact, using open body language, and offering some encouraging responses ("Wow!" "Then what happened?" "Really?" "I understand") and actions (nodding, smiling, and so forth).

Follow-up skills include making certain that we understand what the other person has said, and intended to say, restating the content, asking clarifying questions, summarizing the information, and reflecting on the ideas. If these steps feel a little forced at first, keep digging. If your child is following the example of the Chinese tang when he/she is listening, listening will automatically improve. Adding these social behaviors will dramatically expand two-way understanding.*

No discussion of social expectations and behaviors about listening is complete without a bit of self-examination and soul-searching. How well do you listen to your children? Given the pace of our busy lives, we often find ourselves doing two or three things at the same time. Listening—really listening—is not something that can be done while thinking about something else. Undivided attention, says Chinese wisdom. And that means stopping all else and really listening.

Active listening begins with parent modeling and grows when parents insist upon it as a family code for caring interaction and mutual respect on a daily basis.

Listening Is Not a Passive Pastime

Listening is not a passive pastime. When we lose our concentration, we also lose much of the information. Teach your child to be proactive. Teach your child that there are specific things he/she can consciously do to help tune in to a speaker. For example, we can:

---

* However, social skills alone cannot overcome lack of neural wiring needed to process language.

- Limit distractions. If something is interfering with our ability to attend, we must take action to eliminate or significantly reduce what is bothering us, e.g., change positions, shift so that competing sounds aren't coming directly into our ear, go ask the person responsible for the sound in the environment to turn the volume down (such as music in a restaurant), and so forth

- Look at the speaker. Observe body language (open versus closed), listen to the tone of voice (pitch, quality, and timbre), and note facial expressions as clues to emotions. In many instances, the medium is the message—most of the message is communicated non-verbally*

- Focus our attention on the meaning of words used; create pictures in our mind of what is being said

- Visualize how this information fits with what we already know and what it means to us. Expect to act upon what we are hearing. Always ask the question: What should I do with this information?

WHAT DOES ACTIVE LISTENING LOOK LIKE IN THE REAL WORLD?
We

- Really listen to the response when we ask a child how the day at school went, taking time to listen to his/her fears, joys, and under-the-surface feelings and thoughts

- Listen for relevant information before expressing an opinion

- Listen attentively and with an open mind while serving on a jury

- Attend and enjoy concerts, plays, movies, shows, and professional workshops and trainings

- Listen to guest lecturers and ask pertinent questions

- Listen carefully to new tax laws explained by our accountant

- Visit doctors who listen to our symptoms; retain lawyers who listen to our problems

- Pay attention when customers return broken, damaged, or unsatisfactory merchandise

- Attend/listen to political rallies/caucuses/debates to hear what the candidates have to offer; evaluate politicians' speeches and promises

- Offer solace by being present and quiet while our child, spouse, co-workers share their tale of sorrow or distress

- Stop to listen when adults and children share ideas, concerns, and problems

- As a family, are genuinely interested in what each member has to say when together for day-to-day happenings such as during meals, while car pooling, and so forth

---

* "The Importance of Effective Communication," Northeastern University, College of Business Administration, October, 1999. http://www.cba.neu.edu/~ewertheim/inter/commun.htm

WHAT DOES ACTIVE LISTENING LOOK LIKE AT HOME?

Adults

- Put newspaper and work down while a child is talking to us
- Look at family members when they talk to us
- Respond to information by commenting and asking questions
- Share thoughts and feelings yet remain open to other ideas
- "Read between the lines" to hear our child's real concerns
- Listen with our heart and give undivided attention as our child or other family member brainstorms solutions to his/her problem
- Listen attentively when children tell us where they are going, with whom, and when they will return
- Listen carefully as our child teaches us to operate the computer, VCR, and other new technical wizardry
- Evaluate the news for accuracy and truthfulness and listen to how our child evaluates events and happenings; discuss with him/her any concerns, thoughts, or feelings he/she may have about the reported incidents; discuss how we may "hear" the news differently and why

Children

- Wait patiently while someone gives his/her side of the story
- Track the plot of a story read to them
- Easily memorize slogans from TV/radio commercials and movies
- Readily recall instructions and conversations with others (verbatim and accurately paraphrased)
- Monitor and adjust voice volume to fit the situation (e.g., church vs. football game)
- Hear and follow directions and procedures at public events
- Use attentive behaviors during family discussions, with club members and neighbors, and during other collaborative activities
- During family outings to performances and shows, follow agreed upon procedures such as sitting calmly, remaining silent, listening to the words, songs, or speeches, and showing appreciation by applauding when appropriate
- Listen closely to conversation in order to ask thoughtful questions of a guest

OPPORTUNITIES TO PRACTICE ACTIVE LISTENING

AGES 4-8

- Listen while Mom/Dad reads the story *It Could Always Be Worse* by Margot Zemach. Explain why the woman in the story listens to the Rabbi. Share your favorite part with a family member or friend.

- Discuss with a family member the miscommunication problems that occur in the story, *The Cat Who Wore a Pot on Her Head* by Jan Slepian [or a book your family chooses].

- Memorize two favorite nursery rhymes. Illustrate each one using crayon and paper. Recite them at the next family gathering and share your artwork.

- Invite a family member to read your favorite story/book to you. Ask them to leave out some words or parts. Say "STOP" when you realize something has been left out. Offer to fill in the missing parts. Have the adult check in the book to see how your memory is.

- Play a guessing game. Record some sounds from around the house (e.g., door opening, computer game, mechanical toy, washing machine cycles). Ask different family members to listen to the tape and identify the noises. Give them one point for each correct answer.

- Learn to sing a favorite song from a tape or CD. Practice singing with the music until you know the words and tune by heart. Perform the tune for your family at dinner time (dinner theater).

- Clap different rhythm patterns. Ask a family member to repeat each pattern after you clap it out. Switch roles. Invite the family member to clap some patterns. Repeat each pattern after she/he makes it. Keep track of the longest pattern you can remember and repeat.

- Close your eyes (or wear a blindfold) while riding in the family car. Listen to the sounds you hear and identify them. Ask someone to write down the objects as you name them and to keep track of how many are correctly identified.

- Create a poster that illustrates at least two skills needed for active listening. Display your poster on the refrigerator door or another visible location.

AGES 9-12

- Interview a parent about your ability to actively listen. Ask him/her to estimate how many times he/she has to repeat something before you respond to the directions. Create a method to record for a week your ability to actively listen and respond to directions. Compare your performance at the end of the week to the original estimate. If the results have improved but aren't 100 percent, develop a plan to further improve your ability to use the Lifelong Guideline of Active Listening. Discuss your plan with a family member. Enlist his/her support for implementing the plan and sticking with it for two weeks.

- Choose a story to read to a younger brother/sister/neighbor. Brainstorm three questions that will help you determine if your young listener uses the Lifelong Guideline of Active Listening. Read the story and then follow up with the questions. If the answers are incorrect, look for the answers in the book and point them out to the listener. Repeat this exercise with new books for three more weeks to check for improvement in listening, collecting information, and answering questions.

- Attend a concert or Broadway-type musical. Check the program as the music is performed. Afterwards, share the names of your favorite pieces or songs with the adult who attended the concert with you. Inquire as to his/her favorites and compare to your own. Share how you think the Lifelong Guideline of Active Listening helped you understand and enjoy the performance.

- Practice collecting information from what you hear (rather than from TV or reading). Listen to what someone is telling you. Repeat the information back to the person who is sharing with you. Ask him/her to check your recollections for accuracy.

    ~ Listen to a television interview of a favorite movie or sports star. Take notes as you hear the information. Use the information to write a paragraph with interesting facts about the star and then share what you wrote with a friend. Explain to your friend how using the Lifelong Guideline of Active Listening helped you gather and remember the information you used in writing your paragraph. Send your paragraph to the star's fan club.

    ~ Create a list of your ten most favorite sounds in the world. Make a tape of these sounds. Play them for someone else and ask him/her to try to identify all ten sounds. If needed, give clues until the person can accurately guess the source of the sound.

    ~ Listen to your grandmother/grandfather share three or more family stories. Write them down for a family photo/journal collection book. Retell the stories at the next family gathering. Ask for feedback about the accuracy of the information in your story.

- Turn off the TV for one week. Invite your parents and other family members to play board games, charades, and other indoor and outdoor activities. Listen to the conversations your family has during this sharing time. Compare these conversations during the no-TV week with those your family has when the TV is playing. Share your reflections with your parents. Consider repeating this activity one week during every month.

- Design a symbol or picture to represent the Lifelong Guideline of Active Listening. Label it and write a descriptive sentence explaining your reasons for choosing that symbol. Share the symbol/picture with a family member. Use it as a reminder about the Lifelong Guideline of Active Listening for yourself and other family members for one week. Discuss the sign's effectiveness with your family during dinner time.

AGES 13+

- Select a piece of popular music. Obtain a copy of the lyrics either from the musical score, a web search, or by listening to the song over and over until you have collected all of the words. Review the words and make a connection between the lyrics and each of three LIFESKILLS of your choice. Do the lyrics describe what each LIFESKILL looks like, feels like, and sounds like or what happens in their absence? Share your thoughts with a parent .

- Choose a TV talk show (e.g., "Maury," "Oprah," "Crossfire") that your parents approve for viewing. Watch one show and keep a tally of the number of times that the guests interrupt each other. Write a letter to the host of the show sharing your observations.

- Volunteer your services for at least six months at one of the following organizations: your church, Red Cross, Salvation Army, Candy Stripers, Big Brothers, Big Sisters, Boys Club, Girls Club, etc. Record in a personal journal the stories you hear and the important things you've learned through listening. Reflect monthly on what you are learning as a result of your volunteer work and how the Lifelong Guideline of Active Listening is helping you learn how to do your job there.

- Interview an older family member (grandmother/grandfather, great aunts/uncles, and cousins). Collect experiences that he/she remembers of his/her childhood. Tape record or video this interview for your family archives. Share the stories you have heard with younger siblings/cousins. Be as accurate as you can.

- Visit an elderly neighbor once a week. Offer to do two or more chores that need to be done. Invite him/her to share a "life story" each time you visit. Share your favorite of these life stories with a parent. Reflect on how the Lifelong Guideline of Active Listening helped you remember the details of the story.

- Choose 25 basic, helpful phrases in ASL (American Sign Language). Find someone to teach you the "signing" for these phrases. Practice until you can "sign" with ease. Teach these phrases to a friend. Share with this friend what you have learned about the Lifelong Guideline of Active Listening while learning to sign these phrases.

- Select a children's story to read to a group of younger children—siblings, cousins, and/or neighbors. Choose one that teaches a LIFESKILL lesson. Read and reread the story until you know it from memory. Add vocal expression, body language, and simple props. Before you begin to read the story, explain to your audience the Lifelong Guideline of Active Listening and the LIFESKILL they are to listen for. After the story, invite your audience to make connections between the story and the LIFESKILL. Ask them how the Lifelong Guideline of Active Listening helped them follow the story. Share your experience with a parent. Reflect on what you learned about how others use the Lifelong Guideline of Active Listening.

- Listen to three different kinds of music. Choose from classical, jazz, country/western, new age, disco, reggae, Celtic, and rock-and-roll. Take three pieces of drawing paper and write the categories of these three kinds of music at the top of the sheet, one to a page. Illustrate your feelings for each of the separate selections on the appropriate paper. Share the results with a family member and share how the Lifelong Guideline of Active Listening helped you complete this task.

- Create an active listening self-evaluation form that you and your family can use to evaluate yourselves on a regular basis. Include four or more attributes of someone who uses the Lifelong Guidelines of Active Listening really well. Discuss your progress with your family at the dinner table.

SIGNS OF SUCCESS

Congratulations! Children are showing signs of Active Listening when they

- Pay attention to what someone tells them the first time
- Can follow directions without having to have them repeated
- Can accurately repeat a message they just heard
- Interrupt the speaker—peer and adult—only for emergency reasons
- Listen attentively to concerts, movies, videos, and plays
- Understand the plot of a movie or play
- Stop whatever they are doing to listen to someone share a story or situation

Keep trying! Children need more practice when they

- Keep repeating "What?"
- Frequently ask people to repeat directions
- Overlook the speaker's feelings
- Expect everyone to listen to them but don't listen in return—for example, ignore someone who is talking to them, interrupt others and/or talk over the top of them, or create a disruption
- Talk during concerts, movies, and plays
- Can't follow the conversation and join in appropriately

Literature Link ~ Active Listening

Ages 4-8

Dance Away	George Shannon (New York: Mulberry Books, 1998)
Great Kapok Tree: A Tale of the Amazon Rain Forest	Lynne Cherry (New York: Harcourt Brace Company, 1990)
It Could Always Be Worse: A Yiddish Folk Tale (TE)	Margot Zemach (New York: Farrar, Strauss & Giroux, 1990)
Listen Buddy (TE)	Helen Lester (Boston: Houghton Mifflin Company, 1997)

Ages 9-12

Brother Eagle, Sister Sky: A Message from Chief Seattle (NA) (TE)	Susan Jeffers, Illustrator (New York: Dial Books for Young Readers, Simon & Schuster, 1991)
Harriet, the Spy (TE)	Louise Fitzhugh (New York: HarperTrophy, 1990)
Joyful Noise: Poems for Two Voices	Paul Fleishman (New York: HarperCollins Juvenile Books, 1992)
Talking Earth, The (NA)	Jean Craighead George (New York: HarperTrophy Publishing, 1987)

Ages 13+

Dogwolf (NA)	Alden R. Carter (New York: Scholastic, 1994)
Nothing But the Truth: A Documentary Novel	Avi (New York: Avon Flare, 1993)
Speak	Laurie Halse Anderson (New York: Farrar, Strauss & Giroux, 1999)

Multicultural books: **(AFA)**=African American, **(ASA)**=Asian American, **(HA)**=Hispanic American, **(ME)**=Multi-Ethnic, **(NA)**=Native American, **(TE)**=listed in the teacher edition of this book, *Tools for Citizenship and Life: Using the ITI Lifelong Guidelines and LIFESKILLS in the Classroom*, **(BFE)**=available through Books for Educators

Family Resources

How To Talk So Kids Can Learn: At Home and in School — Adele Faber, Elaine Mazlish, Adele Faber, Elaine Mazlish, Lisa Nyberg, Rosalyn A. Templeton (Columbus, OH: Fireside, 1996)

How To Talk So Kids Will Listen and Listen So Kids Will Talk — Adele Fabor and Elaine Mazlish (Dresden, TX: Avon Books, 1999)

Listening: The Forgotten Skill — Madelyn Burley-Allen (Toronto, Canada: John Wiley & Sons, 1995)

No Put-Downs

Chapter 5

"Care about others."

no put-downs *v* **1a:** not to degrade **b:** not to disparage or belittle **c:** not to disapprove or criticize **d:** not to humiliate or squelch.

No Put-Downs: Never to use words, actions, and/or body language that degrade, humiliate, or dishonor others

WHAT ARE PUT-DOWNS?

Put-downs are words and body language that imply, "I am better than you. I have more money than you, I am smarter than you, or I have more options than you." The objective is to elevate the speaker's social standing and power. By creating a laugh at someone else's expense, the speaker gains power in the situation by controlling the behavior of others and undermining relationships between the targeted person and those in the audience. Put-downs are also a way of avoiding the real issues of the moment. They often mask unconscious feelings of jealousy, anger, fear, or inadequacy. Whether from one person or a group, the goal of put-downs is always the same—humiliation, power, control, and increased social status.

The body language of put-downs, such as rolling the eyes, tapping the forehead, caricaturing, are honed to an art form in sitcoms and other popular media in our society. They are every bit as powerful as words.

Sometimes put-downs affect us more deeply than usual. For example, when they're spoken by people we like and trust or by people we want to like us, the results are devastating. We feel betrayed. If the people whose opinion we so value express something negative about us, then it must really be so. Children under stress are especially vulnerable to the sting of put-downs. If the comments are aimed at a sensitive area (e.g., physical changes during puberty, being overweight or underweight, being an immigrant with beginning English skills), children often feel shame about something over which they have little or no control. Similarly, when we receive put-downs in front of our peers, the humiliation and shame deepen as we lose face.

WHY PRACTICE NO PUT-DOWNS?

Put-downs among adults produce a lack of trust which is extremely detrimental to one's marriage and parent-child relationships; over time they severely erode the basis of a happy, healthy, cohesive home life. If a sense of family is to survive and thrive, put-downs must be eliminated.

Also, to be open to learning is to be vulnerable. We're open to snickers when we make mistakes or admit we can't answer a question. Every child should be able to approach new opportunities and learning experiences without dreading verbal abuse.

When we refuse to allow put-downs within and by the family, at home and wherever we go, we're teaching respect for all people, ideas, and situations. We're building a positive emotional climate so that our children feel comfortable enough to risk an answer, offer a thought, and try a new skill without worrying about mocking remarks or gestures. This is particularly important for middle children whose skills and knowledge can't match the older sibling but who don't have the safety of "being the baby." Prohibiting the use of disparaging remarks is akin to constructing an invisible shield that protects and nurtures.

HOW DO YOU PRACTICE IT?

To change a negative habit to a more positive one, we first must recognize the negative behavior for what it is. And, because put-downs are so pervasive in our mass media and society, we must first teach children to recognize put-downs and become sensitive to their effects. Many children look on the word plays of put-downs as a form of humor, overlooking that it's at the expense of others.

Next, we must create an action plan to eliminate put-downs and encourage respect for others. If families do this planning together, all members feel more responsible for making the plan work.

Recognizing the Need to Change. Select a video clip ripe with put-downs. Have your child identify and count the put-downs he/she hears and sees. Discuss with your child how he/she would feel if he/she were on the receiving end of these put-downs. Next, focus on comments heard at home, around the neighborhood, at the grocery store, and even at church. Ask your child to observe the participants. Who is handing out put-downs to others? Who is the brunt of the put-downs? Who has power and social position and who doesn't?

Changing negative behaviors can occur more readily if we understand why we tend to behave as we do. Psychologist William Glasser developed a list of needs that all humans have—children and adults. To fulfill these needs, children and adults often embark on self-defeating, unpleasant behaviors without consciously knowing why. The four fundamental human needs identified by Glasser are: belonging, power, fun, and freedom.* When we hear a put-down, we should ask ourself which of these fundamental human needs is the speaker missing? If put-downs occur in your

---

* See *Choice Theory: A New Psychology of Personal Freedom* by William Glasser M.D., New York: HarperPerennial, 1998), pp. 31-41.

home, what's missing from your family environment? Look for patterns that demand change and then, with your child's help, identify why and create an action plan to change them.

The Importance of Modeling. Creating an environment free of put-downs requires constant modeling by all adults. All family members and close family friends need to understand their positions as role models for your child. It cannot be a "Do as I say but not as I do" atmosphere. Post the Lifelong Guidelines and the LIFESKILLS around the house for all to see and follow. Initiate discussions about the harmful effects of put-downs. When you hear a put-down, deal with it immediately using a calm, rational manner before the situation escalates.

Taking Responsibility for Eliminating Put-Downs. Everyone plays a part in eliminating put-downs. Begin cleansing your home of put-downs by eliminating the put-down banter that is passed off as humor. Recall a comment that had dual interpretations and then the speaker quickly said, "Just kidding!"—but you never knew the intent for sure. As the saying goes, "Many a true word is said in jest."

Second, agree on a "cancel" signal. Whenever someone says a put-down, other family members simply say, "Cancel." The hurt is canceled, the "power play" is canceled.

Practicing the Lifelong Guideline of No Put-Downs requires a concerted effort from all members of the extended family and close family friends or the realization of a caring, risk-taking, nurturing, family fellowship has little chance to succeed.

WHAT DO NO PUT-DOWNS LOOK LIKE IN THE REAL WORLD?

We

- Model the use of humor that does not "bite" or leave the listener wondering exactly what your message was

- Ban the put-down mentality from interactions with our friends, social groups, and co-workers by refusing to listen to or find humor in offensive racial, ethnic, or religious jokes

- Offer constructive criticism without the addition of demeaning comments or terms

- Ignore stereotypes and learn about each person on a one-to-one basis

- Refrain from racial slurs, disparaging remarks about ethnic groups, and negative comments about religious views that differ from our own

- Support co-workers through learning curves by providing encouragement and assistance until they are successful

- Decry the use of put-downs in TV programming, movies, and speeches by politicians and others in the public arena

- Refuse to become victims and instead empower ourselves to be strong enough to ignore put-downs

What Does No Put-Downs Look Like at Home?

Adults

- Ensure that all extended family members understand and adhere to the "No Put-Down" policy and remind ourselves and others of the policy when needed
- Refuse to allow the use of put-downs in our presence
- Practice positive support strategies while attending children's sports activities
- Refuse to laugh or find humor in racial, ethnic, or religious jokes or comments that degrade or belittle an individual or group
- Refrain from put-downs during discussions and disciplinary actions aimed at correcting behavior or attitude of a child or other adult
- Build a strong sense of family in which each person feels special, wanted, and a part of the group; value each person—adult and child—as an individual and a "work in progress"
- Model the use of humor that does not "bite" or leave our child wondering exactly what the message was
- Support family members' learning experiences through failures as well as successes
- Teach children the value of the old saying, "If you don't have anything nice to say, don't say anything"
- Teach children ways to counteract the use of put-downs

Children

- Identify words and phrases that are put-downs and replace them with statements of honest respect (terms that are positive and affirm the self-worth of other individuals)
- Explain the reasons behind the "No Put-Downs" policy to family, friends, and guests
- Recognize put-downs in newspaper articles, magazines, and literature and do not transfer these terms into everyday living
- Understand that the Lifelong Guideline of No Put-Downs is an important part of good sportsmanship at sports events both as a participant and as an observer
- Provide encouragement for family members as they practice new skills
- Acknowledge that every individual has unique gifts and talents that make for a well-rounded family and community and that differences should be respected, not ridiculed
- Understand that the use of put-downs in movies and television programs does not need to be a model for real-life relationships
- Refuse to give others power by believing a put-down that others may dump on them

OPPORTUNITIES TO PRACTICE NO PUT-DOWNS

AGES 4-8

- Draw a picture of a smiling face. Listen for put-downs as a family member reads *The Rag Coat* by Lauren Mills. Each time you recognize a put-down, tear off a piece from the smiley face. Replace one piece each time you hear a statement of respect. Discuss with a family member how you felt during this activity. Share what you learned about the power of put-downs to hurt and destroy.

- Watch a segment of a Charlie Brown movie. Tally the number of put-downs that you hear and see. Watch the segment again and determine which characters are using the put-downs and which characters are receiving them. Explain to a family member how you would feel if someone said those things to you.

- Design a family "No Put-Downs" poster. Use crayons, paints, or markers on a large sheet of white or colored paper. Write a slogan (e.g., "This Family Has a No Put-Down Policy" or "No Put-Downs Allowed in This House") and illustrate your words with matching pictures. Sign your name in the lower right hand corner and hang the poster where everyone will read it every day.

- Create a skit (short play) to teach about how hurtful put-downs are. Invite other family members to play parts. Use puppets, stuffed animals, or action dolls to tell the story. Base your skit on the song "Don't Put Me Down" from *Spread Your Wings* by Jeff Pedersen (or another song of your choice that will help teach how hurtful put-downs are). Practice your skit at least three times before you present it. Videotape your best rehearsal and present the videotape or your play live for an audience of extended family, friends, and/or neighbors.

- Brainstorm with family members some strategies to use the next time someone zaps you with a put-down. Create some statements that "cancel" the comment without escalating the situation, e.g., "Cancel" or "I don't value what you say," followed by turning and walking away. Practice using these cancel statements until you can say them naturally (mini-skits are a good way to practice). One week later, describe to a parent what happened the first time you used one of these "cancel" strategies; also explain what you learned about this experience and what you will do differently the next time.

- Design a card of encouragement for a family member who seems somewhat sad or feeling badly about a put-down they received. Illustrate the front page with a cheerful picture. Write a message of support on the inside page and explain how to "cancel" a put-down without escalating the situation. Include two things that you appreciate about the family member on the inside and sign your name. Read and give it to him/her at dinner time.

- Listen to the song "Don't Put Me Down" (from *Spread Your Wings* by Jeff Pedersen). Practice singing the song until you know it by heart. Add some hand/body motions that share your feelings about the lyrics. Teach it to everyone at the next family get-together. [You may choose a different song with a no put-down message if you wish, e.g., "Don't Laugh at Me" (*Wish You Were Here* by Mark Wills).]

AGES 9-12

- Watch a ten-minute segment of a Charlie Brown movie/video. Tally the number of put-downs you hear. Determine who is receiving the put-downs. Ask family members to act out this segment in real life. First, perform the skit with the put-downs. Then perform the skit with "put-ups." (Make sure these put-ups pass the test of the Lifelong Guidelines of Truthfulness and Trustworthiness.) Share your feelings about the difference between the two skits.

- Memorize the lyrics and tune for ""Don't Laugh at Me" (*Wish You Were Here*, Mark Wills). Write two additional verses and teach them to your family. Learn to play the song on an instrument and play along while your family sings the lyrics.

- Compose a family pledge that reflects how you will use the Lifelong Guideline of No Put-Downs at sports events. Write the pledge on special paper and decorate the page with sports memorabilia. Share this pledge with your coach.

- Write a skit showing a situation in which put-downs are used. Rewrite the skit eliminating put-downs and inserting statements of respect. With a friend, perform the skit both ways for your family. Ask them to brainstorm other statements of respect that would be appropriate for another version of the skit.

- Brainstorm a "secret signal" to use when a put-down is heard. Make it one that only your family members will recognize and understand. Use this signal as an instant reminder when a family member forgets to speak in a respectful manner towards others. Tally the number of times this signal is used during a four-week period and reflect on what you observe. If put-downs haven't been eliminated by the fourth week, ask a parent to gather the family together to create an action plan for eliminating all put-downs by the end of the next four weeks. Keep a tally to see if the plan is working.

- Identify a classmate/neighborhood child who is the recipient of put-downs. Create a plan with your family to bring this child into one of the community groups you belong to (e.g., Girl Scouts, Boy Scouts, 4H, church fellowship). Bring your plan to completion by befriending this child and inviting him/her to join this organization. Provide support by using friendly introductory comments the first few visits and by eliminating put-downs when he/she is with you.

- Introduce yourself to new kids/families on the block. Offer to show where they can find the nearest grocery stores, libraries, malls, and other places of interest. Volunteer to be a "tour guide" and show the children around the neighborhood parks and playgrounds. Include them in some traditional community events (e.g., barbecues, parades, games, festivals).

- Study commercials and advertisements for subtle forms of put-downs against males or females. OPTION ONE: Choose one example and compose a letter to the president of the company describing your concerns. Educate the agency about the personal and emotional hurts caused by the use of such put-downs. Send the letter to the company. OPTION 2: Create a new commercial/ad that sells the product or service without the use of put-downs. Perform your version for your family.

- Interview an adult about the use of put-downs at their workplace. Ask such questions as: Why do you think people use put-downs at work? What are some signs that your employer treats you with respect? How does your boss discourage or encourage the use of put-downs? In what ways does the use of put-downs affect your ability to learn at school? In what way are put-downs at work and at school similar? Different? Share what you have learned with your family at dinner time.

AGES 13+

- Watch five or more MTV videos (ask your parents' permission). Write the title of each video on a separate sheet of paper. As you listen to the lyrics, write down any examples of put-downs referring to gender, race, ethnic heritage, or religion. Create new lyrics for one of these songs. Omit the use of put-downs by inserting in their place statements of respect, sometimes called "put-ups." (Make sure that the put-ups pass the test of the Lifelong Guidelines of Truthfulness and Trustworthiness.) Sing the song for/with family members at dinner time.

- Read/watch the book/video of *The Outsiders* by S.E. Hinton. Decide which group you would have been a part of at the beginning of the story. During the reading/viewing, write down any information that might convince you to change allegiance to the other group. Decide which group you would rather belong to by the end of the tale. Share your reactions to this story with a parent or grandparent.

- Become a "Put-down" detective for one day at school. Track the number of offensive, sexist, or racist remarks that you hear. Record who gives them and who receives them. Look for any pattern(s) in the comments. Create a "one person" plan to begin the eradication of put-downs. After two weeks, reflect on the results of your action and share your conclusions with a parent, teacher, or coach.

- Watch ten or more people when they are involved in a discussion. Note six or more ways people use their bodies (e.g., rolling eyes) to send a put-down message. Create a skit that exaggerates these messages. Perform the skit for your family. Ask them to identify the negative body language used during the skit. Discuss which are most offensive and why. Brainstorm three ways to help someone break the habit of using put-down body language.

- Read a biography about someone living with a physical/mental disability. Find examples of situations where he/she was put-down. Send away to a national/state organization for information regarding this disability. Create a 3-paneled pamphlet that will teach people respect for this individual. Include who the biography was about, the typical put-downs he/she endured, and advice for eliminating such put-downs. Send the pamphlet to the national/state organization dedicated to helping people with that disability.

- Compare the main candidates campaigning for a major political office (such as president, senator, congressman, governor). Listen to their commercials and debates and read their pamphlets and other campaign literature. Record any put-downs of their opponents that you hear or read. Based on the information you have gathered and the level of disrespect inherent in the put-downs given, decide whom you would vote for. Share with your parents whom you would vote for and three or more reasons why.

- Construct a personal inventory of ten questions or more regarding talents (e.g., sports, music, dance, art) and interests (e.g., collections, hobbies) of your family members. Invite each member to take the inventory. Chart the results. Determine areas of similarity and difference. Design a family poster honoring all of the talents and interests you most admire. On a separate piece of paper, list the most common put-downs of people with such talents and interests. Then, identify what you most respect about each such talent and interest. Share your findings with your family at dinner time.

- Interview an adult about the use of put-downs at their workplace. Ask such questions as: Why do you think people use put-downs at work? What are some signs that your employer does or does not treat you with respect? How does your boss discourage or encourage the use of put-downs? Are there some people that seem to be the targets for put-downs? In what ways does the use of put-downs affect the quality and quantity of your work? Afterward, write two or three paragraphs about what you learned and share them with your family at dinner time.

- Learn to "sign" the phrase, "No Put-Downs." Practice until you can repeat it from memory. Teach your family to sign the phrase and show them when to do it during the singing of "Don't Put Me Down" (*Spread Your Wings*, Pedersen)* or "Don't Laugh at Me" (*Wish You Were Here,* Mark Wills). Add other sign language or appropriate gestures as you choose.

- Design a brochure explaining the Lifelong Guideline of No Put-Downs. Add graphics to illustrate this policy. Make copies of the pamphlet available for visitors to your home (extended family and friends) so that they will understand this policy.

- Read the following quotation by Eleanor Roosevelt, "No one can make you feel inferior without your consent." Write a paragraph about what this quotation means to you. Share your thoughts with a family member.

SIGNS OF SUCCESS

Congratulations! Children are showing signs of not using Put-Downs when they

- Teach family members and friends about the harmful effects of put-downs
- Consciously stop themselves before any negative words pop out of their mouths
- Apologize when they slip and use a put-down and take immediate action to make it up to the person
- Avoid humor based on ethnicity, race, sex, religion, or disability
- Feel uncomfortable in the presence of others who are using put-downs

---

* Available through Books for Educators.

- Include the Lifelong Guideline of No Put-Downs in their definition of sportsmanship-like behavior after winning/losing a game

- Stand up for someone who is receiving put-downs from others

- Include all neighborhood children in clubs and activities

- Extend themselves to become acquainted with someone in the neighborhood who receives put-downs because he/she is considered different

- Understand that true power and influence arises from who we are—our character and values—and that put-downs provide only an illusion of empowerment of the speaker

Keep trying! Children need more practice when they

- Laugh at put-downs

- Repeat put-downs that they've heard that make fun of another's race, religion, gender, ethnicity, nationality, disabilities, or economic status

- Mock/mimic/imitate others actions in an exaggerated manner and think it's funny

- Taunt/tease other children about their abilities, talents, and/or interests

- Encourage other family members/friends to use put-downs

- Hear/see put-downs but do nothing to stop them

- Can't give genuine compliments to family members or friends

Literature Link ~ No Put-Downs

AGES 4-8

Fanny's Dream	Carolyn and Mark Buehne (New York: Dial Books, Simon & Schuster, 1996)
Rag Coat, The	Lauren Mills (New York: Little, Brown and Co, 1991)
Squids Will Be Squids: Fresh Morals, Beastly Fable	Jon Scieszka (New York: Viking Childrens Books, 1998)
Stranger in the Mirror (ASA)	Allen Say (Boston: Houghton Mifflin Publishing Co, 1995)

AGES 9-12

Blubber (TE)	Judy Blume (New York: Simon & Schuster, 1983)
Crow Boy (ASA) (TE)	Taro Yashima (New York: Viking Press, 1976)
When Zachary Beaver Comes to Town	Kimberly Willis Holt (New York: Henry Holt & Co, 1999)
Yolanda's Genius (AFA)	Carol Fenner (New York: Aladdin Books, Simon & Schuster, 1995)

AGES 13+

Autobiography of a Face	Lucy Grealy (New York: HarperPerennial, 1995)
Light in the Forest, The (NA)	Conrad Richter (New York: Fawcett Juniper Press, 1995)
Warriors Don't Cry: A Searing Memoir of the Battle to Integrate Little Rock's Central High School (AFA)	Melba Patillo Beals (New York: Archway Paperbacks, Simon & Schuster, 1995)

Family Resources

Bringing Kids Up Without Tearing Them Down: How to Raise Confident, Successful Children	Dr. Kevin Leman (Nashville, TN: Thomas Nelson, Inc., 1995)
Positive Discipline from A-Z: From Toddlers to Teens, 1001 Solutions to Everyday Parenting Problems, Revised and Expanded 2nd Edition	Jane Nelson, Lynn Lott, H. Stephen Glenn (Rocklin, CA: Prima Publishing, 1999)

Multicultural books: **(AFA)**=African American, **(ASA)**=Asian American, **(HA)**=Hispanic American, **(ME)**=Multi-Ethnic, **(NA)**=Native American, **(TE)**=listed in the teacher edition of this book, *Tools for Citizenship and Life: Using the ITI Lifelong Guidelines and LIFESKILLS in the Classroom*, **(BFE)**=available through Books for Educators

Personal Best

Chapter 6

"Do your best."

personal *adj* 1: done in person without the intervention of another
2: relating to an individual, or his character or conduct
best *adj* one's maximum effort

Personal Best: One's best possible performance given the circumstances and available resources

WHAT IS PERSONAL BEST?

For those using the ITI model, the Lifelong Guideline of Personal Best is defined by the 18 LIFESKILLS: Integrity, Responsibility, Common Sense, Problem Solving, Organization, Resourcefulness, Effort, Perseverance, Sense of Humor, Initiative, Curiosity, Courage, Flexibility, Patience, Friendship, Caring, Cooperation, and Pride. To pursue one's personal best means working to develop and strengthen each LIFESKILL. (See the LIFESKILLS and their definitions on the next page.)

Quality work is never an accident; it is always the result of combining clear goals, high standards, knowledge and skills, and genuine effort. It represents the wisest choice among many options matched with commitment, perseverance, and wise use of time, talents, and resources. There is no one way to achieve a sense of fulfillment but doing one's personal best on a consistent basis is the best road we know of.

The Lifelong Guideline of Personal Best is not about treats, rewards, or bonuses; it's about a deep sense of personal satisfaction* for a job well done, for mastering a skill, or for making a contribution to one's family, community, and world.

---

* The term "deep sense of personal satisfaction" was coined by Brenda Wyckoff, fourth grade teacher in Sedona, Arizona. Her ability to enable students to experience who they could be is an extraordinary gift to her students.

 LIFESKILLS

CARING: To feel and show concern for others

COMMON SENSE: To use good judgment

COOPERATION: To work together toward a common goal or purpose

COURAGE: To act according to one's beliefs despite fear of adverse consequences

CURIOSITY: A desire to investigate and seek understanding of one's world

EFFORT: To do your best

FLEXIBILITY: To be willing to alter plans when necessary

FRIENDSHIP: To make and keep a friend through mutual trust and caring

INITIATIVE: To do something, of one's own free will, because it needs to be done

INTEGRITY: To act according to a sense of what's right and wrong

ORGANIZATION: To plan, arrange, and implement in an orderly way; to keep things orderly and ready to use

PATIENCE: To wait calmly for someone or something

PERSEVERANCE: To keep at it

PRIDE: Satisfaction from doing one's personal best

PROBLEM SOLVING: To create solutions to difficult situations and everyday problems

RESOURCEFULNESS: To respond to challenges and opportunities in innovative and creative ways

RESPONSIBILITY: To respond when appropriate; to be accountable for one's actions

SENSE OF HUMOR: To laugh and be playful without harming others

Personal Best Is Not a Fixed Standard

Personal Best is not about perfectionism. Personal best is the result of our consistent pursuit of a moving target over an ever-changing terrain. Thus, our performance in the same activity looks different over time. As our competence grows, our performance improves. As the tools, time, and resources available to us improve, our performance improves.

For example, while supporting your family (emotionally, financially, and physically), you might take up jogging. You may try hard to improve your running technique but you struggle to complete the course. You're doing your personal best in both areas—family life and jogging—but your jogging skill and capabilities in no way compare to those of a professional athlete who can and does devote full focus and time to his/her athletic pursuits. Personal best is using the utmost effort possible and striving for a heightened stage of excellence. This may or may not translate into being Number 1, the winner, the hero; in the real world, such status is rare. But all of us can achieve our personal best if we are willing to apply ourselves.

Personal Best Defined. Personal Best isn't perfection or a fixed standard. Personal Best is one's best possible performance at the time, given the time and resources available at the moment, under the circumstances of the moment, while fully using one's knowledge, skills, and talents. (This, of course, takes into account the LIFESKILLs of Resourcefulness and Organization!)

PERSONAL BEST IS A MINDSET

What drives you to do your personal best? The most important element is a clear vision of your goals and personal performance standards plus love of what you are doing. When such vision and love are united, you want to do your best! The secret about goals is to make them personal—focus on your performance, not on the status or glamour of the project. Athletes strive to surpass their previous personal accomplishments. This provides a vision that pushes them to constantly improve. Like an athlete, love the process of working toward your goals, celebrating each step toward your vision even if you don't win the Olympic gold.

Doing one's personal best is a way of life, not an isolated incident.

WHY PRACTICE PERSONAL BEST?

As Aristotle wrote, "We are what we repeatedly do. Excellence, then, is not an act, but a habit."* The Lifelong Guideline of Personal Best is transferable from one sector of life to another—in family and social life, on the job, in religious experiences, and during recreational activities. You can't work on excellence in one area and not have it show up in other areas. But the converse is also true: Refusing to do your personal best in one area will show up as laziness or avoidance in others.

---

* *Nicomachean Ethics* by Aristotle, 350 BC, translated by W.D. Ross. *The Internet Classics Archives/Works by Aristotle,* http://classics.mit.edu/Browse/browse-Aristotle.html

Some people start out by thinking, "Doing my personal best is too difficult! I'll have to work really hard." But think of the opposite. Do you really want to work toward personal worst or mediocrity? You may have to expend the same amount of effort to achieve less. Does that make sense? Self-respect—and the respect of others—depends heavily upon performing consistently at our personal best.

HOW DO YOU PRACTICE IT?

As we're sure the Army has discovered, the slogan "Be the best you can be" is far easier said than done. Not that it is a mystery. But to achieve our personal best requires a broad range of personal and social skills that need to be learned early and practiced daily until they become dependable habits of mind rather than now-and-then skills we dredge up when we're in a pinch.

The Lifelong Guideline of Personal Best is defined by 18 LIFESKILLS as shown on page 6.2. To the surprise of many, children seem to have an intuitive grasp of the LIFESKILLS. The word and concept of "perseverance," for example, is no hurdle at all for kindergartners. And they seem delighted to be let in on the secret of how to succeed at things—when they want something, they know how to go about getting it. A wonderful gift so early in life. One might say that the road to success in life is paved with 23 yellow bricks: the 18 LIFESKILLS and five Lifelong Guidelines.

In addition to keeping our feet on the yellow brick road, we must also:

- Identify a vision and set personal goals

- Continuously self-evaluate in order to improve (attitude, performance, or goal-setting) and to revise or completely redesign our plans as needed

- Welcome suggestions from others with a different perspective and who may thus have unique experiences to share

- Understand that we will make mistakes but that we can turn them into life lessons, realizing that we have discovered a way *not* to do something, a necessary fine-tuning of our thinking. Thomas Edison, for example, discovered over 2,000 ways not to make the light bulb before he found a way that worked.*

- Expect to continually refine our methods, thinking, and techniques throughout our lives, looking for any variation that might improve us or our products

- Allow ourselves to feel pride when all of these LIFESKILL efforts combine as one and provide us with the experience of doing our personal best.

Does this sound like a recipe for adults only? Not true. Even five-year olds can set a vision of what they would like to be when they grow up although it may, and often does, change weekly. At age five, many of the skills being learned have feedback built into the learning event; our children don't have to ask, "Mommy, mommy, is this right?" They are able to judge for themselves. As for welcoming suggestions from others, they are used to getting plenty of advice from

---

* *A 2nd Helping of Chicken Soup for the Soul: 101 More Stories to Open the Heart and Rekindle the Spirit* by Jack Canfield and Mark Victor, Health Communications, Inc., Deerfield Beach, Florida, 1995, p. 253. See also *Thomas Alva Edison Home Page,* http://www.thomasedison.com. Webmaster: Gerald Beals, October, 1999, Online AOL

grownups. And when it comes to learning from mistakes, young children do it with much more grace than adults do.

Can children younger than five learn these aspects of doing the Lifelong Guideline of Personal Best? In their own age-appropriate ways, absolutely! It may in fact be more difficult for high-school students and adults to learn the Lifelong Guideline of Personal Best because there is a lot of unlearning of old attitudes and habits of mind that must first be shed.

WHAT DOES PERSONAL BEST LOOK LIKE IN THE REAL WORLD?

We

- Go the "extra mile" for our family, work, and community
- Willingly retrain for another line of work or work more than one job if necessary to provide for our family
- Forget about time clocks and contractual hours and persevere until we complete a project or task as promised
- Guarantee services from our business and products from our company; offer money-back guarantees; recall unsafe and dangerous products
- Volunteer time for service organizations such as the neighborhood school, Red Cross, American Cancer Society, and Ronald McDonald House as well as keep up work and home responsibilities
- Dedicate the necessary time and effort to do our personal best
- Continue learning throughout our lives, always with the thought of improving ourselves; be open to advice and coaching of others—child and adult

WHAT DOES PERSONAL BEST LOOK LIKE AT HOME?

Adults

- Present a smiling, welcoming face each morning to family and friends
- Consistently model the LIFESKILLS even when frustrated or angry in order to provide a stable, consistent home atmosphere for children and spouse; teach our children to also model the LIFESKILLS at all times
- Maintain family schedules as agreed despite work and personal pressures; handle personal responsibilities so we can participate fully in family events, school functions, and other activities in which our children participate
- Perform duties and tasks to a personal standard of excellence; complete chores and responsibilities fully, cheerfully, and on time

- Tackle tough tasks and follow through to completion
- Make time for each child to share his/her events and experiences of the day
- Do all we can to ensure our children will succeed in school, such as arrange for medical care, glasses, dental care, hearing aides, and other care that our child might need to equip him/her for succeeding academically and personally; read notes, newsletters, and information sent by the school personnel and respond as requested; and read books and articles that explain the learning process so we can do our part

Children

- Consciously work at applying the Lifelong Guidelines and LIFESKILLS at home and the world beyond
- Set goals and develop an action plan to reach them
- Say "I can!" rather than "I can't!"; take on and complete challenging projects
- Complete work that requires intense personal investment, a high level of accountability, and continuous growth
- Try different activities and develop new interests (such as learning to play a musical instrument, do woodworking, play a new sport or a different position in a current sport)
- Apply the LIFESKILLS to school work and chores at home especially when the subject/task is not easily mastered/carried out

OPPORTUNITIES TO PRACTICE PERSONAL BEST

AGES 4-8

- Practice the following skills using the Lifelong Guideline of Personal Best: buttoning, zippering, buckling, and tying a bow. Pick out the clothes you will wear the next day before going to bed at night. Dress yourself the next morning. Practice until you master each skill.
- Decide where you are going to keep your toys. Draw a picture of each toy and place the drawing on the shelf or on the box where the toy will be kept. Put the toys in their proper places before going to bed each night.
- Choose two procedures that you need to do more of in order to have a healthier body (e.g., brushing teeth twice a day, washing hands after using the toilet, bathing daily, drinking five glasses of water a day, playing outside). Create a plan (e.g., chart, discussion, reminder, song) with an adult to practice these procedures until they become habits (do them every day without reminders). Once these first two are mastered, add one more and maintain all three for a month.

- With your parents, write "Visiting Procedures"—the behaviors you are expected to use when you are a guest in someone else's home. Identify three LIFESKILLS you think you will most need to use during the visit, e.g., Friendship, Cooperation, and Patience. Determine what you will need to do to carry out each LIFESKILL. Also, include what kind of voice to use, e.g., indoor, outdoor, 24" inch (distance you can be heard), how you will move (e.g., run, walk, skip, jump, climb), what you can touch (e.g., nothing, non-breakables, toys), and manners to follow (e.g., say hello to the adult in charge and thank him/her for allowing you to visit, determine when and how to ask for permission and to say please, thank you). Illustrate these procedures and review them before you visit anyone's home. After visiting someone's home, discuss with your parents how well you think you followed these procedures.

- Choose two chores that you feel capable of completing every day. Offer to do these chores for a two-week period. Set up a calendar so that you can record your actions. Use a checkmark for one chore and a smiley face for the other. Put these symbols on the calendar for each day you complete the chore. Review your performance with your parents at the end of two weeks. Choose two new chores and repeat the activity.

- Choose one skill you are trying to improve/master (e.g., rollerskate, make a bed, pack a book bag, play a computer game). Ask an adult to help you figure out two ways you could use the LIFESKILLS of Perseverance and Patience (two ways each) that would help you master/greatly improve that skill. Ask the adult to help you set goals, (such as when you want to be able to do the skill and for what purpose). Analyze your beginning skill levels. Set up a practice schedule for a two-week period. Every time you use one of the ways to practice the LIFESKILLS of Perseverance and/or Patience to improve the skill, put a checkmark next to it. At the end of the two weeks, ask the same adult to help you decide if you have improved. Discuss how doing the Lifelong Guideline of Personal Best, especially using the LIFESKILLS of Perseverance and Patience, has helped you improve. Repeat for another two weeks if necessary. When that skill has been mastered, set a new goal.

AGES 9-12

- Write "Getting Ready for School Procedures"—things you can do every night before going to bed that will make getting ready for school in the morning easier (such as fewer things to be done and having things better organized). Include choosing the clothes you will wear, packing homework, getting special items ready (e.g., gym clothes, library books) and selecting lunch options (e.g., buying, bringing). An hour before bedtime, complete each procedure to guarantee a "hassle-free" start in the morning. Practice these procedures nightly for three weeks until they become a Personal Best "habit of mind." Continue these procedures as one way to do your personal best on a day-to-day basis. Review these procedures periodically and make any changes needed.

- Review the "character development" comments on your report card. Determine any areas that need improving such as citizenship, attitude, cooperation with others (e.g., talks out of turn, pushes ahead in line), and work habits (forgets materials, doesn't complete homework). With a parent's help, create an action plan to help improve your performance in one of these areas. Think of two LIFESKILLS that would be most helpful. List three or more specific ways you could use each LIFESKILL. Work on these actions daily and review the comments on your next report card to see if more practice is necessary.

- Learn two or more of the LIFESKILLS songs from *LIFESKILLS* (tape or CD)* by Russ and Judy Eacker. Choose one of the songs to teach to your family at your next family gathering or reunion. Explain to them why you chose that particular song to share.

- Brainstorm "Homework Procedures" that will build strong work habits. Include the following information: work place, time schedule, necessary materials, how to get assistance when needed, etc. Write these procedures in chart form using crayons or markers. Add graphics that match your ideas. Hang this chart in your room and follow it daily. Discuss your results with a family member.

- Join a sports team of your choice (e.g., baseball, football, volleyball, basketball, soccer, gymnastics). Determine your current skill levels. Create a plan for using the Lifelong Guideline of Personal Best to improve one or more skills. After each practice and/or game, discuss (with parent/coach/another player) progress toward your new goals. After the new skill level is in place, repeat the process with another skill.

- Join a chorus or choir in your school, church, or community for one year. Commit yourself to doing your personal best to master the part you are to sing, including memorizing the lyrics. Invite all your family members to come hear you and your group sing. Share with a family member how using the Lifelong Guideline of Personal Best has improved your singing and your enjoyment of singing.

- Become a member of one of the following organizations: Girl Scouts, Boy Scouts, 4-H, or other service club. Participate in weekly meetings. Plan four or more projects for the year and how you will use the Lifelong Guideline of Personal Best to complete them. Invite your family to be present for the awards ceremony when you will receive badges or certificates to celebrate your accomplishments.

- Choose four chores (two that you like to do, two that you don't like to do) and volunteer to be responsible for these tasks for one month. First determine the time frame for each chore (e.g., daily, weekly, bi-monthly, monthly). Decide the proper procedures for performing the chore correctly. Write the procedures for each chore on separate sheets of paper; add appropriate graphics and place in a folder for easy reference. At the end of two weeks, ask your parents for feedback on your performance. Readjust the procedures if necessary. Request final feedback at the end of four weeks. Choose four new chores and repeat the process.

- Identify a family member, friend, or other acquaintance who always demonstrates the Lifelong Guideline of Personal Best. Create a card, badge, or write a letter explaining to this person what you have learned from observing him/her and how you plan to use this information to improve your performance/behavior in the future.

AGES 13+

- Reflect on this quote from Oprah Winfrey: "My philosophy is that not only are you responsible for your life but doing the best at this moment puts you in the best place for the next moment." How would your life change if you followed Oprah's advice?

---

* This song collection is not generally available through bookstores. However, it can be ordered through Books for Educators 888/777-9827, fax 253/630-7215, E-mail books4@oz.net, www.books4educ.com

Commit yourself to acting on this quote for one week. Share your successes with a friend or family member.

- Review your school report card with your parents. Determine which areas (such as subjects, attendance, tardies, social skills/judgments) need to improve. Create an action plan to implement for the next marking period. Include your goal, three or more ways you will use the Lifelong Guideline of Personal Best to reach the goal and some form of evaluation (discussion, chart, reflection) to determine if the goal has been reached. Meet with your teacher every two weeks for a report on your progress. Share this information with your parents. Judge the effectiveness of your plan when you receive your next report card. Determine whether or not to continue with this goal or to set up a new one. Share this information with your parents/teacher.

- Complete a job application. Include all of your LIFESKILL strengths. Ask a parent to help you practice for the interview. Be prepared to share your thoughts on how well you use the Lifelong Guidelines and LIFESKILLS and any plans you are working on to strengthen areas of weaknesses.

- Compile photographs and other memorabilia to complete a photo journal essay detailing your family's history over the past 40+ years. Use a scrapbook/videos/audiotapes to collect additional information. Identify at least three Lifelong Guidelines/ LIFESKILLS that each person is/was best known for. Write in comments where appropriate. Display the product at the next two family gatherings. Include additional information as it becomes available.

- Graduate from a babysitting course offered by a local hospital or service organization. Create an emergency binder that will hold the following information for each of your clients: emergency numbers, emergency contact names, allergies of each child, phone number of place where parents will be. Volunteer to practice the skills and information learned at the babysitting course by caring for younger siblings without charge. Ask your parents to write a recommendation that you can use as a reference.

- Volunteer to donate time at a local senior citizens center. Offer to help in one of the following ways: snow shoveling, grocery shopping, heavy cleaning, visiting, food preparation, organizing and carrying out a 30-minute musical or drama performance. Keep a record of whom you visit and the activity(ies) you perform. Request feedback on your job performance from the agency's staff, especially how well you used the Lifelong Guideline of Personal Best.

- With your parents' consent, obtain a driver's permit when you reach the legal age for your state. Sign up for driving instruction through your local school, a driving agency, or with a responsible family member. Learn the laws of the road as required by your state driver's handbook. Ask someone to explain the automobile insurance policy your family has and how your beginning to drive will affect it. Keep a token in the car (e.g., picture, stuffed animal, talisman) that will remind you to use the Lifelong Guideline of Personal Best (especially the LIFESKILLS of Common Sense, Cooperation, Patience, and Responsibility) at all times. Arrange for your driver's test. With your parents, write "Family Car Procedures" regarding where, when, by whom, and how the family car may be used and how it should be cared for. Also decide on consequences if the procedures are not followed. Carry a copy of the procedures/consequences in the car.

- Interview several neighbors who work in different fields (e.g. medical, engineering, computers, education, advertising, food service, maintenance). Ask them to share how the Lifelong Guideline of Personal Best appears in their job/profession. Identify five common attributes that appear in most of the occupations you explored. List three or more ways you can use what you learned to improve how you use the Lifelong Guideline of Personal Best.

- Choose a LIFESKILL (e.g., Responsibility, Caring, Friendship) that you feel you need to practice more. Establish a time frame for improving this skill. List three or more practical steps to reach your goal. When you feel that you have improved, reflect on the process of goal setting and record your thoughts in a journal to read to a family member or during dinner time.

- Read the biography of a successful athlete. List two training techniques taught to him/her by coaches that led to success. Interview a trainer/coach to speak about improving your skills in sports. If possible, also interview a sports player (perhaps one who graduated from your school) now playing for a high school/college/professional team to explain his/her own process for reaching personal best. Record your findings in your journal.

- Research the work standards and customer satisfaction policies of four local businesses. Choose which company you would prefer to work for or buy from because of its employment practices and customer service record. Share your reasons with a family member.

- Interview a local politician to discuss his/her concept of "personal best." Ask about information such as their attendance at meetings, voting record, and introduction of new legislation. Do you believe they did their personal best to represent you? Decide if you would vote for them at the next election.

SIGNS OF SUCCESS

Congratulations! Children are showing signs of Personal Best when they

- Stick to a task until it is completed; redo any task to improve on the quality of the work if it doesn't meet the specified criteria or their own standards for personal best

- Practice self-evaluation and use these observations as guidelines for setting goals and working on tasks

- Recognize the Lifelong Guideline of Personal Best in others and congratulate them for the effort put forth

- Identify heroes who live(d) the Lifelong Guideline of Personal Best and want to emulate them

- Feel a deep sense of personal satisfaction and pride in their hearts and minds when they've done their personal best

Keep trying! Children need more practice when they

- Use personal best only when it suits their own interests
- Set goals but don't work toward accomplishing them
- Do sloppy work and try to pass it off as their personal best; show no interest in improving skills or work habits
- Ignore responsibilities and wait for others to take over the job
- Turn down opportunities for help from family and friends and refuse to listen to suggestions
- Ridicule someone else for doing his/her personal best
- Expect to be exempt from family chores; don't do their share of the work on cooperative projects
- Have more privileges than others
- Don't feel honest pride in what they are doing

Character Begins at Home: Family Tools for Teaching Character and Values

Literature Link ~ Personal Best

Ages 4-8

Bat Boy and His Violin, The (AFA)	Gavin Curtis (New York: Simon & Schuster, 1998)
Little Scarecrow Boy, The	Margaret Wise Brown (New York: HarperCollins Juvenile Books, 1998)
Painted Dreams (HA)	Karen Lynn Williams (New York: William Morrow & Company, 1998)
Story of the Jumping Mouse, The (NA)	John Steptoe (New York: Mulberry Books, William Morrow & Company, 1989)

Ages 9-12

A Boy of Tache (NA)	Ann Blades (Burnsville, MN: Econo-clad Books, Sagebrush Corporation, 1999)
Baseball Saved Us (ASA)	Ken Mochizuki (New York: Lee & Low Books, 1995)
Richard Wright and the Library Card (AFA)	William Miller (New York: Lee & Low, 1997)
Skin I'm In, The	Sharon G. Flake (Boston, MA: Jump at the Sun, A Division of Hyperion Books, 2000)

Ages 13+

Hug a Thousand Trees With Ribbons: The Story of Phyllis Wheatley (AFA)	Ann Rinaldi (New York: Gulliver Books, A Division of Harcourt Brace, 1996)
Lyddie	Katherine Patterson (London: Puffin Books, 1995)
Nightjohn (AFA)	Gary Paulsen (New York: Doubleday Books, 1995)
Zach (AFA)	William Bel (New York: Simon & Schuster, 1999)

Family Resources

Another Sip of Chicken Soup for the Soul: Heartwarming Stories of the Love Between Parents and Child
Andrews McMeel (Kansas City, MO: Health Communications, 1998)

Emotional Intelligence: Why It Can Matter More Than IQ (B4E)
Daniel Goleman (New York: Bantam Books, 1997)

Multicultural books: **(AFA)**=African American, **(ASA)**=Asian American, **(HA)**=Hispanic American, **(ME)**=Multi-Ethnic, **(NA)**=Native American, **(TE)**=listed in the teacher edition of this book, *Tools for Citizenship and Life: Using the ITI Lifelong Guidelines and LIFESKILLS in the Classroom*, **(BFE)**=available through Books for Educators

Caring

Chapter 7

"Show you care."

caring *vi* **1 a:** to feel trouble or anxiety on behalf of another's situation; to feel concern or interest; **2:** to give care **3:** to have a liking, fondness, or taste **4:** to have an inclination

Caring: To feel and show concern for others

WHAT IS CARING?

Caring is a visceral feeling arising from empathy for another's situation when we detect their distress or anxiety. The feeling prompts us to provide support for others in day-to-day living experiences or during crisis situations. Caring is a gift from our *bodybrain's* "information substances"* that detect and transmit information about the emotional status of those around us.

Caring and empathy are innate qualities in humans; we are born with a sensitivity to the plight of others. Consider, for example, the toddler who bursts into tears because another child in the room is crying. Unfortunately for some children, hard circumstances conspire over time to freeze their feelings and emotions.

WHY PRACTICE CARING?

Caring is a key ingredient for our personal and social lives and for citizenship.

Caring As a Glue. Caring is a critical glue that binds us to family, friends, and community. Without it, we would interact like ships passing in the night—indifferent, detached. Without it, community—even on a small scale within family life—would be impossible. In family life, healthy and enduring relationships depend on caring.

---

* For a fascinating and understandable yet scientific explanation of our inner emotional life, see *Molecules of Emotion: Why You Feel the Way You Feel* by Candace Pert (New York: Touchstone, 1997).

Life in the work place would also be a nasty experience without the element of caring. There would be no cohesiveness, nothing to look forward to when showing up in the morning. Work would amount to 40 hours a week spent with strangers. In contrast, effective teamwork is built on three foundations: Genuine caring for members in the group, interest in what is to be accomplished, and concern about what might happen if the task isn't accomplished.

Caring says: "What happens to you matters to me," "I want the best for you," "I am here for you," "I am willing to help provide support when you cannot stand alone, "I want life to work for everyone." A nurturing relationship with even one other caring person can spell the difference between despair and success.*

Caring As Antidote to Egotism and Prejudice. Egotism—the well-known "me first" attitude that has flourished many times during our history—and prejudice, in all its many forms, are real threats to society and citizenship. Caring is perhaps our best antidote to both. Caring lowers the expression of egotism and prejudice and speeds healing for those who bear the brunt of them. Also, as caring and empathy increase, we begin to see each individual as unique and valuable; in so doing we begin to unlearn prejudices and raise our concern for what happens to others, not just ourselves.

Caring As Key Ingredient for Citizenship. Caring is also a key ingredient for citizenship. When we go to the polls, we must vote for the good of the many, not the special interests of the few. The search for solutions that work best for all concerned requires that we genuinely care about the welfare and happiness of others. The attitude of "Not in my backyard" must be widened to a concern about that issue on behalf of others as well.

HOW DO YOU PRACTICE IT?

The motto for practicing caring could be John Donne's statement, "No man is an island; every man is a piece of the continent, a part of the main."** That is true from birth onward.

Caring comes from our deepest-held convictions about the value of the human race and of the individual. To model caring, it must be lived.

Start Early

Nurturing a child's innate sense of caring starts in the home. To no one's surprise, the number one strategy is modeling. Caring must be experienced; it is based in emotions, not intellectual thoughts. And, it must be carefully cultivated; we must encourage a child's gentle, empathetic nature. For boys, we must guard against society's pressures to be macho, the tough guy.*** For

---

*   Coontz, Stephanie, *Phi Delta Kappan,* March, 1995, p. 16.
** "Devotions Upon Emergent Occasions," *Meditation XVII,* 1624. *John Donne Society Home Page* http://www.csus.edu/org/
*** Michael Gurian, *The Wonder of Boys: What Parents Can Do to Shape Boys into Exceptional Men* (Los Angeles,: J.P. Tarcher, 1997). See also James Garbarino, *Lost Boys: Why Our Sons Turn Violent and How We Can Save Them* (New York: Free Press, Simon & Schuster, 1999).

girls, we must focus on the ability to care and detect the feelings of others as a key skill for leadership—in the community and on the job as well as within the family.

At Home

There are several ways parents can help children practice caring. Modeling is, of course, the most important. Next come curriculum content, guided practice, friendships, and community work.

"Curriculum" Content. Parents are not used to thinking in terms of "curriculum content." However what you talk about with your children from moment to moment and the experiences you plan for your children, such as conversation at the dinner table, the stories you read, trips to the zoo, a play, a vacation spot, and so forth, are all loaded with messages or curriculum content. To teach the LIFESKILL of Caring, make the most of your selections of content for their eyes and ears. This chapter is intended to give you a place to start, after which content can be tailored to your child's needs and environment.

Guided Practice. Practicing caring requires thoughtful observational skills. Who is hurting? What steps will provide support? What problem-solving strategies will be most effective? In day-to-day relationships, help your child discern opportunities that will enable him/her to extend heartfelt concern. And help your child recognize, and change, the behavior(s) that is the cause of pain or discomfort to others.

The Opportunities to Practice on pages 7.6 to 7.9 provide opportunities for lots of guided practice which will in turn open up many golden teachable moments for modeling, target talk, and "processing the process."* Also, an inappropriate remark can open up in-depth discussion about caring; learning how to "clean up" our insensitive words is an important skill.

Caring Through Friendship. Help your child develop his/her childhood friendships into the kinds of caring interactions that will last a lifetime. These special relationships—with their intense feelings of camaraderie, their secrets, codes, clubhouses, and long hours spent together—are the perfect vehicle for developing caring.

Listening to a friend's problems is one of the simplest ways to feel caring at a visceral level and one of the best opportunities to show caring. Not only do we listen but we also feel and respond with phrases like, "I understand," "Is there something I can do to help support you while you sort this out?" and "Explain it to me." Although the friend may not need advice or should be left to figure it out on his/her own, just having someone listen and empathize provides release from stress and deepens self-confidence. Make sure that family circle times focus on expressions of caring as well as resolution of issues. Think of family circle** time (when the family gathers to talk through a problem) as an opportunity to deepen positive behaviors as well as resolve negative behaviors.

---

* "Processing the process"—reflecting on what went on during a process/project such as selecting a leader or group recorder or helping each other on a project or disagreeing about something—is an important way to help children become more aware of and sensitive to what's going on for others and themselves. Processing the process is a way to slow down the movie of one's daily life in order to study our interactions with others and learn more about ourselves and human nature. It is especially useful for extending and enriching the Lifelong Guidelines and LIFESKILLS. See *TRIBES: A New Way of Learning and Being Together* by Jeanne Gibbs, p. 403.

** See *Positive Discipline* by Jane Nelson (New York: Balantine Books, 1996), Chapter 7.

Caring Through Serving the Community. Since the average life span keeps increasing, assisting elderly relatives and neighbors who can't navigate on their own is a humbling look at our own future. Many of us are part of the "sandwich generation," caught between growing children and aging parents. Tasks that the older generation once handled automatically now require monumental effort and must be taken over by the younger population who possess flexible knees, a steady heart, and sturdy limbs. On a practical level, if we are unwilling to care now, what would make us think that others would be willing to care about us later?

Neighbors form another link in the caring chain. We should be there to help each other celebrate and grieve, laugh and cry, and cheer and admonish. We should band together for common causes and concerns.

Make community service a weekly or biweekly activity. We can serve our community and live the LIFESKILL of Caring by volunteering to work with the homeless, Red Cross, a food bank, a Ronald McDonald House, or the Special Olympics, for example.

And, in the really big scheme of life, we must also care about our planet and learn ways to express that caring. Global caring is a necessity, not a luxury. Our very existence is at stake—environmentally, socially, and economically. Help your child create action plans meant to improve the quality of life for all citizens in our neighborhood and the world.

WHAT DOES CARING LOOK LIKE IN THE REAL WORLD?
We

- Welcome a new family to our neighborhood
- Shovel the snow from an elderly neighbor's sidewalk
- Volunteer for community organizations that reach out to assist others in crisis such as a local food bank or soup kitchen
- Provide comfort and support for other families when serious illness or death occurs
- Take care of older, fragile relatives
- Organize collections to send flowers and other goodies when co-workers are ill
- Help a lost child find his/her parents
- Bring stray dogs and cats to animal shelters
- Help to clean litter and trash from the streets around the neighborhood
- Listen to friends as they try to solve a problem
- Recycle plastic and paper "throw-aways"; help take care of the environment by practicing the 4 R's of waste management—Refuse~Reduce~Reuse~Recycle

WHAT DOES CARING LOOK LIKE AT HOME?

Adults

- Demonstrate our love for each family member on a daily basis

- Work cooperatively to share the challenges and demands of household and family tasks

- Give special attention to washing/ironing the family's clothes, cooking favorite meals, paying bills, and saving for a "rainy day"

- Tend to family members who are ill; take in parents and grandparents in order to provide physical, emotional, and monetary support as needed

- Organize birthday parties for family members

- Delay buying something new for ourselves in order to buy something for someone else

- Show an interest in the lives of those working in our community businesses, our church, our neighborhood

- Help one another (family, friends, and neighbors) in times of need or stress

Children

- Are genuinely concerned about what happens to siblings, parents, and other family members—how they feel (emotionally and physically), how things turn out for them

- Demonstrate on a daily basis that they care about family and close friends

- Offer to help a parent when he/she is not feeling well, taking on extra chores and so forth

- Take care of clothing, toys, and other personal belongings

- Share toys, tools, ideas, and dreams with family and friends

- Offer help with everyday tasks

- Exercise, feed, and play with pets with their best health in mind

- Befriend a child new to the neighborhood

- Offer support to friends who are having tough times

- Notify an adult who can assist when a friend is crying or very upset

- Participate in community service projects at least twice a month

OPPORTUNITIES TO PRACTICE CARING

AGES 4-8

- Offer to care for the family pet for one month. Make a chart with this heading:

FOOD	EXERCISE	PLAY

  Set up a schedule to feed, walk, and play with the pet every day. Put a smiley face in each column after you do the activity. Count the smiley faces for each category when the month ends. Discuss with Mom/Dad how well you completed the project.

- Design a special card for "Grandparents Day." Use markers, paints, or crayons to color a picture of yourself on the front of the card. Write a two-line poem (e.g., "I just want to say 'Have a Happy Grandparents' Day'") on the inside of the card. Sign your name and mail or deliver the card to grandma and grandpa in person.

- Find two or more ways (e.g., play peek-a-boo, read a story, play a game, sing a song) to entertain a younger brother or sister. Ask Mom or Dad to show you the correct way to do these tasks. Wait for the next time you are needed. Do one of the fun things to keep the child happy. Find out from your parents if what you did was helpful.

- Listen to a family member read *The Butterfly House* by Eve Bunting. Share two parts of the story that show caring by an adult. Ask the family member if he/she agrees or disagrees with your choices.

- Watch a 10-minute video clip of *Charlotte's Web*. Identify two or more examples of caring that humans show toward animals or that the animals show toward other animals. If you could be one of the animals in *Charlotte's Web,* which one would you choose to be? Why?

- Help Mom/Dad go through your old clothing. Decide which are now too small for you. Pick a few outfits to donate to the Salvation Army or similar organization. Make sure they have been washed, mended, and pressed. Design a card thanking this group of people for all that they do to help others and deliver your donation to the organization.

- Collect 100 or more empty soda cans. Return them to a recycling center to receive the deposit money. Donate this money to the local zoo to be used for the endangered species collection.

AGES 9-12

- Write, direct, and act in a play about caring people and the actions they take. Ask friends to be in it. Sell tickets to your family, neighbors, and other friends to watch the play. Take the money you have earned and donate it to a local charity group that provides shelter and food for the poor.

- Design a poster for a shelter that takes in stray and unwanted animals. Include the following information: name of the shelter, address, phone number, hours of service, and types of donations appreciated (e.g., money, food, blankets, newspapers, toys). Meet with the manager of a nearby supermarket and ask for permission to hang the poster on their community action board.

Chapter 7—Caring

- Ask your family to adopt a needy family for the holiday season. Prepare a food basket with healthy, nourishing items and a few special treats. Provide a few gifts for the children and the adults. Tiptoe quietly (with an adult) to their front door, ring the doorbell and quickly walk away. Share your adventure with the rest of your family.

- Volunteer to help the younger children at church or school events. Escort them to the restrooms, to get snacks, to find the playground, and help them put their coats and jackets on when it's time to leave. Stay with them until they get picked up. Ask the adult in charge for any feedback that would help you to better use the LIFESKILL of Caring during the next church or school event.

- Illustrate three or more ways to show your family you care about them. Share your drawing with your family. Do these things daily for two weeks or until it becomes a "habit of mind."

- Videotape your grandparents sharing childhood stories. Prepare three or more questions to ask in case they are shy talking in front of the camera. Make "Oscar" statuettes from Plasticine gold–colored clay. Show the videotape at the next family gathering. Present grandma and grandpa with their "Best Actor" and "Best Actress" awards. Invite the family to offer a round of applause for this memorable occasion.

- Organize your family members at the holiday times. Practice singing special Christmas, Chanukah and Kwanzaa songs at least five times. Walk around the neighborhood and serenade your neighbors. Offer them good wishes for a happy holiday season.

AGES 13+

- Volunteer to be a candy striper at a local hospital. Sign up for the training. Develop skills such as: hospital bed-making, flower arranging, information dispensing, and intensive listening. Work out a schedule that will not interfere with your schoolwork. Keep a record of the hours you volunteer. Continue as a candy striper for at least one year.

- Research your five favorite rock/rap/pop superstars. Find out the names of their favorite charities or causes. Write one of the stars a letter offering your support for this organization. Ask for specific action(s) you can take to make a difference. With your parents, choose one of the options suggested to you and follow through with the project. Donate any profit to the charity/cause with a letter of appreciation for all the organization does to help others.

- Choose a local college/professional sports team (e.g., Syracuse University Orangemen, Buffalo Bills). Write/call one of their managers to find out which charitable causes the team supports. Offer your help to organize the families on your block to provide assistance for this charity. Advertise the event(s); collect money, food, books or clothing; organize the donations; and deliver to the manager of the team. Invite a friend to photograph the exchange. Write a short article for a local newspaper; then submit it with a photo for possible publication.

- Organize your friends/neighbors to support a local home for abused women and children. Contact the director of the organization to determine what kind of support/materials they need to provide a safe and caring environment. Make a list of items and visit your neighbors for donations. Clean/repair any items that are less than perfect and take them to the shelter at a predetermined time. Then, write a personal "thank you" note to each family that provided donations.

- Create a list of endangered species in your area. Choose one of the animals, birds, reptiles, or insects from the list. Discover why this critter is important for the ecology where you live. Create a tri-fold, black-and-white pamphlet detailing this information. Make 100 copies of your educational brochure. Put one on every doorknob on your block (attach with a rubber band) and present the remaining brochures to the closest nature center for distribution.

- Brainstorm with your parents 10 or more ways caring people can provide comfort and support when there has been a death in someone's family. Include ordinary tasks as well as special responsibilities that will need to be completed. Communicate your feelings about illness and death with your parents. Ask them to share their experiences with grief—how they used the LIFESKILL of Caring with others and how others used Caring to comfort and support them during their grief and sadness.

- Identify another student your age who seems to be the target of everyone's jokes and put-downs. Introduce yourself to this person and make an honest effort to be his/her friend. Learn his/her hobbies, interests, and family. Face up to anyone who verbally attacks this student. Share your knowledge of put-downs and the harm they cause.

- Provide support for a friend or neighborhood family whose child has been diagnosed with a life-threatening illness. For example, provide free baby-sitting services for other siblings, offer to do chores (e.g., washing/folding clothing, dusting, vacuuming, lawn mowing), or organize fund-raisers to defray the cost of medical expenses. [*Note:* There are many ways to be supportive, for example, male students, teachers, and relatives of a young cancer victim, Joshua, in Cummington, MA, all shaved their heads to make him feel more comfortable when he lost all of his hair due to chemotherapy treatments.]

- Search your block for an elderly neighbor that needs help with chores around the house. Knock on the door, introduce yourself, and offer to do two chores each week as a good neighbor. Mark the chores on the calendar to help you remember your promise to help. Reflect with an adult how doing this activity makes you feel.

- Read the daily newspaper. Find an article recognizing someone's efforts to help others in your community. Design an appreciation card for this local resident who demonstrates caring actions. Mail the card to the newspaper and then ask that the newspaper editor forward it to the resident.

- Design a pop-up "Get Well" card for a friend who has been in the hospital for awhile. Practice first using scrap paper. Write a short note explaining one thing that has happened while he/she was away and one reason why he/she is missed. Mail it so that the card will be there when the friend returns home.

- Collect newspaper stories about people helping animals. Research one local organization that cares for animals that are mistreated, abused, and/or abandoned. Organize a neighborhood fund-raiser and donate the money to that organization for food, toys, and medical needs for animals that are waiting to be adopted.

- Create "caring" posters for a service organization (Red Cross, United Way, etc.) that extends help to people in your community on a regular basis. Also write lyrics to a familiar tune that will teach the public about this organization. Record yourself singing the song and send the posters and tape to the organization in appreciation for their caring for others.

- Call your local Red Cross, the Salvation Army, or a similar group. Ask them what supplies are needed for disaster victims. Organize a disaster relief collection center in your

neighborhood. Tally the items as they are donated. Deliver them to the organization with the help of an adult.
- Organize a neighborhood collection center for food bank items. Design posters advertising the collection. Explain this service project to your friends and neighbors. Provide decorated containers for the goods. Arrange to have the items delivered to a local food bank.
- Contact the League of Women Voters for their voter pamphlet. Design your own brochure encouraging citizens to vote in the next election. Propose two reasons why a caring citizen should exercise his/her constitutional duty to vote. Distribute your brochure to voters in your neighborhood (attach to doorknobs with a rubber band). Then, offer it to the League of Women Voters for their voter education project.

SIGNS OF SUCCESS

Congratulations! Children are showing signs of Caring when they

- Share their own feelings and also care about the feelings of other people
- Notice someone needing help and volunteer assistance
- Inquire as to why someone is upset/crying/angry
- Feel upset over another person's unfortunate circumstances or situation
- Work to save local stray animals or an endangered species
- Organize services (food, shelter, clothing) for people experiencing hard times
- Write notes appreciating the good deeds of others
- Think less about themselves and more about other people
- Right an injustice
- Offer to help a friend

Keep trying! Children need more practice when they

- Need reminders to think of others' feelings
- Ignore someone in need
- Choose not to help someone struggling with a task
- Think it is funny that someone else is different from themselves

- Toss trash directly on the ground instead of using a trash can; won't recycle
- Disregard others' obvious signs of distress and need for care and concern
- Overlook an opportunity to ensure fair play/justice
- Use put-downs
- Put their own wants ahead of the pressing needs of others
- Abuse an animal or physically hurt another person

Literature Link ~ Caring

Ages 4-8

Butterfly House	Eve Bunting (New York: Scholastic Press, 1999)
Patchwork Quilt, The (AFA) (TE)	Valerie Flourney (New York: Dial Books, A Division of Penguin Books, 1985)
Quiltmaker's Gift, The	Jeff Brumbeau (Duluth, MN: Pfeiffer-Hamilton Publishers, 2000)
Sam and the Lucky Money (ASA)	Karin Chinn (New York: Lee & Low, 1995)

Ages 9-12

Everywhere (ASA)	Bruce Brooks (New York: HarperCollins, 1990)
Goodnight Mr. Tom	Michelle Magorian (New York: HarperTrophy, 1986)
Number the Stars (TE)	Lois Lowry (Boston, MA: Houghton Mifflin, 1989)
Pink and Say (AFA) (TE)	Patricia Polacco (New York: Philomel Books, 1994)

Ages 13+

A Door Near Here	Heather Quarles (New York: Laureleaf Books, A Division of Random House, 2000)
California Blues	David Klass (New York: Point, Scholastic Books, 1996)
Chicken Soup for the Teenage Soul: 101 Stories of Life, Love and Learning	Jack Canfield (Ed.), Mark Victor Hansen (Ed.), and Kimberly Kirberger (Ed.) (Deerfield Beach, FL: Health Communications, 1997)
Puppies, Dogs, and Blue Northers: Reflections on Being Raised by a Pack of Sled Dogs	Gary Paulsen (New York: Bantam Doubleday Dell Publishers, 1998)

Multicultural books: **(AFA)**=African American, **(ASA)**=Asian American, **(HA)**=Hispanic American, **(ME)**=Multi-Ethnic, **(NA)**=Native American, **(TE)**=listed in the teacher edition of this book, *Tools for Citizenship and Life: Using the ITI Lifelong Guidelines and LIFESKILLS in the Classroom*, **(BFE)**=available through Books for Educators

Family Resources

Beyond Sibling Rivalry: How to Help Your Children Become Cooperative, Caring and Compassionate — Peter Goldenthal (New York: Henry Holt and Company, Inc., 1999)

Five Love Languages of Children, The — Gary D. Chapman and Ross Campbell (Chicago: Northfield Publishers-A Division of Moody Press, 1997)

Get A Clue!: A Parents' Guide to Understanding and Communicating with Your Preteen — Ellen Rosenburg (New York: Owl Book, Henry Holt and Company, 1999)

Common Sense

Chapter 8

"TAKE A PRACTICAL APPROACH."

common sense *n* **1:** the practical opinion of ordinary people **2:** sound and prudent but often unsophisticated judgment **3:** intuitive application of natural principles

Common Sense: To use good judgment

WHAT IS COMMON SENSE?

Look at the people around you. Some seem to have a natural inclination toward making commonsense decisions. Even as youngsters, they were able to choose the down-to-earth, straightforward solution without much effort. When asked how they did that, these children might have answered, "It's just the way it's supposed to be. How else would you do it?" When they reach adulthood, they are known by family, friends, and co-workers for coming up with sensible, workable solutions.

Common Sense Isn't Common

In truth, common sense isn't common. It requires the use of five LIFESKILLS: Curiosity (look closely at the problem and see it in its entirety), Flexibility (approach the problem with an open mind; don't get attached to a prescribed approach or easy solution), Organization (keep a clear head; be thorough), Patience (have faith that there is a solution and continue to think through the problem/situation), and Resourcefulness (work with what you have; the best solutions are often the most simple, economical, and/or low-tech).

Common sense doesn't stop there. It in turn is a prerequisite for the LIFESKILLS of Initiative and Problem Solving. Initiative without common sense is going off half-cocked; problem solving without common sense creates more problems.

In short, people with the LIFESKILL of Common Sense are extraordinary people and invaluable in any environment—at home, work, and in our communities. They are also astute and effective citizens.

---

* Note to the reader: Your child may be confused by "common sense" appearing sometimes two words—when a noun—and sometimes as one word—when used as an adjective.

It's the "Not-So-Obvious" Obvious

One of the hallmarks of a commonsense solution is that, once it's been found, it appears perfectly obvious. It's the simple solution to a complex issue, a low-tech solution to a high-tech problem. It's one the farmer can see but the college professor can't. It is often the most time-efficient, the quickest, and the least costly.

Sometimes the commonsense solution is based on ordinary, everyday experiences and knowledge. Sometimes it's based on data from previous, similar problems. At other times, however, the solution comes from a simple, straightforward examination of the problem, an analysis unclouded by prior knowledge or expectations.

It's Intuition at Its Best

Some people believe that common sense is an accidental "Aha!" by the uneducated or unsophisticated. Sometimes this is true but more often common sense is the intuitive application of natural principles. Co-author, Karen Olsen, tells of her farmer stepfather, Henry Miller, whose high school physics, geometry, and chemistry stuck with him for a lifetime, not just long enough to bring him an "A" on tests. Henry practiced the principles of those subjects daily; his commonsense solutions to problems were renowned throughout the area. For example, if he needed a more efficient disk and harrow, he designed one, bigger than anything on the market. A representative from John Deere came out, took a look, and patented it (how to patent an invention wasn't taught at Henry's high school!). If he had a runaway harvester that broke its header in a ditch, he combined a little physics and geometry to bring together several tons of metal for a welding job out in the field. When Mother Nature dumped too much rain during a 24-hours a day seeding operation, he got creative; he asked a crop-duster friend to modify his plane to fly seed on and became the first in the area to prove its economic feasibility. When he thought Cargill Grain and the other giant grain conglomerates had him and the other little guys by the neck, he figured out how to hold grain several months after harvest until the prices went back up. He designed and built truck scales, a grain elevator and pit, and half a dozen storage tanks from the brief instruction manuals from the manufacturers.

Karen Olsen's mother had a favorite motto: "Just think about it and you can figure it out." To Karen's mother, not coming up with a commonsense solution was unthinkable, even inexcusable. If "build it and they will come" rings a bell, try "Think and you will know"! Both stepfather and mother were powerful models and their expectations for their children were high. We need to hold the same expectations for our children. Common sense is in them. We need to draw it out.

It's a Solution That Works

However we arrive at it, the commonsense solution is one that works. It's immediately recognized as workable; "That's it!" says the onlooker. "Now, why didn't I think of that?"

A Comical Example of No Common Sense

Do you remember the fairy tale about a young boy, Foolish Jack, and his mother? She is always sending him on errands which he muddles up each time. Now, being a good mother who is trying to instill common sense into her son, she carefully explains what he should have done in each situation. Jack then conscientiously applies her words of wisdom to the next problem but, of course, the situations are never the same. He is always one lesson behind and quite off the mark.

As the story moves from one ridiculous scene to another, children howl with laughter. Once the children recognize the pattern, they love to predict what Jack will do next. While Jack lacks common sense, he is great at following directions!

WHY PRACTICE COMMON SENSE?

Common sense helps us choose practical solutions. Our lives are easier if we can apply sound judgment early in the thinking process, thereby eliminating chaotic and hasty solutions. This is vital during a crisis when poor solutions escalate the very problem we're trying to solve.

Common sense opens doors which allow us to go places and to do things we would otherwise only dream about. It also keeps us grounded in what's real.

HOW DO YOU PRACTICE IT?

Strengthening the LIFESKILL of Common Sense builds upon the LIFESKILLS of Patience, Flexibility, and Problem Solving and requires lots and lots of practice solving problems and dilemmas of consequence. We must, therefore, be willing to allow our child to risk the consequences of solutions that are off the mark (so long as they aren't life-threatening or catastrophic) and be willing to nurture their learning from the results, both good and bad.

Model

As with all of the Lifelong Guidelines and LIFESKILLS, modeling is critical. To develop common sense, modeling is all the more important because, when it comes to common sense, there are no rules or pat formulas to follow. Two very important qualities to model are attitude and self-talk.

More than anything, children tune in to our attitudes. If we act as if every problem that comes up is a big hassle, they and we are unlikely to be able to calm down enough to allow common sense to surface.

Second, always model the attitude and belief that "I can do it." Self-confidence is everything when it comes to conjuring up common sense. "Talking out loud" as you go gives your child the benefit of hearing someone else solving problems in ways that let their common sense surface.

Provide Practice with Real Problems

Too often we shield children from participating in family problem solving either because we don't want to worry them or because it would require more time to involve them. The time problem can't be solved; learning takes time. Period. But we can easily identify those problems that would provide good practice in solving problems without causing undo worry. To help children develop the LIFESKILL of Common Sense, involve them in the process of solving problems, problems, and more problems.

Practice Reflection

Children should reflect on the results of their solutions and evaluate if they were effective and practical. Did their solutions really deliver what was hoped for or did they compromise what they wanted to achieve? Did their decision make the most sense? Were they practical? Were the choices developed in a thoughtful way? Did they resolve or intensify the circumstances?

The answers to such questions increase our children's ability to reach wise, commonsense decision making—just as it does for us. A good example of such reflection on life shines through Oprah Winfrey's comments during a commencement address at Wellesley College. Her five lessons in life are: 1) life is a journey, 2) be yourself, 3) when people show you who they are, believe them the first time, 4) turn your wounds into wisdom, and 5) be grateful.* What wonderful commonsense reflections about life!

WHAT DOES COMMON SENSE LOOK LIKE IN THE REAL WORLD?

We

- Find the most practical and economical way to complete a task or solve a problem
- Watch/listen to how other people solve problems and learn from their thinking processes
- Read manuals and "how-to" books for practical problem-solving advice
- Seek advice from someone who has experience in the area and knows what works
- Plan ahead for assignments, jobs, and events to make sure we're prepared
- Learn from one experience and transfer that knowledge to new situations
- Practice common sense when caring for our bodies by eating the right foods, sleeping an adequate amount of time, exercising both body and mind, and wearing clothing appropriate for the climate and weather

* Oprah Winfrey, "Five Lessons in Life," Commencement Address, Wellsley College, May 30, 1997.

WHAT DOES COMMON SENSE LOOK LIKE AT HOME?

Adults

- "Live" the Lifelong Guidelines and LIFESKILLS because our life works when we follow them consistently
- Treat spouse, parents, and children with respect
- Say "No" when we have no extra time for more committees and volunteer organizations
- Use effective problem-solving strategies
- Model problem-solving thought processes so that children can imitate them
- Brainstorm strategies because we know that "two heads are better than one"
- Model a variety of effective problem-solving skills; show good judgment when making decisions
- Recycle materials because it saves money and is good for the environment

Children

- "Live" the Lifelong Guidelines and LIFESKILLS because practicing them makes home a safe and welcoming place to be
- Believe that "I know that if I think this through I can find good, workable solutions"
- Use lessons from previous situations to solve new problems
- Don't rush headlong into a solution; take time to contemplate decision making
- Ask for advice when stuck solving a problem
- Organize materials and belongings so they can find any object on a moment's notice
- Figure out how to make do with the materials on hand to complete a project
- Are flexible in their thinking and don't get stuck in mental ruts
- Wear appropriate clothing for the weather

OPPORTUNITIES TO PRACTICE COMMON SENSE

AGES 4-8

- Listen to the story *Silly Jack*. Choose two of Jack's silly responses and come up with your own commonsense choices that Jack could have followed. Create a "Silly Jack" skit with your own characters, setting, situations, and props. Practice and present the story for your family after dinner.

- Play "I Spy" with a partner. Look around the room and choose something that you see; think of one clue that describes the object (e.g., for a banana, "I see something yellow"). Ask the other person to guess what object you have chosen in 10 guesses or less by asking a question such as: "Is it round?" "Is it bigger than a microwave?" "Can you eat it?" "Does it taste sour?" After each guess in the form of a question, answer only "yes" or "no" to that question. If your partner is unable to correctly guess your item after 10 questions, tell him/her what it is. Discuss how the LIFESKILL of Common Sense could have helped your partner ask better questions. Then, trade roles and play the game again.

- Use three pieces of drawing paper measuring at least 8" x 11" inches. At the bottom of each one, write one of these three words: rain, snow, heat. Decide the kind of clothing you should wear for each kind of weather. Draw a picture of yourself on each sheet. Dress yourself for the weather conditions described at the bottom of the page. Explain how you used the LIFESKILL of Common Sense when you chose the clothing you drew.

- Select a jigsaw puzzle of 35 or more pieces. Set the box top with the puzzle picture where you can look at it. Use the LIFESKILL of Common Sense to decide what steps you will follow to do the puzzle (e.g., outside edge first, inside center part first) and how you will organize the pieces (e.g., according to colors or shapes). Put the puzzle together. Explain to a brother or sister how use of the LIFESKILL of Common Sense helped you put the puzzle together.

- Ask a grandparent to describe to you a funny situation that happened to them when they were your age because he/she didn't use the LIFESKILL of Common Sense. Then ask him/her to tell you a sad story that occurred due to lack of common sense. Share with your grandparent a situation that happened to you because you didn't use the LIFESKILL of Common Sense. Explain how your situation could have occurred differently had you used common sense.

AGES 9-12

- Read the story *The Miller, the Boy and the Donkey* by Brain Wildsmith or *It Could Always Be Worse* by Margot Zemach. Find the pattern used by the author to make the story silly and to show that the main character had no common sense. Write a story of 100 words or more. Include a main character with no common sense and create some silly actions that happen because of that. Illustrate your story. Read it to a younger child (sibling or neighbor) and see if he/she "gets" the humor.

- Think about the following famous sayings. Compare each of them to a recent mishap you have had. What do they tell you that could have helped you prevent each mishap? Discuss these with a parent. After discussing this list, what two habits of mind do you most need to change? Make a plan for changing those two habits and implement it for two weeks. Ask your parent to help evaluate your progress.

    ~ "A stitch in time saves nine."

    ~ "A bird in the hand is worth two in the bush."

    ~ "Don't kill the goose that lays the golden eggs."

    ~ "Let sleeping dogs lie."

    ~ "The early bird catches the worm."

    ~ "Don't throw the baby out with the bathwater."

    ~ "Don't cry over spilled milk."

- Choose two or more ways to go to school. Plan one safe way for walking. Plan a second way for going in the car. Explain how you used your LIFESKILL of Common Sense to select these two routes. Ask a parent to help you mark the routes on a map. Use a green marker to highlight the walking route and red marker to highlight the car route. Walk to school (with an adult) using the map. Ask a parent to drive you to school using the map. Ask him/her what routes he/she would have chosen using the LIFESKILL of Common Sense. Compare the choices and why they were made.

- Create a first-aid kit for your family. Choose a plastic case and clean it out. Create a design for the top of the box; include a big red cross (symbol for first-aid). Include eight or more items that will help during an emergency injury. Think about the kinds of emergencies that are most likely to occur; use the LIFESKILL of Common Sense when selecting the eight items. Visit a drugstore. Ask a pharmacist which items he/she thinks should be included and compare them to the list you made. Share your plan with an adult. Put the box in an accessible place.

- Organize your clothes closet. Use the LIFESKILL of Common Sense to simplify what it contains and how you organize it. Discuss with a parent what "rules" you will use to guide your work. Several things to keep in mind include: what won't fit the next season that this item is appropriate to wear, what do I have too much of, where can I store things I won't wear for another four or five months, how could I organize things to keep from wasting my time when I'm looking for something? Tell a friend what you learned about using the LIFESKILL of Common Sense by doing this task.

- Find a real life "Silly Jack" story in the newspaper. Read the whole article to a friend or family member and discuss the silly choices made. Brainstorm wiser choices. Share what you would have done under the same circumstances.

AGES 13+

- Read *The Safe Zone: A Kid's Guide to Personal Safety* by Donna Charet and Francine Russell. Choose one chapter that you find particularly interesting. Discuss the "What if's . . .?" with a friend. List the commonsense safety steps you both agree to follow as a result of your discussion. Share the list with a counselor at school for any other input.

- Watch the nightly news with a parent. Listen carefully to what the newscaster is reporting. Identify three different stories that could have been solved using the LIFESKILL of Common Sense. Explain what you think the problem is in each instance and how you would go about solving it. Ask a family member how he/she would go about solving those same problems. Compare your commonsense solution to his/hers. How are they similar and different? Draw a one-frame, black-and-white cartoon to illustrate a silly solution to one of the problems you chose. Post it on the refrigerator door.

- Collect three newspaper articles illustrating problem-solving situations. In each article, highlight examples of following commonsense decisions and ignoring them. Draw a political cartoon illustrating a lack of common sense by people in one of the articles. Share it with a parent and then submit it to your local newspaper for possible publication.

- Think about the following famous sayings. Compare each of them to a recent mishap you have had. What do they tell you that could have helped you prevent each mishap? Discuss these with a parent. After discussing this list, what two habits of mind do you most need to change? Make a plan for changing those two habits and implement it for two weeks. Ask a parent to help evaluate your progress.

    ~ "Don't make a mountain out of a mole hill."
    ~ "Use the right tool for the right job."
    ~ "Keep your ear to the ground."
    ~ "Better late than never."
    ~ "He's an accident waiting to happen."
    ~ "Actions speak louder than words."
    ~ "Sail close to the wind."
    ~ "You're barking up the wrong tree."
    ~ "Don't count your chickens before they're hatched."
    ~ "An ounce of prevention is worth a pound of cure."

- Write to a local drug prevention center/organization and request literature regarding the drugs of choice for teens. Choose one of the top three drugs on the list and research the long-term effects of this drug on a young person's body.

    ~ Design an educational, drug-prevention pamphlet (including graphics) intended for peers ages 9-12. Include the following information about the drug: description, ingredients, effects (short and long-term), danger signs (physical and emotional), and local organizations that will provide help for users. Include convincing, commonsense reasons why kids should not use this drug. [*Hint:* If the reasons for not

Chapter 8—Common Sense

using the drug don't sound convincing, you may not have addressed the reason kids go ahead and use it.]

~ Bring the pamphlet to either your church youth leader or the guidance counselor at your school. Offer it for reprint and distribution.

- Choose a sport that you play or like to watch. If you were charged with the responsibility of reducing serious injuries, what changes in equipment, conditioning of the athletes, and rules would you recommend? Use the LIFESKILL of Common Sense. Share your recommendations with a friend. Discuss with him/her why you think such changes haven't already been made. Enlist his/her help in carrying out your recommendations— designing one of the pieces of equipment you recommended and/or write the rules you would change/add/delete. Share your work with a coach to get his/her ideas.

- Investigate a credit card holder's responsibility for meeting financial obligations and how the advertising of those cards is intended to override people's common sense. Collect current advertising and application forms for three or more of the following credit cards: Visa, Master Card, American Express, and/or Discover (check mail, newspapers, magazine, and TV ads). Compare the information about each—what's similar and different. Do the ads reflect reality? Read the small print to determine introductory rates (how much and for how long) and regular rates (how much). With this information, compute your answers for each of the scenarios below. Use your LIFESKILL of Common Sense and math skills.

Scenario #1: You still owe $5,000 on your car at 12% a year for 18 more months. You decide to transfer this $5,000 to your credit card to take advantage of the 2.9% introductory rate. The introductory rate is for six months. The regular interest rate is 19.7%. There is no time limit for payoff so you decide to go with the minimum payment each month. Did you use the LIFESKILL of Common Sense when you made this transfer decision? Explain why or why not. Share your analysis with your math teacher.

Scenario #2: You have a $2,000 balance on a credit card that carries a 15% interest rate. You decide to take advantage of the 3.9% introductory rate on another card. The introductory rate is for six months. The regular rate for this card is 19.1%. Decide what amount you would be able to pay each and every month. Using that figure, did you use the LIFESKILL of Common Sense when you made this transfer decision? Explain why or why not. Share your analysis with your math teacher.

- Read the following quotation attributed to Frank Lloyd Wright: "There is nothing more uncommon than common sense." Ponder over these words and discuss with your parents or grandparents what you think Frank Lloyd Wright meant. Invite them to share their understandings of this quote. Write your own quote regarding the LIFESKILL of Common Sense. Design a banner to highlight your words; hang it up in the family/living room for a week. Explain the banner and quote to your siblings and friends.

- Select a problem from a list provided by a family member. Brainstorm three or more solutions for the problem. Test each solution by asking, "If I do 'x' then does it seem likely that 'y' will happen?" Rate your solutions from "Most Common Sense" to "Least Common Sense." Explain each of the three choices to a family member and provide an explanation for your ratings.

- Locate two or more outrageous examples of lack of common sense by people in local, state, and/or federal government. Share the information with your family. Brainstorm commonsense answers for the problems. Write letters to the appropriate elected officials sharing your thoughts on the topic.

SIGNS OF SUCCESS

Congratulations! Children are showing signs of Common Sense when they

- Think and plan before they speak or leap into action
- Weigh choices for possible positive and negative results
- Prioritize choices in commonsense ways
- Understand the humor in stories about foolish decisions
- Readily identify cause-and-effect relationships and likely consequences of various courses of action
- Use prior knowledge and experiences as a basis for current and future decisions
- Make simple decisions with ease

Keep trying! Children need more practice when they

- Have a hard time finding commonsense solutions for simple problems
- Refuse to consider alternative ideas when solving problems
- Choose solutions that have worked in the past but are unrelated to the current problem
- Repeatedly choose solutions to a problem that haven't worked in the past and aren't likely to
- Consistently feel that everyone else is wrong and they are always right
- Neglect to brainstorm or weigh options but just jump right in with the first idea
- Don't understand the humor in stories based on characters lacking common sense

Literature Link ~ Common Sense

Ages 4-8

Amelia Bedelia (TE)	Peggy Parrish (New York: HarperCollins, 1992)
Benny's Had Enough	Barbro Lindgren (Stockholm, Sweden: R&S, 1999)
Frog Girl (NA)	Paul Owen Lewis (Berkeley, CA: Tricycle Press, 1999)
Seven Blind Mice	Ed Young (New York: Philomel Books, 1992)

Ages 9-12

Stone Fox (NA) (TE)	John Reynolds Gardiner (New York: HarperTrophy Books, 1988)
Eighteenth Emergency, The	Betsy Cromar Byars (New York: Viking Press, 1996)
Tales of a Fourth Grade Nothing (TE)	Judy Blume (New York: E.P. Dutton Childrens Books, 1972)

Ages 13+

Ballad of Lucy Whipple	Karen Cushman (New York: HarperCollins Juvenile Books, 1998)
Canyons	Gary Paulsen (New York: Bantam Doubleday Dell Publishing, 1990)
Day No Pigs Would Die, A	Robert Newton Peck (New York: Random House Childrens Publishing, 1994)
Into the Wild	Jon Krakauer *(New York: Bantam Doubleday Dell Publishing, 1997)*
Joyride	Gretchen Olson (Honesdale, PA: Boyds Mill Press, 1999)

Multicultural books: **(AFA)**=African American, **(ASA)**=Asian American, **(HA)**=Hispanic American, **(ME)**=Multi-Ethnic, **(NA)**=Native American, **(TE)**=listed in the teacher edition of this book, *Tools for Citizenship and Life: Using the ITI Lifelong Guidelines and LIFESKILLS in the Classroom*, **(BFE)**=available through Books for Educators

Family Resources

Common Sense Parenting: A Proven Step-by-Step Guide for Raising Responsible Kids and Creating Happy Families

Ray Burke, Ph.D. and Ron Herar (Boys Town, NE: Boys Town Press, 1996)

Secret of Parenting: How to Be in Charge of Today's Kids—From Toddlers to Preteens—Without Threats or Punishment

Anthony Wolf (New York: Farrar Strauss & Giroux, 2000)

Uncommon Sense for Parents with Teenagers

Michael Riera (Berkeley, CA: Celestial Arts Publishing, 1995)

Cooperation

"Work with others."

cooperation *n* **1:** the act of cooperating: common effort
2: association of persons for common benefit

Cooperation: To work together toward a common goal or purpose

WHAT IS COOPERATION?

Cooperation is a working relationship that develops between two or more people as they perform certain tasks. It is characterized by a sense of "give and take" among the group members, of shifting smoothly between the roles of leader and follower, of agreement on goals being pursued.

In *TRIBES: A New Way of Learning and Being Together,* Jeanne Gibbs defines the phases of collaboration as inclusion, influence, and community. If you haven't discovered this book,* it is a "must have" resource, filled with ready-to-go activities that develop each of these stages plus the research behind them.

Attributes of Cooperation

Certain attributes or qualities of interaction help us identify the LIFESKILL of Cooperation as people work together—at work, for community project, and especially to ensure the success of the family unit. Participants share goals, brainstorm solutions, listen to each others' ideas, delegate duties, and readily volunteer assistance. If the group works together cooperatively for a long time, especially on a highly-charged topic that promotes emotional bonding, a strong sense of camaraderie develops.

Cooperation requires a delicate balancing act or dance in which members alternate between the role of leader and follower as the tasks of the group require different expertise, knowledge, and skills. Through this natural shift in roles, each person in the group comes to feel that his or her contribution is important and essential for a completed project or goal; any one person working alone

---

* This invaluable book is not generally available through bookstores. However, it can be ordered through Books for Educators 888/777-9827, fax 253/630-7215, E-mail books4@oz.net, www.books4educ.com

would probably find it difficult, if not impossible, to complete the entire task. In true cooperation, the whole is greater than the sum of the parts.

WHY PRACTICE COOPERATION?

Because of today's hectic schedules and the increase in time children spend on individual pursuits such as TV and computers, many children develop fewer personal and social skills for cooperating than ever before. Yet we live in a time when such skills are vital for current and future success.

Changes in Technology

There are many reasons why children are less adept at cooperating but two significant culprits are overuse of TV and computers.

Television. The popularity of television, and its frequent misuse as baby sitter and educator, has hindered the development of a range of social skills, not just cooperation. According to James Garbarino, "Besides teaching that violence is an acceptable means of conflict resolution, television has another and more insidious effect on human development. By crowding out activities that used to be shared with family and friends, thus substituting passive observation for real interaction, television deprives people of lessons in living together. The less experience people have with face-to-face interaction, the more they distrust one another, the more hostile and defensive their social maps become, and the more toxic the environment becomes."*

Computers. A second technological advancement that, if used incorrectly, can hinder children's socialization is the computer, now found in an increasing number of homes and children's bedrooms. Again, time before the computer screen is primarily a solitary act, thus limiting opportunities for conversation and interaction. Recent studies have shown that the greater the time spent on the computer, the greater the sense of isolation and deterioration of family interaction**—all of which is counterproductive to developing cooperation.

So, TV and computers, while for many years considered a great gift for all of us, may instead be compared to the Trojan Horse because of the hidden consequences of misuse and overuse. To compensate for these unintended effects of technology, we must actively teach students how to cooperate, skills that were formerly picked up through more comprehensive social interactions. We can no longer assume that our child will learn them without focused effort by the family.

On the Job

It is hard to imagine a job or occupation today that does not require some form of cooperation. Workers in the future will, more often than not, need to know how to produce new knowledge

---

* See *Raising Children in a Socially Toxic Environment* by James Garbarino (San Francisco: Jossey-Bass Publishers, 1995), p. 35. Also see *Smart Moves* by Carla Hannaford, pp. 93 and 171-172.

** See *Failure to Connect: How Computers Affect Our Children's Minds—For Better and Worse* by Jane Healy (New York: A Touchstone Book/Simon & Schuster, 1998), pp. 194-196 and 273-274. Also see *Smart Moves* by Carla Hannaford (Arlington, VA: Great Ocean Publishers, 1995), pp. 66-67.

and ways to make things happen rather than being able to draw upon a previously developed bank of knowledge and old ways of doing things.

Reinventing the wheel by oneself is very inefficient and costly to businesses and organizations. It is expedient to brainstorm, debate, and make decisions based upon a pool of ideas, rather than upon one person's experience and ideas. Working with at least one other person enriches the experience base for shared decision-making, conflict resolution, and lifelong learning. Cooperation provides an opportunity to do just that.

For Family Life

Cooperation is fundamental to harmony in the home. Control (it has to be like this; my way or the highway) and ego (me first) are killers. A sense of family depends upon all being fully included, having influence, and liking as well as loving other family members. Cooperation is a must.

For Citizenship

Cooperation skills are also essential for citizenship, especially in an increasingly diverse national population.

HOW DO YOU PRACTICE IT?

To practice cooperation we must work in harmony with other people toward a mutual goal. This means creating the necessary conditions for a group such as: Each member must have a basic understanding of what it takes to make groups work; there must be clear procedures to follow; and leaders must understand how to create meaningful group jobs,* assign individual responsibilities, and set project time lines. Your child may lack sufficient experience in cooperating. If so, start small: Set up procedures for cooperating; keep the beginning projects uncomplicated; model the process; continue to provide adequate support; and include time at the end of each collaborative work session for your child to "process the process." Processing the process is a simple, quick, yet powerful way to encourage your child to reflect on the growth of their cooperative skills and his/her ability to achieve goals through cooperation. Again, *TRIBES: A New Way of Learning and Being Together* by Jeanne Gibbs is an excellent source of activities for processing and reflecting.

Start Slowly and Plan for Many Experiences

Start slowly;. Don't assume your child has developed by osmosis the social and personal skills for cooperating. Have your child start with a partner—a group of two—a sibling or friend. Then, gradually increase group size and the complexity of the tasks. [*Note:* If siblings find it difficult to

---

* See *Designing Groupwork: Strategies for the Heterogeneous Classroom* by Elizabeth Cohen, Foreword by John I. Goodlad (New York: Teachers College Press, 1986).

work together, you may want to first team your child with one of his/her friends. This helps sidestep competition from old sibling rivalries and eliminates age differences that may make shifting between the roles of leader and follower more difficult.]

Make cooperative learning experiences fun. Within the family, use vacations and special outings such as camping, visiting grandparents, and so forth, as well as the usual home/yard chores.

In addition to providing opportunities to practice cooperation within the family, seek out well-run youth organizations such as scouts, 4-H, sports, and so on. Select carefully. Most such organizations are run by willing volunteers who may *not* have any training in helping groups work cooperatively and in accordance with the Lifelong Guidelines.

Role playing also provides opportunities for immediate feedback when a skill is modeled correctly. Please realize that any one experience is not going to provide enough practice for cooperation to happen. Only daily opportunities with different situations over an extended period of time and with a variety and number of partners will build the skills children need.

Pursuing the LIFESKILL of Cooperation takes time and effort, by both parent and children, but it is time well spent when we see the positive, harmonious results.

WHAT DOES COOPERATION LOOK LIKE IN THE REAL WORLD?
We

- Avoid trying to control situations and people so that all members of a group may contribute ideas, talents, and skills

- Support, rather than sabotage, efforts to improve behaviors and relationships at home, in the community, and in our schools

- Work together on a variety of projects, such as "Earth Day" and "Clean Up Your Neighborhood Day," to provide a cleaner, healthier, and safer environment

- Volunteer to improve local conditions by being active members of neighborhood watch, the PTA, hospitals, community action groups, and other nonprofit and governmental organizations

- Share information to create a true sense of security for our community

- Provide materials, equipment, and assistance during times of disaster (e.g., tornado, flood, fire, earthquake) in the United States, as well as in other countries around the world

- Work together to ensure that products or services serve the general good

- Collaborate with others to research, present, and lobby for changes in legislation

WHAT DOES COOPERATION LOOK LIKE AT HOME?

Adults

- Work cooperatively to build a strong family foundation, to keep the home and yard in good condition, and to share other household responsibilities

- Consciously create time to develop a sense of community among family members and friends*

- Make adherence to the family rules a cooperative rather than dictatorial experience by discussing misdeeds as a family issue and enlisting offender and other family members in arriving at reasonable, fair consequences

- Collaborate with extended family members to build a true sense of inclusion for each person; welcome intergenerational gatherings and communication

- Use the LIFESKILL of Patience when our child is experiencing difficulty in completing a task; help our child analyze why he/she is stuck, suggest ways to get the job done, and coach him/her in a positive and consistent manner

- Provide help and support for each family member's efforts to grow

- Offer to assist friends and neighbors with tasks; loan tools to those who are trustworthy

- Orchestrate the day to best meet each person's (adult and child) needs and schedules

- Develop a practical budget (include provisions for savings and retirement) within income limitations and enlist the understanding and support of all family members to keep spending within the monthly budget

Children

- Assist family in maintaining the house and yard without having to be reminded and cajoled

- Include family members (including younger siblings) and friends in work, study, and play groups

- Work, talk, and play with siblings in caring and supportive ways; contribute to group harmony

- Share materials, gifts, and treats without prompting; offer to help other children

- Avoid "me-me" demands and place the needs of the group equal to their personal interests; avoid giving in to short-term personal wants while holding to long-term needs of the family

---

* For an excellent resource for building a sense of community among family members and with friends, see *TRIBES: A New Way of Learning and Being Together* by Jeanne Gibbs; for ways to organize family meetings, see *Positive Discipline* by Jane Nelson, Chapter 7.

- Support their parents in decisions made for the good of the family as a whole, e.g., restrictions on monthly expenditures

- Work to improve interpersonal skills (e.g., sharing, mediating, discussing) and a greater understanding of personal and social differences

- Organize and use materials cooperatively

- Mediate differences

OPPORTUNITIES TO PRACTICE COOPERATION

AGES 4-8

- Listen to the words of the song "Cooperation" on the LIFESKILLS tape/CD* by Russ and Judy Eacker. Create pictures in your mind of what the words mean. Listen to the song again. Learn the tune and lyrics for the "Cooperation" song. Teach it to your family. Sing the song next time you are all working on a project together.

- Organize all the tools and materials in your room and those in the kitchen that you are allowed to use (such as markers, scissors, crayons, colored pencils, rulers, glue sticks). Place them in a designated drawer so that family members can use them in a cooperative way. Devise a plan for you and other family members to follow so that the drawer is kept organized and all materials are returned after use.

- Ask a parent or older sibling to show you your family's pattern for folding towels after laundering. Watch him/her fold the towel at least five times. Practice folding the towel by yourself for five times. Volunteer to fold the family towels after they come out of the drier and then to put them back on the shelves in the linen closet or on the towel racks in the bathroom where they belong.

- Learn the correct way to set the table for dinner. Set the family table including folded napkins, plates, silverware, salt and pepper shakers, butter container, and serving dishes and utensils. Perform this task every night for one month. Determine if you have learned this chore by explaining to an adult the steps you follow every night to set the table. Teach this task to a younger sibling and help him/her do the task every night for two weeks. After that, ask your mom if she would like to have you continue doing this task as your contribution to the work of the family.

- Choose a recipe for a favorite dessert. Ask a parent to help you make it for the family. Read the recipe. Organize the materials and ingredients. Follow the directions. Serve dessert that night after the main course is completed. Repeat this three times in the next month with a different dessert each time.

- Organize your family's recycling process. Find three similar containers (e.g., blue bins, cardboard boxes, bags). Using a piece of light-colored paper (at least 10"x12"), a black

---

* This song collection is not generally available through bookstores. However, it can be ordered through Books for Educators 888/777-9827, fax 253/630-7215, E-mail books4@oz.net, www.books4educ.com

marker and all capital letters, make the following three labels: GLASS, PLASTIC, PAPER. Tape one label to each container.

Show your recycling center to the family; ask them for their cooperation and teach them the procedures for placing discarded materials in the correct container.
Check each container at the end of the day and make any corrections. Go with an adult to the recycle center or put the materials out on the sidewalk for pick-up of recycled materials according to collection company's schedule. Carry out this process for one month. Ask your mom if she would like to have you and your sibling(s) continue doing this task as your contribution to the work of the family.

- Read a book about magic. Choose a trick/illusion that requires a partner. Invite a parent to be your assistant. Practice the trick at least 10 times or until you can do it with ease. Perform the trick at a family gathering.

- Name an early spring day as "Clean Up the Yard Day." Gather rakes, shovels, garden gloves, wheelbarrow, and trash can with plastic liner. Recruit at least two friends or siblings to join you. Together, walk around the yard. Pick up papers, cans, and bottles, place them in the trash can, and rake up old leaves. Put twigs, branches, and other debris in the wheelbarrow. Dispose of your debris in accordance with your community's laws. If you need help organizing and/or carrying out a particular task, ask an adult to support you and your team' efforts (not do the work for you). When the yard looks neat and clean, put away all of the tools and admire your cooperative "Yard Day" clean-up.

AGES 9-12

- Organize a "Family Entertainment Night." Ask each family member to help by volunteering a talent such as singing, playing an instrument, performing a magic trick, reading a favorite poem or excerpt from a story, writing and performing a standup comedian routine, telling a ghost story, and so forth. Hold the performance during or immediately after dinner. As master of ceremonies for the evening, make sure that each performance is in good taste and will be appreciated by each person in the audience.

- Sign up to play an organized team sport in your neighborhood. During the first three practices, listen for two or more strategies the coach teaches your team about how to work together. Share these strategies with an older brother/sister/friend. Discuss with him/her how these strategies could be applied to family life.

- If interested in becoming a newspaper carrier in your neighborhood, research the job. Read the rules and requirements. If you still want to be a carrier, organize your information before you talk with your parents to get their permission. Be ready to answer questions/concerns that your family may have in regard to this opportunity. Also, role-play the following situations with a friend to see what kind of cooperation and support you might require of family members and friends in order to carry out your job as newspaper carrier. Share the results of this role playing with your parents.

    ~ A friend's birthday party is scheduled for the same time the paper delivery is to occur

    ~ Chickenpox strikes and you will be in bed for two weeks

    ~ A great TV special is on during delivery time

- ~ Mrs. Smith calls and in a very angry voice tells you that she did not receive her newspaper today

- ~ This is your third trip back to Mr. White's house to collect his payment

- ~ The first paycheck arrives and is more/less than your expectations

- Read about a bird that nests in your neighborhood. Check out a book about making bird nests from the library. Find plans to build a birdhouse that meets the nesting needs and specifications for your chosen bird. Ask an adult family member to work with you to build this birdhouse. When the project is finished and in place, write and deliver a "thank you" note of three or more sentences expressing your appreciation for his/her cooperation and support.

- Organize a group of relatives/neighbors to celebrate Arbor Day (the last Friday in April) by planting a tree in a nearby park. Research which trees grow best in your area. Provide a way for members of the group to vote on the most popular tree from that list. Obtain permission from local park officials to plant the tree on park grounds. Fundraise or accept donations to pay for the tree if necessary. Check with local gas and utility companies for any restrictions on digging in the area where you plan to plant the tree. Designate a person(s) to water the tree until its own root system develops; follow up to make sure the tree is watered as needed. Celebrate the group's accomplishment by having a "tree party." Visit the Arbor Day website (http://www.arborday.org/) for additional ideas and activities.

- Enlist the assistance of two friends to help design a "Welcome New Neighbor" kit for a new kid your age that will help him/her feel comfortable in new surroundings. Choose a special box and decorate it with interesting graphics. Enlist the cooperation of your friends to help you decide what to put in the box and to gather the needed information such as sign-up dates for the local sport league; map and walking/driving directions to the school he/she will be attending; school phone number, address, and calendar, walking/driving directions of your favorite library, museums, theaters, and malls; phone numbers for local youth organizations such as Boy Scouts, Girl Scouts, Boys/Girls Club, and 4-H; and a list of city, town, and state parks within a 10-mile radius with walking/driving directions. With two of the friends who helped gather and organize the information, deliver the kit to the new kid at his/her house; introduce yourselves and offer to show this new friend around the neighborhood.

- Brainstorm with sport teammates how the team can improve its performance and skills. Decide on two or more strategies that the team will practice together. Include these strategies in daily practice sessions. Ask your coach to evaluate any changes in the team's performance as a result of the team's cooperative efforts to improve.

- Brainstorm five or more attributes or qualities of a cooperative group. Choose three of those qualities and include them in a pledge that describes how you and your friends and family members can work together. Present your pledge to your family after dinner.

- Research two people who work cooperatively in your community. Illustrate in a color drawing three examples of how they work together to get the job done. Present the picture to them.

Chapter 9—Cooperation

- Choose one of your family's jigsaw puzzles with up to 350 pieces. Divide the pieces among you and your family. Work silently to complete the puzzle. After 20 minutes, stop and discuss what cooperative strategies are helping your family complete the task. Work silently together for another 30 minutes. Again stop and discuss how the process is going and how each member feels about it. Is each member truly cooperating? Is each person contributing fully or dropping out of the process? If so, why and what can be done to make the person feel welcome to participate fully? When the puzzle is completed, "process the process." What have you learned as a family?

- Organize a group of five or more friends and work cooperatively to provide assistance for two homebound senior citizens in your neighborhood for one month. For example, provide a special basket of treats twice a week (brainstorm appropriate items to place in the baskets given any special diets, illnesses, and allergies), take care of their yard, do grocery shopping, provide companionship (playing checkers/chess, sharing a hobby—yours or theirs, etc.). Hold a neighborhood fundraiser for money or accept donations to buy gifts for the baskets, flowers for the yard, etc. Cooperatively develop the plan. Explain to a parent what your role will be and get their permission before you begin. Take any ideas from your discussion with your parent back to the group to see if your plan can be improved. When the final plan is approved by the group and each member's parents, carry out your plan as written. Share with your family at dinner each night how the plan is working and what you are learning about the LIFESKILLS of Cooperation and Caring.

AGES 13+

- Brainstorm 10 ways to encourage/teach the LIFESKILL of Cooperation. Write a script for three skits that use some of the ideas you brainstormed. Each skit must appeal to children age 13+ and demonstrate two or more ideas for working together in a cooperative way. Invite a few friends to practice performing the skits until you are all comfortable with your lines, gestures, and timing. Videotape the three skits, add a title, and offer the tape to your middle school for classroom use.

- Write "Cooperative Group Procedures" to help your family work together in organizing chores for meals and for tidying the house before bedtime. Record these procedures in your journal and practice the new steps for two weeks. Review the procedures to determine if any changes need to be made.

- Interview a neighbor about his/her job. Invite him/her to describe the job and ways it requires cooperation. Produce a classified advertisement of 25 words or less about the position. Ask five friends if they would like this job some day. Share the survey results with a member of your family. Design and send a thank-you note to the person you interviewed, sharing one idea you have learned from him/her about cooperation.

- Develop a list of six or more books about cooperation that you enjoyed reading. Include both fiction and non-fiction stories. Share the list with your family. Read at least two of these books aloud to your siblings or younger neighbors. Ask them what they learned from the stories about the LIFESKILL of Cooperation. Share their reactions with a parent.

- Join an organization or club that caters to a special interest of yours (e.g., chess, ice skating, model trains, youth group, YMCA/YWCA, FTA, FFA). Learn two or more new skills/strategies from other members that will improve your abilities to follow this interest. Clarify how the use of the LIFESKILL of Cooperation will support your growth as a club member and, in turn, enable you to help others.

- Discuss with your parents/music teacher which musical instrument you would like to learn to play. Choose one that fits well in a band or an orchestra. Practice learning the notes for easy tunes. Join an orchestra or band (this may depend on your choice of instrument) and learn to play in unison with other musicians. Discover four or more ways the LIFESKILL of Cooperation supports your musical group; share these ideas with your music teacher.

- Choose to help out at a food pantry or soup kitchen in your community. Set up an appointment with the director or person in charge of volunteers. Explain why you want to spend time helping the hungry. Share any strengths you have that will benefit the organization (e.g., great at talking on the phone; good at raising monetary and food donations; terrific at working and talking with people; able to lift heavy cartons). Attend the required trainings. Sign on for a specific time period. Once a month, request feedback from your immediate supervisor in relation to your cooperation skills and ask for any ideas to improve.

- Establish a business with a partner (for example, babysitting, car washing, pet-sitting, and so forth). Plan to create and run this business together for six weeks. Write a business plan that describes: the name of your business; what service(s) it will provide; who your customers will be; the amount of money needed for start-up expenses; where your funding will come from; the amount you will charge customers; how you will provide the service/product; where/how you will advertise your service; and how you will keep records of income and expenses. When you need assistance, ask a family member or neighbor to assist you; elicit as much cooperation from others as you can.
Evaluate your cooperative skills on a weekly basis. Determine if further training in cooperative skill building is necessary. Share your experiences and what you are learning about the LIFESKILL of Cooperation with your family at dinner time at least twice a week.

- Design a board game for two to four players that teaches about cooperation. Write two or more rules to help the players understand the goal and how to play. Create the board, choose some tokens for the players, add dice or a spinner, and create some game cards. Play the game with a partner and ask for feedback on how well the game teaches the LIFESKILL of Cooperation.

- Create a unique gift for grandpa/grandma as he/she enters a physical rehabilitation center/nursing home. Put together a photo journal that includes photographs of many family members and antidotes about their lives. Invite Grandpa/Grandma to add to the comments. Design a special cover with the title, "Family Memories for a Special Grandpa/Grandma" (or another of your own choice). Add more pages as new family members are born and as new events occur.

- With the assistance of your parents and/or siblings, organize a family reunion.
    ~ Create a list of family members with addresses and phone numbers

- Work with others who will be attending to decide on an acceptable date (month, day, year) and time for the reunion
- Determine a central location for the event (e.g., area, city, state) and place (e.g., house, restaurant, hotel, amusement area, park, convention center); make the necessary reservations
- Decide if the reunion will be catered or pot luck; notify all attending how much money to send (if the reunion is catered) or what dish to bring (if pot luck)
- Design invitations using Print Shop, Printmaster, Adobe, or another similar program. Mail them out and keep track of the acceptances/regrets
- Provide a surprise memento (e.g., group photo, floppy disk with photos, specially designed T-shirt, hat, key chain, mug) for each family/person in attendance
- Share examples of family cooperation with everyone at the closing event

* Interview a business person whose business has created a partnership with a nonprofit community organization. Plan three or more questions, at least one focusing on cooperation, to help you and a family member understand the reasons behind this particular business-community service partnership. Write your questions down and be prepared to share them during the interview. Design a billboard/commercial/advertisement for the company to explain the partnership. Mail this drawing to the business partner along with a short thank-you note.

SIGNS OF SUCCESS

Congratulations! Children are showing signs of Cooperation when they

- Feel that the contributions of others, as well as themselves, are important and necessary for the completion of the task
- Have learned how to "give and take" in their relationships
- Work collaboratively on household chores and other projects
- Problem solve with siblings and friends
- Shift easily between roles of leader and follower
- Understand that when it comes to the family, as with other relationships and things, they must cooperate in order to make the "whole greater than the parts"
- Understand that good citizenship requires cooperation among people of all races, religions, and ethnic origins

Keep trying! Children need more practice when they

- Involve themselves in power struggles
- Always insist on being the leader
- Talk about but forget to follow the Lifelong Guideline of Active Listening
- Refuse to work with other children because of their race, religion, or ethnic origin
- Believe their part is more important than anyone else's
- Feel that their contribution is *not* important and needed
- Argue and bicker over every little thing
- Refuse to share toys and other belongings
- Decline to do their share of chores around the house

Literature Link ~ Cooperation

Ages 4-8

Aani and the Tree Huggers (ASA)	Jeannine Atkins (New York: Lee & Low Books, 2000)
Araminta's Paint Box	Karen Ackerman (New York: Aladdin Paperbacks, a Division of Simon & Schuster, 1998)
Buford, the Little Bighorn	Bill Peet (New York: Houghton Mifflin, 1991)
Lulie the Iceberg: Her Imperial Highness Princess Takamado No	Miya Hisako (New York: Kodansha International, 1998)

Ages 9-12

Active Citizenship Today: Field Guide	Charles Degelman (California: Close-Up Foundation, 1994)
Frightful's Mountain	Jean Craighead George (New York: E. P. Dutton, 1999)
Not-Just-Anybody Family, The (TE)	Betsy Cromer Byars (New York: Yearling Books, A Division of RandomHouse, 1987)
View from Saturday, The	E. L. Konigsberg (London: Athenium, 1996)

Ages 13+

Lord of the Flies	William Gerald Golding (New York: Perigree Books, Putnam House, 1959)
Endurance: Shackleton's Legendary Antarctic Expedition	Caroline Alexander (New York: Knopf, 1998)
Snow Bound	Harry Mazer (New York: Dell Publishing Company, 1975)
Steal Away Home (AFA)	Lois Ruby (New York: Simon & Schuster, 1999)

Multicultural books: **(AFA)**=African American, **(ASA)**=Asian American, **(HA)**=Hispanic American, **(ME)**=Multi-Ethnic, **(NA)**=Native American, **(TE)**=listed in the teacher edition of this book, *Tools for Citizenship and Life: Using the ITI Lifelong Guidelines and LIFESKILLS in the Classroom*, **(BFE)**=available through Books for Educators

Family Resources

Kid Cooperation: How to Stop Yelling, Nagging and Pleading and Get Kids to Cooperate — Elizabeth Pantley (Oakland, CA: New Harbinger Publications, 1996)

Easy to Love, Difficult to Discipline: The 7 Basic Skills for Turning Conflict into Cooperation — Becky A. Bailey (New York: William Morrow Company, 2000)

Chapter 10

Courage

"BELIEVE IN YOURSELF AND JUST GO FOR IT."

courage *n* mental or moral strength to venture, persevere, and withstand danger, fear, or difficulty

Courage: To act according to one's beliefs despite fear of consequences

WHAT IS COURAGE?

Do you remember the lion from *The Wizard of Oz*? He was afraid all the time and was known as a coward. What he wanted more than anything else from the great Wizard of Oz was the gift of courage. What he eventually learned is that courage is not something you can get from someone else; instead, it comes from within—from a belief that what you're summoning your courage to do is the right thing to do and that you are committed to do it.

Courage is having the mental or moral strength to do what needs to be done despite problems, fear, danger, or consequences. A courageous person is one who repeatedly faces the difficulties and challenges that life delivers and perseveres no matter what the barriers or consequences may be. When we hear the word "courage," other terms such as bravery, heroism, determination, and risk-taking come to mind; each one of these implies a sense of strength, both physical or moral, that empowers an individual to move beyond fears when confronting any dilemma.

Courage Begins Early in Life

By our very nature, humans are born courageous. Think of a baby taking that first step without holding on to anything. Does fear of falling prevent further attempts? No, the baby just gets up and tries again. Do you remember your first day of school at the tender age of four or five? The butterflies in your stomach? Wondering if you would ever have any friends? Wondering if you would ever learn to read? Courage helped you meet new people, learn new skills, and appreciate adventure in the real world. Life is full of uncertainties and challenges but courage makes progress possible. Reflect on the words of Eleanor Roosevelt: "You gain strength, courage, and confidence by every experience in which you really stop to look fear in the face. You are able to say to yourself, 'I lived through this horror. I can take the next thing that comes along.'"*

* *You Learn by Living* by Eleanor Roosevelt (New York: Harper & Brothers, 1960).

Kinds of Courage

Courage includes moral (of the mind) as well as physical (of the body) acts; many demands for courage call upon both.

In Western culture, courage is primarily thought of in terms of physical courage rather than moral courage; for example, an exhilarating, personal risk-taking task, such as free-fall parachuting, deep-sea diving, rappelling down a mountain. Or, courage may be seen as a more spontaneous response to a situation that is thrust upon us with little time for conscious decision-making, such as jumping into raging flood waters to save a child, dashing into a burning building to rescue a trapped person, or passing the helicopter's dangling lifeline to an injured fellow airline passenger as you both float in shark-infested waters. In both kinds of physical courage, the body responds by producing chemicals to help us confront the fear and perform superhuman tasks. We feel fear, recognize it, control it, and then make it work for us. While taking the first step may be the most difficult decision, courage grows and expands once the action has begun.

Moral courage encompasses knowing right from wrong and standing up for our convictions. Moral cowards, those who either give up or give in, never win in the game of life. They may feel they're winning the occasional conflict but their triumphs are seldom glorious, rarely last long, nor do they inspire future generations. Despite our ingrained views of courage in the physical realm, in everyday life, it is moral courage that carries the day.

Moral heroes face up to ethical challenges in daily life. This same courage over day-to-day issues and events can be drawn upon during times of great stress and controversy. Gandhi and Martin Luther King, Jr. are internationally recognized heroes of moral courage. They remind us that the greatest battleground on which courage is fought is within us. They placed integrity above fear, dread, or acute embarrassment to hold true to their visions.

WHY PRACTICE COURAGE?

Character development is impossible without the LIFESKILL of Courage for it is not easy to do the right thing; if it were, the world would be a much kinder and gentler place than it is. We have to have courage to act upon what we know to be right.

Courage is a critical element in three important areas of our life: relationships, leadership roles, and teamwork.

Courage in Relationships

In friendships and in the intimacy of marriage and parent-child interactions, it takes courage to say "No" when it's easier to say "Yes"; it takes courage to say "Yes" when the truth is "No"; it takes courage to say what is really so rather than what's expected or what the person wants to hear, especially when it's about our feelings and needs. Where and when we are vulnerable, courage is needed so that we may face situations with integrity rather than indifference or lies. Courage is not for wimps!

Courage in Leadership

The home demands many acts of courage each and every day, especially moral courage. Because few places have such profound influence upon future generations, it is critical that we acknowledge the need for courage in leadership in the home. As a parent you are leader of your family. And courage is one of the defining attributes of that leadership role.

Among many challenges confronting us are those of embracing change, committing to personal best, and thinking "outside the box."

Embracing Change. Perhaps no other work place in the world experiences the degree of change that the family unit does. Due to their rapid developmental and intellectual growth, children appear at the breakfast table as different people each day. Then add the impact of births and deaths in a family over one's lifetime, typically three or more generations. And, how about fluctuating income and household moves to follow jobs?

Although we may understand that change is inevitable, it still takes courage to embrace change because the outcomes are unknown. Extreme discomfort and disappointment, even failure, could be just around the corner. How we face these changes makes a lasting impression on our children.

Committing to Personal Best. Think how our lives would change if we modeled the Lifelong Guideline of Personal Best 100 percent of the time. To do so takes enormous courage because while we are striving valiantly to "walk our talk" (model what we say and expect of others), we must at the same time accept the reality that our personal best doesn't mean we're perfect. It takes humility and courage to walk our talk. Holding others to their personal best is not a job for shrinking violets either. To the extent that our personal best is not perfect—and whose is?—we're put in the awkward position of expecting of others more than we might be able to deliver in some areas ourselves. In our role as parent, admitting to mistakes and lapses isn't comfortable and would seem to undermine our position of authority. In applying the Lifelong Guidelines and LIFESKILLS we, like our children, are works in progress.

It takes courage to ask the question: How good is my personal best? If we have areas of weakness, and who doesn't, what are we doing about them? What are we doing to keep improving? How can we expect others to work on their behaviors if we aren't genuinely in the process of working on ours?

The stakes are high and the process painfully visible.

Thinking Outside the Box. Thinking outside the box in parenting means thinking beyond "what other parents do," beyond how we ourselves were raised. Sometimes tried and true solutions no longer achieve the desired results. We must think "outside the box" for more creative answers and some that may have been rebuffed and rejected by our family or work colleagues. At this point, the LIFESKILLS of Courage and Perseverance go hand in hand as we guide ourself and others out of complacency and habit to true moral courage. On other occasions, it's essential for leaders to hear and face the truth, especially when it contradicts our perceptions and opinions. The willingness to admit the possibility that our viewpoint is fallible and to change our opinion requires great courage.

HOW DO YOU PRACTICE IT?

Practicing courage takes courage! Compare it to going swimming in a cold, spring-fed lake on the first hot day of summer. Are you the kind of person who, ignoring the frosty temperature of the water, lets out a holler and dives right in, emerging within seconds to declare through chattering teeth, "The water's great! Come on in!" Or, do you cautiously dangle one big toe into the shallow water and slowly begin to immerse one body part at a time, answering, "It's freezing! I don't know if I want to do this or not!"

You can approach the LIFESKILL of Courage the same way. You can either jump right in—and commit yourself to practicing courage in all aspects of your life—or you can start gradually by selecting only a few areas of your life and then expand from there. Either way, the job gets done.

There are some variables, however, that may affect your comfort level and thus your starting point. First, is the issue insignificant or highly-charged for you? Second, are you standing alone or are others standing with you? Third, what are your tolerance levels for things such as uncertainty, risk-taking, non-agreement, or disapproval?

Look for Personal Examples

Think about all of the times you have called upon inner strength and personal conviction to be courageous. Reflect on those experiences. Why did you stand up for your beliefs? What was the driving force behind you? What feelings did you have afterward?

Learn to distinguish nervous excitement from true anxiety. Do some soul searching; know yourself, your feelings, your beliefs, and your opinions.

Establish and/or clarify your personal goals. This will guide your decision making and will keep you on the path to what is most important in your life.

Act on your moral convictions. Share your opinions with others but, at the same time, listen to theirs. Don't be swayed by ineffective arguments, group size, or fleeting feelings of self-doubt. Know where you stand.

Path of the Warrior

A big part of courage is the willingness to give up control of the outcome and stop playing it safe. The world is bigger than we are; a plan for the common good is often larger than our own personal vision for it. If we try to control events, we invariably squeeze problem solving down to less powerful solutions than could be accomplished through the participation of others, however messy the process. We can't control events, we can only do our best at playing our part.

To practice courage, travel the path of the warrior. First, show up. Second, pay attention. Third, tell the truth. And, fourth, let go of the consequences.

WHAT DOES COURAGE LOOK LIKE IN THE REAL WORLD?
We

- Embrace change
- Take calculated risks
- Take an unpopular stand when we feel the cause is just; speak up for ideas and policies that benefit all people
- Speak our minds but always apologize for inappropriate actions and words
- Ignore the limitations people place on us and always work to our personal best
- Own up to our mistakes and make amends
- Start businesses; develop new products
- Dare to change occupations when we are dissatisfied with our work; seek a different position that may be a better match for our interests and skills
- Return to school or college to earn a degree or acquire new skills and knowledge
- Taste different foods and explore new places
- Believe in ourselves when others don't

WHAT DOES COURAGE LOOK LIKE AT HOME?
Adults

- Tell the truth regardless of the consequences or damage to our image
- Dare to commit ourselves to "walk our talk" (model the Lifelong Guidelines and LIFESKILLS) with our children and own up to any failure to do so
- Create an atmosphere of trust so that all members of the family feel free to take risks
- Establish behavior guidelines for our children despite what "other moms and dads do" and enforce those rules consistently and fairly "no matter what other parents do or think"
- Support children when they believe their actions are correct, even if such actions are unpopular
- Take night classes to improve our skills
- Relocate to find work; find another job when downsizing occurs

Children

- Respect and follow behavior guidelines set by their parents, including dating and dress standards, despite what "our friends are allowed to do"

- Accept enforcement of those guidelines despite what their friends think they should be allowed to do and whether it is considered "cool" or not

- Accept responsibility for their own behaviors and actions; acknowledge when they make a mistake

- Take that first step without being cajoled

- Open their minds to learn new ideas, approaches, and skills; willingly accept new challenges

- Ask questions or say "I don't understand. Please explain it to me again."

- Face illnesses with grace

- Befriend someone whom others ignore, tease, or attack with put-downs

- Defend siblings from verbal and physical attack

- Develop strategies to deal with the neighborhood "bully"

OPPORTUNITIES TO PRACTICE COURAGE

AGES 4-8

- Listen to/read the book *The Bully Brothers: Making the Grade* by Mike Thaler or *Just a Bully* by Gina Mayer. Discuss how you feel about bullies with your parents. Identify two things a bully does to frighten people. Choose two strategies (e.g., walk away, tell the teacher) you will use to deal with a bully. Share the results with a parent.

- Watch the video *Charlotte's Web*. Identify three or more instances when the characters showed great courage. Draw a picture of the character that impressed you the most. Act the scene out for a brother or sister. Ask them to play a part if you need additional cast members.

- Listen to a family member read from *The Wizard of Oz*. List five acts of courage that the lion performed before he realized he already was courageous. Create a diorama that illustrates the scene when the lion finally understands he has the LIFESKILL of Courage. Display it in the family room or your bedroom.

- Choose a familiar tune such as "Twinkle, Twinkle, Little Star" and compose lyrics that will teach a family member two or more attributes of a courageous person. Write two or more verses. Add motions that will further explain courage. Teach the song to your family at dinner time.

- Enter the Future Problem-Solving Program Contest (grades K-6)
    ~ Form a team of four (including yourself)
    ~ Ask a teacher or other adult to be your coach
    ~ Learn the FPSP six-step process
    ~ Tackle three problems (topics provided by FPSP) during the school year
    ~ Mail solutions to evaluators
    ~ Prepare for further competition if your answers are accepted
    ~ Contact Future Problem Solving Program, 318 West Ann Street, Ann Arbor, MI 48104-1337; E-mail: fpsolv@aol.com; Website: http://www.fpsp.org; Phone: 313/998-7377

- Brainstorm an activity (e.g., playing chess, knitting, baseball card collecting) or sport (e.g., soccer, roller skating, jumping rope) you want to learn. Ask a family member to be your coach/teacher or sign up for the activity/sport at a neighborhood center. Complete the entire training session. Share three or more skills you are learning with grandpa/grandma each week. Prepare a demonstration for your family when the lessons/classes have ended.

- Study the correct way (etiquette) to introduce yourself to someone you are meeting for the first time. Ask for help learning: the words to say, the correct way to shake someone's hand, who speaks first, and what to say at the end. Practice with another person at least 10 times or until you can repeat the pattern without feeling anxious or embarrassed. Use your latest skill with the next new person your parents bring into your home. Share with a parent how this has increased your courage when meeting strangers.

- Watch a wildlife video or TV program. Share five or more times when an animal showed courage. Read more about one of the animals and the courageous actions it uses to defend itself and its young. Describe and demonstrate one of the actions for your brother/sister/friend. Reflect on what you can learn about the LIFESKILL of Courage from this animal.

AGES 9-12

- Choose a cartoon character that you feel shows the LIFESKILL of Courage. Pick a song whose tune you can easily sing (e.g., "On Top of Spaghetti," "Happy Birthday") and write one verse that will teach someone two ways to recognize courageous acts. Pretending to be this cartoon character, sing the song to your family. Ask them to share with you what they learned about courage from your lyrics (words). Teach them the song.

- Identify a child on your block that is the target of "put-downs." Befriend him/her. Introduce yourself, inquire about personal interests, share your hobbies and skills, and offer to teach/play with him/her. Stand up to the other children and teach them to use

"Put-ups" (kind comments and positive feedback) rather than "Put-downs" (unkind comments). Role-play responses that will provide him/her with strategies to use in put-down situations. Provide support as he/she attempts his/her new skills. Share what you have learned about the LIFESKILL of Courage with an adult.

- Follow current articles in your newspaper. Read through the stories and identify a neighbor or local citizen who has used the LIFESKILL of Courage in one of the following ways: physical bravery, standing up for his/her beliefs, facing a challenge, learning some new skill. Design a COURAGE-O-GRAM that identifies: the person, the way he/she used the LIFESKILL of Courage, what his/her actions have taught you about courage, and why you appreciate what he/she did. Send this COURAGE-O-GRAM to the newspaper and ask them to forward it to the subject of the article.

- Discreetly observe (it's not polite to stare) someone who has a challenging condition such as blindness, deafness, a form of paralysis. Identify five or more ways this person uses the LIFESKILL of Courage every day. Design a bookmark honoring such a quietly courageous person, an unsung hero, who exhibits courage daily. Present this bookmark to your local librarian to put on display with books on this subject.

- Read one or more biographies about one of the following people: Eleanor Roosevelt, Elizabeth Cady Stanton, Ruby Bridges, Jacques Cousteau, John F. Kennedy, or Leonardo da Vinci. Gather information/facts explaining the kinds of courageous actions your subject demonstrated. Prepare a soliloquy (a dramatic monologue that gives the illusion of being a series of unspoken reflections) describing the courageous actions attributed to your subject. Without sharing the name of the person, dramatize the monologue for family and friends. Invite them to guess who you are in the monologue.

- Offer your technology services to an older member of your family (e.g., Mom, Dad, grandpa, grandma). Teach them the following skills: starting/closing the computer, writing/sending/opening E-mail, accessing the World Wide Web, and completing a search on a topic of his/her choice. Demonstrate each skill 10 or more times; be a guide-on-the-side while he/she practices each skill a dozen times or until he/she can do it with expertise. During the training and practice sessions, analyze what parts of the learning session required the LIFESKILL of Courage by your trainee. Design and present him/her with a "Techie Diploma" when the training is complete. After awarding the diploma, ask your trainee how the LIFESKILL of Courage helped them. Share with a family member what you have learned about the LIFESKILL of Courage.

- Design a "courage" card to present to a local citizen whose courage has improved life for others in our community. Illustrate the card with a drawing that further identifies what he/she did. Mail the card to that person.

- Skim the book *The Ultimate Guide to Student Contests: Grades K-6* by Scott Pendleton. Choose a topic that matches your interests. Study the different contests; choose one that looks interesting. Follow the directions for creating your contest entry. Complete the entry process and actually send it in to be judged. Explain to someone how the LIFESKILL of Courage helped you enter the contest. Celebrate your entry into the contest with your family.

Chapter 10—Courage

AGES 13+

- Read this quote by author Ambrose Redmoon: "Courage is not the absence of fear but rather the judgment that something else is more important than fear." Design a diorama that demonstrates a time in your life when this quotation was true for you. Plan a background, characters to include, other props, and a written description of the action as it happened. Display this in your family room or living room.

- Choose one of the following books to read: *The Red Badge of Courage* by Stephen Crane, *Always Courage* by Frederik Weller, or *Call It Courage* by Armstrong Sperry. Identify four or more ways the LIFESKILL of Courage was demonstrated in the story. Reflect on four or more times in your life that you have used the LIFESKILL of Courage. Compare/contrast your personal examples with the examples you chose from the novel. Share your comparisons with an English teacher, guidance counselor, or parent.

- Research 15 or more songs that have been on the top 100 list of hits in the past year. Identify one or more that centers on a form of courage. Learn the tune and the lyrics. Create two or more verses sharing your personal reflections on courage. Teach the entire song to your family/friends.

- Watch three or more local TV news programs for one week or longer. Identify three local heroes who have overcome or ignored his/her fears and, in doing so, performed a courageous act. Discuss these acts of bravery with your best friend. Compare these situations with similar ones during which no one stepped forward and displayed the LIFESKILL of Courage.

- Direct a video based on the format of the *Chicken Soup for the Soul* books. Interview 10 or more local children and/or neighbors who show acts of courage daily. Choose five of the most definitive examples and write a screenplay to tell these stories of courage to friends and relatives. Invite the actual subjects to participate or obtain permission to use an actor/actress friend to play the part. Add a title and other dialogue to enhance the video. Preview it with a Girl Scout/Boy Scout troop, 4H Club, or other youth group. Show it for your family and friends.

- Explore the possibility of becoming a candidate for a class or school office (e.g., student council member, president, treasurer, publicity chairperson). Itemize the skills necessary for each of the positions you find interesting. Inventory your personal strengths and compare them with those required for office. Decide which office or position is the best personal match. Obtain the paperwork for becoming an official candidate and follow the directions (e.g., submitting grades, list of extracurricular events, signed petitions, election plan). Choose a campaign manager and cooperatively form a positive campaign plan based on the issues. Design posters, write speeches, and plan debates. Whether you win or lose, reflect on how the LIFESKILL of Courage helped you throughout your candidacy.

- Sign up to participate in a program such as Outward Bound or a ropes/climbing course that tests your physical abilities as well as emotional strength and courage. Keep a journal detailing your feelings and any examples of personal courage you show during the training period. Invite two or more special relatives/friends to your graduation ceremony. Frame your certificate of completion and hang it in your bedroom.

- Observe a toddler between the ages of one- and two-years old for at least 30 minutes. List three or more examples of the child's courage. Note what the child does if its courageous attempt fails. Share your observations with the child's mother and a family member.

- Choose an issue that is important to your community, such as pollution, the condition of parks and playgrounds, or dangerous traffic conditions. Collect and read four or more newspaper articles on the topic. Listen to someone speak about the issue on radio, TV, or at a public lecture or community meeting. Learn the different points of view. Make a visual aid (sign, poster, video, photo album) to show your family and friends how you feel about the issue. Be prepared to answer questions. Share how the LIFESKILL of Courage helped you take a stand, explain it, and hold firm to your beliefs.

- Read a non-fiction book with the theme of courage. Choose a part in which one of the characters learns about the LIFESKILL of Courage. Act out this part of the story for family members. Explain why you chose this particular scene.

- Learn 10 phrases in a different language and practice them with a family member. Brainstorm three emotions you might feel if you were visiting a family in the neighborhood and weren't fluent in English. Explain how you would need the LIFESKILL of Courage to handle such situations. Record in your journal three ways you could assist students at your school who don't speak English well.

SIGNS OF SUCCESS

Congratulations! Children are showing signs of Courage when they

- Stand against the group to follow their conscience
- Speak out against injustice and prejudice
- Speak up for themselves and their beliefs
- Analyze their feelings after taking an unpopular but courageous stand and feel pride in demonstrating the LIFESKILL of Courage
- Investigate a new activity
- Willingly try new foods and new experiences
- Practice skills even though the skill/material is difficult and failure is likely early on
- Combine courage with common sense and good judgment before taking risks
- Protect siblings and other family members from racial slurs and ethnic put-downs

Keep trying! Children need more practice when they

- Don't say what they feel or believe because they fear other people's opinions (friends, neighbors, relatives)

- Disregard their conscience and ignore "gut" feelings about right and wrong in favor of peer decisions and pressure

- Break family rules in order to join in with what their peers are doing

- Stay silent when they witness incidents of racial, religious, and ethnic prejudice

- Refuse to try new activities, skills, or projects

- Deny personal responsibility for their actions

- Avoid confrontations; take the easy way out of a situation

- Avoid/neglect an opportunity to demonstrate courage

Literature Link ~ Courage

Ages 4-8

Dancing Man, The	Ruth Lercher Bornstein (New York: Clarion Books, 1998)
Little Polar Bear and the Husky Pup	Hans de Beer (New York: North-South Books, 1999)
Red Flower Goes West	Ann Warren Turner (New York: Hyperion Books, 1999)
Sitting Ducks	Michael Bedard (New York: Grosset and Dunlap, 1998)

Ages 9-12

Chicken Soup for the Kid's Soul: 101 Stories of Courage, Hope and Laughter	Jack Canfield, Ed. (Deerfield Beach, FL: Health Communications, 1998)
It's Our World Too! Stories of Young People Who Are Making a Difference (ME)	Philip Hoose (New York: Little, Brown & Company, 1993)
Johnny Tremain	Esther Forbes (New York: Yearling Book, Random House, 1987)
Julie of the Wolves (TE)	Jean Craighead George (New York: HarperTrophy, 1974)

Ages 13+

Anne Frank, the Diary of a Young Girl (TE)	Anne Frank (New York: Bantam Books, Division of Random House, 1993)
Hold Fast to Dreams	Andrea Davis Pinkney (New York: William Morrow & Company, 1995)
Kids With Courage: True Stories About Young People Making a Difference (ME)	Barbara A. Lewis (Minneapolis, MN: Free Spirit Publishing, 1992)
I Know Why the Caged Bird Sings (AFA)	Maya Angelou (New York: Random House, 1969)
Jemmy (NA)	Jon Hassler (New York: Fawcett Books, 1991)

Family Resources

Endangered Minds: Why Children Don't Think and What We Can Do About It	Jane Healy, Ph.D. (New York: Simon & Schuster, 1990)
Why Johnny Hates Sports	Fred Engh (East Rutherford, NJ: Avery Publishing Group, 1999)

Multicultural books: **(AFA)**=African American, **(ASA)**=Asian American, **(HA)**=Hispanic American, **(ME)**=Multi-Ethnic, **(NA)**=Native American, **(TE)**=listed in the teacher edition of this book, *Tools for Citizenship and Life: Using the ITI Lifelong Guidelines and LIFESKILLS in the Classroom,* **(BFE)**=available through Books for Educators

Chapter 11
Curiosity

"Always seek to understand."

curiosity *n* 1: desire to know   **a:** inquisitive interest in others' concerns   **b:** interest leading to intellectual inquiry

Curiosity: A desire to investigate and seek to understand one's world

WHAT IS CURIOSITY?

Curiosity is a delightful, compelling, and sometimes annoying characteristic of our favorite mammals—puppies, kittens, otters, and, most of all, human children. It guides us to learn about the world and its possibilities and limits, to discover what is fun and what is harmful, and to practice old skills and experiment with new ones. Perhaps because we can remember the past and project the future, we're the most curious animals on earth. We are constantly exploring our world and everything that's in it. Human curiosity is a constant search for answers—how things work, why they work, and what if. Curiosity is the wellspring of human learning and the inner engine of creativity.

Curiosity Is Innate

Curiosity is a craving, a longing, a passion for knowledge. It is innate in young children. With their passion for exploring and learning new things, babies' drive to explore is taken for granted. Increased neurological connections are created by such exploration and rapidly used as the basis for more curiosity and more learning. Investigating the unusual creates new pathways in the brain. The more pathways, the more connections we can make.

Natural curiosity is easily seen in babies who explore their bodies and immediate environment—toes, fingers, crib, and toys—reaching for everything within sight. When crawling begins, a baby's world expands to include anything within range, creating the need to carefully examine the house for any dangers such as plugs, open doorways, and stoves. As the toddler conquers the rudiments of speech, the endless "Why?" emerges as a recurring question.

Curiosity Can Be Fragile

Yet as innate as curiosity is, it can be quite fragile, often diminishing as people are squelched by regimented, sterile learning and living environments that don't satisfy or reward curiosity. For many children, their curiosity slowly begins its spiral descent from wanting to know the "why" about everything to not even caring enough to ask a question. Boredom is not a natural state for humans. Children who need to be "motivated" to learn are children who have experienced adverse, spirit-crushing circumstances.

Curiosity and Creativity

Creativity often originates from dissatisfaction with the way things are or seem to be. Curiosity—"How could this be made to work better?"—pushes us to investigate and invent. By encouraging and strengthening the LIFESKILL of Curiosity in childhood, we are creating future inventors, scientists, writers, artists, composers, and thinkers. After all, it is curiosity that gives birth to our theories and pushes us to prove, disprove, or improve them. We often use other LIFESKILLS, such as Patience, Caring, Perseverance, and Resourcefulness in conjunction with Curiosity to facilitate our search for answers. Curiosity is the driving force that stimulates and renews the spark needed in our search.

WHY PRACTICE CURIOSITY?

Without the LIFESKILL of Curiosity, life would be very different. An almost endless list of creations would be missing from our lives such as electronic technologies of all kinds, stories, symphonies, buildings, poems, medicines, rock music, cars, planes, and rocket ships. All of these became reality because somewhere along the way, a caring adult took the time to stimulate and encourage a child's curiosity. That child, once grown, rewards us with the products of the LIFESKILL of Curiosity.

Lack of curiosity is detrimental for society. When too many of us stop asking questions and seeking answers, human accomplishments will decline. On the other hand, questions about such issues as pollution of the Earth's water can lead to answers that improve the quality of life for all living things. It's vital that we practice the LIFESKILL of Curiosity by continuing to ask "Why."

Lack of curiosity on a personal level is severely limiting. Opportunities pass us by. Those without curiosity are poor learners. Their knowledge and skill base grows like an inch worm rather than by leaps and bounds. They make poor conversationalists who have little to say that hasn't been heard before. Their personal satisfaction level is low and employment options and income are limited.

Curiosity propels us to ask *what* and *why* and *how* questions in the search for meaning, for new way to do old things. It prompts us to observe more closely, analyze more thoroughly, formulate theories to test, and question the obvious. Curiosity makes us think. For the uncurious, life is a bore, a thing to be endured rather than enjoyed.

HOW DO YOU PRACTICE IT?

It is important to understand that not all children will demonstrate curiosity for the same topics because no two brains are the same. We must allow space and time for children to pursue individual interests. Having said that, however, some things are important to learn for citizenship and family harmony, whether they immediately "tickle our fancy" or not. But a heightened sense of curiosity, like sugar, makes the medicine go down and opens doors to expanding careers, lifelong interests, and hobbies that we might not otherwise have discovered. Nurture curiosity.

Curiosity Is Contagious: Model It

Not surprisingly, the best way to encourage and nurture our child's LIFESKILL of Curiosity is to model curiosity ourselves. Do we still avoid learning how to program the VCR? Do we continue to avoid computers, are we web-less? Do we wait for others to figure out new equipment so we can get the quick "explanation for dummies"? If so, we're killing our child's curiosity by example.

Instead, we should be a lover of books and web surfing, devote our conversations with others to ideas and "what ifs" rather than gossip. Read daily, especially non-fiction, and share what we find exciting and fascinating with our family. Be an active hobbyist—practice your hobby weekly if not daily. Learn at least one new, significant skill a year, such as playing a new instrument, learning to sing, weave, hang glide, sew, cook a new area of ethnic foods, ride a horse.

Formalize Curiosity

As your child's curiosity grows, teach him/her formal ways to use it as well as letting it flow in formless, undirected ways such as daydreaming. Help him/her hone skills for theorizing, articulating questions, researching data, organizing information, and sharing wisdom. These aren't just "school topics." These are the stuff of clear thinking.

Also, teach your child to honor the interests and creativity of others. In the process he/she may discover new interests and new pleasures in life.

WHAT DOES CURIOSITY LOOK LIKE IN THE REAL WORLD?

We

- Examine the natural world and ask "Why?"
- Wonder, "What if. . . ?" "How can we. . . ?" "Let's try it this way. . . ."
- Embrace lifelong learning in vocations and avocations

- Visit the World Wide Web frequently for information on varying topics
- Join organizations, clubs, and interest groups
- Are eager to introduce ourselves to new neighbors and welcome them to the neighborhood
- Frequently visit information sources such as the library and World Wide Web for information on varying topics
- Discover new and better ways to accomplish a task
- Experiment in life activities such as cooking, gardening, exercising, traveling, and reading
- Return to high school or continue with extended learning programs
- Seek answers to the unknown
- Ask theoretical, speculative, and hypothetical questions
- Invent products that will improve the quality of life

WHAT DOES CURIOSITY LOOK LIKE AT HOME?

Adults

- Reflect on personal capabilities
- Open our minds to new ideas, implement new strategies and techniques for doing things
- Develop personal interests, hobbies, and pastimes and share with family and friends
- Learn many subjects in-depth as well as explore widely; share our wisdom and delight with our child, other family members, and friends
- Desire to know the "workings" of things such as computers, TVs, engines, microwaves, dishwashers, and other mechanical apparatus as well as the world of nature
- Model our thinking processes aloud for our child
- Ask our child thought-provoking questions and encourage him/her to question
- Develop interests in the natural world of birds, insects, and animals
- Graph out genealogy information about our family tree
- Read daily, including at least one daily newspaper and always have at least one book, magazine, or journal in progress

Children

- Ask questions, questions, and more questions
- Wonder "Why?" about nearly everything they encounter
- Make hypotheses and test them
- Brainstorm more than one answer to a question, more than one solution for a problem
- Participate in organizations, clubs, sports, and other interest groups
- Try new experiences
- Crave environmental learning experiences; find ways to learn outside of the school and home environments
- Look for ways to use skills and knowledge in real-world applications
- Read biographies of scientists, inventors, statesmen, composers, and artists
- Admire and respect artists, musicians, scientists, inventors, statesmen, and writers
- Design new and innovative projects

OPPORTUNITIES TO PRACTICE CURIOSITY

AGES 4-8

- Listen as a family member reads *Curious George* by H. A. and Margaret Rey. Make a list of five things that puzzled George. Choose two of them to illustrate. Title your drawing "Curious George." Read the list again and check which things you also would like to know more about. Share what you are curious about with a family member. Ask a family member to help you find answers to satisfy your questions about this thing(s).

- Take a magnifying glass outside of your house. Choose 10 or more items in the yard that pique your curiosity. Select one object and carefully study it on all sides. Look at the same object through the magnifying glass. After studying each of the remaining nine objects, choose the one that makes you most curious. On one side of a piece of paper, draw what you see when you look at the object without the magnifier. On the back side of the paper, draw how the object looks when you look at it through the magnifying glass. Sign your name in the bottom corner of the paper. Share with a parent what surprised you the most about doing this and what you learned about the LIFESKILL of Curiosity. Ask a family member to help you find answers to satisfy your questions about what you saw and experienced.

- Ask Mom/Dad for an old wind-up clock that is no longer used, such as a Big Ben. Predict what the inside of the clock will look like. Then, borrow some tools and ask for help to carefully open up the clock and take it apart, studying it as you go.

- Draw a picture of what the inside looks like. Learn the names of two inside parts.
- Wind the clock and watch what happens on the inside.
- Predict which cogs drive the hour hand, the minute hand, and the second hand (if the clock has one).
- Put the clock back together. Look to see if the clock is working. If the hands are not moving, take the clock apart and try to get it working.

Share with a parent what you learned about the clock and about the LIFESKILL of Curiosity.

- Borrow a beginner's birding book from the library. Sit in the yard very quietly and observe any birds that come for a visit. Choose 10 different kinds of birds to observe closely. Note each one's size, color, shape of beak, type of legs and feet, the sounds it makes, and what it eats (Is it a herbivore, carnivore, or omnivore.). Look for each different bird in the book. Match names with pictures. Go out a second day and try to name the birds without using the book. Keep practicing until you can name all 10 with accuracy. Ask yourself what else you would like to know about these birds. Find someone who can answer all your questions. Share what you have learned with your grandpa/grandma or other family member.

- Listen to one of the Curious George stories by Margaret Rey. On a piece of paper, draw a picture of each object that made George curious. Count them up. Now draw a matching number of pictures/objects about which you are curious. Use an encyclopedia to learn more about one of those objects. Teach someone else the information you learned.

- Lie on your back outside on the grass on a beautiful, warm, partially-sunny day. Watch for clouds. Use color, shape, size, and height to describe any clouds to Mom/Dad. Choose three special clouds; try to picture them as animals, people, or objects. Name what you think each one looks like. Go back inside. Using a piece of blue construction paper, cotton balls, and white glue, re-create a model of one of the clouds you saw.

- Invent a special toy for your pet that will arouse its curiosity. Use safe materials. Leave off small objects that your pet might swallow. Offer the toy to your pet and show him/her one or two ways to play with it. Observe your pet with the toy to see if it keeps his/her interest. If it does, that's great! If it doesn't, try making some changes that will make your pet curious and retry the toy. Make a copy of the toy and offer it to someone who has the same kind of pet that you do.

AGES 9-12

- Choose two items (smaller than your two hands together) from around the house or yard that fire your curiosity. Use a magnifying glass to study each object. Identify three or more ways the items are different and three or more ways they are the same. Share with a parent how the LIFESKILL of Curiosity led you to learn more about the two items during this examination than you have learned since these items came to the house.

- Create a list of six or more quotations containing the word "curious" or "curiosity." Start with "Curiosity killed the cat. Satisfaction brought it back." Design a banner for each quotation; include both the quote and an illustration of each. Display them in the family room. Explain to your family how you interpret each quotation.

- Memorize the quotation, "Curiosity killed the cat. Satisfaction brought it back." Discuss its meaning with a friend. Design a cartoon of four or more frames with "CURIOSITY CAT" as the main character. Add one other character of your choice. Then, put the title in the first frame, upper left hand corner. Write your name directly beneath the title. Use the above quotation to develop the story line and plot. Add dialogue in "conversation clouds" for the characters. Color the drawings and mount the cartoon on a slightly larger piece of heavy cardboard. Submit the cartoon to a children's magazine for possible publication. Share with a family member what you learned about the LIFESKILL of Curiosity by making this cartoon.

- Choose four items from your home. Draw a picture of each object on an index card (5" x 8") plus write the object's name on the card. Use a magnifying glass to examine one of the objects. Focus on one special part. Draw what you see through the magnifying glass on another index card that is also 5" x 8" but do not label what the item is. Do the same for each of the other items. Then, ask a friend or family member to match the magnified picture with its picture drawn to scale. Provide feedback to your friend or family member on his/her matching skills. Ask him/her how he/she used the LIFESKILL of Curiosity to match the pictures.

- Choose an insect that you're curious about. Identify five body parts and predict how each one helps the insect. Research the body parts, their design, and their function or purpose. Use clay or paper to create a large model of the insect. Label the five parts and why they're important to the insect. Make a threefold title card with the insect's scientific name, the name we know it by, and one more question you have about this insect. Explain what you learned to an interested friend. Use your LIFESKILL of Curiosity to explore what this insect would do and eat if it were as big as you are.

- Collect five or more wildflowers from your yard or a nearby field. Carefully draw each flower on its own sheet of paper. Make each life size and in true color. Use a reference book for your part of the country to help identify the plant (such as *Roger Tory Peterson's Field Guide: Wildflowers* or Ruth Heller's *The Reason for a Flower*). Write the plant's name beneath its drawing. Then, select one of the flowers and dissect it. Inspect the following parts: pistol, stamen, petal, stem, and pollen. Scotch tape each part and label it on the page with the drawing. Ask yourself what you would like to know about each of these parts of a flower, for example, what it does, how it helps the plant survive and thrive, what parts are edible, and so forth.

- Locate the nest of three or more birds that live in your neighborhood. Without touching the nest and disturbing the parent birds, examine each shell for color and approximate length and width. Compare your data. Using a *Roger Tory Peterson Bird Guide*, find out what birds built the nests you found. Ask yourself what other birds have eggs similar in color and in size. Ask yourself why some small birds lay big eggs and some big birds lay relatively small eggs. Ask why some birds build in trees, some on the ground. Find books or a bird expert to help you answer questions you are curious about.

- Locate David Macauley's book, *The Way Things Work.* Select six drawings that arouse your curiosity and study their descriptions. Ask Mom/Dad for an old appliance or piece of machinery that has similar parts or functions. Ask for one that doesn't work so you are free to use your LIFESKILL of Curiosity without worrying about getting it back to working order. Take it apart and examine the parts inside. Make a detailed pencil/paper drawing of the inner workings. Identify three or more parts by name and function. Question an adult about any parts you cannot identify. If doing this has you wondering about the innards of more machinery, start a book of your own. Ask other family members and neighbors for castaway mechanical things.

- Select a foreign language (e.g., French, Italian, German, Japanese) that is part of your cultural heritage. Borrow a beginner's book and audiotape in that language from the library. Set aside a specific amount of time every day to practice learning the meanings of words and their pronunciation. Choose 10 basic phrases that will help when you visit that country. Say the phrases for someone in your family who speaks the language and see if he/she can determine what you mean.

- Choose one of the following technological products (television, computer, smoke detector, audio cassette player, radio, or VCR) and find out how it works. Ask an adult for help to look inside the product. Draw a diagram of the inner workings. Take the diagram to your backyard. Using a scale of 1":20", create a model from recycled and/or readily-at-hand materials that will help others understand how this product works; you can also use people (yourself and/or friends) to represent parts or actions. Demonstrate your project for your family and friends.

- Interview a parent or other family member. Ask him/her to share five or more topics he/she wanted to learn more about as a child. Next, ask your interviewee to describe what he/she currently finds to be most interesting. Compare both lists to determine if any of the interests match. Discuss with a family member your finding and whether or not they surprised you.

- Interview your parent or another family member about his/her job. Think up questions that most arouse your curiosity. Identify eight words key to their explanation that you don't understand. Visit the family member's job site for at least an hour. Ask the family member to check that you understand the words and what they mean to the job the family member does. Add any other words about his/her job that you want to understand.

AGES 13+

- Use the LIFESKILL of Curiosity to learn more about yourself. Read five chapters in *Please Understand Me: Character and Temperament Type II* that most pique your curiosity. Take the test and read about yourself. Ask a parent to also take the test and compare his/her personality type to your own. In what ways are you alike and different? What does the test tell you about how to appreciate differences and get along better with family members? Also ask to take a job aptitude/interest inventory through the guidance counselor's office at school. Review the results with the counselor as well as with your parents. Identify the top five jobs on your inventory. Rank these five in the order of your current interests and level of curiosity about them. Create a personal business card with logo for your number one choice. Include your name, address, phone number, and E-mail address. Share it with the guidance counselor.

- Borrow 10 or more college catalogs from the guidance office. Include a variety of schools: private, public, in-state, out-of-state, large and small, expensive, and inexpensive. Check the courses of study they have and the degrees offered. Rank the colleges from #1 (your favorite) to #10 (your least favorite). Compute the cost for four years at your #1 college choice and at your #10 choice. Discuss both amounts with your parents and determine how much you will be expected to pay toward expenses each year.

- Turn the book *Alice in Wonderland* into a play. Include the really curious changes that occur to the characters. Organize some other neighborhood kids to be the actors/actresses for parts you assign. Practice the play until it is letter perfect and then perform it for a group of younger children. Invite them to share the parts they can identify as "curious-er and curious-er."

- Volunteer to become an intern for a candidate running for office. Create a resume listing credentials and previous experiences that will help you to perform the duties. Arrange to meet with the campaign director, present your resume, and offer your services. To prepare for your new job, examine two important campaign issues and assemble background information on the topics. Answer the important 5Ws: who, what, when, where, and why. Design a "fact" sheet that organizes the information for ease of understanding.

- Discover three or more ways technology is used to create special effects for modern movies. List one movie for each special effect. Construct a miniature movie set and experiment with special effects to create four of the following images (or those of your own choosing): lightning, thunder, dinosaurs larger than buildings, space ships hurtling through space, giant ants, and an ocean liner sinking with hundreds of people on deck.

- Read a biography about one of the following people: Alexander Graham Bell, Rachel Carson, John Muir, Madame Curie, Leonardo da Vinci, Thomas Edison, Albert Einstein, or Christa McAuliffe. Write a paragraph of 50 words or less nominating your person to receive the National Curiosity Award. Design the award you think should be presented to the winner. Include in your design key ways your candidate demonstrated the LIFESKILL of Curiosity.

- Design a toy for a younger child, four- to eight-years old. Develop a prototype to use for modeling and demonstration purposes. Produce a one-minute (or less) commercial (audio/video) that introduces the toy's name, how it is used, and the proposed cost. Air the commercial for your family and survey them to determine how many would purchase the product.

SIGNS OF SUCCESS

Congratulations! Children are showing signs of Curiosity when they

- Ask questions, questions, and more questions
- Relentlessly search for answers to questions
- Improve a new skill or develop a talent

- Observe the people, actions, and objects in their world
- Express an interest in how mechanical objects work
- Become an expert in a field of interest
- Accept responsibility for their own learning and generate their own motivation to learn
- Observe people, actions, and objects in their world; reflect on their ideas and learning
- Show excitement about learning widely and deeply both in and out of school
- Express wonder over amazing happenings
- Stop and examine the natural world
- Share their interests with others

Keep trying! Children need more practice when they

- Stop asking "Why?"; show no wonder about the world around them
- Act bored much of the time
- Can't entertain themselves on their own (without TV, videos, computers, or people)
- Spend too much time watching TV and videos and/or using the computer
- Complain that they are being asked too many questions
- Are afraid to ask questions or share ideas because others might laugh
- Put down other children's ideas, excitement, and projects as dumb, stupid, or insignificant because they are unable to see/not curious about the potential excitement of the ideas/project
- Feel it's a "waste of time" to explore significant questions; won't take the time to formulate some ideas and test them for accuracy
- Neglect trying any new idea or activity because it will be too hard to do

Literature Link ~ Curiosity

Ages 4-8

Abuela (HA) (TE)	Arthur Dorros (New York: E.P. Dutton, 1991)
Armadillo from Amarillo, The (HA)	Lynne Cherry (New York: Harcourt Brace, 1994)
Polar the Titanic Bear	Laurie McGaw (New York: Little, Brown & Co, 1994)
Tar Beach (AFA)	Faith Ringgold (New York: Crown Publishers, 1991)

Ages 9-12

Chasing Redbird (NA)	Sharon Creech (New York: HarperCollins, 1998)
Friends, The (ASA)	Kazumi Yumoto (New York: Farrar, Straus & Giroux, 1996)
Girls and Young Women Inventing: 20 True Stories About Inventors Plus How You Can Be One Yourself (ME)	Frances A. Karnes, Suzanne M. Bean, and Rosemary Wallner (Minneapolis, MN: Free Spirit Publishing, 1995)
Story of Thomas Alva Edison, The	Margaret Cousins (New York: Random House, 1997)
Ultimate Lego Book	Kjeld Kirk Kristiansen (New York: DK Publishing, 1999)

Ages 13+

Fahrenheit 451	Ray Bradbury (New York: Simon & Schuster, 1993)
Midnight Hour Encores	Bruce Brooks (New York: HarperTrophy, 1988)
To Be a Slave (AFA)	Julius Lester (New York: Scholastic, Inc., 1988)

Multicultural books: **(AFA)**=African American, **(ASA)**=Asian American, **(HA)**=Hispanic American, **(ME)**=Multi-Ethnic, **(NA)**=Native American, **(TE)**=listed in the teacher edition of this book, *Tools for Citizenship and Life: Using the ITI Lifelong Guidelines and LIFESKILLS in the Classroom*, **(BFE)**=available through Books for Educators

Family Resources

Awakening Your Child's Natural Genius: Enhancing Curiosity, Creativity, and Learning Ability (B4E) — Thomas Armstrong (New York: J. P. Tarcher, 1991)

Playing Smart: A Parent's Guide to Enriching, Offbeat Learning Activities for Ages 4 to 14 — Susan K. Perry (Minneapolis, MN: Free Spirit Publishing, 1990)

Sharing Nature With Children — Joseph Cornell (Watertown, NY: Dawn Publishing, 1998)

Simplify Your Life With Kids: 100 Ways to Make Family Life Easier and More Fun — Elaine Saint-James (Kansas City, MO: Andrews McMeel Universal, 1997)

Effort

"Do your best."

effort *n* **1:** conscious exertion of power: hard work **2:** a serious attempt: try **3:** something produced by exertion or trying **4:** the total work done to achieve a particular end

EFFORT: To work hard and do your best

WHAT IS EFFORT?

In ordinary speech and general writing we use "effort" to describe both process and product—the way we work (a serious attempt to attain our goal) and the outcome (something produced by our exertion). For example, "Their effort to get the job done today was commendable." "Our defense worked hard; it was a good effort and carried the day for us."

Effort is both mental and physical. Tasks such as computing, reading, and studying are mostly mental. Shooting hoops, running laps, riding a bicycle, and washing dishes require mostly physical effort. Other tasks, such as performing music, acting on stage, conducting science experiments, and acting out simulations require both mental and physical effort.

Also, the amount and kind of effort exerted for various activities differ from person to person. Some of our friends, for example, are extremely high-energy people while others are laid back. Effort can also vary with the circumstances. For example, if we lack the knowledge and skill to do a task, it will require much more effort of us than of someone who has expertise in doing the task. Or, if people pretend they want something—they say they want it but make only a half-hearted attempt to reach their goals—effort expended is minimal versus the effort expended by someone passionate about achieving a particular goal.

Effort can be a solitary endeavor or part of a team project. In either case, it is the willingness to give something our best shot, to use all of our energy, skill, knowledge, and commitment to go the extra mile. Both solitary and team efforts are crucial to personal as well as group success.

Questions To Ask

Effort doesn't automatically result in the desired product—it simply keeps us going. To make sure we're headed in the right direction, we must ask ourselves some questions: What do we want? Why? What plans do we have to make to get there? Setting priorities, choosing goals, reflecting about our progress (or lack of it), are all pieces of the effort puzzle. If one piece is missing, we can't complete the picture.

In team efforts, we ask similar questions but must also define each person's role as well as our own. Once these questions are answered, we can examine how the LIFESKILL of Effort can help us achieve our goals.

Baby Steps

Even when we're babies, the LIFESKILL of Effort is firmly in place. Watch a baby learning to master sitting, crawling, standing, speaking, and walking. "That baby has a one-track mind," someone may say, as the child pushes harder and harder, without a rest, to reach the objective. If he doesn't succeed, the child is even more determined and tries harder. When he succeeds, his glee and satisfaction are obvious in his body language, expressive eyes, and contented look. The joy we see on the infant's face continues into adulthood as "a deep sense of personal satisfaction"* that arises from concentrating on a goal, putting forth full effort, and, finally, achieving that goal.

It takes effort to explore our world, acquire knowledge, and master needed skills. The educated mind is a mind that can muster energy, long attention spans, and focused effort throughout the day every day. There are few shortcuts but many baby steps to be taken. Too often students define studying as work beneath their dignity (who wants to be a "school boy" or teacher's pet?) or something for which they should receive a reward (an M & M, a smiley face, or money) rather than something that gives them a deep sense of personal satisfaction.

WHY PRACTICE EFFORT?

The best laid plans are worthless if we don't put out the effort necessary to implement them. The LIFESKILL of Effort bridges the gap between dream and reality, wishes and accomplishments.

Effort Moves Our Personal Lives and Civilization As a Whole

Think of some examples of effort in action. No doubt your list would include such descriptors as: applies, attempts, uses elbow grease, endeavors, exerts, labors, pushes, strives, and ventures. Lack of effort might be described as: inactive, half-hearted, neglectful, quits, doesn't try, and

---

* "A deep sense of personal satisfaction" is a phrase used by Brenda Wycoff, Arizona, to lead students to recognize that external trappings of money and power aren't as nurturing as the internal rewards of satisfaction, contentment, and respect of self that arise from one's accomplishments.

defeatist. Which list identifies the attributes you want in your doctor, lawyer, car mechanic, child's teacher, airplane mechanic, pastor, friend, and family members?

The qualities associated with the LIFESKILL of Effort are those that push civilizations and individuals forward. The efforts of those around us contribute significantly to the quality and success of our own lives.

Increased Self-Esteem

Practicing the LIFESKILL of Effort is crucial to our self-esteem. A sense of satisfaction and pride springs from deep within when we give our best and strongest effort to complete a task. Such accomplishments are self-perpetuating; the more successful our efforts, the more we want to try. The LIFESKILL of Effort pushes us to experience, to learn, to excel, and to become. As we do so, our sense of self and our confidence in our capacities increases.

In Times Of Need

Practicing the LIFESKILL of Effort is crucial in helping us to work our way through hard times and difficult situations. When the bills are bigger than our paycheck, when family obligations pile up, when we're slogging through our work but don't seem to be accomplishing anything, when miracles seem few and far between, effort over time will pull us through. By following a strong work ethic and never giving up to failure, we can prevail.

HOW DO YOU PRACTICE EFFORT?

Getting children to embrace the LIFESKILL of Effort may seem like a difficult sell job. Not true. Each day there are a number of opportunities to apply effort, some as simple as climbing out of bed on time when the clock radio chimes its wake-up tune, smiling at the breakfast table, pleasantly greeting family members and neighbors. Other examples of the LIFESKILL of Effort in action on a daily level require more energy of us, such as diligently working to complete our assigned responsibilities in a timely way and offering help to others with a task.

When teaching students about the LIFESKILL of Effort, begin small and start with things they care about. Allow your child to experience a deep sense of personal satisfaction each step of the way. Increases in difficulty, complexity, or size of tasks to be done shouldn't leapfrog ahead of their abilities. This kills incentive to put forth effort and shreds self-confidence.

The American Dream Versus a Pipe Dream

While reading the newspaper's classified section or advertisements, have you ever been tempted by notices that read, "Full-time income! Part-time effort," or "Amazing income! No effort." Don't you find them hard to believe? With little, or no effort, great amounts of money will quietly steal into your pockets? The American pipe dream for sure!

Even with best efforts, wallets often end up short-changed. Do you remember your parents admonishing you as a child, "You don't get something for nothing"?

The first step in practicing the LIFESKILL of Effort is to stop looking for the easy way out, the short cut, the all-American pipe dream to instant riches. Help children distinguish between the dream that can guide a life of accomplishment and satisfaction versus the pipe dream that drags its owner through false hopes and leads to fool's gold at the end of the rainbow. Once they're on the right track, the sensible choice is to put forth effort, exert themselves, use elbow grease, and labor over meaningful tasks.

Choose to Try

Implementing the LIFESKILL of Effort means doing whatever it takes to achieve the goal. Phone calls? Letters? Personal visits? Extra hours at work? Either we choose to go for it or we don't. It's as simple as that. If we choose to try, we should give it our best effort. If we decide that we want something, we choose to apply ourselves in ways necessary to attain the goal.

Teach children the importance of the act of choosing and committing oneself to a course of action. Only they can do it, only they can feel it, only they can summon the LIFESKILLS of Patience and Perseverance to stick to it. Only they can kindle the motivation to sustain the necessary efforts to complete their commitments and reach their goals.

Celebrate Successes

Unfortunately, all too often even we adults lose the sense of contentment that comes from successful efforts. We become so focused on moving to the next task that we forget to celebrate our accomplishments. This cheats us of an important source of motivation that is essential to maintaining our willingness to apply the LIFESKILL of Effort year in and year out throughout our life. Celebration of success is a powerful antidote to burnout.

Teach children early on to stop and smell the roses, to celebrate success of both the processes and products of their efforts. Teach them to celebrate the fruits of their efforts, to bask in the exhilaration that results from working hard and using the LIFESKILL of Effort to attain their goals.

Develop Yardsticks for Self-Assessment

Celebrating success hinges on knowing that we have succeeded—because *we* believe so, not because someone else says so.* To judge our success, we must develop internal yardsticks that will allow us to measure our expectations. Such yardsticks must be realistic. If our standards are too high, we are always disappointed in ourselves; if too low, we will never succeed in life. If our standards are set and held by someone else, we won't own them and they won't bring us satisfaction. If our standards don't grow with us—if our ego is too inflated and our perception of self

---

* See *Punished by Rewards* by Alfie Kohn ((New York: Houghton Mifflin, 1993). Also see the chapter on the eighth bodybrain-compatible element, mastery/application, in the ITI book appropriate for your grade level (see Appendix A).

artificially positive— we will have difficulty adjusting to the world of work and adult-level standards with any grace. We need the LIFESKILL of Effort to continue to propel us forward.

WHAT DOES EFFORT LOOK LIKE IN THE REAL WORLD?

We

- Work to discover better ways to design or present a product
- Send out numerous resumes and participate in many job interviews
- Service a new product or help find a replacement if unsatisfactory to a customer
- Learn and practice technological skills
- Improve a process or technique
- Work more than one job when our family is in need
- Choose opportunities for lifelong learning
- Work overtime to complete a task or project
- Strive to do our personal best on every task

WHAT DOES EFFORT LOOK LIKE AT HOME?

Adults

- Work hard on projects that benefit the family, completing them fully and on time
- Give our full concentration and commitment to a task; do what is required and more
- Work with determination and high energy on each household/family task
- Work as long as it takes to complete a task
- Learn new parenting skills and techniques
- Support each child's interests and personal growth
- Attend extracurricular activities and events at child's school
- Acknowledge the efforts of other family members
- Plan thoroughly so jobs/tasks will go smoothly/efficiently
- Provide support for our children and spouse consistently and dependably

Children

- Say "I can" rather than "I can't" and "I will" rather than "I don't want to"

- Offer to help family members when they need help

- Work hard at listening to others, waiting their turn, supporting others, and getting a job completed; use manners with family members

- Willingly redo jobs that are less than their personal best

- Start and complete school assignments with a minimum of reminders from family

- Keep their rooms (or personal space) neat, clean, and in order

- Keep trying to learn a skill or technique without whining

- Arrive on time as agreed

- Work to develop social skills that will enhance family life

- Volunteer for jobs in addition to their regular chores

- Meet deadlines in a timely fashion

OPPORTUNITIES TO PRACTICE EFFORT

AGES 4-8

- Listen to a story about Thomas Alva Edison. Whenever you hear a part of the story that tells about Mr. Edison using the LIFESKILL of Effort, clap your hands three times. When the story is finished, recall three or more examples of Mr. Edison using the LIFESKILL of Effort.

- Read the LIFESKILLS list with your parents and other family members. Choose one LIFESKILL behavior that you feel is a strength for you. Share with your family some examples of how and when you have used this LIFESKILL. Choose another LIFESKILL—one that you would like to use more fully. Identify two or more ways you will practice using that LIFESKILL for one week. For example, if you choose the LIFESKILL of Effort: 1) I will not say "I can't . . ."; instead I will say "I can . . ." whenever anyone asks me to do or try something new; and 2) Before going to bed, I will pick up all of my toys and put them away for the night. To record your progress doing these two tasks, make a chart. On a piece of paper, make three columns. At the top of the column on the left, write the names of the days of the week starting at the top of the page and going down. At the top of the middle column, draw a smiley face to represent "I can" at the top of the column on the right, draw toys on a shelf or in a box. Each day when you practice the LIFESKILL of Effort by doing these two things, put an "X" under the right picture(s). At the end of the week, count the Xs. Fewer than 14, means you have to use more effort.

- During a family meeting, share appreciations (thank-yous) with brothers or sisters who have shown the LIFESKILL of Effort around the house that week. Sharing needs to be specific. Use the person's name "Mike," and the word "effort" and describe how Mike used the LIFESKILL of Effort. For example, "Mike, you used the LIFESKILL of Effort when you mowed the entire lawn even though the temperature was over 90 degrees."

- Design a plan to help you become a better rope jumper. Practice jumping with both feet landing at the same time. Then practice jumping with a little jump between each big jump. Locate two people to turn the long rope. Practice stepping into the center to jump when the rope is turning. Do this every day (for at least seven days) until you can safely jump twenty-five jumps without stopping. Show your best friend your new skill.

- Write the numbers 1 through 5 going from top to bottom on a piece of paper. Construct a tower using as many blocks as you can. Count how many blocks you can use before the tower falls down. Next to number one, write the number of blocks you used. Build the tower again. When it falls down, count the blocks again and write that number next to number two on your paper. Do this three more times until you have built five towers. Circle the number that shows the most blocks you were able to use building a tower. Explain to an older sibling or friend how the LIFESKILL of Effort helped you improve your performance.

- Learn to draw an object found in your house, such as a ball, doll, dog, apple. First, sketch it in lightly in pencil on paper. Then choose crayon colors to match the colors on the object. Fill in the drawing with color. Put your drawing next to the object and compare them. Make changes to improve the way your drawing looks. Show your final sketch to a parent. Explain how the LIFESKILL of Effort helped you improve your sketch from first to final version.

- Listen as a family member reads a biography of Helen Keller. Find three examples of how Helen Keller practiced effort in her life. Dramatize these examples for your family at dinner time by presenting a short skit (four to five minutes). Include family members and friends in the skit as needed.

- Train your dog to follow three or more basic commands such as sit, stand, roll over, speak, or sing. Read a dog training book or watch a training video that offers good tips on how to teach the three commands of your choice. Watch how your dog uses effort to learn. Train your dog every day. Start with the first command; when that is learned, begin the second command. Then, add the third command. Practice each one daily until your dog responds quickly and quietly to each. Offer your dog a small treat for doing what you taught him to do.

AGES 9-12

- Read a book, such as *Stone Fox* by John Reynolds Gardiner, and list examples of the main character using the LIFESKILL of Effort to solve problems. Share your list with a family member or friend.

- During a family meeting, discuss the pleasures of a job well done and the feelings that accompany its completion.

- Design and assemble a model of your choice (e.g., airplane, train, car, dollhouse). Record the number of minutes you spend putting the model together. Compute the total amount of time from beginning to the completion of the project. Celebrate the final product by having "Opening Night" for your family. Answer any questions they may have about your model, your work, and your use of the LIFESKILLS of Effort and Pride.

- Develop a plan to organize your personal belongings in your bedroom. Write a personal procedure for organizing your personal belongings each day. Write procedures for tidying your clothing, making your bed, and putting away anything you have used before going to school and procedures for putting things away at the end of the day. Include procedures for putting away things and preparing for the next morning. Make a "mini" two-week calendar. Choose two symbols, one for marking completion of the morning procedures and another for marking completion of the end-of-the-day procedures. Stamp those symbols on your calendar each day to indicate completion of procedures for that day. Share the calendar and the results of your effort with a family member. Share what you have learned about the LIFESKILLS of Effort and Organization by doing this. Write in your journal the things you want to remember about this experience and what you want to remember to do each day. Enlist help from a family member to remind and support you each day.

- Choose a math idea (e.g., times tables, subtraction, fractions) that is not easy for you to do. Assemble a special study place with classical music, pencils, markers, paper, and some small collections of things. Arrange for a family "tutor" to help you master the math idea. Work each day for 20 minutes or more. Use music, movement, and art to help you learn the skill. Design a "thank-you" card for your tutor; use catchy number phrases in the saying, such as "2 a Great Math Tutor—2 Good 2 Be 4 Gotten!" Sign the card and hide it someplace where your tutor will find it such as in his/her drawer, closet, or under the pillow.

- Try out for the cheer leading squad. Ask a current member to teach you the cheers and the movements. Practice every day until you know both by heart. Ask someone you trust to offer feedback on your performance and plan to make any changes that are necessary to improve your routine. Use the LIFESKILL of Effort to give you the extra edge in preparing your performance.

- Use the LIFESKILL of Effort to concoct a new dessert for dinner. Use five or more ingredients to make it tasty. Arrange the treat so that it is appetizing to the eye as well as the taste buds. Serve it to your family. Observe their body language for reaction to the taste of the dessert.

- Read a biography of Amelia Earhart, Helen Keller, Benjamin Franklin, Jim Thorpe, or Harriet Tubman. Create a time line showing five or more examples of when he/she used the LIFESKILL of Effort to push forward towards a goal. Use chronological dates, descriptive words, and colorful graphics to make the time line of his/her effort and achievements informational. Take it to school and share it with your math/history teacher.

- Develop an "Effort Scrapbook" containing newspaper articles from your area. Find, cut out, and paste into a homemade scrapbook 15 or more articles that show a variety of people using the LIFESKILL of Effort. Use a colored pencil to underline those words in an article that illustrate the LIFESKILL of Effort. Place the scrapbook on a living room table where guests may browse through it. Leave the last page for "Guest Comments."

Chapter 12—Effort

- Discuss with your parents a chore you really don't like to do (e.g., clean the cat's litter box, dry the dishes, take out the trash). Volunteer to take on the responsibility of this task using the LIFESKILL of Effort for at least one month. Write an "Effort Cheer" that will get you going each day. For example,

    > "Hurray! Hurray! Hurray!
    > Today is the day
    > I throw the cat litter away
    > Then I get to play!"

    Add some hand motions or a little dance step to the cheer. Design a poster that reminds you to do the chore cheerfully and with the LIFESKILL of Effort.

AGES 13+

- Share examples of exemplary use of the LIFESKILL of Effort in your family. Invite Grandpa/Grandma to reminisce about old family stories and the effort your ancestors put forth to come to America. Tape record or videotape these sessions so that you can refer back to them with your own children when you are grown.

- Create a list of 10 or more genealogy websites that assist people in locating "lost" family members. Research and design your family tree for three generations or more. Include as many relatives as you can. Decorate your tree, have copies made, and distribute it throughout your extended family. Add more information as it becomes available. Create a "LIFESKILL of Effort Hall of Fame" for family members who, according to family stories, showed exemplary use of the LIFESKILL of Effort in some field or interest.

- Assemble a collection of candid photos that illustrate family members under the age of four using the LIFESKILL of Effort. Order the photos chronologically, youngest to oldest. Compare the activities that have captured their interest and elicited such effort. Judge for yourself if the LIFESKILL of Effort is developed and used by children in this age group. Share with a parent what you have learned about the LIFESKILL of Effort by analyzing these photos.

- Compare the behaviors of four or more of your favorite movie stars or sports heroes. Select three LIFESKILL strengths and three LIFESKILL weaknesses for each person. Identify examples of behavior that illustrate each strength and weakness. Determine which of the stars/sport heroes uses the LIFESKILLS the most. Assemble a collage of photographs, drawings, and articles that represent his/her LIFESKILL strengths. Mail this LIFESKILLS collage, along with a brief letter of explanation, to the fan club of that person.

- Design a LIFESKILLS word search puzzle for the younger members of your family. Start with an empty grid of squares (17 by 17). Using all capital letters, spell out each of the LIFESKILLS (the words may go from top to bottom, bottom to top, left to right, backwards, horizontally, and diagonally). Start with the longest LIFESKILL word. Then write in the next longest and so forth until you have filled in all of the LIFESKILLS. Complete the word search puzzle by filling in each blank box with letters at random. Provide this as a fun activity someday when your siblings are bored and need something to do.

- Imagine how athletes prepare, not only physically but emotionally, for the Olympics. Analyze the practice sessions of three or more Olympians in regard to time, procedures, and repetition of movements. Rank, using your opinion, the three most important LIFESKILL behaviors for contestants in the Olympics. Share with a parent how your life might be different if you used the LIFESKILL of Effort to do these three LIFESKILLS each and every day.

- List examples of exemplary use of the LIFESKILL of Effort that you see at home, school, and outside of your home and school. Share these examples in family meetings.

- Recall when you have recently used the LIFESKILL of Effort to practice the skills needed to play a sport, play a musical instrument, or to learn to dance. Share with a family member or friend two examples of how you used the LIFESKILL of Effort to improve your personal performance at something in the past two weeks.

- Pursue a "make something" hobby (e.g., model making, woodworking, knitting, photography, sculpting, or weaving) that will require use of the LIFESKILL of Effort. Obtain the necessary materials and practice working on new skills you will need for the hobby. Find someone who can teach you the necessary construction techniques and skills. Stick with your practice of these skills until you've created three or more products. Choose two products to share with your family and demonstrate two of the most important new skills you needed to make them. Also share how the LIFESKILL of Effort helped you throughout the learning processes and construction.

- Begin a "collecting" hobby, such as rocks, shells, coins, stamps, autographs, or postcards. Collect and catalog 25 or more items. Include each item's name or classification, when you acquired it, any cost involved, and something special about it. Display your collection in the family room. Explain to a friend how and why you needed the LIFESKILL of Effort to assemble your collection.

- Select a "doing" hobby, such as playing a sport or an instrument, singing in a choir, gardening, cooking, or birding. Practice your "doing" hobby for a month or more. Choose a tune you know, such as "Happy Birthday To You," and write three or more verses to teach younger family members how to use the LIFESKILL of Effort to do your particular hobby. Teach your song to your younger siblings or friends.

- Read a biography about Thomas Edison, Rachel Carson, Jim Thorpe, Wolfgang Amadeus Mozart, or Walt Disney. Design a poster illustrating at least four of his/her most significant contributions to society. Hang this poster in your bedroom for one month. During this time, think about what contribution to society you want to make with your life. Share with a friend how the LIFESKILL of Effort can help you prepare yourself to make that contribution to society.

- Observe athletes in training. List the attributes of the LIFESKILL of Effort needed for their sport and discuss your list with a family member or friend. Describe 10 ways that your home, family, and you would be different if such effort was applied by you and each member of your family every day.

- Create a role-playing scenario for six everyday situations; write each on a separate piece of note paper. Invite each family member and/or friend to pick one and role play that situation with two different solutions—one that requires the use of the LIFESKILL of Effort and one that doesn't. Discuss the consequences of each choice.

SIGNS OF SUCCESS

Congratulations! Children are showing signs of Effort when they

- Practice mastering a new skill until they can do it with ease
- Offer to do something over because it isn't their personal best
- Offer to help other family members with a project or task
- Go out of their way to do something extra, something that is not required or expected of them
- Say "I can . . . and I will" instead of "I can't . . ." or "I don't want to"
- Are eager to learn something difficult
- Try and try again; never give up until they succeed
- Are motivated by success to put forth even more effort

Keep trying! Children need more practice when they

- Don't care to improve themselves; refuse to learn or try
- Refuse to complete work or redo work containing errors
- Pretend to do their chores
- Give up after one or two tries
- Blame others for their poor results
- Ignore opportunities to improve
- Insist work is their personal best when they know that it isn't
- Lack diligence; act plain lazy
- Believe that everyone else has it "easy" except them

Literature Link ~ Effort

Ages 4-8

100th Day Worries — Margery Cuyler (New York: Simon & Schuster, 2000)

Fly, Eagle, Fly: An African Tale (AFA) — Retold by Christopher Gregorowski (New York: Simon & Schuster Publishing, 2000)

Hawk, I'm Your Brother (NA) — Byrd Baylor (New York: Athenium, 1976)

Alejandro's Gift (HA) — Richard E. Albert (San Francisco: Chronicle Books, 1994)

Ages 9-12

Hostage To War — Tatiana Vasileva (Greenville, SC: Polaris, 1999)

Me and My Little Brain — John D. Fitzgerald (New York: Yearling Books, A Division of Random House, 1972)

Sign of the Beaver, The (NA) (TE) — Elizabeth George Speare (New York: Yearling Books, A Division of Random House, 1994)

Where the Red Fern Grows (TE) — Wilson Rawls (New York: Bantam Books, 1984)

Ages 13+

Daily Reflections for Highly Effective Teens — Sean Covey (New York: Simon & Schuster, 1999)

Her Story: Women Who Changed the World (ME) — Ruth Ashby, Ed. and Deborah Gore Ohrn, Ed. (New York: Viking Childrens Books, 1995)

Kidstories: Biographies of 20 Young People You'd Like to Know (ME) — James R. Delisle and Pamela Espeland (Minneapolis, MN: Free Spirit Publishers, 1991)

Within Reach: My Everest Story — Mark Pfetzer and Jack Galvin (New York: E.P. Dutton, 1998)

Family Resources

Cooperative Sports and Games Book: Challenge Without Competition, The — Terry Orlick (New York: Random House, 1978)

Simple Fun for Busy People: 333 Ways to Enjoy Your Loved Ones More in the Time You Have — Gary Krane and John Bradshaw (Berkeley, CA: Conari Press, 1998)

Multicultural books: **(AFA)**=African American, **(ASA)**=Asian American, **(HA)**=Hispanic American, **(ME)**=Multi-Ethnic, **(NA)**=Native American, **(TE)**=listed in the teacher edition of this book, *Tools for Citizenship and Life: Using the ITI Lifelong Guidelines and LIFESKILLS in the Classroom*, **(BFE)**=available through Books for Educators

Flexibility

Chapter 13

"Be open-minded."

flexibility *n* **1:** capable of being flexed: pliant **2:** yielding to influence; tractable
3: characterized by a ready capability to adapt to new, different, or changing requirements

FLEXIBILITY: To be willing to alter plans when necessary

WHAT IS FLEXIBILITY?

Are you a person who easily adapts to change or do you become frustrated and upset if plans are altered? Since nothing in this world is certain except death and taxes, mastering the LIFESKILL of Flexibility allows us to adapt to changes, problems, and unexpected situations without undue emotional strain and unpleasantness for ourselves and those around us.

Flexibility indicates our willingness to alter specific plans and ideas to serve our needs and/or satisfy the needs of others.

What Flexibility Is Not

To be flexible is not to be rudderless, wishy-washy, or lacking opinions or goals. It doesn't mean giving up our values, following the crowd, or caving in to peer pressure. It's the ability to dance through life, flexing when needed, altering our path for the moment, and then returning to our goals and tasks as originally planned or recently revised based on experience.

Possible Pitfalls

Powerful emotional and personal beliefs can prevent us from embracing opportunities to change our plans or methods. Such intense feelings can produce negative character traits such as stubbornness and rigidity which often destroy, rather than nurture, productivity, relationships, and reputations.

WHY PRACTICE FLEXIBILITY?

Flexibility is a key ingredient in our ability to flow with others in a give-and-take environment of mutual respect and appreciation. Without such flexibility, succeeding socially—with friends, co-workers, even family—is all but impossible. Furthermore, being flexible often exposes us to new and better options because it enables us to "hang loose," to tolerate ambiguity while additional possibilities become available.

Just completing a task often requires flexibility. Things seldom go as expected. Refusal to be flexible often leads to impossibly long hours to complete a task or to quitting altogether.

Increase In Knowledge

Due to the increasing volume of knowledge in this Age of Information, our minds are continually exposed to new and invigorating ideas. Keeping an open mind to information that is inconsistent with our experiences and beliefs allows us to consider new ideas, update information, and to sometimes realize that what we had considered conjecture has recently become fact. Flexibility empowers us to change our minds and know that this is acceptable. If we aren't flexible enough to study new ideas and philosophies thoroughly, then we quickly become "out of touch" and ineffective in work place, parenting, and with friends.

Because we can't predict what life will bring, it is imperative that we always be ready to alter plans when necessary.

Unpredictable Environment

Change is hard to accept. It is much easier, and far more comfortable, to follow a set routine and hope everything will happen as anticipated. However, when people, events, and situations interact, the whole becomes bigger—and often unpredictably different—than the sum of the parts. This, in turn, affects our plans, thoughts, and actions. If we can bend a little,* adjust our plans or think in diverse ways, life usually becomes easier and our chances for succeeding often increase. The LIFESKILL of Flexibility is a learned behavior: so give children many different experiences with choice and change in order to give them practice developing and using the LIFESKILL of Flexibility.

HOW DO YOU PRACTICE IT?

It's no surprise that practicing the LIFESKILL of Flexibility requires work both personally and professionally. The desire to control people and circumstances cuts deeply across both areas.

---

* This does not mean to bend one's sense of right and wrong, of morality and immorality, but rather to take a different approach to a problem or situation.

Staying flexible is easy for those people whom the Myers-Briggs/Keirsey-Bates personality inventory places at the perceiving end of the lifestyle scale.* These are the open, spontaneous, flexible folks. At the other end of the scale, people described as judgers (those who live by decree, not by judging as in good or bad) are organized, methodical, insist on closure, and work persistently from stated goals and priorities until they achieve those goals and finish those priorities. For people on the judging end of the scale, being flexible is an act of will, a conscious and often not very comfortable choice.

It definitely helps to keep our eyes on the outcomes of our efforts rather than on a near-sighted focus on the processes of the moment.

Flexibility Is a State of Mind

Flexibility is a state of mind that requires giving up control, a letting go of attachment to our ideas so we can be open to the ideas of others, and accepting that our way isn't the only way.

Giving Up Control. We must be willing to give up controlling things, people, and events. If children are to learn to take ownership of and direct their learning, we must learn to share control of learning and behavior with them in meaningful and responsible ways. If we want our children to share the challenges and hard work of creating and maintaining a harmonious family, we must learn to share leadership, power, and control with them. If we want to enjoy life with family and friends, we must learn to not only go with the flow but to enjoy the journey as well. We must begin to trust that two heads are better than one, that group wisdom will emerge however messy and inelegant the process. "My way or the highway" is not the motto of a flexible person.

Letting Go. We must put aside emotional allegiance or attachment to what we want for and from our children. We must be willing to let them develop into who they are and let go of our pictures. This doesn't mean "anything goes" or that families shouldn't have guidelines and standards but that, within these matters guidelines and standards, we are open to the development and expression of different aptitudes and personality traits.

Accepting That Our Way Isn't the Only Way. Until we understand and accept that every brain is different and thus every child and adult learns and does things differently, we will continue to expect that our way is *the* way. And, as night follows day, we will thus continue to teach our child the way we ourselves learn, operating the way we prefer for our comfort zone rather than in ways that would most enhance learning for our child.** The LIFESKILL of Flexibility asks us as teachers/parents to do the stretching, that we interact in multiple ways with our child, accepting and anticipating his/her different ways of learning and building on his/her ways of learning and doing.

The LIFESKILL of Flexibility is especially important when appraising your child's work and behavior. Look not for what you would have done but for how and why your child did the task

---

* For an entertaining as well as enlightening exploration of personality preferences, see Chapter 7, *Making Bodybrain-Compatible Education a Reality: Coaching for the ITI Model* by Karen D. Olsen. (Kent, Washington: Books for Educators, 1999.) Lifestyle is defined here as how we want our life to unfold, its level of predictability and orderliness, not as in living high on the hog.

** For user-friendly discussions of important concepts from recent brain research, see Chapter 1 of the ITI book appropriate for your grade level. See also *Human Brain and Human Learning* by Leslie Hart.

the way he/she did. As your child's teacher, learn to truly appreciate and genuinely value the different ways our child thinks and goes about doing things. Teach your child that differences are a function of unique brain wiring and that there is no one right way to think or to go about doing something. The yardstick of assessment should be your child's previous performance. The important question is: Is he/she growing in competencies?

Flexibility Is Not Merely Going with the Flow

Being flexible requires more of us than merely going with the flow—"Whatever you want is fine with me," "You choose . . . whatever," or the bureaucratic versions, "We do it this way because it's how we've always done it," or "That's how I was raised," or "We must do it this way because 'they' said so."

Flexibility requires that we own the new decision or choice—not blindly or mindlessly but because our common sense and values convinces us it's the better way.

Flexibility also requires that we implement the ideas of others *to which we have agreed* with the same vigor and commitment as when implementing decisions of our own making.

Helping Children Shift from "Me First" to "Us"

By focusing on the LIFESKILL of Flexibility, we help teach our children, in ways they understand, the concept of "us" rather than "me first." For example, they can see how to make their life with siblings and friends work better, to be a family/community rather than a loose collection of strangers. This LIFESKILL also requires that our child distinguish between being flexible and agreeable versus slavish adherence to the group norms of cliques and gangs and other forms of peer pressure.

Opportunities to practice the LIFESKILL of Flexibility are everywhere. In addition to formally planned inquiries such as those on pages 16.6-16.10, be sure to take advantage of teachable moments that pop up throughout the day.

WHAT DOES FLEXIBILITY LOOK LIKE IN REAL LIFE?

We

- Change schedules as necessary with as little fuss as possible
- Keep an open mind and listen to both sides of a case when friends argue
- Cheerfully take other roads to work when the regular route is temporarily closed
- Purchase a different brand when our favorite one is out of stock and consider it an opportunity to explore rather than an irritation or inconvenience

- Stretch a paycheck and/or do without "extras" to ensure that bills are paid on time
- Go out of our way to pick up a neighbor's child from soccer practice when his/her car is disabled
- Carpool to work
- Practice a little "give and take"
- Offer to cook different foods for our in-laws who have special dietary needs
- Allow our thoughts to flow from one topic to another with smooth transitions

WHAT DOES FLEXIBILITY LOOK LIKE AT HOME?

Adults

- Exude a positive attitude about unexpected schedule changes
- Juggle daily schedules to allow for illness, special appointments or events, or a budding interest of one or more family members
- Agree to reschedule our event in order to allow the schedule of another family member to take precedence
- With a chuckle and smile, change from one dinner menu to another because all of the necessary recipe ingredients are not in the pantry
- Change our entire day's plans when a child is ill
- Use public transportation when our car is being repaired
- Attend night school and college courses in between work and family responsibilities
- Stop what we are doing to attend to a serious and/or heartfelt need of another member of the family
- Create educational experiences and choices for our child through activities such as those described in this book for practicing Lifelong Guidelines/LIFESKILLS, family outings, and other community, co-curricular, and after-school activities
- Work two jobs with different schedules so that one parent is always home when our child is home

Children

- Can entertain themselves as well as play with others
- Understand that "change" is a part of life

- Without grumbling, look for another outfit to wear when the favorite one isn't available

- Choose to buy another label (e.g., sneakers, clothing, bicycle, computer game) when the family cannot afford the "in" or "designer" name item

- Complete a different chore than the one on their list because it needs to be done

- Ask another family member or friend for assistance when a parent is temporarily unavailable

- Demonstrate a positive and optimistic attitude when a special event has been canceled or postponed

- Choose many kinds of projects and inquiries

- Offer several alternative ideas for solving a problem/situation during family discussions

- Choose alternative materials when their first choice isn't available

- Play/work with other people when their best friends are busy

- Play a different position on a sports team to fill in a gap

OPPORTUNITIES TO PRACTICE FLEXIBILITY

AGES 4-8

- Learn to sing a song, such as "Happy Birthday to You," and create new lyrics describing two ways to use the LIFESKILL of Flexibility. Teach the song to your family. Take the same words and use them in a chant or rap. Ask each family member which way they most enjoyed learning—through the song or chant/rap.

- Prepare for using the LIFESKILL of Flexibility in the morning. Before you go to bed, set out two different outfits to wear. Watch the morning weather report and listen to the meteorologist's predictions. Choose the set of clothing most appropriate for the temperature and weather conditions for that day. Return the other outfit to its place in the closet or dresser.

- Arrange a weekly schedule for watching TV so that each family member has the opportunity to watch one favorite show. Determine a way to include special programs. Create a poster with words or pictures that will remind everyone of the arrangement. Post it near the TV as a reminder. Be prepared to make changes if shows are delayed or canceled.

- Brainstorm ways for each family member to be safe while traveling in the car. Examine your car's safety features, such as car seats design, safety belts, air bags, and the age and weight of the passengers. Simulate a car ride by having each family member sit in the safest place (according to federal guidelines). Determine if there is any room for flexibility with these arrangements. For instance, is there more than one place where the two-year old can sit and still be safe? The eight-year old? The baby? Review the final seating arrangement each time a child in your family has a birthday to see if the plan needs revision.

- Arrange the games and activities for your birthday party. Choose two or more games that can be played inside (e.g., pin the tail on the donkey, musical chairs) and two or more that can be played outside (e.g., hide and seek, tag, jump rope, baseball). One week before the party, organize any equipment needed to play the games or complete the activities. On the day of the party, determine which games best match the weather and temperature. Evaluate the success of your games/activities selections after your guests have gone home. Explain to a parent how planning ahead allowed you to use the LIFESKILL of Flexibility.

AGES 9-12

- Choose a favorite cartoon (e.g., "Peanuts," "Calvin and Hobbes," "Garfield") and read at least 35 of the story frames. Follow the actions of one of the main characters (e.g., Snoopy, Charlie Brown, Calvin) and express your opinion as to whether or not he/she uses the LIFESKILL of Flexibility with ease. Support your conclusion with evidence from the story line.

- Read the book *The Family Under the Bridge* by Natalie Carlson. Arrange to visit an organization that helps homeless families in your community. Interview the director about homelessness in regard to education of the children and at least on one other issue of your choice. Identify three or more ways that the homeless need to be flexible. Name two or more educational problems that you anticipate occurring among homeless children. Choose one of them and ask your family to brainstorm some ideas that might help to minimize the effect of the problem. Select the most realistic solution and work to make it happen.

- Practice playing a different position on your sports team. Learn the skills necessary for success at that position. Discuss the possibility of changing to this new position permanently with the coach's assistance. Explain to your teammates how the LIFESKILL of Flexibility enabled you to make the switch.

- Read several fables written by Aesop. Develop a fable of your own that teaches about the LIFESKILL of Flexibility. Print your fable on the computer. Add graphics or illustrations. Dramatize your fable for your family after dinner. Ask them to predict the moral of the story.

- Choose a tune you know, such as "Row, Row, Row Your Boat," and write new lyrics that teach two advantages of using the LIFESKILL of Flexibility. Use the same lyrics in an alternative form (rap, chant, or poetry). Perform both for family after dinner. Explain which is your favorite way and why.

- Sign up to be in the school or community center drama group. Try out for those parts that interest you. Learn other parts by memory also. Use the LIFESKILL of Flexibility to become an understudy for more than one part. Practice your lines every day until they are committed to memory.

- Volunteer to be in a different project group in class to balance the number of students per group. Thank your previous group for showing understanding for the switch. Greet your new group, actively listen to their plans, and offer to work in any capacity so the project will be everyone's personal best and be completed in a timely fashion.

- Take a song that you or your parents know (such as "Personality" sung by Lloyd Price) and rewrite the lyrics to teach about the LIFESKILL of Flexibility. Perform the song at a family celebration and then teach it to everyone who is there. Capture the moment on video.

- Experiment with different types of exercise that develop flexibility in your body. To improve your large muscle skills, choose two or more kinds of movement that require you to run, skip, hop, or jump. Practice two or more other activities that develop your small muscle skills, such as coloring, painting, working with clay, building with Legos. Demonstrate the kind of movement you like to do best for Grandpa/Grandma the next time you see them. Explain to him/her what this quote tells you about the LIFESKILL of Flexibility and your body: "Use it or lose it." Do you agree or disagree and why?

AGES 13+

- Attend a professional arts performance (e.g., "Riverdance, BackStreet Boys, your local symphony). As you watch the program, identify five or more areas where the performers might have to use the LIFESKILL of Flexibility so that the "show goes on!" Transfer this information to your personal life and reflect on ways you can use it.

- Observe two or more insects in their natural environment. Place different materials or objects in their pathways and observe what occurs. Compare/contrast the two insects as to their reactions to an obstacle. Identify which insect was more flexible when dealing with the barrier and which found the quickest way around to get back on its path.

- Join the debate club at school. Learn how to identify a topic, research information, identify key points, provide supportive data, and summarize your viewpoint. Develop your ability to be flexible by offering to present either side in the debate.

- Design puppets/marionettes that represent different storybook characters (e.g., Goldilocks, the three bears, three pigs, Little Red Riding Hood, the wolf). Present each puppet show using a main character (Goldilocks) from one story and another main character(s) (e.g., three pigs) from another story. Perform the story with the characters intermingling to make a new version of two old favorites (e.g., Goldilocks and the Three Pigs). After your performance, check the audience's ability to retell the new story and to correctly identify sections that are missing from the original version. Share with a parent how the LIFESKILL of Flexibility helped you develop this new, integrated version of two old stories.

- Interview an architect, engineer, or construction worker in order to collect information about the different kinds of building materials. Identify the five tallest buildings in the world and find each one's sway factor (the number of inches the top of the building moves back and forth when winds pass by). Investigate and identify which materials are most often used to build the skeleton, or framework, of a skyscraper. Analyze your findings and hypothesize why these particular building materials are the ones of choice. Hypothesize what would happen to a skyscraper if its framework was not flexible enough to move in the face of wind and to roll with earthquakes.

- Join an exercise group to help increase your strength and body flexibility. Check your pulse rate before, during, and at the end of the session. Learn a variety of exercises (e.g., isometric, cardiovascular, limbering, warm-up, cool-down) and rhythmic routines that you can perform alone or in a group. Teach some of the simpler routines to a younger "couch potato" in your family.

- Learn to speak a second (or third) language. Study this new language at school, through audiotapes, and/or by speaking with someone in your family conversant in this language. Identify those phrases which would be most helpful if you are:
    - ~ in trouble
    - ~ a tourist looking for a place to stay the night
    - ~ lost
    - ~ hungry

    Locate someone in your neighborhood that knows this language and is willing to provide some extra practice in conversational skills. Share how study of a new language required you to use the LIFESKILL of Flexibility.

- At the end of the day, identify 10 situations when you, family members, and/or friends used the LIFESKILL of Flexibility that day. Describe to a family member how the LIFESKILL of Flexibility was used in each situation; then, identify two other possible ways to have responded in each situation. Share with this family member what you have learned from these observations about the LIFESKILL of Flexibility.

- Listen to the same song recorded by three different jazz musicians. [The library is a good source of music.] Study the variations of each group. Interview a musician to determine the importance of flexibility in a jam session. Write a rap, chant, or poem that teaches two or more ways to use the LIFESKILL of Flexibility when playing music. Design a bookmark that shares these strategies and give it to a family member or friend who is taking instrumental music lessons.

- Investigate flexibility in the human body (such as in muscles, tendons, joints). Design two charts (with assistance from a physical therapist or P.E. teacher at school) illustrating one exercise on each that will increase body flexibility. Share the information on the charts with a family member or friend and demonstrate the two flexibility exercises.

- Learn about Howard Gardner's theory of multiple intelligences. Design a visual representation (such as a poster, brochure, video, or overhead) of the "8 Kinds of Smart." Using music and movement, teach your family and friends about the intelligences and how use of the intelligences invites using the LIFESKILL of Flexibility. Explain to them how knowing how to use all the intelligences increases your ability to be flexible.

- Create an emergency plan for your family. Include three or more alternate exits that will provide safe access to your yard. Determine a site outside to gather together. Explain the plan to your family and ask them to try all of the emergency routes. Make any safety adjustments as needed. Share with your family what you learned during this task and how planning ahead often increases one's ability to be flexible.

- Choose a location in your community that you would like to visit. Use a map to plan the most direct route from your home to the site and highlight that route in one color. Pretend that route is closed. Use the LIFESKILL of Flexibility to determine three or more other routes. Highlight each of these alternate plans using a separate color for each. Ask an adult to check these plans for accuracy.

- Interview an architect, builder, carpenter, engineer, mason, or construction worker. Ask him/her how to determine what materials he/she will use to build his/her next structure. Create a visual aid that will demonstrate to your family and friends two or more reasons for using flexible building materials on some structures. Explain the reasons for this to your family and friends.

- Design three bridges to test the flexibility and strength of these materials: toothpicks, paper, and clay. Make the bridges and test them by using objects of different known weights.

SIGNS OF SUCCESS

Congratulations! Children are showing signs of Flexibility when they

- Openly listen to others' ideas and change their opinions accordingly
- Volunteer to change seats with siblings in the car
- Willingly change their schedule to help a friend or to accommodate family members' special needs
- Practice new methods and skills in many different ways until mastery is reached
- Help negotiate settlement of disagreements
- Embrace change as exciting rather than frightening
- Attempt a new activity, hobby, or sport
- Are a pleasure to be around when things change

Keep trying! Children need more practice when they

- Refuse to try a new experience
- Reject other opinions before even hearing them
- Decline an opportunity to negotiate; won't settle differences amicably
- Rebuff an opportunity to apologize; refuse to accept an apology
- Are upset by small changes in daily schedules and activities
- Do not want to accommodate other people just because it would inconvenience them
- Are rigid in their decisions and actions
- Automatically dispute wisdom and usefulness of directions or suggestions from others, especially a sibling

Literature Link ~ Flexibility

Ages 4-8

Alexander and the Terrible, Horrible, No Good, Very Bad Day (TE) — Judith Viorst (New York: Aladdin Books, 1987)

Amelia's Road — Linda Jacobs Altman (New York: Lee & Low, 1993)

Anthony Reynoso: Born to Rope (HA) — Martha Cooper (New York: Clarion Books, 1996)

Chester's Way — Kevin Henkes (New York: Mulberry Books, Simon & Schuster, 1997)

Ages 9-12

All for the Better: A Story of El Barrio (HA) — Nicholas Mohr (Austin, TX: Raintree Books, Steck-Vaughn Publishing Company, 1996)

Autumn Journey — Priscilla Cummings (Toronto, Canada: Cobblehill Press, 1997)

Barn, The — Avi (London: Orchard Books, 1994)

La Mariposa (HA) — Francisco Jimenez (Boston: Houghton Mifflin, 1998)

Sounder (AFA) — William H. Armstrong (New York: HarperCollins, 1989)

Ages 13+

Crazy Horse Electric Game, The — Chris Crutcher (New York: Dell Publishing Co, 1991)

100 Men Who Shaped the World (ME) — Bill Yenne (Blue Wood Book, 1994)

100 Women Who Shaped the World (ME) — Gail Meyer Rolka (Blue Wood Book, 1994)

How the Garcia Girls Lost Their Accents (HA) — Julia Alvarez (New York: Plume Press, 1991)

Multicultural books: **(AFA)**=African American, **(ASA)**=Asian American, **(HA)**=Hispanic American, **(ME)**=Multi-Ethnic, **(NA)**=Native American, **(TE)**=listed in the teacher edition of this book, *Tools for Citizenship and Life: Using the ITI Lifelong Guidelines and LIFESKILLS in the Classroom*, **(BFE)**=available through Books for Educators

Family Resources

Explosive Child, The: A New Approach for Understanding and Parenting Easily Frustrated, "Chronically Inflexible" Children — Ross W. Greene (New York: HarperCollins, 1998)

Family Manager, The — Kathy Peel (Westport, CN: Word Books, Greenwood Publishing Group, 1996)

Chapter 14

Friendship

"FRIENDSHIPS IMPROVE LIFE."

friendship *n* **1:** the state of being friends **2:** the quality or state of being friendly: friendliness
friend *n* a person whom one knows well and is fond of; an ally, supporter, or sympathizer

FRIENDSHIP: To make and keep a friend through mutual trust and caring

WHAT IS FRIENDSHIP?

Friendship describes the caring, affectionate, playful, and usually strong emotional bond we experience with an assortment of companions during various stages of our lives. It is a relationship in which we can share who we are and who we want to become, our hopes and our fears.

Friendships Are Like Rainbows

Friendships, like rainbows, come in a wide spectrum. Some friendships are intimate and can have enormous impact on our lives. Some are more limited, even if long-standing, when we chat about the weather and less consequential things. Some are new with people we know little about but with whom we feel a kindred spirit.

Friendships can command our complete trust and affection; over time they can evolve into an intimate relationship. Unlike family ties, we choose these relationships and we must continue to earn them.

Some friends know us inside and out—our private self and our public persona. Their impact in our lives is huge; because they know our roles in life and how we carry them out, they can give us accurate, honest feedback. Other friendships are limited to specific contexts such as work, social circles, church, our child's preschool, the neighborhood homeowners' association, political organizations, hobbies, or sports.

Whatever the degree of intimacy, friendships are not static, made one day and forever the same thereafter. Making a friend is one thing, but continuing to earn his/her respect and trust is another. Friendships are dynamic, ever changing. They are gifts we give ourselves.

Choice of Close Friends

Because of their power to influence and nurture us, we should choose our close friends with deliberation and care rather than wait for accidental meetings, e.g., who moves in next door, who belongs to the country club, who sits next to us in a high school class, or who agrees with us when we whine.

Every parent's worst nightmare is that his/her child will "fall in with bad company," that an acquaintance will prove to be "a bad influence." And well they should worry because friendship is a two-way street, mutually self-sculpting. Our friendships virtually change the course of our lives, for better or for worse.

Be clear, the friends we make and keep are the result of choices we make day by day, by default or by deliberate decision.

Friendships and Developmental Stages

Like other LIFESKILLS, the capacity to make and keep friends is developmental. With maturity and experience, most of us add the personal and social skills that make richer friendships possible.

In the Beginning. The art of friendship develops slowly. Young children tend to be egocentric. They don't share toys unless an adult is there to prod them. Before the ages of four or five, children generally play side by side, not necessarily together. Adults determine many of these early experiences, choosing the who (participants), where (location), when (time schedule), why (occasion), and how (transportation).

Growing Up. Gradually, children begin to reach out to others and tenuous relationships form. Think back. There is nothing like that first best friend. Who was yours? Do you know where he/she is now? Do you keep in touch? What drew you to each other? While in the elementary grades, friendships are usually drawn from classmates at school or from peers sharing sports, neighborhood playgrounds, scouts, hobbies, and such.

This early practice often involves play more than the skill of friendship but as children grow older and become more interested in others, they interact consciously with others in ways that encourage them to want to be a friend. As children become more independent, their friends come from ever-widening circles. Common interests, proximity, and age are common factors that influence forming and sustaining friendships.

Initially, lacking experience and judgment, children often make errors in determining who they want for a friend and who they don't. Hurt feelings often result when the friendship is terminated by one and not understood by the other. Only after many experiences can we finally conclude who is a likely candidate to become a trustworthy friend and who is not.

Moving On. During teen and young adult years, a young person's peer group is the most important source of friends. At this stage of life, he/she is highly mobile—riding bikes, taking buses, and driving to local hang-outs. Groups of teen friends may walk, talk, and dress alike just to point out that they are different! Status within the peer group is all-important.

The teenager's highly charged emotional state generally carries over into friendships, making them extremely volatile—often, best friends one day and worst enemies the next. As social skills lag behind a keen desire to have friends, relationships sometimes unfold in hurtful ways (e.g., put-downs, embarrassing comments, and rude noises) as the young person attempts to connect with others. Extremely close, tightly knit friendships often form in this emotional atmosphere and often last a lifetime. Even if we haven't seen our friend in years, we pick up the conversation as if we had never been apart.

Adult Friendships. Fortunately, most of us continue to grow in our ability to reach out beyond ourselves to enter into adult friendships, linking with neighbors, co-workers, church members, club or interest group members, and companions. Many of the same components that were present in our childhood friendships form the core of adult skills to make and keep friends such as the Lifelong Guidelines and the LIFESKILLS of Caring, Cooperation, Flexibility, Integrity, Responsibility, and Sense of Humor, to mention but a few. Happily, however, previous experience with forming and keeping friendships makes the process easier and more comfortable. Adult judgment, tempered by years of experience, helps us make wiser decisions about who to choose for a friend and what degree of friendship is appropriate to seek with that person. More refined personal and social skills make it easier to carry out our decisions.

WHY PRACTICE FRIENDSHIP?

We humans are social animals. If isolated for lengthy periods at any time in our lives, but particularly when young, we often become out of kilter, estranged from others and ourselves, less than we are and can be.

Friendship: A Personal and Social Imperative

Being with others is a personal and social imperative. Mastering the LIFESKILL of Friendship is a necessity, not a luxury. In the long run, our success at forming friendships shapes our lives more powerfully than our grasp of the 3Rs. In 1991, the U.S. Department of Labor, in its report *What Work Requires of Schools*, listed the personal qualities that young people must have upon entering the work force. High on the list was sociability,* defined as the ability to demonstrate understanding, friendliness, adaptability, empathy, and politeness in group settings.

The skills for making and keeping a friend are the same skills for making and keeping the long-term relationships of marriage and parenting. Whether at home or work, within the family or in the community, making and keeping friends is critical to our success and personal well-being. As family, we need to invest considerable time and effort in helping our child practice and master this critical LIFESKILL.

---

* Quoted in *TRIBES A New Way of Learning and Being Together* by Jeanne Gibbs, p. 33.

Friends As Mentors

A good friend has our best interests at heart and, having earned our trust and respect, is well-positioned to help us find our way through life. For most of us, our professional as well as personal lives would be very different were it not for the mentoring/peer coaching of our close friends. Through them, we develop areas of expertise and interest we would not otherwise have and go on adventures full of life-enriching experiences we would not have planned for ourselves. (For a discussion of mentoring and coaching in the context of the ITI model, see *Making Bodybrain-Compatible Education a Reality: Coaching for the ITI Model* by Karen D. Olsen.)

Friends As Mirrors

Friends are a kind of mirror of who we are (our values and our dreams) and want to be, and, often, who we are afraid we are. Friends with dreams help us to get past yesterday's problems, to see today more clearly, and then look beyond today to prepare for our future. They help us clarify who we want to be and to test our dreams against reality. Their accurate feedback helps us see our lives more objectively.

As we develop the LIFESKILL of Friendship, our circle of friends grows wider and more diverse. This diversity in friends helps us to know about the world beyond people like ourselves. On the other hand, consistency of values among our friends tells us how truly we hold to our values.

Friends As a Source of Nurturing and Support

However tough-skinned, worldly, and self-sufficient we may think we have become, all of us need a hug, a long heart-to-heart talk, and some outside opinions from time to time. Support from an informed source, one who knows us well, is much more comforting than a blanket "Gosh, what a tough break" rejoinder. Sometimes just knowing we have a "3:00 A.M. friend" is all it takes to get us over the hump. Just knowing that we have options based on the support of our friends (a loan or a work team over the weekend) helps us get through our difficulties.

Friends who have dreams and work to make them a reality help us plan our own dream-inspired courses of action to get us where we want to go, by a path consistent with our goals. Good friends are the most important gift we can give ourselves.

HOW DO YOU PRACTICE FRIENDSHIP?

Making and keeping friends is not automatic or an act of luck; it requires intention and effort. All the Lifelong Guidelines are needed plus the LIFESKILLS of Caring, Cooperation, Flexibility, Integrity, Responsibility, and Sense of Humor. Lucky are the children who learn early in life to use these skills consciously and consistently.

Success at friendship is a two-step affair: We must carefully select and cultivate a friend; then, we must continue to earn his/her friendship.

Making a Friend

The skills needed to make a friend come from the very core of who we are. Here are some pointers. As you adapt this list and brainstorm other ideas with your child, keep in mind your child's developmental level.

The "Gift of Gab" with People We Have Yet to Meet. We can't make a friend of someone we don't know. Therefore, we must work on our capacity to chat comfortably with people we don't know so that we can begin to uncover areas of common interest and values. This ability immediately widens our potential circle of friends. Even introverts, to their surprise, find that such chance encounters have greatly enriched their circle of friends.

Go for Quality, Not Quantity. Making friends is not a competition. More is not necessarily better. "Better" comes from depth and richness. It is useful to make a clear distinction between "an acquaintance," "a friend," and "a close friend." Because maintaining a friendship takes time and attention, it is unrealistic to think that everyone we meet and like will become and remain a close friend. How big our circle of friends can become depends heavily upon our social skills and the nature of our responsibilities to self and others, job and community. Being a party animal and friend to one and all may not balance well with our responsibilities to our employer and our family or even our responsibility to ourselves to become our own person. Be realistic. To "have" a friend, one must "be" a friend.

Acting on the belief that we must belong at all costs is always—*always*—detrimental in the long run. Go for quality, not quantity.

Know Thyself. Life puts many people in our path. Some are great candidates to be a friend but most—yes, most—are not. We must know ourselves well enough—who we are now and who we want to become—to choose people who will bring out the best in us, not our worst; people who will complement us, not necessarily copy us; people who will challenge us, not stagnate with us. Friendship is not a "search and rescue" operation. Getting into relationships "because he/she needs me" is dangerous territory. Such a relationship is not friendship, it is co-dependency. The difference is huge.

Conquer Your Ego. No emotionally healthy, well-balanced person wants to be around a self-centered, egocentric person or one who is emotionally needy. And that cuts both ways. If we want to succeed at having friends, we must get beyond ourselves and be someone that others want to be with. Getting beyond self requires that we continue to grow and learn and to commit ourselves to making a contribution to the world. It's a bore to be around someone who isn't growing, who isn't in the process of becoming, who is stuck in his/her current point of view, and whose conversations stay centered on the same topics.

Keeping a Friend

To keep a friend, we need all of the Lifelong Guidelines and LIFESKILLS plus the common courtesies. In addition, keep in mind the following.

Be Caring and Show It. If you care, show it in tangible, unmistakable ways. If you feel too reserved or too quiet to do so, make a commitment to move beyond your sense of limitations and comfort zone. Friendship is as much about the other person as it is about you. To keep a friend, make sure that person knows you value them, care about them, are there for them. Friendship is about the other person. Plus, what goes around comes around. In a good friendship, that person lets you know they value you, care about you, are there for you.

Don't Take a Friend for Granted. Too often, we treat relatives and close friends with less regard and fewer courtesies than we treat more distant friends and acquaintances. As the old saying predicts: "Familiarity breeds contempt." We exhibit less civility and a double standard. For example, we yell at our siblings in ways we would never yell at a classmate or we "dress down" a spouse in ways we would never criticize an employee or colleague. Just because someone is a close friend doesn't mean that they don't deserve our best social graces and genuine care. Send them thank-you cards when they've done something especially helpful and nice. Remember their birthdays with cards and presents. Be as punctual with friends as you would with business clients. Diamonds might be forever; friends are not. We must continue to earn their respect and regard and we must continue to value them and show them that we do.

Friends Aren't Crutches. A mark of maturity is that we know where our friends end and we begin. We don't "need" our friends to make our life work; nor do we assume that they will always be there supporting us. We are a whole and complete person but we do appreciate and value each friend for the contribution they make to our lives.

Give and Take. Good friendships are balanced interactions, working to the benefit of both. Expect to follow as well as lead, support as well as be supported. The goal of a good friendship is accelerated growth and the well-being of both.

Get—and Stay—Beyond Yourself. Life is about making a difference, making a contribution. View your close friendships as opportunities to make a difference—to them directly and, in partnership with them, performing acts that enrich your community and the world.

Most accomplishments in life are team efforts; learn to be a good team player and expect your friends to be your accomplices. Time with friends should further you on your life's path, not distract you.

WHAT DOES FRIENDSHIP LOOK LIKE IN REAL LIFE?

We

- Take the time and care enough to truly understand those we call "friend"
- Really listen when a friend is in need; can be depended upon to provide both support and accurate feedback
- Tell friends the truth but do so tactfully; offer positive feedback and don't use put-downs
- Are understanding when friends make mistakes and support them in making amends
- Offer support to face problems rather than take the problem away
- Interact in ways that keep the friend's best interests in mind (as well as our own)
- Share personal memories but do so without dumping sad or angry feelings
- Welcome new families to the neighborhood and make them feel included
- Guide a new employee around the company and teach him/her the ropes
- Stand up for our friends and acquaintances by seeking out the truth behind rumors and setting the record straight
- Write cards, letters, and e-mail to relatives and friends in times of celebration, joy, sympathy, and stress
- Keep in touch with friends after moving; attend reunions
- Visit during times of stress or illness

WHAT DOES FRIENDSHIP LOOK LIKE AT HOME?

Adults

- Greet family, friends, and neighbors in a pleasant way; are consistently even-tempered
- Listen carefully to what our spouse and child is saying before preparing a response
- Tune into the feelings and emotions of family members and offer help when needed
- Laugh together often and genuinely
- Spend time together to develop and deepen relationships and connections

- Work consciously at creating and sustaining the role of "friend" with spouse and children as well as the role of spouse and parent
- Avoid social cliques; are pleasant and friendly with everyone in the neighborhood

Children

- Enjoy doing things with parents, grandparents, and siblings; are considered good "conversationalists"; genuinely care about people and enjoy getting to know more about them
- Play with siblings and neighborhood children
- Invite friends home to play; visit friend's homes; participate in sleepovers
- Share toys, materials, and belongings
- Laugh with friends
- Support friends through tough times
- Respect differences in interests, hobbies, and learning abilities of friends and acquaintances
- Are interested to learn more about friends' lives and interests
- Provide truthful feedback in tactful ways
- Keep secrets when asked (unless someone is endangered)
- Are friendly to all in the neighborhood and in the organizations in which they participate
- Offer to share tasks, even when not asked

OPPORTUNITIES TO PRACTICE FRIENDSHIP

AGES 4-8

- Read a story about friendship (see the "Literature Link" at the end of this chapter). Create two lists. In one, identify actions that "Help Friendships" to develop and on the other identify actions that "Hurt Friendships." Share the lists with friends or family.

    Invite a new neighbor child to visit your house and yard. Offer to share your toys. Talk about the different games you like to play. Ask what games and activities he/she likes to do. Introduce this new "friend" to your friends and acquaintances. Exchange telephone numbers and talk with him/her at least once a week for three months.

- Design a special card for your best friend's birthday. List the sports, toys, or games that your friend enjoys. Choose one of them for the illustration on the front cover. Include the number that shows the age of your friend. Express your feelings of joy and happiness on the inside of the card using crayons or markers in his/her favorite colors. Sign your name and present the finished card to your friend on his/her special day.

- Ask an older brother, sister, or cousin to teach you a skill he/she can do. Explain your reasons for wanting to learn how to do this skill. Set up practice times and use the LIFESKILLS of Effort and Perseverance until you can do it all by yourself. Demonstrate the new skill for your parents. Thank the person who taught you the skill by giving them a great big hug!

- Identify three or more qualities that you look for in a friend. Explain why you feel each quality is important. Determine three qualities you have that make you a good friend to someone. Make a friendship bookmark using these three descriptions. Use crayons or markers, punch a hole in the top, add a piece of ribbon, and present it to a good friend. Compare the words on your bookmark to the list of Lifelong Guidelines and LIFESKILLS in this book. If you find a new character trait that you would like to know more about, ask a parent or older sibling to teach you more about it.

- Investigate behaviors that help or hurt friendships. Create a T-chart* poster with the word FRIENDSHIP at the top. Make two columns and label the first one "YES" and the second one "NO." In each column, write behaviors that encourage or discourage friendships. For example:

FRIENDSHIP

HELPS	HURTS
Sharing toys	Grabbing toys
Saying kind words	Using put-downs

Offer this chart to your Sunday School teacher, brownie leader, or den mother to use during a meeting.

- Compare two different kinds of friends—human and animal. Compare two or more ways that human friends and animal friends are alike. Identify two or more ways they are different. Draw a picture of your best friend (human), write his/her name at the top of the paper and add your own name at the bottom right corner. Hang this where your friend can see it and feel special.

- Read/listen to the book *The Adventures of Sugar and Junior* by Angela Shelf Medearis. Identify one part of the story that you enjoyed. Make a list of six friends; count the number of boys and girls on your list. Share five ways being friends worked for Sugar and Junior. Reflect with a parent on what you have learned from Sugar and Junior's friendship that you could apply to the way you make and keep friends.

- Brainstorm the attributes of the "perfect friend." Create a T-Chart (Looks Like, Sounds Like, and Feels Like **and** Does *Not* Look Like, Does *Not* Sound Like, and Does *Not* Feel Like) listing the characteristics of a good friend. Write a paragraph, short story, poem, song, or essay using some of the phrases from the chart to honor this ideal friend.

---

* T-charts are a simple means of organizing and displaying information in ways that highlight comparisons and make information memorable. See Chapter 26, page 26.5, for a model of a T-chart.

AGES 9-12

- Read the book *50 Nifty Friendship Bracelets, Rings, and Other Things* by Sharon McCoy and plan a small business to manufacture items to sell. Choose an interesting project, gather the materials, and assemble the product. Invite two or three friends to join you as business partners or employees. Set a target number of products for each person to craft. Inspect the finished products to ensure that they are defect and flaw free. Analyze the cost for you per unit. Decide how much to charge customers so your business will make a profit. Place a table and two chairs at the front of the yard near the sidewalk. Design a colorful sign that includes the name of your business, the name of your product along with the price for one unit. Invite an adult or friend to sit with you. Donate the profit to a local charity such as Ronald McDonald House, the Salvation Army, or a Veterans' Hospital.

- Research three or more written or spoken codes (e.g., Morse Code, Braille, Pig Latin, Roman alphabet). Analyze each code to see how it works. Visualize a code that you and a best friend can use to communicate messages. Brainstorm with your friend a symbol (e.g., letter, number, picture) for each letter of the alphabet. Begin by writing each of the following in this new code:

    ~ Your name

    ~ Your friend's name

    ~ Your town/city name

    ~ School name

    ~ Pet's names

    ~ Secret messages

    Offer one message to Mom/Dad to see if they can break the code and decipher the message. If he/she does, consider revising your code to make it more difficult to solve.

- Recommend a collection of 20 or more fiction books with a friendship theme. Arrange an alphabetical annotated bibliography using this collection. Design an attractive cover including a title and your name. Organize the pages in order and staple the sheets in the upper left-hand corner. Present one copy to each of the following people: English teacher, school and local librarian, and the salesclerk at a nearby bookstore (e.g., Barnes & Noble, Media Play, Borders). Contact Amazon.com by e-mail to see if they are interested in having this information for reference purposes.

- Create a directory of 12 or more famous pairs of friends from any of the following categories: movies, stage, comedy, armed forces, medicine, religion, politics, sports, and technology. Hypothesize four or more strategies and skills that strengthened these friendships. Identify three Lifelong Guideline and/or LIFESKILL behaviors that you believe all 12 pairs had in common. Explain to a parent how you now use these three Lifelong Guideline/LIFESKILL behaviors and what behaviors you will use in the future. Reread this directory whenever you and a friend are experiencing relationship problems.

- Analyze three or more Lifelong Guideline/LIFESKILL behaviors that you expect a friend to use. Reflect on why these particular Lifelong Guidelines/LIFESKILLS are so important to you. Write two pages in your journal about what you want to remember about the LIFESKILL of Friendship. On another page list the Lifelong Guidelines and LIFESKILLS that you think are important for making and keeping a friend.

- Choose one Lifelong Guideline/LIFESKILL you believe helps strengthen friendship. Picture what it looks like, sounds like, and feels like **and** does *not* look like, does *not* sound like, and does *not* feel like. Construct a T-chart to organize the information. For example:

Lifelong Guideline/LIFESKILL OF _____

LOOKS LIKE	SOUNDS LIKE	FEELS LIKE	DOES NOT LOOK LIKE	DOES NOT SOUND LIKE	DOES NOT FEEL LIKE

Ask your parents to share personal stories of their experiences with friendship and contribute additional phrases to the T-chart.

- Review five or more movies that you have viewed that have a friendship theme. For each of the five main characters:

    ~ Judge his/her actions as either using or not using the Lifelong Guidelines/LIFESKILLS

    ~ Identify one Lifelong Guideline/LIFESKILL strength for each main character with supporting evidence from the movie

    ~ Recommend one Lifelong Guideline/LIFESKILL that needs more practice and offer an explanation for your choice

    ~ Use the following key to rate these movies as far as showing Lifelong Guidelines/LIFESKILL behaviors

    ***** = 5 stars   Modeled 20-23 Lifelong Guidelines/LIFESKILLS behaviors
    **** = 4 stars   Modeled 15-19 Lifelong Guidelines/LIFESKILLS behaviors
    *** = 3 stars   Modeled 10-14 Lifelong Guidelines/LIFESKILLS behaviors
    ** = 2 stars   Modeled 5-9 Lifelong Guidelines/LIFESKILLS behaviors
    * = 1 star   Modeled 0-4 Lifelong Guidelines/LIFESKILLS behaviors

Share with a parent what you have learned by analyzing these movie characters for their use of the LIFESKILL of Friendship. What new skills and behaviors will you apply to your life?

- Read a story about friendship (see the "Literature Link" at the end of this chapter). Create two lists. In one, identify actions that "Help Friendships" to develop and on the other identify actions that "Hurt Friendships." Share the lists with friends or family.

- Write your own story about friends and friendship. Add illustrations/graphics as desired. Create a "Chicken Soup for Friends" book. Put your story in it and ask three family members and/or friends to write a story, poem, or song about the LIFESKILL of Friendship to add to your book. Bind and display in a prominent place in the family room.

- Choose a pen pal from a list provided by a parent. Write an introductory rough draft of a letter sharing your personal interests (e.g., favorite books, hobbies, sports, organization memberships). Ask a family member or older friend to edit your letter for any errors. Design special "pen pal" note paper and copy the letter in your best handwriting. Address and mail the letter and respond to any answers you receive.

- Prepare a statement of appreciation for the friendship of two of your best friends. Use the format for giving an acknowledgement: "_____ (name of friend), you used the LIFESKILL of Friendship when you helped me learn how to improve my baseball swing. Thank you for being my friend." Offer a paper copy for the person to keep.

AGES 13+

- Design a survey of 10 or more questions that will collect information about the durability of high school friendships after graduation. Evaluate the survey material and select the two most outstanding deterrents to maintaining friendships beyond high school. Hypothesize as to why these two deterrents cause the greatest rift between two friends. Propose one or more solutions to the problem and share them with your best friend.

- Reflect on the LIFESKILLS that support friendship and encourage people to reach out to one another. Design a book that will convey your ideas to children 4-8 years old. Include a cover, title page, dedication page, and 14 or more story pages, each one beginning with these words: "Friendship is. . . ." Illustrate your ideas with colorful drawings. Leave a few blank pages at the end of the book for the reader to add his/her own thoughts about the LIFESKILL of Friendship. Read the story to some siblings, neighbors, or cousins; invite them to write a page of their own.

- Investigate the importance of the Lifelong Guidelines/LIFESKILLS in making and sustaining two of your most valued friendships. Rank the 23 Lifelong Guidelines/LIFESKILLS from 1 (most important) to 23 (least important). Next, set up a notebook page for each Lifelong Guideline/LIFESKILL following this model:

    Lifelong Guidelines/LIFESKILL of _____

Name of Friend #1	Name of Friend #2
_____	_____

For one month, track the number of times each friend uses a Lifelong Guideline/LIFESKILL in your friendship. Determine if there is a correlation between your ranking of the Lifelong Guidelines and LIFESKILLS and the behaviors of your two friends. Reflect in your journal on what you have learned about yourself and the LIFESKILL of Friendship.

- Analyze the LIFESKILL of Friendship behaviors as they relate to marriage, which in the best of situations is the joining of two best friends. Create and dramatize three scenarios that you frequently see when you are out and about; role-play each of the scenarios from two different viewpoints (not using the LIFESKILL of Friendship vs. using the LIFESKILL of Friendship). Select someone to be your partner and improvise the two interpretations. Invite family members to be your audience. Invite your audience to discuss what they have learned about the LIFESKILL of Friendship by watching your scenarios.

- Analyze the LIFESKILL of Friendship and other related Lifelong Guidelines and LIFESKILLS. Dramatize each of the following situations from two different viewpoints (not using the Lifelong Guidelines/LIFESKILLS vs. using them).
    ~ One of you wrote a check and forgot to record it in the checkbook; therefore, there is less money in the account and the bank is starting to bounce checks
    ~ The baby is running a high fever, can't go to daycare, and both of you have important meetings/presentations that day
    ~ It's the first beautiful day of spring; the yard is a mess and you think the day should be spent in cleaning up while your spouse wants to go and play ball
    ~ Identify the LIFESKILLS you and your partner found helpful in preparing these skits and explain your choices

    Select someone to be your partner and improvise the two interpretations. Invite family members to be your audience and ask them for examples of how they would have used the Lifelong Guidelines/LIFESKILLS in these situations.

- Compile a list of 20 or more songs that refer to friendship. Listen to each one, choose your favorite, and print the lyrics onto decorated computer paper. Select each phrase that you can match with a specific LIFESKILL behavior by underlining it. Write at least two additional verses relating to friends and friendship. Teach the song (including your verses) to your best friends and perform it in a variety of ways (e.g., rock, rap, country, reggae, pop).

- Investigate 10 or more quotations that include the word friendship. Compare their sentiments and judge which one best matches your views on friendship. Design a piece of art (e.g., needlepoint, calligraphy, stenciling, stamping, embossing) containing your chosen quotation. Frame the finished piece and donate it to your church bazaar, neighborhood fundraiser, or a charity auction.

- Arrange a chronological list of your friend's birthdays beginning in January and ending in December. Compare three or more websites (e.g., Blue Mountain Arts, American Greeting Card) that provide card-making services. Design a different card for each friend on your list and arrange for it to be delivered via e-mail on his/her birthday.

- Interview an adult in your family about one special childhood friendship. Ask questions such as: How did you meet? How old were you when you met and how long did the friendship last? What common interests did you share? Where is the friend today? How is your best friend today different from that friend in terms of their use of the Lifelong Guidelines and LIFESKILLS? Share the interview in a brief presentation (five minutes or less) to your family at the dinner table.

- Create a classified advertisement that identifies four or more personal qualities you look for in a friend. Remember that ads are short, to the point, and may use capital letters and graphic symbols to attract the attention of readers. Share this "WANTED: FRIENDS" ad with a family member or friend. Post your ad on the refrigerator door.

- Design a handmade or computer-generated "Get Well" card for a friend experiencing an extended illness or a "sympathy" card for someone who has recently lost a family member or close friend. Include appropriate expressions for a speedy recovery or condolences over his/her loss. Mail the card to that person when you feel you have done your personal best to express your thoughts and feelings.

- Create a friendship bracelet by using either embroidery yarn and fancy knots or a paper bead necklace. [*Note:* To make a paper bead necklace, roll strips of colored advertisements from magazines or colored paper to form beads. String the beads onto a 17" piece of fishing line and knot.] Present this friendship jewelry to a special friend.

- Study a pair of famous friends from any time period. Design a poster about how the pair achieved their fame because of their friendship. Describe five or more characteristics that strengthened their friendship and two other interesting facts. Share the information with a family member or friend.

- Research one of the following people: Henry David Thoreau, Jane Goodall, Jacques Cousteau, Rachel Carson, or someone else approved by a parent. Learn how this person was a friend to animals or nature. Prepare and present a five minute skit that conveys this special kind of friendship to your family or friends in an entertaining and informative way.

SIGNS OF SUCCESS

Congratulations! Children are showing signs of Friendship when they

- Greet family and friends in a pleasant, sociable way each time they meet
- Give to a relationship as much as they take; don't take their friendships for granted
- Provide support for someone who is scared, hurt, or sad
- Offer to share him/herself by sharing something special and dear
- Honor a promise to a friend
- Remain loyal to a friend even if other friends don't seem to appreciate this person
- Protect a friend from put-downs
- Respect the ways a person is different from themselves
- Introduce themselves to the "new kid on the block" and introduce this newcomer to their friends
- Include all neighborhood children in a variety of games
- Ensure that everyone on their team has a fair chance to participate in the game
- Participate in organizations such as scouts, YMCA, 4-H, and neighborhood clubs

- Create a handmade gift for a friend on a special occasion; design a get-well card for a sick friend

Keep trying! Children need more practice when they

- Can't seem to keep friends over a period of time
- Act silly to get their peers' attention; lie to exaggerate their personal qualities
- Hit, bite, or kick people when they are angry
- Call people names or use put-downs as part of their daily language
- Harass or tease someone because of his/her general appearance, race, religious, or ethnic background
- Spread lies about people
- Refuse to share a friend with others
- Deliberately ignore some children in the neighborhood
- Bribe someone to be their friend with toys or money
- Torment or tease animals
- Steal other children's belongings
- Abuse the environment
- Form cliques and gangs and contribute to a sense of "if you're in, you're someone" but "if you're out, you're nobody"

Literature Link ~ Friendship

Ages 4-8

Elizabeth and Larry	Marilyn Sadler (New York: Simon & Schuster, 1990)
George and Martha: The Complete Stories of Two Best Friends	James Marshall (Boston: Houghton Mifflin Company, 1997)
Marshmallow	Clare Turlay Newberry (New York: Smithmark Publishing, 1999)
Mightiest Heart, The (AFA)	Lynn Cullen (New York: Dial Books, 1998)

Ages 9-12

Cliques, Phonies and Other Baloney (TE)	Trevor Romain (Minneapolis, MN: Free Spirit Press, 1998)
Lily's Crossing	Patricia Reilly Giff (New York: Yearling Books, 1999)
Mouse of Amherst, The	Elizabeth Spires (New York: Frances Foster Books, A Division of Farrar, Strauss & Giroux, 1999)
Night the Bells Rang, The	Natalie Kinsey-Warnock (New York: Cobblehill, Dutton, 1991)

Ages 13+

Cay, The (AFA)	Theodore Taylor (New York: Camelot Books, 1995)
Holes	Louis Sachar (New York: Farrar, Strauss & Giroux, 1998)
Last Days of Summer	Steve Kluger (Austin, TX: Bard Books, 1999)
Outsiders, The	S.E. Hinton (London: Puffin Books, 1997)

Family Resources

Good Friends Are Hard to Find: Help Your Child Find, Make and Keep Friends	Fred Frankel (Pasadena, CA: Perspective Publishing, 1996)
Let's Make a Memory: Great Ideas for Building Family Traditions and Togetherness	Gloria Gaither, et al (Westport, CN: Word Books, Greenwood Publishing Group, 1994)
Playground Politics: Understanding the Emotional Life of Your School-Age Child	Stanley I. Greenspan, M.D. (Reading, MA: Perseus Books, 1994)

Multicultural books: **(AFA)**=African American, **(ASA)**=Asian American, **(HA)**=Hispanic American, **(ME)**=Multi-Ethnic, **(NA)**=Native American, **(TE)**=listed in the teacher edition of this book, *Tools for Citizenship and Life: Using the ITI Lifelong Guidelines and LIFESKILLS in the Classroom*, **(BFE)**=available through Books for Educators

Initiative

Chapter 15

"Do it now."

initiative *n* **1:** an introductory act or step **2:** energy or aptitude to initiate action: enterprise

INITIATIVE: To do something because it needs to be done

WHAT IS INITIATIVE?

Of all the Lifelong Guidelines and LIFESKILLS, Initiative and Integrity are the most inner-driven. They can't be forced from outside; they must be formulated, nurtured, and put into action from within. Initiative and Integrity are twin LIFESKILLS. Initiative without Integrity becomes bossiness or bullying; Integrity without Initiative becomes guilt or cowardice.

Initiative is sparked by an inner voice that propels us not only to pay attention but to act. It can be as simple as picking up a towel left on the floor or as complex as whistle blowing on corporate fraud or government malfeasance. It fires our actions, inventions, and creative endeavors. It runs on high octane—an inner motivation fueled by success with past challenges and our deep commitment to live up to our values and beliefs. It compels us to do something because it needs to be done and to redo something until it meets our internal standards for quality and correctness.

Initiative differs from responsibility. The root of the word "responsible" is to respond—to respond to situations moment by moment as they occur. Initiative is prompted by an internal, rather than an external, source. Initiative prompts us to anticipate situations and play a significant role in creating them.

WHY PRACTICE INITIATIVE?

Initiative is important on many levels. Quite simply, if we don't practice the LIFESKILL of Initiative, how will anything get done? Who will be the inventors, the "doers," and the volunteers in our family, community, state, nation, and world? Who will start the work that needs to be done? Who will further science, technology, and the arts? Who will carry the work of a democratic society? Who will further civilization?

Initiative and Citizenship

The LIFESKILL of Initiative is an essential quality of citizens in a democratic society. As Edmund Burke put it, "The only thing necessary for the triumph of evil is for enough good men to do nothing."* As participating citizens in a government "by the people," we must practice initiative. When we see something that needs to be done, we must do it. We must inform ourselves and push the wheels of government to solve problems and ensure a just society. We can't wait to be told what to do; we must act based on our own internal urgings. The ITI model recommends frequent social/political action projects to give students practice taking the initiative to solve problems using our democratic processes. (Such projects also provide opportunities to apply the knowledge and skills your child is learning at home and studying at school in order to master them and store them in long-term memory.) The LIFESKILL of Initiative makes the difference between wishing for more effective learning and behavior outcomes for our child versus making them a reality.

Life abounds with adventure as we challenge ourselves to take chances while other people are still calculating the risks and puzzling over decisions. Initiators step out boldly and blaze a trail for the hesitant to follow.

Initiative and Personal Well-Being

On a personal level, taking action—taking the initiative—is fundamental to our expression of self. Without it, our personalities would be beige, flat, unremarkable. Without it, we can't reach out to form relationships with family, friends, or co-workers. Taken to the extreme, lack of initiative contributes to powerlessness, hopelessness, isolation, and, eventually, death of the self.

The LIFESKILL of Initiative is essential to our well-being.

HOW DO I PRACTICE INITIATIVE?

Because the LIFESKILLS of Initiative and Integrity are so closely connected and because both are at the core of who we are, surface applications or the "Do what I say when I say it" practice of initiative are worthless, even counterproductive. We must model the LIFESKILL of Initiative from the beginning, day in and day out. We must help children create a foundation which they can build on.

Building a Foundation

The LIFESKILL of Initiative requires that we have well-defined, clearly articulated values, goals, and standards for behavior and workmanship. In short, we must know who we are and what we stand for. And, we must have the courage of our convictions and the willingness to act on them.

---

* Edmund Burke, letter to Sheriff of Bristol, dated April 3, 1777.

To help our children develop the LIFESKILL of Initiative, we must help them clarify their values, establish high expectations and standards for themselves, and set short- and long-term personal and academic goals they are passionate about. These are the foundations of the LIFESKILL of Initiative.

Using Real Life Experiences

As with the other LIFESKILLS, Initiative is developed and strengthened through its use. Give your child meaningful problems, dilemmas, and issues to wrestle with. Home and community are rich with examples. Still others pop up in the daily news. When watershed events in history occur, such as the fall of communism, the cloning of Dolly the sheep, the Columbine High School killings, the advent of colleges on the Internet, and so forth, encourage your child to discuss how his/her life might be affected by such events. Encourage him/her to use the LIFESKILL of Initiative to examine the issues in terms of how they will affect his/her personal plans for the future, however tentative such plans may be.

Using Management/Leadership Strategies

Make the LIFESKILL of Initiative a daily focus of your parenting and home management leadership strategies. The development of the values, standards, and goals necessary for using the LIFESKILL of Initiative can easily be incorporated into collaborative work, family meetings, leadership opportunities, and genuine choices.

Collaborative Work. Collaborative work requires enormous amounts of initiative, individually and as a group. To focus on the LIFESKILL of Initiative in the context of collaborative work and play, teach your child to use the skills for planning ahead, stopping mid-stream to analyze how things are going, and analyzing product and process upon completion. Learning to ask such questions—of self and others—is an essential skill for applying the LIFESKILL of Initiative. A project unanalyzed is no more successful or rewarding than a life unexamined.

It is easy to add a question or two to help children focus on the LIFESKILL of Initiative. While the questions below may sound rather formal, try them for family meetings. We think you'll discover that they will greatly enrich the dialogue. Also, if things go awry in twosomes or other "play" events, use them to help the children learn how to avoid similar problems in the future. Possible questions to ask:

- Planning ahead: What are our family/group/team goals for this task? What do we hope to accomplish personally? What Lifelong Guidelines or LIFESKILLS will we most need to succeed at this task? How will this task help each of us achieve our group and/or personal goals?

- Mid-way analysis: How are we doing so far? Are we on track? Will we reach our goals? Are we proceeding as we had planned? If not, why not? Are our methods working? Are they consistent with our values and standards or have we stopped using needed Lifelong Guidelines or LIFESKILLS? What do we need to change to succeed? Does each member of the family/group freely volunteer effort and ideas? If we're stuck, how can we get ourselves moving again?

- Analyzing the completed project or action: What worked? How well did we work together as a family (as a whole or teams within the family) to provide both leadership and support? What did we learn about ourselves as family/group members and about ourselves personally? Did we avoid perfectionism yet complete the task on time and meet expected standards? How can we improve our process and product next time?

Family Meetings.* Encourage your child to bring issues to family meetings. Support him/her in speaking his/her mind fully, accurately, confidently. Teach your child to initiate conversations to resolve interpersonal issues, an invaluable skill throughout life. Help him/her see that how this operates is as much the child's concern as it is yours as parent.

Leadership Opportunities. Create opportunities for your child to be in leadership roles on a daily basis. Serving successfully as a leader is one of the most powerful ways to practice the LIFESKILL of Initiative. It is also the quickest and surest way to elevate self-esteem and confidence,** prerequisites for living the LIFESKILL of Initiative.

Genuine Choices. Of all the areas in which to demonstrate the LIFESKILL of Initiative, one of the most important is initiative in directing one's own learning. For example, some of the family's reading time (being read to and reading alone) should allow your child genuine choices. Encourage your child to explore, to discover lifelong interests, hobbies, and vocations.

WHAT DOES INITIATIVE LOOK LIKE IN THE REAL WORLD?

We

- See a job that has to be done and do it
- Recognize a problem and lead efforts to resolve it; don't whine about it but instead go directly to the person with the authority/power to change the situation
- Create organizations to help solve community problems
- Raise money for schools and churches
- Run for political office
- Tackle the hard problems of the community as pro-active citizens
- Invent new machines to make work easier
- Study scientific research on ways to improve our health
- Volunteer for both local and global efforts to solve social and environmental problems

---

* See *Positive Discipline, Revised Edition* by Jane Nelson (New York: Ballantine Books/Random House, 1987.

** For a fascinating, research-based discussion of the power of leadership roles to change social status and self-perception, see *Designing Groupwork: Strategies for the Heterogeneous Classroom, Second Edition* by Elizabeth Cohen (New York: Teachers College Press, 1994), Chapters 6 and 8.

- Organize a Neighborhood Watch group
- Offer help to family members, neighbors, and friends during a crisis
- Embrace change as a fact of life and work toward finding positive answers
- Act in spite of others' possible negative reactions
- Make things happen, sometimes against great odds

WHAT DOES INITIATIVE LOOK LIKE AT HOME?

Adults

- Perform a distasteful job because it has to be done
- As consumers and persons responsible for household finances, do research to find the best buy, e.g., compare prices before buying, inspect houses before submitting a purchase offer, inquire about schools before purchasing a home, read the small print in contracts
- Evaluate financial resources long before retirement
- Report physical and emotional health problems during their early stages of development
- Take action to secure the health and safety of our families, e.g., create escape plans for emergency evacuations from the house, gather essential emergency preparedness items
- Reach out to children, family, and neighbors when they are hurting or need assistance
- Take courses and read books to continually improve relationship and parenting skills
- Volunteer to be a community leader, e.g., 4-H, scouts, neighborhood improvement projects

Children

- Initiate and complete projects without being prompted or nagged
- Contribute suggestions for family projects
- Volunteer to do tasks that are important but uninteresting to do
- Volunteer to perform extra chores when a family member is ill or out of town
- Choose to save money for a special purchase
- Decide to investigate new interests; have more than one project going at a time
- Initiate ways to organize clothing, toys, and other belongings into some kind of order
- Start investigating working in the real world long before they are of age to do so

- Ask family and friends for help to understand and master knowledge and skills
- Introduce themselves to new children in the neighborhood
- Stand up for others who are being put down

OPPORTUNITIES TO PRACTICE INITIATIVE

AGES 4-8

- Listen as a family member reads *The Hole in the Dike* by Norma Green (or another story about the LIFESKILL of Initiative that the family chooses). Brainstorm five or more ways the hole in the dike could have been repaired. Rate them from "most practical" to "least practical"; share your opinions with the person who read you the story. Discuss with him/her what you discovered about yourself and the LIFESKILL of Initiative.

- Identify one household chore that you want to do for your family for two weeks. Pick one that is not your favorite and offer to complete the job once each day. Make a calendar and draw a smiley face on each day you finish the task. Count the smiley faces at the end of two weeks. Did you do the job every day? Explain to a parent what you learned about the LIFESKILL of Initiative.

- Memorize your name, address, and phone number. Tell an adult how you would get help in an emergency. Demonstrate what you would do by role playing a telephone call. Explain what you will do to get help if the phone is not working.

- Take photographs of 10 or more people in your community who are using the LIFESKILL of Initiative, such as food bank volunteers, disaster clean-up crew, meeting of civic leaders and citizens to solve problems. Create a photo essay with captions that express the message, "I am taking the first step to help solve a problem." Share this collection with a member of your family.

- Learn how to make your favorite Jello dessert. Invite a relative to take pictures each step of the way. Choose the box with your flavor name and picture on the front. Read (ask for help if you can't read yet) the directions. Gather all of the ingredients and materials you need. Show how you would complete each step (ask an adult for help with the boiling water). Put the Jello in the refrigerator to set. Decorate with fresh fruit/whipped cream and serve for dessert. When the photos are developed or printed, glue them in order on a sheet of paper to show what you did first, then second, and so on. Show the finished sheet to the person who took the photos and ask them to recheck the order to see if it follows the instructions on the Jello box. Keep this "recipe" handy so you can refer to it when you make Jello the next time.

- Collect coupons from magazines, the daily newspaper, and Sunday papers to help your family save money at the supermarket. Demonstrate cutting on the line so all of the information will be on the coupon. Set up your materials (e.g., scissors, magazines, and newspapers) and clip out the coupons. Classify the coupons into the following categories: meat, vegetables, fruit, treats, cereals, beverages, and cleaning materials. Place each coupon in its category. Paper-clip each category together when you are finished. Estimate how many coupons there are and offer them to the family shopper.

- Discover two or more nursery rhymes that teach about the LIFESKILL of Initiative (to do something because it needs to be done). Memorize two of them and draw an illustration for each. Create your own nursery rhyme of four or more lines that teaches young children how to use the LIFESKILL of Initiative in family life or school. Recite it for your family at dinner time.

- Identify two or more places in your house that would be great spots for reading. Investigate each place to find out how quiet it is, how private it is, how comfortable it is, and whether the lighting is adequate for reading. Compare the information and choose the best place for your new, private reading nook. Design a sign to hang up that says: "Quiet, please!" and add a graphic that will provide a picture of quiet and reading. Add a piece of yarn; then hang up the sign to let other family members know that this is your place for reading.

- Use the LIFESKILL of Initiative to safeguard your clothing from being lost. Write your name on a label using black permanent marker for easy identification. Add your name to any item that needs it, including your sneakers, boots, and shoes.

AGES 9-12

- Develop and demonstrate a plan to ensure you are prepared to act in the following emergency situations:
    - ~ Report an injury of a serious nature
    - ~ Report a fire
    - ~ Operate a fire extinguisher
    - ~ Turn off the water in a sink as well as for the entire home
    - ~ Report a prowler

    Ask a parent for feedback on your plans. Share with him/her what you have learned about the LIFESKILL of Initiative by developing and demonstrating your plans.

- Demonstrate how you are prepared to use the LIFESKILL of Initiative to do the following:
    - ~ Order a meal from a menu, check the subtotal for accuracy, add approximate sales tax, and add a 15% tip
    - ~ Demonstrate how to write a check and pay by credit card
    - ~ Identify three alternate routes home from school
    - ~ Locate a timetable for your local bus service, train station, and/or subway system, and one airline; determine a set of connections that will get you to the home of a relative who lives far from you

- Determine which five items would be most important to have in your house to prepare yourself for a local disaster (e.g., tornado, earthquake, flood, hurricane, blizzard). Ask your parents to purchase these and then place them in a special crushproof container. Create a "Disaster Box" label for the box and keep it in a readily-accessible area.

- Start a business—a sole proprietorship with you as the only employee (for example, e-mail or website set up, a newspaper route, lawn mowing, dogwalking, poop scooping, and so forth). Operate this business for at least two months. Keep track of expenditures and income. Share with a parent what you have learned about the LIFESKILL of Initiative by setting up and running your own business.

- Volunteer once a week for a community service project such as a food bank, food kitchen, Salvation Army, scouts, and so forth. Volunteer for at least two months. After the first month, share with your family at dinner what you are learning about the LIFESKILL of Initiative. Share your challenges and ask for any suggestions. After the second month, again share with your family what you have learned and how you plan to make it part of your everyday family and school life.

- Read *Charlotte's Web* by E.B. White and pretend that you are Wilbur, the little pig in the story. Figure out three other ways Charlotte's egg sac could have been brought back to Fern's farm. Rank them from most possible to least likely. Explain to a family member your reasoning for choosing these possible ways and why you ranked them as you did.

- Learn to "sign" at least ten emergency phrases that would help you communicate an urgent message to a deaf person in danger. Practice these signs until you can make them with ease. Teach them to a family member and review them once a week for four months.

- Read a biography about a scientist, inventor, or artist who demonstrated the LIFESKILL of Initiative in some special way(s). Dramatize a monologue that this person might have spoken explaining three or more reasons why the LIFESKILL of Initiative is vital to succeeding in life. Present this for your family before Sunday dinner. Lead a discussion on the importance of this LIFESKILL while everyone is eating. Invite family members to share three examples of their use of the LIFESKILL of Initiative that helped them succeed at a critical point in their life.

AGES 13+

- Attend a CPR class in your area that will prepare you to handle certain emergency situations. Identify the signs/symptoms that will be present and require the use of CPR. Rehearse the procedure as many times as necessary in order to perform it correctly. Demonstrate the maneuver correctly for your instructor. Prepare and share a demonstration of your training for family members.

- Investigate the LIFESKILL of Initiative in your neighborhood or community by using careful observation skills. Rove around with a camera and snap candid shots of children and adults using the LIFESKILL of Initiative. Complete an essay with photographs sharing information about these "good Samaritans" and submit it to the local Pennysaver or community newsletter for publication.

- Start and expand a collection of things (e.g., baseball cards, seashells, marbles, postcards, rocks) that interests you. Begin a journal in which you reflect on any knowledge you are gaining from collecting these items—about the items themselves and about how you use the LIFESKILL of Initiative. Inventory your collections and record the name, size, identifying marks, and approximate worth of each piece. Photograph any exceptionally valuable item for insurance purposes. Display this collection at a nearby show or exhibit for the

Chapter 15—Initiative

general public. Share with friends interested in your collection what you've learned about the items you collect and share highlights from your journal.

- Inform yourself about a local issue (e.g., hunger, pollution, human rights, gender equity). Identify two or more local organizations that are working toward solving this issue. Contact the local group, as well as any national organizations, for further information on the services they perform or provide. Compare the budget of the local group to its national counterpart and judge the effectiveness of their spending. Determine if this is a cause that you want to support.

- Arrange to start a small business that is needed in your neighborhood. Determine the product or service you will provide, funding your start-up fees, choosing a professional name, setting prices/rates, and hours of service. Consult with an adult familiar with advertising practices, evaluate the choices generated, and decide on the method(s) best for your company. Print some business cards, hand out flyers, and fulfill promises made in your advertising. Review your financial books each month to determine if the business is on its way to making a profit. After six months, decide whether or not to continue your business.

- Compose a song (at least three verses and a chorus), dance (three minutes or more), or sculpture (clay, wood, metal) that represents your hero's experiences with the LIFESKILL of Initiative. Choose a title appropriate for the piece and submit it for judging in a local/regional exhibit. Write and send your hero a note sharing how his/her actions inspired you to create this piece of art. Include a tape, video, or photo of the product.

- Organize a food collection from your neighborhood, church, or youth group. Ask the director of a food bank what kinds of food (fresh, canned, preserved, dried) they most need. Create posters, advertisements, and flyers to educate the neighbors about the project and encourage them to donate. Divide the products into categories, such as fruit, vegetables, food staples, as they are brought to the drop-off site. Record the number of items in each category. As soon as the collection date is set, arrange for adult drivers to deliver the items directly to the food bank.

- Investigate the lives and experiences of three relatives who own their own business. Select three who are different from one another in age, gender, educational background, and the products/services their business provides. Write an article, create a collage, or design a poster exhibiting at least three of the most important ways the LIFESKILL of Initiative helps them make their business a success. Share your product with family and friends.

- Plan to be prepared for the following emergencies. Demonstrate your plan for each.
    ~ Report a fire and report a prowler
    ~ Operate a fire extinguisher, explain how to extinguish different kinds of small household fires, and ways to check a smoke detector to ensure it's working
    ~ Read a timetable for your local bus or subway system and identify three alternate routes to a relative's home outside your area who could temporarily house you if needed
    ~ Turn off the water in a sink and for your entire home
    ~ Prepare a list of emergency numbers to be posted in your home

- ~ Call 911 to report an emergency. Be prepared to include your name, address, phone number and the nature of the emergency

- Learn to "sign" at least ten phrases that would help you communicate with a deaf person in distress. Practice these signs until you can make them with ease. Teach them to a family member or friend.

- Attend a babysitters' training course to prepare you to take care of babies/young children. Demonstrate four of the following: feeding and burping a baby, changing a diaper, dressing the baby for a cold/hot day, entertaining a toddler, choosing and reading a story to a three-year old, and three of the most important danger signals to watch for. Prepare and share this demonstration for other interested friends. Upon completion of the course, design business cards that emphasize your training and advertise your services.

- Invent a tool, machine, or aid that will provide a solution for a problem currently affecting your life. Draw plans to scale, list the materials you need, and create a prototype. Demonstrate your invention for your family.

- Investigate five or more major corporations or local businesses. Send a letter to the CEO asking for information about how the company encourages development and use of the LIFESKILL of Initiative. Ask about procedures that encourage employees to use the LIFESKILL of Initiative by sharing ideas, coming up with creative alternatives, developing new products, and so forth. Also ask if the company has statistics on the effectiveness of its efforts to encourage the LIFESKILL of Initiative in its employees. Write one procedure of your own that you feel would encourage enterprise and ingenuity. Present your findings to your family.

SIGNS OF SUCCESS

Congratulations! Children are showing signs of Initiative when they

- Try different activities, initiate meeting a wide range of people, and relish travel to new places
- Readily take on leadership roles
- See work that has to be done and do it without having to be told to do so
- Tackle an unglamorous job that no one else is willing to try
- Speak their minds even though others may not agree
- Organize a group to solve a problem
- Suggest divergent ideas for family projects
- Introduce themselves to new neighbors and look forward to getting to know them

Keep trying! Children need more practice when they

- Avoid sharing or trying new ideas because they feel threatened by teasing or put-downs from other children and/or adults

- Follow others and seldom voice or implement their own ideas or solutions; rarely step into the role of leader

- Allow other people to think for them; follow conventional, traditional thinking patterns

- Always wait for someone else to step up to the task

- Refuse to try anything new or different

- Respond to problem-solving opportunities with apathy and listlessness

- Tell themselves that the way it's always been done is the best way no matter what other innovative ideas are introduced and even when the old ways don't work

Literature Link ~ Initiative

Ages 4-8

Arthur's Really Helpful Bedtime Stories	Marc Tolon Brown (New York: Random House, 1998)
Circle of Thanks (NA)	Susi Gregg Fowler (New York: Scholastic Books, 1998)
Garden of Happiness, The (HA)	Erika Tamar (New York: Harcourt Brace Publishing Company, 1996)
Something Beautiful (AFA)	Sharon Dennis Wyeth (New York: Bantam Doubleday Dell Publishers, 1998)

Ages 9-12

Diego (HA)	Jeanette and Jonah Winter (New York: Alfred A. Knopf, 1991)
Legend of Luke, The	Brian Jacques (New York: Philomel Books, 2000)
Planet of Junior Brown, The (AFA)	Virginia Hamilton (New York: Aladdin Paperbacks, 1984)
Sweet Clara and the Freedom Quilt (AFA) (TE)	Deborah Hopkinson (New York: Knopf, 1993)

Ages 13+

Backwater	Joan Bauer (New York: Putnam Publishing Group, 1999)
Boy and the Otter, The	A. R. Lloyd (New York: Holt, Rinehart and Winston, 1984)
Girls Who Rocked the World: Heroines from Sacajawea to Sheryl Swoopes (ME)	Amelie Weldon (Hillsboro, OR: Beyond Words Publishing Co., 1998)
Tall Mexican: The Life of Hank Aguirre, All-Star Pitcher, Businessman, Humanitarian (HA)	Robert E. Copley (Houston, TX: Arte Publico Press, 1998)

Parent Resources

Growing Good Kids: 28 Activities to Enhance Self-Awareness, Compassion and Leadership	Deb Delisle, Jim Delisle (Minneapolis, MN: Free Spirit Publishing Inc., 1996)
Raising Self-Reliant Children in a Self-Indulgent World: Seven Building Blocks for Developing Capable Young People (B4E)	H. Stephen Glenn and Jane Nelson (Rocklin, CA: Prime Publishing, 1989)

Multicultural books: **(AFA)**=African American, **(ASA)**=Asian American, **(HA)**=Hispanic American, **(ME)**=Multi-Ethnic, **(NA)**=Native American, **(TE)**=listed in the teacher edition of this book, *Tools for Citizenship and Life: Using the ITI Lifelong Guidelines and LIFESKILLS in the Classroom*, **(BFE)**=available through Books for Educators

Chapter 16

Integrity

"ALWAYS BE TRUE TO ONESELF AND OTHERS."

integrity *n* **1:** honesty, incorruptible
2: firm adherence to a code, especially of moral or artistic values: incorruptibility
3: the quality or state of being complete or undivided: completeness; unimpaired, soundness

INTEGRITY: To act according to a sense of what's right and wrong

WHAT IS INTEGRITY?

As discussed in Chapter 15, the LIFESKILLS of Initiative and Integrity are the most inner-driven. They can't be forced from outside; they must be formulated, nurtured, and put into action from within. Integrity and Initiative are twin LIFESKILLS. Integrity without Initiative becomes guilt, cowardice, or the worst mix of self-righteousness and "I-told-you-so." Initiative without Integrity becomes bossiness or bullying.

Integrity is our inner voice of wisdom, a voice that speaks the truth about whether there is resonance or discord between our words and actions and our sense of what's right and wrong. Like a tuning fork, it tells us if we are in harmony with our beliefs or living in life-sapping discord. This LIFESKILL lies at the core of who we are, what we believe, and what we stand for. It is the touchstone for all other LIFESKILLS and Lifelong Guidelines.

WHY PRACTICE INTEGRITY?

In a society whose teens and 20- and 30-year-old males wear T-shirts boasting the slogan, "I don't get mad, I just get even" and whose cars sport bumper stickers that say "My kid beat up your honor student," integrity is sometimes seen as old fashioned. Getting even, striking back, "putting a hurt" on someone, seeking retribution, saving face, protecting ego—even if you are the person who is wrong or at fault—are all championed by movies and prime time sit-coms and dramas. Image and status are everything.

What Goes Around Comes Around

So why not go with the flow and forget about the LIFESKILL of Integrity? There are selfish reasons for living a life of integrity as well as selfless ones—practical reasons as well as philosophical and moral reasons. Besides being concerned about how our life impacts others, the sanity and stability of our own lives depend upon a measure of predictability and stability in others; without it, we can't make our own life work. Integrity is a two-way street—what goes around comes around.

This dependability and predictability in relationships comes largely from integrity. When the people around us lead their lives with integrity, we know how they will interact with us, others, situations, and ideas. They are steadfast; they don't waiver depending on who or what or circumstances or whim. Who they are today is who they will be next week and the month after. We know where we stand with them. We trust them. We respect them. We value being in their presence.

If we want integrity in others, we must deserve it by having integrity ourselves.

Integrity As a Source of Personal Power

Of all the LIFESKILLS, Integrity generates the most personal power. People with integrity are in high demand as trusted counselors, dependable politicians, effective business partners, treasured spouses, and valued friends. We listen to what they have to say and consider it carefully. We can depend on their word; we trust who they are and what they stand for. In our lives, we willingly give them our respect and we honor their strength.

Integrity Opens Doors. Because first impressions are often misleading, reputations built up over a lifetime are much more reliable. One of the centerpieces of a person's reputation is integrity. If someone is known for his/her integrity, doors open; if integrity is questionable, many doors close. The number and kinds of doors that open to us often make the difference between success or failure in life, satisfaction or discontent, dreams realized or fantasies that float beyond our reach. Integrity plus opportunity is a powerful mix.

Integrity Is Fragile. As the boy who cried wolf too many times discovered, once your reputation is lost, it's extremely hard to rebuild it. Susan Kovalik's father often warned his young daughter: "It takes a thousand acts to build a good reputation but only one lapse in integrity to lose it." Integrity is not an on-again, off-again quality. It is a lifetime endeavor, a lifetime work of art.

Integrity As Basis for Society and Government

Democratic societies cry out for citizens of integrity who in turn demand integrity in those they elect and in those who serve on juries, vote in elections, pay just taxes, and stand up for the less fortunate and less powerful members of society. And, of course, leadership based on integrity— a government with effective leaders of strong character, immune to corruption, opportunism, or moral decay—is fundamental to sustaining and nurturing a democratic society. When integrity wanes, nations fall.

HOW DO YOU PRACTICE IT?

We develop integrity primarily by seeing it in action—modeled by those we admire and respect. If we model taking the high road, children will learn to make decisions based on principles rather than expediency. If we model sticking to standards rather than giving in to short cuts, children will commit to doing their personal best. If we model doing a job from beginning to end and taking pride in our accomplishments, children will willingly adhere to codes of excellence. If our behaviors consistently match the words we speak, children see integrity. What we do always out-teaches what we say should be done.

Start Early

Parents are the first and most powerful models of the LIFESKILL of Integrity. Through daily example, they teach their child to share, to be fair, to respect ownership, and to use self-restraint. By example of acts and attitudes, they also teach their beliefs about everything from law-based government to how their religion's fundamental teachings direct one's life.

Building integrity starts in the cradle and proceeds throughout life. Many of life's lessons come from making mistakes, using bad judgment, and then agonizing over the results. From these errors, we determine which actions do not correspond to our sense of right and wrong and the person we want to be. Some decisions make us feel bad while other choices make our heart sing. Initially we look to the responses of families, friends, and coworkers; eventually our sense of right and wrong becomes sufficiently internalized that we make our own judgments.

Teaching the LIFESKILL of Integrity must be central to how each family member operates. In a democratic society, integrity of its citizenry is a necessity, not an option; it is a requirement.

Use the Teachable Moment

The goal of character development is to educate the conscience in such a way that a person does what is right without being told and without being watched. This can't be done through a series of rules or exercises on worksheets; it can only be done through modeling and use of the teachable moment.* Helping children solve a real dilemma at the moment it occurs is one of the most effective learning experiences. For example, your child bursts through the door all abuzz about a pushing-shoving incident down the street; discussion ensues about what act of integrity could have stopped the incident before it escalated out of control. Or, your child points out similarities between organized crime during Prohibition and the rule of neighborhood gangs today; this prompts a discussion of loyalty versus integrity. Family members must nurture and guide such discussions rather than simply cutting them off or giving a stern sermon about them.

---

* The "teachable moment" is a deliberate instructional strategy in the ITI model. Teacher—and parents—are encouraged to stay focused in the present and use what comes up at the moment as a teaching opportunity to connect the Lifelong Guidelines and LIFESKILLS to real world situations.

Help Children Build an Inner Foundation

Help your child develop his/her sense of what's right and wrong by framing dilemmas for discussion that are important to and understandable by him/her. Focus on family and neighborhood issues. Insist that your child continually examine who he/she is and what he/she stands for through journal writing, discussion during family meetings, and one-on-one conversations. Help him/her clarify his/her own values, establish high expectations and standards, and set personal and academic goals. Don't let a day go by without giving your child opportunities to make the LIFESKILL of Integrity relevant to his/her life and perspective of what's right and what's wrong. The LIFESKILL of Integrity is developed by degrees and inches over time. If it were an easy task, the percentage of our citizenry considered to be people of integrity would be sharply higher.

Using Management/Leadership Strategies

Make the LIFESKILL of Integrity a daily focus of your parenting and home management and leadership strategies. The development of the values, standards, and goals necessary for living a life of integrity can easily be incorporated in many ways. For tips for teaching the LIFESKILL of Integrity through collaborative work, class meetings, leadership opportunities, and genuine choice, see Chapter 9.

WHAT DOES INTEGRITY LOOK LIKE IN THE REAL WORLD?

We

- Remain true to our goals by continuing to work on them without selling out to shortcuts
- Keep promises made to ourselves and others
- Tell the truth even when it gets us into trouble
- Try to locate the owners of found objects
- Point out an error to cashiers even when the error is in our favor
- Use accurate figures when computing income taxes
- Follow through to complete projects
- Remain loyal to family and friends yet help them own up to their problems and misdeeds
- Live within our means
- Honor others by showing up on time for appointments

WHAT DOES INTEGRITY LOOK LIKE AT HOME?

Adults

- Understand that some of the best lessons come from making mistakes; we thus own up to them and learn from them
- Remain faithful and loyal to our spouse
- Model all the Lifelong Guidelines and LIFESKILLS for our children
- Keep promises made to family members
- Fulfill commitments and complete projects as agreed
- Go above and beyond what the job descriptions require to complete important tasks
- Remain true to our beliefs and values
- Uphold high moral principles
- Insist that gossip and put-downs be eliminated
- Provide honest appraisals of children's accomplishments
- Keep our word to others—adults and children, friends and family, boss and co-workers
- Model honesty, strength, and firmness of character
- Insist that religious, ethnic, and cultural identities be respected
- Demonstrate fairness in all areas

Children

- Do what they say they will do
- Distinguish between right and wrong
- Readily own up to mistakes of omission and commission (even when known only to them); learn from these experiences
- Determine their own behaviors
- Resist peer pressure and speak and act from their own values and beliefs
- Understand how to mediate
- Work through misunderstandings and grievances

Character Begins at Home: Family Tools for Teaching Character and Values

- Respect family members and neighbors even if they disagree with their opinions
- Sort through cultural, neighborhood, and family values and beliefs to extract universal principles
- Earn the money they spend and only spend what they earn
- Take charge of their own learning and growth and commit themselves to excellence

OPPORTUNITIES TO PRACTICE INTEGRITY

AGES 4-8

- Read/listen to the story *Goldilocks and the Three Bears* by Jan Brett. Draw a picture of each problem that Goldilocks created at the bears' house. Evaluate each action and decide if Goldilocks used, or did not use, the LIFESKILL of Integrity. Explain your choices to Grandpa/Grandma.

- Listen to the fable of *The Boy Who Cried "Wolf!"* by Tony Ross. Explain whether or not you feel this boy's actions show that he knows the meaning of the LIFESKILL of Integrity. List three or more positive ways the boy could get attention from the villagers.

- Learn to play three or more board games (e.g., checkers, Candyland, Monopoly, Life, Scrabble) that require the player to be a person of integrity. Play each game two or more times with different family members. Share how you feel when someone cheats when playing a game; also share how you think others feel when you cheat and what they think about you for doing so. Discuss why it is important to play games fairly using the LIFESKILL of Integrity.

- Memorize a song about the LIFESKILL of Integrity.* Teach it to a grandparent the next time you see them. Ask them to share stories illustrating the LIFESKILL of Integrity from the old days. Design a thank-you note for them. Include something you learned from their stories.

- Create a family pledge based on the LIFESKILLS of Integrity, Initiative, Friendship, and Caring. Use either rhyme or free verse. Make the final copy on the computer using a fancy font, color, and graphics. Teach the pledge to your family and invite them to recite it along with you. Develop a way to check on your growth in matching your behavior to the words of the pledge. Report your successes to a family member once a week for one month.

- Share with a parent the discomfort you feel when you know you've told a lie or not kept an agreement as promised. In what ways does your body tell you that you have not used the LIFESKILL of Integrity, e.g., stomach ache, blushing, ears burning, feeling tired? Ask your parent what bodily sensations he/she feels when he/she doesn't use the LIFESKILL of Integrity. Thank your body for letting you know when such lapses occur.

* See the LIFESKILLS, CD or audiocassette with song book, by Russ and Judy Eacker. Available from Books for Educators.

Chapter 16—Integrity

AGES 9-12

- Read the following situations. Discuss with a parent two different responses for each problem. One answer must reflect use of the LIFESKILL of Integrity while the other choice must show failure to use Integrity. Dramatize and videotape both responses to each situation using both choices. Share the video with your class. Ask your family and friends to vote for the choice they think is best for each problem. Invite your audience to explain why they chose the answers they did and to share other choices that would show the LIFESKILL of Integrity.

    ~ You find a $5 bill on the floor in the hallway

    ~ A friend begins to call some kids on the block "bad" names

    ~ As you walk around the candy store, you see your older sister slip a candy bar into her pocket and walk out without paying for it

    ~ A friend dares you to pull the red-handled fire alarm at school saying, "It will be funny!"

- Create a family pledge based on the following LIFESKILLS: Integrity, Cooperation, and Pride. Use rhyme or free verse for the promise. Name it "The (put your family name here) Family Pledge." Design the final copy by hand or by using computer technology. Add a family picture beneath the pledge. Practice reciting this pledge until you know it by heart. Recite it whenever your family wants to feel united.

- Sketch a LIFESKILL of Integrity flag in pencil. Use symbols and patterns that represent honor, truth, and reliability in your family. Decide on one color that characterizes your family's heritage and use it for the base layer of your flag. Complete your sketch with other complimentary colors. Experiment with different materials and choose those that will make an effective, weather-resistant banner. Complete the flag by sewing or hot-gluing the patterns to the base. Hang the flag from your front porch for special family celebrations.

- Accompany your parent to the supermarket. Bring a calculator to check on the store's accuracy in computing special, advertised sale prices. Compute the prices for any sale items your parents put in the shopping cart. Analyze the computer prices as those items pass through the checkout counter. Politely identify any prices you believe to be incorrectly entered into the store's computer and ask for a price check. Demonstrate the math on your calculator (if necessary). Write a letter to the store's manager or owner expressing your disappointment with their errors. Discuss with your parent whether you think that such discrepancies were an honest mistake or a lapse in the store's use of the LIFESKILL of Integrity.

- Discuss the video *Mathilda* with two or more friends. Contrast the behaviors of the two professionals, the principal and Ms. Honey, and determine which of them uses the LIFESKILL of Integrity more. Identify three or more examples that support your hypothesis.

- Compose a plan that will eliminate the use of put-downs within your family. Select the information, materials, songs, videos, and activities you will need to carry out your plan. Set a time for the training; assemble the group and share your ideas. Get agreement from the group about silent signals to use to remind family members if they still use put-downs after your instruction. Design a certificate of graduation to present at the final ceremony. After one week, lead a discussion at dinner time about how effective they thought your training was and how well the silent signals are working. Re-discuss parts of your presentation that were not clear and change the silent signals as needed. After another week, again lead a discussion at dinner time about eliminating put-downs.

- Judge two or more of your favorite TV programs' main characters and their use, or lack of use, of the LIFESKILL of Integrity during two consecutive shows. Construct a chart for the information you collect.

	Name of TV Program _____	
	Name of Character #1	Name of Character #2
First show: Examples of use of the LIFESKILL of Integrity—		
First show: Examples of lack of use of the LIFESKILL of Integrity—		
Second show: Examples of use of the LIFESKILL of Integrity—		
Second show: Examples of lack of use of the LIFESKILL of Integrity—		

Compare each character's behavior from one show to the next. Judge whether each character's use of the LIFESKILL of Integrity improved or got worse. Write a letter to the producer explaining your feelings about the use, or lack of use, of the LIFESKILL of Integrity on the program.

Chapter 16—Integrity

AGES 13+

- Study the problem of employee theft as reported by businesses in your community. Search through local newspapers and listen to the nightly broadcasts for examples of people ripping off the companies they work for. Interview managers for three or more local businesses (for example, supermarket, hospital, construction company, discount store, convenience market, insurance company). Collect copies of procedures, penalties, and statistics that each business uses to halt theft and prosecute thieves. Estimate how much employee theft costs each member of your community every year. Share your information and ideas with three adults at home, school, and/or interest clubs.

- Design a memorial to all of the youth in your community under the age of eighteen who have died in the past ten years as the result of drunk drivers. Include the name of each child and a small memory clip from someone who knew him/her well. Visit a MADD (Mothers Against Drunk Drivers) meeting, share your own personal views on the LIFESKILL of Integrity and underage drinking. Present your memorial to the president of MADD to be used for educational purposes.

- Know the requirements for voting in local, state, and federal elections. Explain the age requirements and your opinion of their fairness. Select one set of candidates for any election, examine their selected issues, compare their proposals, differentiate from current policies, predict which candidate will win and which will carry out his/her promises with integrity. After six months in office, assess performance versus promises; also ask a grandparent to compare this politician with a previous office holder. Then, write a letter to one of the politicians reminding him/her of the gap in promise versus performance; or, if he/she has done what was promised, thank him/her for using the LIFESKILL of Integrity. Share you letter with the grandparent who talked with you about this project.

- Research the body of fresh water nearest to your home that is a source of drinking water for your neighborhood. Contact local and state officials for information on quality monitoring procedures that determine the bacteria count and safety of this source as water for drinking. Perform some scientific experiments of your own to judge the quality/safety of the water. Also analyze any newspaper stories that relate to safe/unsafe drinking water from this source and attend town meetings and actively listen for facts that will inform you of this water's status. Become involved with a citizens' group that is monitoring any dangerous/toxic chemical levels in the water. Share with a parent the results of your investigation and what you have learned about the LIFESKILL of Integrity.

- Define the term "situational ethics." Discuss with a parent how situational ethics and peer pressure and the LIFESKILL of Integrity are similar and different. Use a Venn diagram* to organize your thoughts as you talk. [Note: There are no right-wrong answers to this question. What is important is clarifying your thinking.]

- Investigate 30 or more websites advertising their content as appropriate for children. Create a chart to assist you in collecting the following information for each site: recommended ages, topics, educational and recreational uses, advertisers, ease of use, links to other sites, and awards/ratings. Review the information and select the top ten websites. Develop your own rating system and rank these ten with #1 being the highest and #10

---

* The Venn diagram is a simple but effective tool for comparing similarities and differences between two objects. See Appendix B for an example of a Venn diagram.

being the lowest. Propose an Internet Pledge for the children in your family to follow when surfing the Web. Arrange "Your Favorites" for younger siblings and block offensive mail from their access. Review the sites periodically for re-evaluation.

- Learn to play five or more games, such as checkers, Monopoly, chess, solitaire, Scrabble, or dominoes, that require integrity by the players. Play each game at least once with family members and friends. Discuss with fellow players why the LIFESKILL of Integrity is an important aspect of each game. Do your friends agree that the LIFESKILL of Integrity is important in everyday life situations such as in playing games? Is winning more important? Do they consider integrity old-fashioned or boring?
Share with a parent your feelings about the importance of the LIFESKILL of Integrity after your discussions with friends.

- Choose a situation from the following list: Finding a lost object, being undercharged for an item at the store, witnessing a friend being put-down, witnessing a stranger being put-down, breaking a school rule, fighting on the playground, or being wrongfully accused. Enlist the support and assistance of family and friends to create a five-minute skit that demonstrates two ways to approach the problem. Have one approach show a lack of the LIFESKILL of Integrity and the other present a strong example of the LIFESKILL of Integrity. Perform the skit for your family at dinner time and then lead a discussion about using the LIFESKILL of Integrity in everyday life.

- Collect five or more newspaper articles about citizens exhibiting the LIFESKILL of Integrity. Create a mindmap of observable behaviors and characteristics. Conversely, find five or more articles about people lacking integrity. Mindmap* your findings; then, create a "Consequence Chart" for each article. Discuss this information with your family.

- Create a chart with the following title: "Ways to Gain and Lose Integrity." List five or more possibilities for gaining integrity and five or more for losing integrity in the eyes of others. Post the chart on the refrigerator door. Discuss with a family member what you have learned about the power of the LIFESKILL of Integrity as you were making the chart.

- Visit a store during a major sale. Take your calculator along and compute the sale price of ten or more items to determine if the store has priced the merchandise accurately. If the prices are correct, create an "Integrity Award" that includes the name of the store, the date you visited, the prices checked, and your signature as a satisfied consumer. If the sale prices are not accurate, write a letter to the general manager expressing your concerns about the inaccurate pricing. Suggest that the prices be corrected to earn back customer trust and respect. Mail either the award or the letter of concern to the store's general manager. Explain to your family the steps you have taken to ensure accuracy in pricing and what you have learned about the LIFESKILL of Integrity and the corporate world.

- Research shoplifting in three or more local stores. Determine how much is taken in a week, month, and year. Compute the average age of the accused shoplifters and the cost to the non-shoplifting customer. Find out what punishment is given for a shoplifting conviction. Share two ways stores are protecting themselves from this kind of theft. Role play three ways to use the LIFESKILL of Integrity to prevent a friend from shoplifting.

---

* Mindmapping is a effective way to organize a large amount of information in ways that make relationships visible, understandable, and memorable. See Appendix B.

Chapter 16—Integrity

- Research local laws about juvenile delinquent behavior. Interview two or more people who work in the juvenile justice system, including policy, court, and rehabilitation. Use the information to write a play, skit, story, or produce a short video (5-10 minutes) for an audience your age. Discuss with a family member how a juvenile could use the LIFESKILL of Integrity to avoid breaking the law by shoplifting, driving while under the influence of alcohol, or using illegal drugs.

SIGNS OF SUCCESS

Congratulations! Children are showing signs of Integrity when they

- Know the difference between right and wrong and choose to do right even if no one is watching
- Recognize when they have made an unwise choice and do all in their power to correct it
- Fulfill a promise or contract and keep their "word"
- Accept responsibility for their actions
- Tell the truth even though there may be unpleasant consequences
- Walk away from peer group pressures to do things that are wrong, unkind, and/or unjust

Keep trying! Children need more practice when they

- Lie to get out of trouble
- Keep items they have found and don't try to locate the owners; steal things
- Break a promise; say one thing but do another
- Are constantly late for work or school
- Violate school commitments
- Understand the difference between right and wrong and deliberately choose "wrong"
- Emulate sub-standard behavior from TV, movies, books, videos, and real life situations
- Believe that "If it doesn't hurt anybody, what's the harm?"
- Believe that it is all right to remove materials from their school because "teachers expect a certain amount of stuff to disappear"
- Refuse to accept responsibility for their actions; make excuses for their behavior

Character Begins at Home: Family Tools for Teaching Character and Values

Literature Link ~ Integrity

Ages 4-8

Gardener, The	Sarah Stewar (New York: Farrar, Straus & Giroux, 1997)
Passage to Freedom: The Sugihara Story (ASA)	Ken Mochizuki (New York: Lee & Low, 1997)
Reuben and the Quilt (AM)	Merle Good (Intercourse, PA: Good Books, 1999)
Sr. Anne's Hands (AFA)	Marybeth Lorbiecki (New York: Dial Books, 1998)

Ages 9-12

Cat Ate My Gymsuit, The (TE)	Paula Danziger (Chicago, IL: Econo-clad Books, 1999)
Catherine Called Birdy	Karen Cushman (London: Clarion Press, 1994)
Maniac McGee	Jerry Spinelli (New York: HarperCollins, 1992)
Wringer	Jerry Spinelli (New York: HarperTrophy, 1997)

Ages 13+

Call of the Wild	Jack London (New York: Tom Doherty, Inc., 1986)
Chocolate War, The	Robert Cormier (New York: Laureleaf Books, a division of Random House, 1991)
Finding My Voice	Marie G. Lee (Boston, MA: Houghton Mifflin and Company, 1992)
Legend of Jesse Owens, The (AFA)	Hank Nuwer (New York: Franklin Watts, Inc., 1998)

Family Resources

Meeting the Needs of Children: Creating Trust and Security	Louis Edward Raths (College Park, PA: Educator's International Press, 1999)
Punished By Rewards: The Trouble With Gold Stars, Incentive Plans, A's, Praise, and Other Bribes (B4E)	Alfie Kohn (Boston, MA: Houghton Mifflin and Company, 1993)
Raising Children With Character: Parents, Trust and the Development of Personal Integrity	Elizabeth Berger, MD (Northvale, NJ: Jason Aranson, 1999)

Multicultural books: **(AFA)**=African American, **(AM)**= Amish, **(ASA)**=Asian American, **(HA)**=Hispanic American, **(ME)**=Multi-Ethnic, **(NA)**=Native American, **(TE)**=listed in the teacher edition of this book, *Tools for Citizenship and Life: Using the ITI Lifelong Guidelines and LIFESKILLS in the Classroom,* **(BFE)**=available through Books for Educators

Organization

Chapter 17

"CLUTTER CAUSES CONFUSION."

organization *n* **1:** the act or process of organizing or being organized
2: arranging or forming into a coherent unity or functioning whole
3: arranging by systematic planning and united effort

ORGANIZATION: To plan, arrange, and implement in an orderly way, to keep things orderly and ready to use

WHAT IS ORGANIZATION?

Organization is a state of mind, an insistence that everything have a place and everything be in its place—in working order and ready to go. It's an internal standard that demands that we not leave projects unfinished or tools and leftover materials lying about.

In this busy world with its competing demands, it has become increasingly difficult to complete responsibilities, satisfied that we've done our "personal best." Many of us have good intentions but lack either the skills for the task or the short- and long-term planning methods to see a job through from its inception to completion. This inevitably leads to crisis planning, frustration, and, often, a deep sense of failure.

The organized mind looks for clear purpose. It ties vision to the task at hand and to ways to accomplish a task.

The LIFESKILL of Organization is not a stand-alone LIFESKILL. Effort is its siamese twin: One without the other leads us to a lifetime of good ideas but little action, a trail of frustration and lesser accomplishments. And, because the best laid plans of mice and men inevitably go astray, the LIFESKILL of Flexibility is essential.

When using the LIFESKILL of Organization, the LIFESKILLS of Effort and Flexibility are essential ingredients to success.

WHY PRACTICE ORGANIZATION?

Have you ever failed to even begin a project because you knew that it would take forever to gather what you needed? Have you ever blown a commitment because it took you so long to get organized you missed the deadline? Do you feel as if you're doing less than you know you're capable of because your desk is disorganized and you can't find what you need when you need it? Have you ever been passed over for a promotion even though you knew more about the business than the person who won the job? But his tidy appearance and work space made him look as if he knew much more than he did?

If you've answered yes to any of those questions, you already know why it's important to practice the LIFESKILL of Organization. Strong organizational skills are a pathway to greater productivity, effectiveness, and spontaneity. They help us release our creativity and vitality. They bring peace to our lives.

Being organized is important: It saves us time because we don't have to search for things (everything is readily at hand); it improves the quality of our work (we have the right tools, information, materials, and resources when they're needed); and it increases our motivation to move on to the next task (there aren't 10 things left over from previous tasks that must be done before we can get started on the next).

Time Is Money and Sanity

The LIFESKILL of Organization is reflected in the book title, *If You Haven't Got the Time to Do It Right, When Will You Find the Time to Do It Over?* by Jeffrey J. Mayer. It drives home the importance of staying organized so that we have time to do the job right the first time.

It appears that the Holy Grail of the 21st century will be *time*—how to find it, where to get more of it. Today, more than ever, saving time by being organized is a personal imperative. Life without time-saving organization is a nightmare. Effectiveness and efficiency depend upon it, as does our sanity.

Organization makes the difference between success and failure in our work and the difference between a life of all work with no time to play or a balanced life of work and personal time.

Improving the Quality of Our Work

Quality work is impossible without the right tools, information, and resources—all available as we need them, not in helter-skelter fashion. Whether in a blue-collar trade or in a white-collar position, our professionalism hinges on our ability to get and stay organized. No matter how gifted, how well financed, how experienced we may be, how superior our idea or approach . . .

all is for naught if we're not organized to fully do the job. According to Oprah Winfrey, "Luck is a matter of preparation meeting opportunity."

Increasing Our Motivation to Move On

In *Human Brain and Human Learning,* brain-compatible learning pioneer Leslie Hart points out that the biochemicals produced when a mental program doesn't work and must therefore be aborted make us feel upset and uncomfortable. In evolutionary terms, mental/physical programs that don't work could be threatening, even lethal.* In an unorganized environment, disruption in mental programs and plans is common and frequent. Such negative emotions make us less adventurous and more conservative in order to avoid failure and its discomfort. We're less motivated to move forward to new things and more ill at ease throughout the project.

Improving Our Ability to Think

It's a little-known fact, and quite unbelievable for some, that tidiness and simplicity in our working environment improve our ability to think. Lack of clutter, the orderly availability of tools and resources, calming colors (not more than two coordinating colors plus accent color), live plants, full-spectrum lighting, and music (soft, instrumental, 60-beats a minute) all help create an environment that enhances thinking. The research on this is clear and commanding.**

Our old pictures of the "enriched environment"—a blast of bright colors, profusion of things covering every wall and hanging from the ceiling and materials and resources from previous and future projects—are simply not supported by current brain research. Visit a five-star hotel and tune into your visceral reactions; you'll experience firsthand what brain research is telling us. Elegant simplicity appeals to the bodybrain not just the eye.

The physical, emotional, mental, and spiritual dimensions of being human are all connected; thus, attaining harmony with our physical environment contributes to greater wholeness in our lives. It is, therefore, essential that we plan our environment (along with actions and emotions) to enhance our quality of life. Our task is to create a mind- and soul-enriching environment in which to live, work, and play.

At home, we can increase the probability that our children will also become adept at organizing their own time—and lives—if we fully develop and model the LIFESKILL of Organization.

What Organization Is Not

Being organized does not mean being inflexible or uncreative nor compulsive about cleanliness and tidiness. For most things in life, knowing where you're going and how you'll get there improve the likelihood that you will reach your goals.

---

* See *Human Brain and Human Learning* by Leslie Hart. (Kent, Washington: Books for Educators, Inc., 1998), p. 160-161.

** For more information, see the ITI model text for your grade level. Each book provides both research references and practical suggestions for applying the research. The ability to get and stay organized depends heavily upon our surroundings. This is particularly true for young children who have limited control over their environment.

Being organized is not slavish adherence to tried and true processes. It's insisting that we select processes that will help us achieve our goals. It's a way to approach life and manage situations.

HOW DO YOU PRACTICE IT?

For some of us, the urge to be organized is innate, a part of our personality preferences or temperament* since birth. For others, the yen to be organized is a low priority.

For those who can depend on inner cravings to be organized and tidy, perhaps this chapter can help you further strengthen and refine your skills.

For those who feel no inner urge to be organized, reread why we should practice organization. For you (and I am among your ranks!), being organized is an intellectual choice rather than an instinct or inner urge—a decision to be made moment by moment, over and over and over again, day after day. First, choose to become organized! Then, use the following tips to help you strengthen your organization skills.

Start with Your Physical Environment

Start with mastering your physical environment. Don't just clean your house, organize it as you clean. To reduce clutter and competition for storage space, ask yourself "Does this support me now?" If you haven't used an item or worn it within the past 12 months, donate it to Goodwill or a recycling agency of your choice. Are you a pack rat? Then limit yourself to two keepsakes per year. (Just the process of determining value among your treasures will enrich your memory bank as well as help cut down on clutter.) Are the tools/materials you use most frequently readily at hand? Are those for emergencies kept handy where you and others in your household can readily find them? If not, put labels on the shelves where things go and create an inventory list showing location of items. If you clear out and reorganize all in the same day, your labeling will fit the amount of stuff you have in each category. Then, stick with it and follow the labels. Remember the old adage, "A place for everything and everything in its place."

Children kindergarten age and up can join in the labeling process. With non-readers, use symbols. Teaching children how to organize—and stay organized—prevents a lifetime of friction over messy rooms, half-completed jobs, and endless nagging over any number of issues.

Learning at an early age to be organized is a gift.** Everyone would like the opportunity to live in a five-star hotel environment. That's what your home can be!

---

* For a fascinating and highly useable description of temperament/personality preferences, see Chapter 7 in *Making Bodybrain-Compatible Education a Reality: Coaching for the ITI Model* by Karen Olsen (Kent, Washington: Books for Educators, 1999) or go to the source: *Please Understand Me II: Temperament, Character, Intelligence* by David Keirsey (Del Mar, California: Prometheus Nemesis Book Company, 1998.)

** Maria Montessori intuitively understood the power of organization and its link to development of the brain almost 100 years ago. Her emphasis on organization, on things having a beginning, middle, and end, and on working at a task at increasing levels of difficulty is seamlessly interwoven into her program. This is one of the reasons her preschool program is so powerful and so popular throughout the world.

Daily Living Is A Management Tool

Why is starting with the physical environment so important? Because, as every architect knows, form dictates function in obvious and subtle ways. The best way to practice the LIFESKILL of Organization is to design and use your environment as an effective management tool—a tool to keep yourself organized. Our best advice is to create an environment that helps shape your behavior, one that helps you get—and keep—organized every minute of the day . . . at home and at work.

Doesn't this make common sense? Yes. Remember, being organized isn't just another task, another thing to do. It is *the* most important thing to do! It shapes the moment and the day, your mood and your effectiveness. It saves time that we can spend on things other than work—family time, hobbies, recreation, time to grow, and so forth. Looked at from this perspective, organizing becomes an intriguing, worthwhile challenge.

Find A Mentor

For many of us, identifying what should be better organized and how to do it is easy. For others, it is more difficult. We might know what's "wrong" but, no matter how hard we have tried, we can't seem to *fix* it! Even harder is keeping the fix going! But you know what? Every family and/or neighborhood has at least one ready-made, super-duper, handy-dandy, natural-born organizer who is willing to share secrets for getting and staying organized—those little tips that allow one to meet deadlines, find any paper within one minute, and rid a room or entire house of used "stuff" that is no longer being used.

Remember, many small successes lead to major accomplishments. We must learn to walk before we can run.

For those of us who aren't organizers by nature, how do we proceed? To begin, ask your organization mentor to "do" your house with you. As you move to each area, have your mentor help you look at the "whole picture," then break it down into smaller, more manageable pieces. Ask for tips on how he/she organizes similar areas. For instance, consider dividing the search for organization into three main topics: personal time management starting with personal items (such as our own laundry, toiletries, hobbies, personal spaces), our work space (desk/office organization and kitchen, laundry room, and family areas such as living room, dining room, and bathrooms), and room organization. For each topic—personal items, our work space, and room organization—identify the patterns that create confusion, disarray, and clutter. Then identify orderly management procedures that will increase productivity—for us and for our family. Take it step by incremental step. Disorganization didn't appear over night nor will spiffiness occur with the snap of our fingers.

Stepping Out on Our Own

Getting organized is one thing, staying organized is another. When our mentor goes home and we've enjoyed a blissful week of being organized, we must learn to mentor ourselves. Practice asking yourself the following questions and then act on your answers:

- Does this item support me now? If not, how do I make myself throw it out or recycle it?

- What are the most common activities that occur here? What common procedures, tools, and resources should be readily available here? How can I create a place for everything and have everything in its place?

- What is the most appropriate organizational system for filing and keeping track of important items/information of this kind? What activities take place in this area and what is needed for them?

- How do I keep my organizational processes alive and well? How much time do I need and how often—daily, twice a day, weekly? How often should I check that the organizational system is working and up to date?

Time Management Strategies

Handling the same piece of paper twice is a time management no-no. And yet, on a once clear desk and work space, papers never seem to go anywhere; even worse, they seem to multiply overnight like rabbits.

To get things moving, we must be decisive, acting quickly on questions such as those above. Don't waffle. Decide within 30 seconds of asking yourself the question, and act on it immediately. Don't allow yourself to even entertain the "later" word. Later never comes and paper never goes.

To practice time management strategies, consider forming a Time Wasters Anonymous Club in the neighborhood. Find friends who want to raise their personal skills in this area. Meet daily at first to share successes and support. Half the battle is remaining conscious of the intention to use time well. Then, follow the time management tips below in a small area of your life, such as handling homework, team planning work, house cleaning, responsibilities for the children, or nurturing your relationship with loved ones.

Once you have mastered one area, expand to a second, still rather small area. With each success, take on another part of your life while simultaneously keeping the earlier plates spinning. Stop expanding when your successes stop. Then, re-examine the areas you've chosen; we weren't all born to be master jugglers. Ask yourself if the areas you are working on are the most important; if not, refocus your energies.

Recommendations for improving time management:

1. Set priorities, with the most important tasks first and the least important last

2. Break the tasks into smaller pieces if necessary

3. Make a list with important "To Dos" on the top

4. Limit the list to tasks you can complete in the time you have allotted

5. Take one task at a time and follow it through to completion

6. Cross out each task on the list as it is completed

7. At the end of each day, ask yourself what you have learned about "doing" organization. Is it becoming more automatic? Are you developing a habit of mind for it?

WHAT DOES ORGANIZATION LOOK LIKE IN THE REAL WORLD?

- Productivity is high, quality of product/service is high
- Transportation systems operate according to schedule
- Governments don't run out of money; they set aside reserves for emergencies
- Bar codes provide a universal system for coding pricing and other information
- The staff at the doctor's office can find our medical records when we arrive; no mistakes are made in hospitals, thus saving the lives of more than 100,000 people annually
- Businesses track their finances in relation to profit/loss on a daily basis
- Bank records accurately reflect the activity of our accounts
- Jobs get completed on time and at a high level of quality because the needed materials and tools were readily accessible
- The Little League sign-up representative notes the check number, date, and amount of our payment and provides a receipt
- We're prepared for local emergencies
- We arrange flowers in the garden by color, size, and bloom period

WHAT DOES ORGANIZATION LOOK LIKE AT HOME?

Adults

- Don't procrastinate; meet deadlines
- Maintain a clutter-free home environment that is welcoming and supportive of family life
- Keep personal space organized (e.g. purse, wallet, desk, car, garage)
- Can immediately locate any important document with ease
- Keep track of the schedules of family members; remember special days such as birthdays, anniversaries, and so forth
- Carefully monitor and document monthly bills, accounts, payments, and bank records; safeguard important documents (e.g., marriage license, birth certificates, passports, deeds, wills, Power of Attorney, health proxy forms)
- Provide clear, concise directions for babysitters and service and repair persons
- Place trash and recycling out for pick-up on assigned days

- Maintain family automobiles in ready-to-go condition at all times
- Complete projects in a timely fashion
- Locate tools, materials, and resources with ease
- Can respond quickly and easily to requests for assistance
- Wash, dry, and put away clothes and dishes in a timely fashion

Children

- Identify and keep track of their own clothing, materials, and toys; each item has a place and is returned immediately to that place after use
- Maintain a clutter-free room; group books/toys by self-developed system
- Maintain a clutter-free mind; able to go about problem solving or producing a project in a systematic, orderly way
- Maintain clutter-free workspaces; clean up after themselves
- Easily locate and gather materials that are necessary for projects
- Pack their school book bag every evening for hassle-free departure to school in the morning
- Show up for special activities according to schedule
- Keep outdoor equipment in secure area
- Save a percentage of allowance or earnings for short- and long-term goals
- Perform chores with minimum request for help for where things are and/or the procedures for getting the job done well the first time
- Bring notes/newsletters/report cards home on the day they are received; take back responses the next day
- Turn in homework, class work, tests, and projects on or before the due date
- Have a system for reminding themselves to take gym clothes, art smocks, and musical instruments to school on scheduled days

Chapter 17—Organization

OPPORTUNITIES TO PRACTICE ORGANIZATION

AGES 4-8

- With a friend(s) dramatize a story (such as *The Seven Chinese Brothers*) that teaches a lesson about the LIFESKILL of Organization. Present it for your family. Ask them to explain any lessons they learned from the skit. Ask them to share their answers with you and your fellow actors and evaluate how well they understood the skit's message.

- Write new lyrics to the tune of "Twinkle, Twinkle, Little Star" (or a song of your choice) that compare a day in the life of an unorganized person versus an organized person. Write three or more verses and include at least one strategy that will help other family members become more organized. Add movements and motions to enhance the message of your lyrics. Teach the song to your family and friends.

- Analyze your Halloween candy and divide it up into three or more categories. Separate each category, count the pieces, and place them in a plastic zip-lock bag; label the bag with the category name and number of pieces inside. Calculate how many pieces of candy there are altogether. Determine how many days your candy will last if you eat one piece a day. Two pieces a day? Three pieces a day? Share your "candy eating plan" with your dentist or whoever pays the dental bills in your family. Select which toothpaste and toothbrush will best clean your teeth after you have eaten your daily treat.

- Create a diagram that shows how all of your personal items in your room, such as toys, clothes, and so forth, should be placed in order to keep it neat and orderly. Label all of the items on the picture. Ask a family member to help you implement your plan. Practice placing frequently used items in their places until you know how to do it by heart. Ask that same family member to come to your room every day for two weeks to see if things are put away according to your diagram. At the end of two weeks, share with your family what you have learned about the LIFESKILL of Organization.

- Brainstorm the steps you should follow at the end of each day in order to leave your room organized and neat. Write the procedures in a positive way. Add visuals to help jog your memory. Post the "End of the Day" procedures in a prominent place. Review them with a family member as needed.

Ask a parent to help you think through procedures you need to follow at night so that your clothing will be organized for the next morning. Discuss ways to determine the weather forecast (sun, clouds, snow, rain, wind), temperature (hot, warm, cool, cold), the nature of the upcoming activities (indoor, outdoor, formal, informal, special, school, no school, church), schedule (play activities first or after another activity), and appropriate accessories (watch, jewelry, hats). Describe the 4-5 steps you should follow every night to get your outfit(s) ready for wearing when you wake up. Write/draw "Choosing Clothes Procedures" with those steps that will help you organize what to wear the next day. After three weeks, compare using these procedures to not using them and explain which way you prefer and why.

- Interview each family member as to which pattern he/she uses to join two socks and keep them together as a pair after laundering. Identify two or more distinct ways. Conclude if either one will work for you by trying both ways a few times each. Make up a method of your own if neither of these help you. Volunteer to fold the family socks for one month. Predict the number of socks that will not have a mate at the end of the month. Write a short story about "The Land of Lost Socks" and read it to your family at dinner time.

- Collect any of the following items: rocks, seashells, bird feathers, leaves, baseball or Pokeman cards, Beanie Babies, models, or something of your own selection. Decide on a system to group your collection in some special way: color, size, shape, location associated with the item, or another way you think will be helpful. Place each item in its own group. Examine your groupings to see if you want to make any changes. Create a sign for each group and a small name label for each item in the collection. Exhibit your collection at the next special family get-together and listen for any comments family members have to offer about your use of the LIFESKILL of Organization.

- Categorize your collection of books and stories. Identify two or more categories (e.g., fiction, non-fiction; large, medium, or small; re-read a lot, re-read sometimes, never re-read) that will help to sort your books. Borrow some colored tape, one color for each category. Begin with one color tape and decide which category it will represent. Cut a one-inch piece and wrap it around the spine about one inch up from the bottom of the books in that category.
Choose a second colored tape and repeat the pattern for all of the books in the second group. Organize all the books in remaining categories in the same way. Place the books back on the shelves or in baskets according to their tape color. After one month judge how this system of organizing your books is working for you.

- Ask to be the person in charge of recycling for your family. Ask a parent to teach you the official categories and symbols for your community's recyclable items (e.g., cardboard, paper, plastic, metal, glass, and other recyclable containers). Identify those categories that can share a container. Check the recycling bins daily. Flatten plastic and milk cartons to provide more room. Help put the bins by the curb for the recycle pick-up. Determine if your efforts are helping your family and the environment by recording the amount your family recycles for one month. Share with a parent what you are learning about the LIFESKILL of Organization by handling the family's recycling.

- Plan a meal for your family. Include salad, main course with two vegetables, bread, dessert, and beverage. List all the items you would need to buy to create this meal. Using weekly newspaper supermarket ads, compute the total cost. Then compute the cost per person. Offer to prepare this special treat for your family.

- Keep a homework notebook or calendar. Write down all of your assignments. Note the date when each was assigned and when it is due. Use two different colors if that will help. Also list any materials, notes, or permission slips you should bring to school. Share this organizer with your family at least once a week.

AGES 9-12

- Learn how to create a mindmap* of important information by using webs, graphics, and various colored markers or pens. To practice, create a mindmap of your life. Make a circle in the middle of the page and smaller circles around the center circle, like the sun and its planets. Write your name in the center circle and the following in the outer circles: Family, school, friends, hobbies, sports, clubs, and pets. See a beginning mindmap below. Add lines for each pet describing their personality, value to the family, and what you most enjoy about them. Use pictures or symbols to make the mindmap interesting to read. Share your personal web with a family member. Ask him/her how you could have better organized the information.

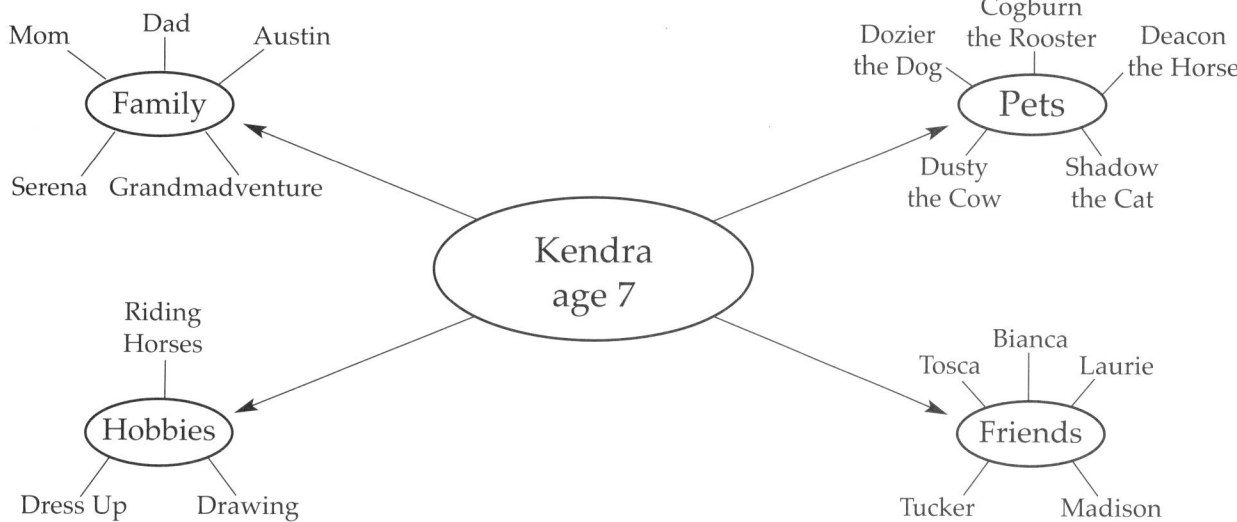

- Keep a homework notebook or calendar. Write down all of your assignments. Note the date when each was assigned, the task, and when the work is due. Use two or more colors if that will help. Also list any materials, notes, or permission slips you need to bring to school. Cross items off the list or calendar as they are completed. Share this notebook with your parents frequently (at least 2-3 times per week) and share with them the LIFESKILL of Organization challenges you face on a regular basis. Ask for any tips they might have: write them in your calendar and, the next time you chat with then about your progress, share which tips worked for you and why.

- Research the recipe of one of your favorite meals or desserts. Ask for permission to make the dish for dinner. Organize all of the materials and ingredients. Follow the steps in the recipe. While you are waiting for the treat to bake, cook, or set, wash your dishes and utensils and clean up spills on the counter and floor. Analyze how you could have been better organized and more efficient. Share your self-evaluation (rating) with a member of your family.

- Plan a meal for your family. Include salad, main course with two vegetables, bread, dessert, and a choice of beverages. List all the items you will need to create this meal. Using weekly newspaper supermarket ads, compute the total cost of ingredients. Then,

---

* For an easy-to-use guide to mindmapping, see *Mapping Inner Space: Learning and Teaching Mind Mapping* by Nancy Margulies (Tucson, AZ: Zephyr Press, 1991).

compute the cost per person. Also plan the presentation of the meal, for example, design a menu, fold the napkins into fancy shapes, prepare and serve the dishes. Provide a survey for each person to complete regarding the tastiness of the dessert and the timing and graciousness of the service. Review these and reflect on what changes you will make next time. Ask the adult who does most of the cooking for your family for any tips to improve your LIFESKILL of Organization.

- Using a calendar program on your computer, create a separate monthly calendar for each member of your family. Check with each person to determine the accuracy of the information for his/her calendar. Compile the information from each calendar to make one "master calendar." On this calendar, choose a different color ink for each family member's activities to make the schedule "user friendly." Give each family member a copy of his/her personal calendar and post the master calendar on the refrigerator door. Maintain these calendars for three months. One night a week at dinner time, lead a discussion about what everyone is learning about the LIFESKILL of Organization by using these individual and family calendars.

- Organize and create posters for the 18 LIFESKILLS and their definitions. Using 12"x18" white construction/drawing paper, design a set of LIFESKILL Posters, one LIFESKILL per sheet. Organize the poster pattern. Print the LIFESKILL name in three-inch capital letters across the top of the sheet. Add the definition at the bottom of the page. Illustrate each LIFESKILL with a meaningful drawing in the center. Sign your name as artist in the lower right-hand corner of each one. Ask a parent to select one LIFESKILL each week (or two) for your family to practice. Hang the poster for the week where everyone can see it.

- Volunteer to organize the family grocery lists for the next month. Draw a circle about the size of a half dollar in the center of a sheet of paper (8.5"x11.5"). Print the words SHOPPING LIST inside the circle. Draw five straight lines (like spokes on a wheel) going away from the center circle. Draw graphics, one at the end of each spoke near the edge of the page, that represent the following categories: protein (meat/dairy/eggs), fruit/veggies, bread/cereal, snacks, cleaning/household items. Draw several straight lines branching out from each spoke (category). Write an item that your family needs from the store in that category on the branch; each item should have its own branch on that spoke (e.g., hot dogs, eggs, milk for protein). Write branches and shopping items for each of the remaining categories. Cross items off the list as you find them in the store and place them in the shopping cart. Analyze at least two other ways to organize a shopping list and share them with an aunt. Ask a parent if this organizational approach is reducing or eliminating the number of weekly trips to the grocery store. Calculate the gas money the family is saving.

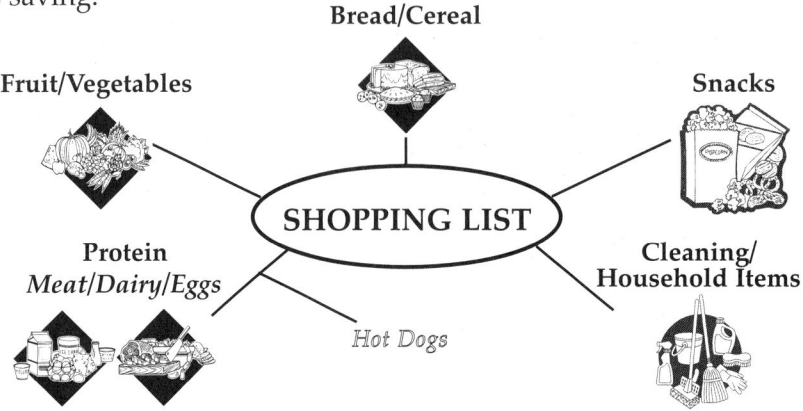

- For insurance purposes, inventory each of the following items in your house: appliances (e.g., washer, dryer, microwave, dishwasher), every machine (e.g., sewing, snow-blower, bikes, lawn mower, power tools, vacuum), and all audio-visual/electronic equipment (e.g., TVs, DVDs, radios, computers, printers, scanners, camcorders, digital and analog cameras). Indicate for each item the brand name, store/date of purchase, original cost, model and serial numbers, age of the item, and apparent condition. Photograph each one and place these photos with the inventory in a safe deposit box in case of an insurance emergency. Update your file at least twice a year. With a parent, discuss what you have learned about the family's use of the LIFESKILL of Organization and make any recommendations that you feel would improve it.

AGES 13+

- Investigate the field of time management. Interview a time management specialist and/or three mothers in the neighborhood who are well known for their organizational abilities. Ask each interviewee to share five or more household organizational strategies that he/she finds particularly valuable. Create a poster as a visual reminder of these strategies. Place it in a prime location in the house so that others can easily refer to it as needed.

- Interview an adult in your family about how they plan their daily schedule. Identify four or more strategies he/she uses to coordinate the day's events so they flow from one to the next. List these strategies in your homework notebook for future reference.

- Buy or make a pocket organizer that includes monthly and weekly calendars, goal-setting, scheduling, to-do lists, and contact information (phone numbers and addresses of extended family and friends). To begin, include all family events and important school events such as homecoming games, class/individual picture taking, and long-term school/homework assignments. Meet with a parent weekly to discuss how you are using your calendar. Ask for any tips he/she might have and incorporate them in what you are doing. Implement any suggestion for at least two weeks before you judge whether it works for you. Share what you are learning about the LIFESKILL of Organization.

- Learn how to create a Venn diagram, a graphic organizer that compares and contrasts information about two topics. With a family member practice making two circles with an overlapping space in the center. Put your name above one circle and a friend's name above the other circle. List attributes that the two of you share in the central overlap area (for example, we both like dogs and cats). In the part of the circle under each name, identify the ways in which you are different (for example, Tommy likes to play soccer versus I like to swim). Pick two other topics to diagram. Share your Venn diagrams with other family members. Identify two advantages of this kind of diagram for helping you organize information. Explain to a parent how you could use it for studying for school.

- Organize your finances by developing a spending and savings plan based on your weekly allowance.
    ~ Identify a long-term spending goal, analyze how much money you will place into saving toward that goal, and how many weeks it will take you to reach that amount
    ~ Research whether to keep this money in a piggybank at home or put it into a bank; explain your choice and reasons for that choice to a parent
    ~ Determine how much money will be available for daily spending
    ~ Create a WARNING LIST (items and services to avoid) if you want to change spending patterns; place it in the bill compartment of your wallet

    At the end of each week, revisit your budget and see how well you are following it. Ask a parent or other adult for any tips he/she might have to help you stay within this budget. After a month, determine if any changes to the budget are needed. Discuss the need for these changes with a parent. Ask yourself if some spur-of-the-moment expenditures are the result of poor planning and organization, e.g., forgetting to pack a lunch for a weekend hike, failing to carry a snack(s) with you when you leave the house and then buying them at a convenience store, leaving a needed item at home, and so forth. If so, plan ways to improve your LIFESKILL of Organization. After another month, reassess your ability to live within your budget. Share with your family at dinner time what you are learning about the LIFESKILL of Organization.

- Prepare a survival kit for the family car. Determine which 10-15 items would best help your family in time of accident, car break-down, or bad weather. Consider some of the following items: rescue blanket, 50 ft. of nylon cord, hard candy, chocolate, beef jerky, matches, steel wool, candle, fire starters, small glass mirror, pen light/spare batteries, small pocketknife, plastic water bottle, water purification tablets, and a clear plastic sheet. Predict how each item on the list could be used in an emergency. Place your final choices in a plastic container (e.g., Rubbermaid), tape it shut, write the date on it, and open it only to replace perishable items or for a real emergency. Pack it in a safe, out-of-the-way space in the car. Assemble additional kits if your family owns more than one vehicle. Collect newspaper articles about people surviving after being stranded; consider adding any items the survivors found to be indispensible.

- Plan a family weekend vacation to a destination at least 300 miles from your home. Determine an itinerary for the group including the route to be followed there and back, plus the cost of travel. Highlight the route on a map for the family driver(s). Request brochures from the tourist bureau or Chamber of Commerce. Select four sights that your family must visit during the weekend. Include one of each of the following: historical landmark, body of water, animal preserve or zoo, and a county, state, or National Park. After the trip, create a memory scrapbook of the weekend by organizing trip photographs into a scrap book.

- Assemble a kit for newcomers to the neighborhood. Brainstorm important categories of information such as: shopping sources, medical facilities (e.g., hospitals, HMO, Medical complexes), professional services (e.g., doctor, dentist, lawyer), houses of worship (e.g., church, temple, synagogue), financial institutions, automotive repairs and gas, and recreational facilities. Create a binder with categories in alphabetical order. Insert names of local stores, business, and services where they belong. Present this information to any new family. After two weeks, ask one of the newcomers for feedback on the usefulness and organization of the binder you gave them.

- Build your own website. Before you begin, use the LIFESKILL of Organization to identify and list each step to be undertaken and the materials (software, connections) and knowledge that you need for each. Consider these design strategies as starters:
    - ~ Choose a web editor
    - ~ Plan the site
    - ~ Organize the content
    - ~ Design the layout (template vs. free-form)
    - ~ Insert information
    - ~ Add special effects (e.g., color, pictures, sounds, links to other sites)
    - ~ Provide an opportunity for feedback
    - ~ Insert a visitor counter
    - ~ Include a guest book
    - ~ Return e-mail

    Maintain this website for six months and update the content as necessary.

- Organize the neighborhood's first annual spring clean up day; coordinate it with Earth Day in April. Arrange for an extra trash and recycle pick-up if possible but emphasize recycling by scheduling clean up the first day and holding a consolidated garage sale the next day (you, and volunteers you recruit, will man the garage sale and return the proceeds to the person who donated each item for sale).

    Create a neighborhood flyer including the following information: date, times, location, materials to bring, goal (clean, neat yards, sidewalks and roadways), how to place items in the garage sale, and details of the group celebration held the afternoon of the cleaning day (bring a pot luck dish to share, place servings for yourself, and beverages for yourself). Deposit the flyers under people's doors or into their hands. Prepare yourself to answer any questions or concerns.

    Record this great event on film and submit it to your local community newspaper along with a request to print a personal thank you (as organizer of the event) to all of the participants. After the event, lead a discussion at dinner time about what all of you have learned about the LIFESKILL of Organization through this event.

SIGNS OF SUCCESS

Congratulations! Children are showing signs of Organization when they

- Locate any article of clothing or other personal belonging within a minute or two
- Complete daily/weekly chores on time
- Have a clean (no old food, dirty plates, beverages, or clothes waiting to be washed) and neat (a place for everything and everything in its place) room or personal space within a shared room

- Rearrange closet space for optimum efficiency
- Bring home personal papers and notices from school and do what's required of each immediately
- Return library books and other borrowed or rented materials on time
- Manage a project from beginning to end with minimum support from others
- Plan ahead, think in a methodical, organized way

Keep trying! Children need more practice when they

- Discover Halloween cupcakes under their bed on Valentine's Day
- Stash old beverage cups, snack wrappers, and food remains (save these for science fair projects!) around their rooms
- Avoid using the closet because everything falls out when the door is opened
- Find mittens in their book bags in June
- Are consistently late for meetings or practices because . . . (you fill in the blank)
- Can't find items they are sure they "put somewhere"
- Miss P.E. class more than twice a semester cause they forget or couldn't find the required outfit
- Receive so many overdue notices from the library that the fine is larger than their allowance or your paycheck!
- Ask you to sign a permission slip for a class trip that took place a month ago
- Never have the materials they need for school or to do chores

LITERATURE LINK ~ ORGANIZATION

AGES 4-8

Franklin Is Messy	Paulette Bourgeois (New York: Scholastic Trade Books, 1995)
From Father to Son (HA)	Patricia Almada (Crystal Liake, IL: Rigby Press, 1997)
I Lost My Bear	Jules Feiffer (New York: William Morrow & Co, 1998)
Mitten, The	Jan Brett (New York: Putnam Books, 1989)

AGES 9-12

Angela Weaves a Dream (HA)	Michele Sola (New York: Hyperion, 1997)
Aunt Harriet's Underground Railway in the Sky (AFA)	Faith Ringgold New York: Crown Publications, 1992)
Be A Perfect Person in Just Three Days (TE)	Stephen Manes (New York: Clarion Press, 1982)
Mayeros: A Yucatec Maya Family (HA)	George Ancona (New York: Wm. Morrow & Co, 1997)

AGES 13+

Absolutely Normal Chaos	Sharon Creech (New York: HarperCollins Juvenile Books, 1997)
Black Hands, White Sails (AFA)	Patricia McKissak and Frederick L. McKissak (New York: Scholastic, 1999)
Buried Onions (HA)	Gary Soto (New York: Harcourt Brace, 1997)

Multicultural books: **(AFA)**=African American, **(ASA)**=Asian American, **(HA)**=Hispanic American, **(ME)**=Multi-Ethnic, **(NA)**=Native American, **(TE)**=listed in the teacher edition of this book, *Tools for Citizenship and Life: Using the ITI Lifelong Guidelines and LIFESKILLS in the Classroom*, **(BFE)**=available through Books for Educators

Family Resources

Don't Sweat the Small Stuff With Your Family: Simple Ways to Keep Daily Responsibilities and Household Chaos from Taking Over Your Life Richard Carlson (Boston, MA: Hyperion Press, 1998)

Family Manager, The Kathy Peel (New York: Word Books, Random House, 1996)

Pick Up Your Socks . . . and Other Skills Growing Children Need: A Practical Guide to Raising Responsible Children Elizabeth Crary (Seattle, WA: Parenting Press, Inc., 1990)

The Only Being There Guide Students Ever Need: Connect Learning, Trips, Kids at School   (B4E) Kari Simmons Kling (Kent, WA: Books for Educators, 1999)

Chapter 18

Patience

"PATIENCE SMOOTHES THE ROAD OF LIFE."

patience *n* **1**: the capacity, habit, or fact of being patient
patient *adj* **1**: bearing pains or trials calmly or without complaint
2: manifesting forbearance under provocation or strain **3**: not hasty or impetuous
4: steadfast despite opposition, difficulty, or adversity

PATIENCE: To wait calmly for someone or something

WHAT IS PATIENCE?

With technology, transportation systems, fast-food restaurants, and life moving along at an ever-increasing rate, we feel as though we are not accomplishing much *unless* we also move at an increasingly fast pace. This interest and fascination with going faster and faster does not bode well for the LIFESKILL of Patience which requires calmness, tranquillity, and tolerance. With adrenaline swirling throughout our bodies, patience often seems a distant goal.*

Patience involves learning to wait . . . and wait . . . and wait . . . and wait . . . until it is our turn to pay at the checkout counter, order ice cream, explain our version of the story, listen to ideas before sharing our own, persevere to learn a skill, or allow the emerging butterfly to dry out its wings on its own time schedule. It means waiting in a quiet and calm manner, not with our eyes rolling, arms folded, and foot tapping. Patience requires us to appreciate that things done well take time, that expertise doesn't come overnight, that much of our sense of satisfaction about something is because we earned it, through patience and persistence, over time.

Patience requires that we give up wanting to control everything and be willing to wait until something runs its course or someone completes what they're doing before they join us. Patience is being able to enjoy the spring without yearning to rush to the swimming pool for summer.

Patience is a vital component of eight other LIFESKILLS: Curiosity, Effort, Flexibility, Friendship, Organization, Perseverance, Problem Solving, and Resourcefulness.

---

* For a disturbing discussion of the long-term impact of a hurried existence, especially about how constant exposure to TV and video games increases impulsivity and sensory overload, see *Ritalin Nation* by Richard DeGrandpre (New York: W. W. Norton & Co., 1999), pp. 19-23.

WHY PRACTICE PATIENCE?

Can you imagine life and everyday occasions if no one used the LIFESKILL of Patience? The noise level would surely increase as people demanded what they wanted when they wanted it and how they wanted it. Traffic lights and other instructions would be ignored. Road rage would be the norm, not the exception. Tagamet, Zantac 75, and other indigestion soothers would be the "candy" of choice at every party and business meeting. Examples of frustration gone awry would be everywhere. Not a pretty prospect.

Why practice the LIFESKILL of Patience? There are many reasons—personal and societal.

Personal Benefits from Practicing Patience

Because the people who will benefit the most from our patience often are those who admonish us to use the LIFESKILL of Patience, we sometimes disregard their advice. After all, our being patient benefits them . . . what's in it for us? It's important that all of us, and especially children, understand that the primary beneficiaries of patience are they themselves. Here's why.

Patience Is a Lifesaver. Patience—truly felt inside, not just restraining the body language that would reveal we are about to blow our top—is our best defense against most stress-related illnesses and premature aging. Overdoses of adrenaline, harmful cortisols, high blood pressure, and most heart disease are significantly reduced when we respond to circumstances with the LIFESKILL of Patience instead of frustration. As we are often admonished, we cannot control events but we can control our response to them.

Patience also saves energy. Anger and frustration eat us up inside. Just mellow out!

Patience Creates More Minutes in the Day. More minutes in the day! Now there's a thought-provoking idea! Falling into frustration or losing our temper is time wasted. Remaining calm and thoughtful gives us more minutes in the day to use as **we** choose. Patience gives us adequate time to think about situations, ideas, and responses in an analytical way which in turn improves our decision making.

Being Patient Improves Learning and Performance. As we know from brain research, when emotional override occurs,* thinking is significantly impaired and learning and performance levels nosedive. If we want to be at our best, now and in the future, mastering the LIFESKILL of Patience is a necessity for us as well as a benefit for those around us.

---

* For a discussion of the powerful effect of emotion on learning and performance, see *ITI: The Model* by Susan Kovalik, Chapter 2 (Kent, WA: Susan Kovalik & Associates, 1997). Available through Books for Educators (see back of book).

Societal Benefits from Patience

Life would be very different if the LIFESKILL of Patience were practiced in our homes, on our streets, and in our governmental agencies. The benefits of patience to society are numerous. They include issues of safety, higher academic achievement, stronger families, and active citizenship.

Physical and Psychological Safety. The LIFESKILL of Patience on our roadways would significantly reduce auto accidents. Patience about becoming rich would significantly reduce crime—on the streets and within the white-collar variety such as the Savings and Loan scandal of the 1980s and inside trading in the 1990s. Patience on Capitol Hill to work on solutions that benefit the greatest number of people would significantly reduce "pork barrel" spending. Patience in stock market investing would make the system seem more secure and less risky. Patience on the street would translate into less racial, ethnic, religious, and class tensions.

Higher Academic Achievement Levels. Imagine the effect of greater use of the LIFESKILL of Patience in schools—better planning and instruction by teachers and better, more thorough learning by students. We believe our embarrassingly low literacy rates would rise significantly and our appalling drop-out statistics would decrease dramatically.

Stronger Families. The LIFESKILL of Patience in the home—spouse to spouse, parent to child, sibling to sibling—would strengthen family bonds. Less frustration, less child and spousal abuse. Less tension and better communication, less drug and alcohol abuse. The more patience with differences and misunderstandings, the lower the divorce rate. Does this sound like pie in the sky? We don't think so. Over and again we hear parents complaining about not having enough time, of feeling harried and rushed and the poor decision making and temper flare-ups that result.

Being Patient Increases Likelihood of Change Occurring. Are there some things that need to change in your home? Are there habits of mind of some family members that make things unpleasant or difficult for others? If so, two important ingredients for making change happen are trust in leadership and overcoming resistance to change. According to J. Edwin Dietal,* patience is key to both. "Being patient is a major element in earning trust." Dietal goes on to say that "Most people resist change. A combination of patience and persistence is needed for change to occur—patience enough for the change to occur and persistence enough so that the status quo does not overwhelm and kill the proposed change."

Citizenship Would Come Alive. If citizens were willing to work at the process of guiding their government instead of impatiently throwing up their hands and saying they're powerless to change things, we would have much more accountability from politicians and better solutions for our pressing problems.

---

* "Exceptional Leadership: Leading Through Patience and Persistence" by J. Edwin Dietal. Practice Development Website. http://www.abenet.org/lpm/newsletters/skills/w98Dietel.html

HOW DO YOU PRACTICE IT?

If the LIFESKILL of Patience is to become a habit, it must first be consistently modeled for children. As parents and our children's first teachers, we must give our children every opportunity to experience situations, both at home and out in the real world, that require patience, forbearance, and moral stamina.

Modeling Patience

As parents, we know that "Do as I do" is much more powerful than "Do as I say." Thus, we have no choice but to model a high degree of patience. This is especially important, and not easy, when dealing with children who may not have acquired the skill of waiting in a quiet, calm manner before they come to us. The LIFESKILL of Patience is learned slowly, through a variety of experiences, over an extended period of time, and absorbed primarily in an atmosphere where it is consistently modeled.

Patience Develops Gradually

Patience takes time. Period. It is a LIFESKILL that exists only when internalized. Externally, it can be coached but not coerced.

Parents Start the Process. Parents start the process by gradually extending the amount of time before they respond to their child's request for their attention. For example, the parents first finish their sentence in a conversation with someone on the phone before responding to the child, then later complete their paragraph, then finally their entire conversation. Parents encourage patience in the form of manners: "Wait your turn for the slide, swing, toy, etc." When toddlers visit the store or the doctor's office, parents teach them that they must wait their turn to pay or before entering the examining room.

Very young children may have all the patience in the world for a favorite toy but may erupt into a temper tantrum when a snack or mother's attention is not immediately forthcoming. Gradually, as a conceptual idea of time emerges, it becomes easier to wait; children learn to endure and to understand that delay doesn't necessarily mean denial. As they develop confidence in the procedures for waiting, they learn to trust that what they need or want will, in the end, be responded to.

In the Classroom. In the classroom, teachers slowly extend the time students calmly wait using techniques such as wait time and having groups discuss their use of the LIFESKILL of Patience when working together. Other ways to practice patience include multi-age classrooms and buddy systems, discussing the benefits of the LIFESKILL of Patience used on a consistent basis, and, above all, modeling patience day in and day out, regardless of events of the day.

WHAT DOES PATIENCE LOOK LIKE IN THE REAL WORLD?

We

- Wait at the intersection while other drivers take their turns
- Politely repeat a question or comment for someone who did not hear it
- Understand if the doctor is called away on an emergency while we're in the office for our scheduled appointment
- Practice a meaningful skill over and over until it is mastered (bike riding, roller skating, keyboarding, painting, etc.)
- Use active listening skills while someone is talking
- Remain cheerful while standing in line at the store, bank, or supermarket
- Remain "on hold" on the telephone while listening to annoying commercials or non-descript music
- Search for employment
- Teach someone to tie shoelaces
- Learn how to use/program the VCR, computer, scanner, printer, and fax machine

WHAT DOES PATIENCE LOOK LIKE AT HOME?

Adults

- Use the Lifelong Guideline of Active Listening as our child shares daily information or explains about his/her behavior or misbehavior
- Re-teach our child as often as necessary and provide adequate practice time until he/she understands the pattern (e.g., walking, shoe tying, bike riding) and learns how to use it/do it
- Wait for someone who is late without losing our temper or grousing about it
- Stop when we see the yellow caution light instead of trying to beat the red light
- Refrain from honking in a traffic jam
- Prune and reconfigure the family budget again and again to fit the household income
- Prepare our annual tax filings
- Pay off a mortgage, car loan, or credit card bill

- Cook a "real" meal with all fresh food from scratch
- Wait our turn for a parent-teacher conference
- Sit through our child's sports practices, activities, and meetings
- Wait for our income tax refund
- Give new strategies a fair chance to work by trying them more than once

Children

- Practice a skill (e.g., crawling, standing, walking, skipping, bike riding) until they master it
- Wait politely until others have stopped talking before they speak
- Wait their turn in school, at sports practices and games, and at meetings
- Persist in waiting for their parents' attention in order to share exciting news
- Search for missing items
- Wait for answers to the many questions they ask
- Investigate the natural world of animals, insects, birds, amphibians, and reptiles
- Listen to parents'/grandparents' childhood memories and stories
- Take the necessary time to become proficient at a skill
- Teach a new skill to a younger child and guide his/her practice of it until mastered
- Stay in line at the grocery store, zoo, hot dog stand, theater, ticket line, etc.
- Wait to use toys and materials that someone else is using
- Take turns in conversations and games
- Wait for others to get organized before starting

OPPORTUNITIES TO PRACTICE PATIENCE

AGES 4-8

- Read one of the stories from the "Literature Link" list. Share with a parent five things that you think are good examples of the LIFESKILL of Patience in action. Explain two instances when the main character did not use the LIFESKILL of Patience and the consequences.

- Choose a special song (e.g., "Happy Birthday", "I Can See Clearly Now") that you can sing, both the tune and the words. Invite someone to time you singing the song out loud with a stopwatch. After you've learned the song, stretch your patience from singing one verse to singing three or more while you wait your turn. Sing the song silently whenever you are trying to be patient. Share with a parent how well you think this strategy is helping you learn and practice the LIFESKILL of Patience.

- Decide on a private signal (e.g., tug on the ear, cough, thumb and pointer finger making a circle) that a brother or sister can send you as a silent reminder to practice the LIFESKILL of Patience. When you see the signal, it is time to sing that song in your head or try a Brain Gym* exercise while you wait. Thank the family member for reminding you to use the LIFESKILL of Patience.

- Think of four quiet activities you can do in the car to entertain yourself. Two of the activities you should be able to do alone while the other two might include a second person (but not the driver!). Make a written or picture list of materials you will need to bring along. Choose a plastic container that will hold your activities in an organized, easy-to-use way. Create a name label for your box. Change the activities on a monthly basis or when you discover that they are no longer challenging your brain. Request feedback from the driver on your use of the LIFESKILL of Patience while being a passenger.

- Learn Brain Gym strategies* with your family. Choose two that will help you to pass the time while you are practicing the LIFESKILL of Patience. Practice them at least ten times during the next week. Keep track of when you need to use them and think about whether or not the exercises are helping you to become more patient. Share your ideas with a parent or grandparent.

- Develop a savings plan so you can purchase a special item such as a bicycle, roller blades, or a gift. Brainstorm at least three ways to earn money. Determine a minimum amount that you will save weekly. Plan your jobs and keep a journal of the work you have done, the date completed, the amount of money earned, and the amount still needed. When you have reached your goal, share the strategies and skills you used with your family and friends and the role of the LIFESKILL of Patience.

- Plant ten or more Russian sunflower seeds in your garden by following the directions on the seed packet. Record in your journal the date that:

    ~ You plant the seeds

    ~ The seeds sprout (peeking through the soil)

    ~ The first leaves appear

    ~ Your sunflower measures 10 inches tall

    ~ You first see a flower bud

    ~ The flower blooms

    Compute how many days you practiced the LIFESKILL of Patience from the day you planted the seed until the day the flower bloomed. Continue practicing the LIFESKILL of Patience as you feed the sunflower seed to the birds by putting out only 30 sunflower seeds each day until all the seeds are eaten.

- Choose a board game or card game that you would like to learn to play. Practice the LIFESKILL of Patience while someone in your family teaches you both the rules and

---

* See *Brain Gym: Teacher's Edition Revised* by Paul and Gail Dennison (Ventura, CA: Educ-Kinesiology, Inc., 1994).

strategies. Show the LIFESKILL of Patience while you wait for your opponent to make his/her move. Play one or more games a day with this person until you feel that you are ready to play someone new. When you have won at least five games, teach the moves, strategies, and LIFESKILL of Patience to someone else.

- Bake a batch of sugar cookies with a parent's help. Arrange the cookies on some wax paper or tin foil to let them cool. Make icing for the cookies. Spread some icing on each cookie top. Decorate the iced cookies with one or more of the following items: colored sprinkles, cinnamon candies, mini-chocolate chips, raisins, chopped nuts (make sure no one in your family is allergic to any of these toppings). Use the LIFESKILLs of Patience and Caring as you decorate so that the cookies will look attractive and appetizing. Serve them for a snack or as dessert after dinner.

AGES 9-12

- Investigate the art of paper folding and cutting—Mexican, Japanese (origami), or German (Scherenschnitte). Discuss how the LIFESKILL of Patience would benefit mastering this art form. Choose books like *Pokeman Origami* by Ryoko Nishida or *50 Nifty Super Animal Origami Crafts* by Jill Smolinski that explain a variety of projects using paper, scissors, and requiring the LIFESKILL of Patience. Choose a beginner's project, read the directions, follow the steps, and compare your completed project with the one pictured in the book. Explain your strategies and techniques to a family member. Learn another project with him/her. Exhibit your products in the family room or dining room (centerpiece for dinner). Then use them to decorate gifts for a special occasion such as a birthday, anniversary, or Mother's/Father's Day.

- Write a poem, story, or book review or create a piece of art. Produce a piece of work with depth and a sense of reality, whether it's about imaginary situations or real ones. Submit your work to: *Stone Soup: The Magazine By Young Writers and Artists*, Children's Art Foundation, P.O. Box 83, Santa Cruz, CA 95063, e-mail: editor@stonesoup.com, Internet: http://www.stonesoup.com/, 1-800-447-4569

  Practice the LIFESKILL of Patience while you wait to receive a reply about the piece you submitted.

- Practice one of the versions of the card game called Solitaire (in Great Britain it is called Patience). Predict the number of games you feel you will win out of 30 games. Create an organizer and record your number of wins and losses. Compare your "win" prediction with the actual number of wins. Explain how the LIFESKILL of Patience affected how you played each game and your level of enjoyment (or lack of). Compare strategies with another player in your house.

- Interview a parent or grandparent about parenthood. Ask permission to take notes or record the interview. Request five or more examples of times when the LIFESKILL of Patience was critical. Identify two or more examples that might offer tips to friends who are babysitting or helping with younger siblings. Create bookmarks that illustrate these examples and hand them out to friends who babysit.

- Recall five examples of your parents or grandparents using the LIFESKILL of Patience when you were between the ages of three and seven. Explain where you were, the circumstances, your actions, their actions, and your feelings. Create a card thanking your parents/grandparents for using the LIFESKILL of Patience with you and how it helped you become a person of character.

- Research your area's growing season and the kinds of vegetables that do well in your soil and climate. Design a garden to feed your family with vegetables at least three nights a week during the growing season. Include early-, mid-, and late-blooming varieties. Practice the LIFESKILL of Patience while you till, seed, weed, and harvest your crop. Keep accurate records of the following:
    ~ Brand(s) of seeds planted
    ~ Amount of seed purchased
    ~ Soil preparation and planting dates
    ~ Harvest dates
    ~ Amount of vegetables harvested
    ~ Three or more times you practiced patience as a gardener

- Put together a model of one of the following: airplane, car, human body, dollhouse, or one of your own choosing. Share with a parent two or more problems you experienced during the building process and the solutions that worked for you. Count the number of hours/minutes you spent creating this model. Share with a friend the step that required the most patience.

- Brainstorm ways to pass the time (e.g., practice the times tables, spelling words, addition facts) while waiting in line or expecting something to happen. Design an individual poster identifying ten quiet, personal activities that will help you spend waiting time in an educational way. Use color and graphics to create a strong visual reminder of these activities. Share your poster with a family member and ask him/her to add two ideas.

- Learn Brain Gym strategies* as a family member explains them to you. Choose two that will help you to develop the LIFESKILL of Patience; practice them at least 10 times in the next week. Keep track of when you use these strategies and reflect on whether or not the exercises are helping you to develop the LIFESKILL of Patience. Share your thoughts with the family member who taught you the brain gym activities.

- Interview a grandparent—yours or a friends—for examples of how adults need to use the LIFESKILL of Patience with children in their care. Ask about age and personality differences that affect a child's ability to be patient. Brainstorm two or more ways children can practice the LIFESKILL of Patience with busy adults. Share what you learned with your family.

- Interview a grandparent—yours or a friends—for examples of how his/her grandparents used the LIFESKILL of Patience with family and work. Ask yourself if you or your parents need to use the LIFESKILL of Patience in similar ways for similar things despite the lapse of years. Record what you learned in your journal. Share what you learned with your family.

---

* See *Brain Gym: Teacher's Edition Revised* by Paul and Gail Dennison (Ventura, CA: Educ-Kinesiology, Inc., 1994).

- Interview an adult about his/her employment. Ask permission to take notes or record the interview. Request five or more examples of times when the LIFESKILL of Patience has been an important part of his/her work day. Share with a parent what you learned from this interview about the LIFESKILL of Patience and what you will do in your family life to better use the LIFESKILL of Patience. Create bookmarks that illustrate these examples and hand them out to family and friends.

- Learn to play a new board game (e.g., Monopoly, checkers, chess, Life, Candyland, Scrabble). Ask a friend to help you learn the rules. Play the game four or more times during the next two weeks. Test your patience level as you learn new strategies. Share your feelings and insights with your game partner.

- Research a new hobby or craft, such as knitting, carving, carpentry, sewing, collecting, painting, photography, sculpting, or birding that you want to learn. Find someone in your neighborhood who is proficient in this skill and is willing to teach you the basic steps. Practice the beginning steps until they feel automatic. Design and create a finished product. As you share the piece with your family, explain how the LIFESKILL of Patience supported you in this task.

- Create your own personal T-Chart (poster, transparency, pamphlet) for the LIFESKILL of Patience. Write four or more phrases for each of the following categories: Looks Like, Sounds Like, and Feels Like (and Doesn't Look Like, Doesn't Sound Like, and Doesn't Feel Like). Add graphic reminders. Volunteer to share your project with two other families in the neighborhood. Invite the children of each family to add more phrases that are age appropriate for them. Create a poster using their phrases and present it to that family to keep.

- Dramatize the following real-life situations with your family at diner time:
    - ~ You're waiting in line for tickets to a movie
    - ~ Your group is lining up to wait for a bus or taxi
    - ~ You want a toy someone else is playing with
    - ~ Someone is pushing ahead of you
    - ~ A new skill is very hard to master

  For each predicament, show two responses, one using the LIFESKILL of Patience and one not using it. Practice each set of skits three or more times until they run smoothly. Present the skits for your family and let them determine which skits exemplify the use of the LIFESKILL of Patience.

AGES 13+

- Apply for a job at a local fast-food restaurant by completing an application; include all of the necessary information. Prepare a "Personal Patience Plan" listing three strategies for using the LIFESKILL of Patience that will most enhance your getting and keeping the job. During the interview process, discuss with the manager/interviewer the importance of using the LIFESKILL of Patience when one is in the fast-food service business.

Chapter 18—Patience

- Become a helper at the Special Olympic Games in your community. Contact the local coordinator and offer your services in one of the following capacities: "go-fer," greeter, first aide assistant, snack server, event organizer. Observe five or more athletes as they compete and identify at least four examples of their use of the LIFESKILL of Patience. Reflect on how these examples can inspire your own growth in using the LIFESKILL of Patience. Share your thoughts with a parent.

- Volunteer as a tutor (for at least one semester) at one of the following: Boys Club, Girls Club, after-school tutoring program, or a community center that provides after-school services for younger children. Review your assignment and plan three or more activities that will increase the understanding of reading (phonics, comprehension, study skills) or math (computational, reasoning, estimating) of the child you are tutoring. List at least four strategies that will help you use your LIFESKILL of Patience when tutoring. Ask your favorite teacher for ideas.

- Find a spider inside or outside of your house. Predict how long it will take this spider to build a web from start to finish. Observe its actions and techniques during the web-building process. List at least two examples of patience the spider uses. Monitor the arachnid's behavior after the web is complete. List another example of the LIFESKILL of Patience during this time. Explain to a younger brother, sister, or neighbor what you have learned about the LIFESKILL of Patience from your observation.

- Volunteer to teach a younger sibling an important, useful skill such as: tying laces, buckling a belt, buttoning a shirt, brushing his/her teeth, riding a bicycle, and so forth. Process the number of steps it takes to complete the action you want to teach him/her; write a rhyme, song, or rap that will teach the skill with music or a rhythmic beat. Ask your sibling to practice this routine until it becomes automatic. Sing/chant the rhyme with him/her while he/she performs the actions. Predict how many times you will need to teach and re-teach this skill before your brother/sister can successfully perform it alone. Compare your prediction with the actual number of times. Discuss with an adult what you have learned about the LIFESKILL of Patience.

- Provide computer lessons for three or more senior citizens at your local senior citizen center. Teach the following basic skills:
    - Turning the computer on and off
    - Accessing the word processing program
    - Writing, saving (hard drive and floppy disk), and printing a business letter
    - Signing on with a server
    - Opening e-mail
    - Sending e-mail
    - Accessing the web
    - Performing a search on the web

    Express your appreciation for your senior citizens' use of the LIFESKILL of Patience on their graduation certificates and during the "graduation" celebration.

- Interview two adult family members about the companies they work for. Request background information about each company's policy regarding commitment to production quality. In reality does the company rush for the bottom line or does it exhibit the LIFESKILL of Patience to achieve quality?

- Interview the manager of a local fast-food restaurant. Request background information about his/her company's entry into the fast-food market. Listen for company policy that provides insight into their production philosophy. For example, McDonald's "a serving a second." Ask about their research on time management, food preparation, and how they deal with unhappy patrons who fail to use the LIFESKILL of Patience. Then interview the manager from one of the best, most expensive restaurants in town. Ask the same questions. Share with a parent what you have learned and three things that you can apply to your own life starting today. Write a thank-you note to the managers for taking time to talk with you; also mention what you found to be most interesting about the LIFESKILL of Patience in the workplace.

- Study the techniques used by three different artists (e.g., Rembrandt, Monet, and O'Keefe) and explain how you think each one used the LIFESKILL of Patience before, during, and after the completion of one of his/her pieces of art. Share your thoughts with an artist or your art teacher.

SIGNS OF SUCCESS

Congratulations! Children are showing signs of Patience when they

- Wait their turn in a line or to talk to someone; don't become angry or disruptive
- Offer to teach someone a skill
- Sit quietly at the doctor's or orthodontist's office waiting for their appointment
- Save money to buy something special
- Wait politely for everyone at the table to get their food before starting to eat
- Work to complete a difficult project without getting frustrated
- Talk politely even when they are feeling upset
- Listen while others complete what they're saying before beginning to inject their own ideas

Keep trying! Children need more practice when they

- Lose their temper because they don't get what they want
- Speak rudely to someone who is trying to help
- Ride their bikes too fast and dart in front of walkers
- Hang up the phone on someone trying to explain something they don't want to hear
- Push or shove people out of the way
- Refuse to share materials
- Grab items from others' hands
- Refuse to wait their turn to use some object/toy/materials
- Give up too easily; don't spend adequate time practicing an important skill
- Demand an adult's immediate attention for non-emergency matters

Literature Link ~ Patience

AGES 4-8

Butterfly Boy (HA)	Virginia Kroll (Honesdale, PA: Boyd Mills, 1997)
Marguerite Makes a Book	Bruce Robertson (Los Angeles: J. P. Getty Museum, 1999)
Not Yet, Yvette (AFA)	Helen Ketteman (Morton Grove, IL: Albert Whitman & Co, 1995)
Story of Ferdinand, The (TE)	Munro Leaf (New York: Viking Press, 1987)
Very Busy Spider, The	Eric Carle (New York: Philomel Books, 1984)

AGES 9-12

Bridge to Terabithia (TE)	Katherine Patterson (New York: HarperCollins Childrens Books, 1978)
Danger Zone (AFA)	David Klass (New York: Scholastic Books, 1996)
Sachiko Means Happiness (ASA)	Kimiko Sakai (San Francisco: Children's Book Press, 1990)
Walk Two Moons (NA)	Sharon Creech (New York: HarperTrophy Publishers, 1996)

AGES 13+

160 Ways to Help the World: Community Service Projects for Young People	Linda Leeb Duper (New York: Checkmark Books, 1996)
California Blue	David Klass (New York: Scholastic Point, 1996)
Summer of My German Soldier	Bette Greene (New York: Puffin Books, 1999)

PARENT RESOURCES

Hurried Child, The: Growing Up Too Fast Too Soon	David Elkind (Reading, MA: Perseus Books, 1988)
Playwise: 365 Fun-Filled Activities for Building Character, Conscience, and Emotional Intelligence in Children	Denise Chapman et. al. (New York: Putnam Publishing Group, 1996)
Teaching Children Patience Without Losing Yours	Jerry Wilde and Polly Wilde (LGR Publishers, 1999)

Multicultural books: **(AFA)**=African American, **(ASA)**=Asian American, **(HA)**=Hispanic American, **(ME)**=Multi-Ethnic, **(NA)**=Native American, **(TE)**=listed in the teacher edition of this book, *Tools for Citizenship and Life: Using the ITI Lifelong Guidelines and LIFESKILLS in the Classroom,* **(BFE)**=available through Books for Educators

Perseverance

Chapter 19

"Stick with it!"

perseverance *n* the act or condition or an instance of persevering: steadfastness

PERSEVERANCE: To keep at it

WHAT IS PERSEVERANCE?

Perseverance can be the crucial difference between success and failure in most aspects of life. We might define it as "stubbornness under control."

Think back to a time when you learned to tie your shoelaces. Did you master the skill the first time you were shown how to do it? No! How about the second time? No! You may not remember the exact number of tries it took before you could make the "x," slip the end under, pull it tight, make a loop, circle the other tie around it, slip the middle of the tie in under the loop, pull, and finally end up with a bow. It required lots of practice and resolve.

Perseverance grows in the face of a challenge. It's the ability to stay with a chore or a goal despite inexperience and problems. It's a crucial ingredient in the development of inner strength and stamina, in the ability to pursue goals, and in the determination to "hang in there" through all sorts of highs and lows in childhood and adulthood.

Fortunately, we are born with perseverance. Babies don't give up! Infants begin to understand this notion as they experiment with mobiles, teething rings, and rattles during their first months. Throughout their first year of life, they continuously persevere as they conquer tremendous physical challenges, such as learning to grasp, turn over, sit, crawl, feed themselves, stand, walk, and run. They fall, they get up, they fall again, they get up again.

Perseverance is a concept children learn naturally through their own discovery processes. However, it is easily squashed if the tasks presented are age-inappropriate (and therefore impossible for a child of that age to do or to understand) or meaningless (why bother). Furthermore, if family or school pressures seem to demand perfection, we are forever disappointed in our performance because it doesn't measure up to the expectations of others and/or ourselves. These are all killers of perseverance.

"Stick to It" Attitude

Perseverance is a combination of endurance, doggedness, and determination. It is believing in yourself, your ideas, and goals—sometimes in the face of criticism and others' lack of faith in who you are and what you're attempting to do. Perseverance is a commitment to yourself to follow through with your plans, a responsibility to yourself to stick with it until you reach your goals, a commitment to honor your word.

Motivation Is Crucial

Motivation plays a huge part in our ability to persevere: If we lack motivation, our level of perseverance falls; conversely, if we are highly motivated, our level of perseverance rises. When it comes to the LIFESKILL of Perseverance, motivation must be internal. We persevere because we say so. During a crisis or challenge, the most basic jobs can become remarkably difficult. At these times, it is important to acknowledge our perseverance to give ourselves a boost and marshal the energy to stay with our plans. At other times, we may take our actions for granted and not recognize our perseverance; this weakens our motivation to keep going.

WHY PRACTICE PERSEVERANCE?

Expert-level skill and knowledge does not grow on sugarplum bushes ready to be plucked by wandering passers-by. Expertise, regardless of the level of God-given talent underneath it, is the result of lots of hard work driven by lots of perseverance. As Calvin Coolidge said: "Nothing in this world can take the place of persistence. Talent will not; nothing is more common than unsuccessful men with talent. Genius will not; unrewarded genius is almost a proverb. Education will not; the world is full of educated derelicts. Persistence and determination alone are omnipotent. The slogan 'press on' has solved and always will solve the problems of the human race."*

Strong Effort Is Helpful

Effort counts! We always remember to appreciate success but often forget to acknowledge the hard work that led to it. Perseverance leads to continuing progress. It's not only the initial effort a child puts forth in conquering a challenge that matters but the staying power as well.

Perseverance is an important trait at all stages of life. It is vital that children learn it as early as possible because it supports many of the other crucial experiences of childhood, especially exploring and making sense of the world. The LIFESKILL of Perseverance is the engine that drives success.

---

* Calvin Coolidge Memorial Foundation. http://www.calvin-coolidge.org/

HOW DO YOU PRACTICE IT?

Conscious practice of perseverance requires several factors.

There Must Be a Clear Goal in Mind. Children must have a vision of what they are pursuing that is strong enough to feed their efforts and fire their internal motivation. The goal must be valued by children; what parents may think is terrific or what politicians think will look "foxy" to the voters are of little consequence here. To persevere, children must understand and value what they're pursuing.

Modeling Is Key. Children must have opportunities to watch others and to visualize what is possible. The one-room schoolhouse and multi-age settings are ideal because older children model what is possible. If you find yourself in the traditional same-age classroom, use cross-age tutoring to bring children together. Also, remember that you are an important source of modeling as well.

Effort. The LIFESKILL of Effort is a twin LIFESKILL. It drives the LIFESKILL of Perseverance, giving it action and reality; without it, the LIFESKILL of Perseverance bogs down into worry and anxiety. On the other hand, the LIFESKILL of Perseverance guides Effort.

Flexibility. The LIFESKILL of Flexibility is indispensable when persevering. As we continue to work at something, we often must change what we are doing and how we are doing it. Unwillingness to make such changes usually dooms us. Perseverance is not compulsive persistence, working over and over at an approach that doesn't work; it is working smart until we succeed.

Processing the Process. "Processing the process" is a phrase that recurs throughout this book. It is a key instructional strategy to help internalize Lifelong Guidelines and LIFESKILLS because it gives people immediate feedback on their behavior and performance. The phrase refers to discussions that immediately follow completion of a group task, focusing on how the group performed as a collaborative unit. It is an excellent vehicle for getting children to reflect on how well they used a Lifelong Guideline or LIFESKILL.*

Self-Talk. "Processing the process" is a group structure for internalizing the Lifelong Guidelines and LIFESKILLS; self-talk is a private, individual way. Through self-talk, we are our own teacher and mentor. Teaching children strategies for processing the process, brainstorming, and problem-solving teaches them "self-talk," the internal dialogue needed to analyze what we do and how and why.

Resiliency. Resiliency is the ability to take failure on the chin and bounce right back, to learn from the experience but not be destroyed by it or forever run ragged by it. If we can't roll with the punches life throws our way, we can't persevere. Teach children that failure is their teacher, not their enemy. Teach them by example how to learn from failure without succumbing to disappointment, frustration, or humiliation.

---

* For a discussion on "processing the process," see *Tribes: A New Way of Learning and Being Together* by Jeanne Gibbs, Sausalito, CA: CenterSource Publications, 1995, pp. 100, 114-116.

Parent As "Guide-on-the-Side"

It's natural to want to "save" or "rescue" children when things go wrong. However, the only lesson learned then is that someone else will fix their problem for them. To persevere is to go through the challenges, the roller coaster emotions, the alternating cycles of success and failure to emerge on the other side. Through such experiences we learn that we are responsible to ourself and that the motivation to carry on comes from within. There are no short cuts on this one—no save-the-pain tricks or labor-saving devices. When it comes to developing and using the LIFESKILL of Perseverance, we must do it for ourselves.

The parent as a "guide-on-the-side" rather than the "sage on the stage" can make the task easier. Here are several strategies:

- Provide daily conversation about, and practice in, problem solving and identifying goals (both short- and long-term)

- Model an optimistic outlook and describe your own tussles with the LIFESKILL of Perseverance

- Encourage the LIFESKILLS of Effort and Flexibility

- Provide stress relief; when times get tense, encourage your child to take short breaks and talk about his/her work ("self-talk")

- Allow your child to set his/her own pace whenever possible

- Help your child identify self and group behaviors that hinder the LIFESKILL of Perseverance and those that facilitate it

- Celebrate genuine accomplishments, not just for reaching a goal but also for "staying with it"

Re-examine Content of Curriculum and Homework Assignments

Many aspects of traditional education chip away at student willingness to persevere with their assignments. The biggest culprits are:

- Curriculum that is meaningless to children—not relevant and/or age-inappropriate
- The negative effects of competitive grading

Too often we expect, even demand, that children persevere at tasks even we would have a hard time completing, such as dull homework worksheets, assignments that repeat what they already know, or the study of concepts that are beyond the child's experience and ability to understand. In truth, much of our traditional school curriculum is inexcusably inappropriate and boring—worksheets are meaningless and repetitive; concepts aren't given a real-life context children can understand or relate to. When we ask our children to persevere, let's make sure that the content and the process of the task are kid-friendly and worthy of their persevering.

WHAT DOES PERSEVERANCE LOOK LIKE IN THE REAL WORLD?

We

- Follow through on ideas
- Complete projects (building a house, making a gift, cooking dinner)
- Keep trying until we succeed (driving a car, graduating from high school, finding a job)
- Work out personal relationship problems and misunderstandings
- Refine an invention or product until it is marketable
- Finish jigsaw and crossword puzzles
- Read a book from beginning to end
- Resubmit claims for medical insurance after they have been rejected and go to the State Insurance Commissioner if necessary
- Get a second, or even third, medical opinion in cases of serious or mysterious illnesses
- Mow, mow, and mow again to keep our yard looking spiffy
- Master a sport or game
- Learn to program the VCR
- Insist that a company abide by its guarantees and customer satisfaction policies

WHAT DOES PERSEVERANCE LOOK LIKE AT HOME?

Adults

- Teach, re-teach, and re-teach again manners and values to our child
- Remain consistent in setting and enforcing rules, boundaries, and consequences for our child
- Invest and re-invest time in building family relationships
- Reschedule appointments until the problem is solved
- Keep working on remodeling projects on a daily/weekly basis until each project is completed
- Maintain our house and yard as a clutter-free environment

- Request additional teacher conferences when better results are not forthcoming; get involved in school improvement efforts

- Volunteer as coaches, troop leaders, den mothers, and 4-H leaders to show our child what family values look like outside the home

- Keep a weekly watch on family finances, revising the family budget as many times as needed to ensure our expenditures stay within the budget; rein in daily expenses so we can pay off mortgages, car, and college loans; put aside money on a regular basis to save for retirement

- Search for the best prices for food, clothing, household goods, automobiles even if it means going to more than one store to get the best prices available or waiting for sales

- Work at a job, sometimes two, to take care of our family

- Keep appliances, machines, and cars going as long as possible

- Read, read, and re-read income tax information until we understand it

Children

- Stick with a project from beginning to end

- Read a book from cover to cover

- Invest time in developing family relationships and friendships

- Have great powers of concentration; can sustain a "one-track mind" on a growing number of topics

- Complete a jigsaw puzzle

- Join scouts, 4-H, YWCA, or other organizations and remain a member for two years or more

- Volunteer to work for fund-raisers such as walk-a-thons, Habitat for Humanity, Special Olympics, food pantries, and homeless shelters

- Learn to crawl, walk, skip, hop, and run

- Invest practice time to improve skills and strategies for various games—mental and physical, such as board games, computer programs, sports, and so forth

- Create reasonable timetables for homework assignments and work as planned until each project is completed

- Work to reach personal, educational, and social goals

- If they feel like quitting, they analyze why, then choose to stick with it until they've gotten value from the experience

Chapter 19—Perseverance

OPPORTUNITIES TO PRACTICE PERSEVERANCE

AGES 4-8

- Choose three or more nursery rhymes to memorize. Listen to someone in your family read the first rhyme again and again. Join in and repeat as many words as you remember until you can say the rhyme all by yourself. Add some body movements and facial expressions to help you remember the words. Draw one picture to match each rhyme. Follow the same steps for the second and third nursery rhyme. Recite them from memory while showing the illustrations to your family at the next family gathering.

- Practice stacking a tower of blocks. First, stack the tallest tower you can make out of wooden blocks. Count how many blocks were in the tower before it fell. Try three more times; try to set a personal-best record. Write your personal-best number on a piece of paper and put it with the blocks when you put them away. Next, stack the highest tower that you can build made out of Lego blocks. Try three more times; try to set a personal-best record. Write your personal-best number for a Lego block tower on a piece of paper and put it with the Legos when you put them away. Third, stack one more tower made of Lincoln Logs. When the tower crumples, count the logs. Try three more times. Write your personal-best number for a Lincoln log tower on a piece of paper and put it with the Lincoln logs when you put them away. Wait a day, then try building each of the towers again. See if you can improve your personal-best records for each kind of tower. Share with a parent what you have learned about the LIFESKILL of Perseverance by building these towers and trying to improve your personal best.

- Volunteer to help with holiday cards. Memorize where the address sticker goes (upper left-hand corner on the flapless side or on the back of the flap) and where the stamp is put (upper right hand corner of the flapless side). Peel off the stamps and stick one on each envelope. Repeat the process with address stickers. Send your own special card to grandpa/grandma. Count the envelopes when you are finished and tell the family how many cards were mailed. Share with them what you learned about the LIFESKILL of Perseverance by helping with this mailing.

- Demonstrate the art of snow shoveling after a storm. Write down your starting time. Mark off the area you intend to clear with some sticks or boards. Pick up the snow with your shovel and dump it away from the sidewalk and driveway. Push some of the snow out of the way if it gets too hard to lift. Rest for a few minutes if you need to but come back to finish the task. When you have finished, inspect your work and compute the number of minutes/hours it took you to complete the entire job. Share with a parent what helped motivate you to use your LIFESKILL of Perseverance. Ask them how they motivate themselves to use their LIFESKILL of Perseverance on a job. Think about their suggestions and decide if any of their suggestions might work for you.

- Ask the dentist to teach you the correct way to brush your teeth. Suggest that he use model teeth and a really big toothbrush. Memorize the pattern that the brush needs to follow to keep your teeth clean and healthy. Practice on the model set. Ask the dentist to judge how you are doing. Practice on your own teeth three or more times each day until your next appointment. Ask the dentist to tell you if you have mastered the skill of brushing your teeth correctly.

- Sit outside in the shade on a warm, sunny day and observe an anthill for fifteen minutes or longer. Estimate how many ants live in this colony. Write down three actions you see (e.g., carrying something, scurrying, and hiding). Each time one of the ants repeats an action on your list put a tally mark beneath the action word. After four tally marks, make the fifth tally line cutting across the other four, e.g., ‖‖‖. Repeat this pattern as you make your tallies. Explain how you think ants show perseverance in the insect world. Share what you have learned from the ants about the LIFESKILL of Perseverance and what ideas you will use when you next have a job to do.

- Play a strategy game, such as checkers, chess, tic-tac-toe, or Othello, with many different partners. Compare and contrast your strategies with those of each partner. Produce a game plan that will increase your probability of winning. Practice by playing against yourself for 10 games. Test your plan with partners for a minimum of 15 games and determine its effectiveness. Share with a family member how you used the LIFESKILL of Perseverance to complete this objective.

- Plan a "perseverance quilt" of 5"x5" squares (fabric or construction paper) with your family and/or friends. Invite each participant to draw a symbol/illustration representing some time when he/she had to use the LIFESKILL of Perseverance. Intersperse appropriate quotations on solid- color squares. Sew or glue the squares together and present the gift to your school or local library to display.

AGES 9-12

- Identify a goal or task that you still want to complete but never seem to get to. Enlist the support of an adult family member to help you identify why you have failed to persevere in the past. Develop a plan for using the LIFESKILL of Perseverance and Effort to resolve these barriers and complete the task. Share with that same family member the results of your plan and what you have learned about the LIFESKILL of Perseverance by completing this task.

- Interview a family member or neighbor who was not born in the United States. Compile a list of the information he/she needs to learn and understand to become a citizen of our country. Create a time line dividing up the material into topics for easier learning. Study and discuss one of the topics each time you meet. Ask questions and discuss answers to help this person learn about our government and constitution. Attend the official awards ceremony and present him/her with a LIFESKILL of Perseverance certificate and card of congratulations designed by you.

- Choose a pattern for a useful project made of wood (e.g., bookshelf, boot jack, bookends, key rack). Read the directions for making this object. Organize the materials and tools you need. Trace the pattern and ask an adult for assistance using a saw or making cuts. Sand any rough edges. Hammer or glue the pieces together in order. Decide whether or not to stain (color) the wood to match other decorative pieces in your home. Identify three or more ways you used the LIFESKILL of Perseverance to finish the job. Present the completed project to a favorite relative.

- Design one paper airplane that will do all of the following moves:
    - ~ Fly in a straight line
    - ~ Fly in circles
    - ~ Turn to the left
    - ~ Turn to the right

  Draw a detailed diagram to scale so that you or someone else can recreate this airplane some other time. Provide a demonstration for your family and explain to your audience how the LIFESKILL of Perseverance helped you complete this task.

- Test your ability to do the following sport skills:
    - ~ Run 55 meters (time)
    - ~ Dribble a basketball five times with the right hand, then left hand, and then alternating hands (number of sets)
    - ~ Balance on one leg, on a still bicycle, on a balance beam or curb, and with a book on your head (time)
    - ~ Jump as far as you can (length)
    - ~ Throw as far as you can at a target (length)
    - ~ Kick a moving ball (number)
    - ~ Bounce a tennis ball up and down on a racquet (number)

  Record for each activity the time, length, height, or number of times you are able to do the activity in a row. Decide which four of these skills need the most improvement and develop a plan for daily practice for two weeks. Record the following in a journal: When you practice, the amount of time spent practicing, and a weekly recount. Use this sentence as a discussion starter with an adult of your choice: "The LIFESKILL of Perseverance and self-discipline are/are not important character traits because. . . ."

- Dramatize each of the following situations with two different endings, one showing the use of the LIFESKILL of Perseverance and one where the LIFESKILL of Perseverance is not used. Perform the skits for your family and ask them to guess which ending shows the LIFESKILL of Perseverance in use.
    - ~ This is your first time on skis (downhill or water) and you have been on the ground/in the water more than you have been standing. All at once you notice a four-year old go whizzing past
    - ~ Your new pet dog, Nicky, misbehaves all of the time and you have been put in charge of training him to behave. He will have to go back to the Humane Society if his behavior doesn't improve
    - ~ A division math test is scheduled for the end of the week; you are very worried because you don't understand how to do the problems

AGES 13+

- Propose a series of hikes that together will total at least ten miles. Explore the land with your family; assign each person a role to play such as navigator, leader, cartographer, botanist, geologist, recorder, and photographer. Define each role and summarize the responsibilities. Brainstorm a motto that will encourage the use of the LIFESKILL of Perseverance as you hike. Design and make a T-shirt for each member of the family. Include a family logo and motto plus the individual's name. Wear them as you hike and sing the song "Perseverance" from the LIFESKILLS tape (or another song about perseverance of your choice).

- Create an annotated bibliography of 25 or more children's books whose stories can be used to teach about the LIFESKILLS. Identify three of the books as containing situations that stress the need for the LIFESKILL of Perseverance as a strong character trait, one well worth developing. Make multiple copies of this bibliography and leave one with every family whose children you babysit. Read one of the three books to the children the next time you babysit them.

- Design a T-chart that will provide examples of what perseverance does look like, sound like and feel like. Begin like this:

LIFESKILL OF PERSEVERANCE

Looks Like	Sounds Like	Feels Like
Trying something again and again	"That's it! Keep going!"	Strength, satisfaction

Make another T-chart show what the LIFESKILL of Perseverance does *not* look like, does *not* sound like, and does *not* feel like. For example:

Doesn't Look Like	Doesn't Sound Like	Doesn't Feel Like
Not trying	"I can't!" — giving up "I don't want to."	Failure

Add as many ideas, words, and phrases to the charts as you and your family can brainstorm. Post both charts on the refrigerator door or some other high-visibility location. After two weeks, revisit your chart and ask the family to add any additional thoughts.

- Create a family museum with art exhibitions, antique collections, craft/hobby displays, and musical performances. Arrange for these items to be available for viewing during family celebrations. Photograph or videotape the display for posterity. Share with your family how the LIFESKILL of Perseverance helped you complete this task.

- Complete an application for each college you would like to attend. Place them in folders that are organized alphabetically. Pursue each application by calling the admissions office to check on the status of your application. Follow up on any rejection notices by calling the admissions office and asking for feedback that might increase your chances of being reconsidered. Offer to redo any paperwork or forward more personal information that might cause the team to reconsider your application.

- Design a four-frame cartoon strip or a political cartoon with the LIFESKILL of Perseverance as the main concept. Include one or more characters and bubbles for dialog. Submit the finished piece to your school newspaper or yearbook for publication.

- Identify one song from each of the following music categories below that has lyrics related to the LIFESKILL of Perseverance (for example, trying hard, never giving up, determination, and will power). Play/sing the songs for your family; add motions and movement to emphasize the meaning of the words. After each song, ask them to share an example from their own life that is similar to that depicted in the song.
    - Rock
    - Country Western
    - Opera
    - Broadway musical
    - Pop

- For one week keep a log that documents the amount of time you spend on each of the following activities: sleeping, eating, attending school, watching television, playing video games, using a computer, and doing physical exercise such as sports, aerobics, dance, hiking, weight lifting. For the second week, create a revised play/recreation schedule that supports a healthy lifestyle on a daily basis by increasing the amount of movement time in your life (outdoor and indoor). Choose specific exercises, games, or movement that you plan to do each day. Keep a journal for at least one month that reflects your use of the LIFESKILL of Perseverance to help you stick to this new plan. Share these reflections with a parent.

- Choose a skill (such as oral reading, paragraph writing, computational math, reading comprehension, physical strength) in which you would like greater proficiency. Devise a skill improvement plan with adequate time for you to practice and experience using the skill. Locate a mentor to help you master this skill; ask for any additional advice. Locate a quotation to help you persevere and remain focused. Keep daily records in your journal of your beginning and ending times, of your work alone or with assistance, your rate of improvement in mastering the skill, and any reflections about your ability to stick to your goal. Share progress notes with your mentor and a parent.

- Read the following famous quotations about the LIFESKILL of Perseverance. Choose two and design a "mock up" business card for its author. Include the quotation, the person's name, and an illustration or graphic that explains the words. Make 10 of these cards and hand them out to five or more special people in your life. Ask them to share their interpretation of the quotation. Create your own quotation teaching about the LIFESKILL of Perseverance and share it with a parent.
    - "Whether you think you can, or think you can't, you're right." Henry Ford
    - "Courage and perseverance have a magic talisman before which difficulties disappear and obstacles vanish into thin air." John Quincy Adams
    - "Few things are impossible to diligence and skill. Great works are performed not by strength, but perseverance." Samuel Johnson
    - "Press on: Nothing in the world can take the place of perseverance. Talent will not; nothing is more common than unsuccessful men with talent. Genius will not; unrewarded genius is almost a proverb. Education will not; the world is full of educated derelicts. Persistence and determination alone are omnipotent." Calvin Coolidge

- Use the LIFESKILL of Perseverance to learn how to use a computer program, e.g., Inspiration, PrintShop, Hyperstudio. Create one finished product, such as a poster, card, bookmark, award, or web page that teaches four or more perseverance strategies. Teach what you have learned to a family member or friend.

- Play a board game, such as Monopoly, Scrabble, mahjong, checkers, or chess, in "tournament" style. Make a graph to represent the players' scores for two weeks. After the tournament, list all the ways that the LIFESKILL of Perseverance was needed to complete the tournament.

- View the Women's Movement in the United States since 1900 as a demonstration of the LIFESKILL of Perseverance. Consider the progress made in your own state and the changes it has made in the lives of women in your family. Narrow your investigation of the Women's Movement to one of the following topics: voting, family issues, employment, obtaining credit, or owning property. Identify a family member who has shown leadership and the LIFESKILL of Perseverance in helping to change the social or legal status quo affecting women's rights. Identify five tangible ways the lives of women in your family have been improved. Share with your family at dinner time what you have learned about the Women's Movement, participation by members of your extended family, and about the LIFESKILL of Perseverance.

- Choose an inventor/scientist who had a difficult time convincing people to produce/use his invention, discovery, or product. List three or more strategies that didn't work in catching the interest of business people. Then identify three or more strategies that did. Create a "Perseverance Award" for your inventor. Include his/her name, accomplishment, and successful strategies. Include graphics and color for an attractive presentation. Explain your reasoning to your audience (family and friends).

- Research one of the following leaders known for his/her leadership in the Civil Rights or peace movements using non-violent strategies: Dr. Martin Luther King, Jr., Mahatma Gandhi, Rosa Parks, or President Jimmy Carter. Chronicle three setbacks and three achievements. Identify a member of your extended family who worked/is working to further advance this leader's beliefs. Design a United States postage stamp honoring this leader and your family member for their LIFESKILLS of Perseverance and Effort.

- Read at least three books on household pets and their care. Choose one of the pets and create a "Pet Care Chart" detailing the following: (1) eating/feeding habits, (2) exercise required, (3) interests/play, (4) peculiarities, (5) training, and (6) life span. Determine four or more examples of occasions when the LIFESKILL of Perseverance will be required during the pet's lifetime. Share your information with a veterinarian, trainer, breeder, or pet store owner for accuracy. Design a pamphlet that prepares people to care for the animal you chose. Use graphics or photographs for added visual appeal.

- Define the following terms: Threatened, endangered, and extinct species. Research an animal listed in one of these categories for your state or region. Determine the conditions of the animal's location, needs, enemies, and any additional factors that hinder its ability to persevere to survive. Educate your family at dinner with a visual presentation (such as a video, computer program, or photographic essay) on this animal's fight for continued existence. Provide addresses of organizations that support your cause and invite interested friends to write letters requesting additional information on ways they can help. Share with your family what you have learned about using the LIFESKILL of Perseverance while preparing for and carrying out this political action project.

SIGNS OF SUCCESS

Congratulations! Children are showing signs of Perseverance when they

- Stick with a difficult task until it is completed
- Ask for help mastering difficult tasks
- Complete short- and long-term goals on time
- Keep working to find alternative solutions to real-life problems
- Ask questions about work, ideas, and concepts until they understand the content
- Learn academic skills through determination
- Master bike riding without wobbling or falling; challenge themselves to master an obstacle course
- Save money for many weeks to buy a special gift for someone
- Join a school or neighborhood club or team and work hard to improve their skills

Keep trying! Children need more practice when they

- Accept failure and lack of completion as normal
- Never seem to complete projects, inquiries, and homework by the due date
- Give up learning something after one or two hasty attempts
- Keep saying "I'm bored!" and give up easily
- Begin to assemble a kit/model but neglect to complete it because they run into problems
- Shy away from new challenges
- Accept the first idea they hear without investigating choices; insist their way is the only one way to do something and forget/refuse to look for other options

Literature Link ~ Perseverance

Ages 4-8

Akiak: A Tale from the Iditarod	Robert Blake (New York: Philomel Books, a Division of Putnam Grosset, 1997)
Shaman's Apprentice, The	Lynne Cherry and Mark Plotkin (New York: Harcourt Brace Publishing Company, 1998)
Mirandy and Brother Wind (AFA)	Pat McKissack (New York: Dragonfly, a division of Random House, 1997)
My Rows and Piles of Coins (AFA)	Tololwa M. Mollel (Boston: Houghton Mifflin, 1999)

Ages 9-12

A Letter to Mrs. Roosevelt	C. Coco De Young (New York: Delacorte Press, 1999)
El Chino (ASA)	Allen Say (Boston: Houghton Mifflin and Co., 1990)
Island of the Blue Dolphins (NA)	Scott O'Dell (New York: Yearling Books, a division of Random House, 1987)
People Shall Continue, The (NA)	Simon Ortiz (Chicago Econo-clad Books, 1999)

Ages 13+

Chinese Cinderella: The True Story of an Unwanted Daughter (ASA)	Adeline Yen Mah (New York, NY: Delacorte Press, 1999)
Juan Gonzalez (HA)	Dennis Tuttle (New York: Chelsea House Publications, 1994)
Quilted Landscapes: Conversations with Young Immigrants (ME)	Yale Strom (New York: Simon and Schuster, 1996)

Parent Resources

Lotions, Potions, and Slime: Mudpies and More	Nancy Blakey (Berkeley, CA: Tricycle Press, 1996)
Loving Your Child Is Not Enough: Positive Discipline That Works	Nancy Samalin and Martha Moraghan Jablow (New York: Penguin Press, 1998)
Raising Your Spirited Child: A Guide for Parents Whose Child Is More Intense, Sensitive, Perceptive, Persistent and Energetic	Mary Sheedy Kurcinka (New York: Harper-Trade, 1991)

Multicultural books: **(AFA)**=African American, **(ASA)**=Asian American, **(HA)**=Hispanic American, **(ME)**=Multi-Ethnic, **(NA)**=Native American, **(TE)**=listed in the teacher edition of this book, *Tools for Citizenship and Life: Using the ITI Lifelong Guidelines and LIFESKILLS in the Classroom*, **(BFE)**=available through Books for Educators

Chapter 20

Pride

"Celebrate your personal best."

pride *n* the quality or state of being proud as in **a:** a reasonable or justifiable self-respect **b:** delight or elation arising from some act, possession, or relationship **c:** proud behavior

Pride: Satisfaction from doing your personal best

WHAT IS PRIDE?

Pride is not a set of skills or a bank of knowledge. We don't *do* pride, we experience pride. It is a gift from our molecules of emotion.* It is the thrill of reaching the top of a mountain and looking out over a fabulous vista, of having done our personal best and accomplished a hard-earned goal. Pride is a combination of feelings that drives us to do our personal best and feeds our sense of self-worth in a respectful, rather than arrogant, way. It is accompanied by a deep sense of personal satisfaction,** well-being, and joy—a natural "high." Pride is the inner engine of motivation and the desire to do well. It is readily recognizable—the individual stands tall, shoulders back, eyes clear and focused, and the walk confident.

Avoiding False Pride

In America, the word pride often conjures up images of someone who has a haughty, disdainful attitude or who gets to the top by stepping on others; for example, the neighborhood bully who takes "pride" in the way people fear him and his reputation as a tough guy. Or, a teenager who has built a reputation around being an intellectual outcast, or a drug king, or Mr. Cool. A sense of pride built upon self-destructive or anti-social behavior is false pride—a feeling of importance that is misguided and fleeting and that masks the gut feeling that things really aren't all that great.

---

* The "molecules of emotion," a term coined by Candace Pert, are ligands, peptides, hormones, and steroids produced by various organs in the body which carry information/instructions to cells throughout the body. These proteins are literally the physical origins of emotion. See her book, *Molecules of Emotion: Why You Feel the Way You Feel.*

** A phrase coined by Brenda Wyckoff, a fourth grade teacher in Sedona, AZ. Brenda is a master at helping children experience the joy and satisfaction that comes from living a life of integrity and caring.

False pride also occurs when someone is praised for inferior work and behavior. This kind of pride is all too often the outcome of programs designed to build self-confidence by asserting that a person's doing great whether they are or are not. Or, even worse, affirming that they're great just because they exist and are "unique"—a conclusion arrived at without taking into account a person's performance, behavior, character, and attitudes. However, as Madeline Hunter, noted educator and professor at UCLA, explained when someone asked her how the lab school's program built positive self-image, "Teach students to be successful readers, writers, and mathematicians. Then they will have something to feel good about." A very wise one-room schoolhouse teacher put the same idea in more direct words: "If a kid is a pain in the neck and he and everybody else knows he is, telling him he's a wonderful person is a lie and he knows it. Teach him how to be successful academically and socially. A positive self-concept will follow."* And teach them she did. She became a magnet for behavior-problem kids from surrounding school districts. Self-respect, positive self-concept, and self-confidence in life are earned, not conferred upon us by others.

WHY PRACTICE PRIDE?

For most of us, many day-to-day tasks such as washing dishes bore us while other tasks such as cleaning the toilet are abhorrent to us. We perform them not because we enjoy the process but because the job needs to be done and we know that we'll feel good when it's done and done well—that we'll experience the dance of the molecules of emotion which produce the sense of pride.

Pride is such a powerful emotion that we are willing to expend enormous effort to experience it. In its pursuit, it perpetuates a self-fulfilling prophesy: "Because I worked hard and did my personal best, I succeeded; I can repeat this experience another time."

Without developing the LIFESKILL of Pride, our self-esteem, self-image, and self-confidence dwindle and our motivation and productivity decrease.

HOW DO YOU PRACTICE IT?

Again, pride is not something you do, it is something you experience. But we can help our child take the prerequisite actions to make experiencing the LIFESKILL of Pride not only possible likely. These actions include consciously practicing the other Lifelong Guidelines and LIFESKILLS, applying oneself to mastering academic and social skills, and learning to accept acknowledgement graciously. Other prerequisites are becoming aware of the difference between personal best and perfectionism and observing and learning from others as models.

Consciously Practice the Other Lifelong Guidelines and LIFESKILLS. Pride must be earned. Mastering the Lifelong Guidelines and LIFESKILLS opens doors to new opportunities and new areas of support. Becoming someone others want to be around attracts friends who support the best you can become. Most

---

* A 1977 conversation with Dulcie Brown, a highly effective teacher who spent the first half of her 30-year career teaching in one-room, K-8 schools, in rural California.

importantly, learning how to be a friend helps you become a friend to yourself, directing the voice inside your head—your self-talk—to provide useful, positive feedback and direction.

Apply Oneself to Mastering Academic Studies. Skills and knowledge expand our opportunities—opening new doors and possibilities in our personal lives and on the job. Encourage your child to love to learn so that learning something new is a source of joy and pride rather than drudgery. Help him/her develop a sense of "knowing when you know and knowing when you don't know." This helps avoid the self-delusion that a little knowledge is all there is to know about a subject or all that he/she needs to know. Insufficient knowledge is the root of poor decision making and, over a lifetime, is enormously expensive personally and economically.

Teach Your Child (and Yourself) to Accept Acknowledgement Graciously. Although we all yearn for acknowledgement, we typically do a poor job of receiving it. We say, for example, "Oh, this old thing? It's nothing; I picked it up last week at Goodwill." Learn to respond first with, "Thank you," and mean it. Then, if you feel anything else should be said, add something like, "I appreciate your noticing." Allow the acknowledgement to sink in. Then, your family can begin to voice acknowledgements and appreciations that too often go unsaid—those heartfelt sentiments typically reserved for funerals and the expressions of love and respect we all hunger for.

Be Aware of the Difference Between Personal Best and Perfectionism. Most of us would like what we do to be perfect, the best, but life is a busy affair. We don't always have the resources, time, and energy we need to reach perfection on every task. If we get caught up in perfectionism, we will be forever disappointed in ourselves and our family. Happiness in life comes from coming to terms with the reality that personal best is just that—the best we could do given the resources, time, skill, knowledge, and the circumstances of the moment. The mark of maturity is allowing ourselves to feel pride in both process and product when we deserve it while refusing to indulge in false pride when our work may look good to others but we know we didn't give it our personal best. These are difficult lessons to learn. Help your child learn them early in life.

What Does Pride Look Like in the Real World?

We

- Accept compliments and acknowledgements with grace
- Offer handshakes, hugs, pats on the back, kisses, and smiles to friends and colleagues when they accomplish something worthwhile
- Allow ourselves to fully experience the joy and deep sense of satisfaction that comes with genuine pride
- Celebrate Founders' Day in our community and are proud of their contributions to our community

- Sponsor awards and other acknowledgements (e.g., Employee of the Week, Realtor of the Year, Mom of the Month, Most Improved Softball Player, Volunteer of the Week) that recognize the efforts of individuals who use the LIFESKILL of Personal Best

- Join organizations (e.g., Lions Club, Optimists, Boys/Girls Clubs, scouts, 4-H, sports teams, choirs, church groups, booster clubs, and professional associations) and actively participate in and enjoy activities that make the organization the effective group it is

- Guarantee any services your company provides

- Vote in local, state, and national elections; march in patriotic parades (Memorial Day and the Fourth of July); participate in community celebrations (Homecoming, May Day)

- Create new businesses and give them our family name

- Attend swearing-in ceremonies for relatives and friends who are becoming naturalized citizens

WHAT DOES PRIDE LOOK LIKE AT HOME?

Adults

- Model for our child the work ethic and pride in workmanship, no matter what the occupation or profession

- Share in our child's joy in accomplishing a task or goal and doing his/her personal best

- Appreciate our child's efforts to succeed at home and in school

- Maintain an organized, clean, tidy house and yard and take pleasure in a job well done

- Take the necessary steps to ensure that the family home is always ready for guests

- Invest time and energy in collecting and trying out new recipes; enjoy our family's appreciation of tasty meals served hot and on time; find pleasure in serving our family's favorite meals

- Acknowledge our family's cultural heritage and pass it on to our child; appreciate that members of other cultures, races, and religions are equally proud of their backgrounds

Children

- Feel a deep sense of satisfaction from a job well done

- Perform assigned jobs with accuracy and care; work to their personal standards

- Acknowledge family members and friends who are using the LIFESKILL of Personal Best

- Understand and appreciate that interrelationships within the family, and not the amount of money that one earns, are the basis for a strong family foundation

- Acknowledge the cooperative effort in family projects and each person's contribution to the end result

- Share positive statements about their culture, heritage, and religion and that of others

OPPORTUNITIES TO PRACTICE PRIDE

AGES 4-8

- Listen to/read the story *Stone Fox*. Share two or more times when you think Grandpa should be proud of Willie's efforts to save the farm. Explain to an adult what actions you would have taken to help Grandpa.

- Watch one of the following Disney videos: *Cinderella, Dumbo, Pinocchio, Snow White,* or *Bambi*. Find two or more times in each film when the hero/heroine should feel proud of something he/she has done. Share your ideas with a special relative in your house.

- Practice printing your first, middle, and last name until you can write it without looking at a model. Ask a family member to explain how your first and middle names were selected for you. Find out the meanings of these two names. Share one way you will make your family proud that this name was chosen for you.

- Learn to roller skate, ride a bike, ice skate, or play a sport. List two new skills that you learned while practicing. Discuss with a family member one other way these new skills might help you in school and then try your ideas. Share with the same family member how well your ideas worked.

- Create a "Personal Best" display (for refrigerator, wall, hallway) in your house. Choose one school or home assignment/project that you are proud of and post it or a picture of it. Ask other family members to add a sample of their Personal Best work. Change the work on the display at least once a week.

- Design a "Choices I am Proud that I Made" scrapbook. Illustrate four or more sensible choices you have made that helped you to be a better, more competent person. Glue the drawings, one to a page, inside the book. Add more pictures as you make more wise choices that you are proud of. Look through the book each time you need to make a tough choice. Remember the smart choices you have made in the past. Share your scrapbook with a parent.

- Teach your pet (e.g., cat, dog, bird, ferret) a special trick (e.g., roll over, fetch, hide, speak, sleep). Write down the number of times you had this pet practice the trick before he/she could do it with ease. Share with your pet (by words and actions) how proud you are of his/her ability to learn something new and your ability to teach. Tell a parent what the LIFESKILL of Pride felt like inside.

- Design an "I am proud of you" card for someone special in your life. Describe at least three reasons why you proud of this person's courage and integrity. Present the card and share his/her reactions to receiving the card with family members.

- Record in your journal five or more of your personality characteristics that make you feel proud to be who you are. Share your thoughts with a family member.

AGES 9-12

- Read a biography of someone whose life interests you. Identify two or more difficult choices this person had to make during his/her life. Discuss the choices and whether or not these decisions were wise or unwise, whether they made him/her proud or disappointed. Explain your thoughts to a parent.

- With two or more relatives, brainstorm the attributes of a great family. Identify five qualities that you agree are most important. Share these five attributes at dinner time and invite family members to give examples of these attributes in action and describe how they experience the LIFESKILL of Pride when they remember these instances.

- Take notes or tape (audio or video) an interview with an older family member (e.g., parent, grandparent, aunt, uncle) about times in his/her life when he/she felt proud of having made a difficult personal choice. Ask for at least three such instances. Design a thank-you card thanking this family member and sharing what you learned from him/her about the LIFESKILL of Pride.

- Write three or more mini-skits demonstrating difficult problems you have faced in the past year. Share both a positive and negative solution for each situation. Perform the skits for family members at dinner time. Explain which choice(s) gave you the greatest sense of the LIFESKILL of Pride.

- Observe a younger sibling and identify two or more skills/tasks that he/she is trying to develop. Offer to assist him/her in practicing the skill/task. Plan a special celebration of the LIFESKILL of Pride when the goal has been reached; present your sibling with a certificate that honors his/her accomplishment. Assist your sibling in setting a new goal. Share with a parent what you have learned about the LIFESKILL of Pride by assisting your brother/sister.

- Research your family's genealogy. Identify one country (e.g., Ireland, England, China, South Africa, Poland) where you believe your family originated. Draw a map showing this country's location in the world. Include the country's flag, two or more famous "native-born" people, and two or more skills/crafts that are identified with this nation. Share your information at the dinner table or the next large family gathering (e.g., Thanksgiving, Kwanzaa, Chanukah, Christmas, family reunion). Invite your relatives to add more information and memories to this map.

- Design a photographic essay recording four or more times you have felt pride in yourself, your family, or as part of a group to which you belong (e.g., Scouts, 4-H, Boys or Girls Club, church group). Paste each photo on a page, record the date the event occurred, and write four or more sentences explaining the action and your sense of the LIFESKILL of Pride because of this accomplishment. Add to this photo journal each time you feel proud of your actions. Review the material when you have difficult or complicated choices in your life. Share with a parent what this project has taught you about the LIFESKILL of Pride.

- Record in your journal each instance where you have taken a stand to do what is "right" even though this choice may have meant doing something different than your friends. Explain your feelings about making and following through on a decision that may be unpopular with your group of friends. Discuss your choices with an older brother, sister, or cousin. Describe the satisfaction you felt. Ask him/her to share a time when he/she made a difficult decision that went against their friends' choices.

- Create a "Community Pride" bulletin board. Clip articles from the daily newspaper(s) that reflect the LIFESKILL of Pride in individual or group projects. Highlight important phrases that reflect pride. Create a web or mindmap organizing these phrases. Update the bulletin board weekly. At the end of one month, invite family and friends to vote on which individual/group most deserves a "Pride Award." Create this award and present it in person or by mail to the individual or group named in the chosen article.

- Design a folder to hold samples of your personal best work that you are especially proud of. Date each paper/project and organize them by subject and topic/task. Brainstorm standards or criteria by which you can judge each paper/project before including it in the folder. Tape these standards to the inside cover of the work portfolio. Once a week, browse through the folder, remove any work that no longer meets your standards. Add any new paperwork, photos, or examples of personal best that make you experience the LIFESKILL of Pride as a student. Share the contents of the folder at a parent-teacher-student conference and explain why you are proud of each one as an example of the Lifelong Guideline of Personal Best. Also offer it to family guests who are interested in learning more about your personal growth and achievements.

AGES 13+

- Watch the movie/video *October Sky* or *Fly Away Home*. Identify three or more actions of the main character that exemplify the LIFESKILL of PRIDE. Explain your choices to a family member and also share a time in your life when you have made a personal decision that has given you that same sense of the LIFESKILL of Pride.

- Observe an older family member (e.g., parent, grandparent, aunt, uncle, guardian) and identify two or more ways you are proud of actions he/she has taken in the past year. Create an award to present to him/her. When you present the award, explain how his/her actions made you proud and how his/her modeling will help you to make better choices in the future.

- With two family members, brainstorm the attributes or characteristics of a great family. Identify five that are most important to all of you. Create checklists for your family members to complete after working together cooperatively on family chores. Include a way to evaluate such interpersonal skills as Active Listening, No Put-Downs, Personal Best, and providing positive feedback. Share your individual observations and feelings. Lead a discussion at the dinner table about how well your family measures up to the attributes of a great family. Identify strengths and weaknesses. As a family, choose an area to work on for the next month.

- Choose two or more popular songs whose lyrics encourage developing a sense of pride in one's accomplishments. Teach the lyrics for one of the songs to your family at the next large gathering or celebration. Invite family members to use their musical talents and skills to accompany you on musical instruments. Vote to determine if this song is worthy of becoming a "family theme song." If the vote is positive, lead the song whenever the family gets together during the next year. If the vote is negative, introduce another song. Keep introducing songs until you find one the family wants to adopt as a way of acknowledging and celebrating the family's sense of the LIFESKILL of Pride.

- Choose one of the following well-known people (Dr. Martin Luther King, John F. Kennedy, Mahatma Gandhi, Harriet Beecher Stowe, Harriet Tubman, Lef Lewenza, Franklin D. Roosevelt, Cesar Chavez, or another person of your choosing). Explain how this person's actions have changed the lives of a segment of some population. Identify a group that should feel the LIFESKILL of Pride in the actions taken by this individual. Reflect on how these actions might impact your life or decisions you may have to make. Share your thoughts with a parent or other adult in the family.

- Choose a skill or talent in relation to the arts (e.g., drama, singing, playing an instrument, dance, drawing, painting, cinematography). Create an action plan timeline that will enable you to develop this skill/talent to a level of Personal Best. Celebrate each success along the way to reaching your goal. Keep a journal of your achievements, thoughts, and feelings in relation to the LIFESKILL of PRIDE for a minimum of three months.

- Participate in a group activity (e.g., Scouts, 4-H, Boys or Girls Club, church group, volunteer, sports team). Select one of your club's/group's goals and develop a five-step plan that you will follow to reach this goal. Share your thoughts with one of the adult leaders and ask for feedback on the potential of this plan. Write a letter of appreciation to this adult when you feel a sense of the LIFESKILL of Pride in reaching your goal.

- Review the requirements that non-citizens must follow to become citizens of the United States of America. Obtain sample questions they must answer correctly before their citizenship is final. Ask for volunteers to take the test and learn if they have the necessary knowledge to become citizens. Contact federal representatives to find out how many new citizens will be sworn in during the next ceremony in your area. Make a congratulatory card that comments on their pride in citizenship for each person. Attend the ceremony and present the cards. Write your feelings about participating in this event in your journal.

SIGNS OF SUCCESS

Congratulations! Children are showing signs of Pride when they

- Bring their friends home to meet their family members
- Introduce their family as "the best family a kid can have"
- Acknowledge the gifts and talents exemplified in the family circle
- Support family members with encouraging words and share in their satisfaction when the task is accomplished and a goal achieved

- Work together as a family unit to accomplish a task and share the joy in a job well done
- Share "personal best" papers and products with their parents
- Research their cultural roots and share the information with family members; learn to speak their native language well
- Chant positive school cheers at sports events
- Take music lessons and perform for family members
- Compliment classmates on their knowledge of different cultures
- Look forward to attending a family and class reunions

Keep trying! Students need more practice when they

- Ridicule someone else's efforts and personal best
- Put-down family members to their face and behind their back
- Don't complete family jobs and homework; are hasty, messy, or inaccurate
- Refuse to be seen with some or all family members in public
- Mock family members for their beliefs, behavior, and interests
- Neglect to use the Lifelong Guidelines and LIFESKILLS in daily life
- Keep a messy, sloppy room, and have little or no regard for personal belongings
- Deface their home and family property
- Boo or use derisive language during an event
- Use put-downs about someone's race, culture, religion, or economic status
- Can't find a sport, club, or activity in which to participate

Literature Link ~ Pride

AGES 4-8

Penny's Worth of Character, A — Jesse Stuart, Jim Wayne Miller, Jerry A. Herndon, James McGifford (Ashland, KY: Jesse Stuart Foundation, 1993)

People Could Fly, The: American Black Folktales (AFA) — Virginia Hamilton (New York: Knopf, a division of Random House, 1993)

Verdi — Janell Cannon (New York: Harcourt Brace, 1997)

Golden Tales: Myths and Legends from Latin America (HA) — Lulu Delacre (New York: Scholastic Trade, 1996)

AGES 9-12

Devil's Arithmetic, The — Jane Yolen (New York: Puffin Books, 1990)

My Name Is Maria Isabel (HA) — Alma Flor Ada (London: Athenium, 1993)

Roll of Thunder, Hear My Cry (AFA) (TE) — Mildred D. Taylor (New York: Dial Books, 1976.)

Trumpet of the Swan, The (TE) — E.B. White. (New York: HarperTrophy Books, 1973)

AGES 13+

Contender, The — Robert Lipsyte (New York: HarperCollins Books, 1967)

Lesson Before Dying, A — Ernest J. Gaines (New York: Vintage Books, 1997)

M. C. Higgins, the Great (AFA) — Virginia Hamilton (New York: Simon & Schuster, 1999)

Runner, The — Cynthia Voigt (New York: Athenium, a division of MacMillan, 1985)

Family Resources

7 Habits of Highly Effective Families, The: Building a Beautiful Family Culture in a Turbulent World — Stephen R. Covey and Sandra Merrill Covey (Trumbill, CT: Golden Books Publishing Company, 1998)

What Kids Need to Succeed: Proven, Practical Ways to Raise Good Kids (B4E) — Peter Benson, PH.D., Judy Galbraith, M.A., and Pamela Espeland (Minneapolis, MN: Free Spirit Publishing, 1998)

Multicultural books: **(AFA)**=African American, **(ASA)**=Asian American, **(HA)**=Hispanic American, **(ME)**=Multi-Ethnic, **(NA)**=Native American, **(TE)**=listed in the teacher edition of this book, *Tools for Citizenship and Life: Using the ITI Lifelong Guidelines and LIFESKILLS in the Classroom*, **(BFE)**=available through Books for Educators

Chapter 21
Problem Solving

"CHALLENGE YOURSELF TODAY"

problem *n* **1:** a question raised for inquiry, consideration, or solution **2 a:** an intricate, unsettled question **b:** a source of perplexity, distress, or vexation
solving *v* **1:** to find a solution

Problem Solving: To create solutions for difficult situations and everyday problems

WHAT IS PROBLEM SOLVING?

Problem solving isn't limited to the weighty and complex questions of life or the realm of nuclear physics. Problem solving is an everyday activity for each and every one of us. When we pop out of bed on a workday and rush to the closet, one problem we face is, "What's not too dirty, not too wrinkled, and matches my slacks?" Then, "Let's see, what can I grab for breakfast that can be put together in the few minutes I have left?" And on and on.

On a more academic level, none of you could read this book if you hadn't become problem solvers somewhere along the way. Readers must solve phonetic puzzles about the sounds letters make and the pronunciation of those sounds to form words (does this set of letters follow the rules or is it an exception). Readers need to solve the meaning of those words in context to understand the message being communicated. Also, how did you get a copy of this book? Did you order it through the mail? Via fax? By a phone call? Over the Internet? Each of these activities requires problem-solving* skills. All day, every day, our brains and bodies work together to decode a multitude of puzzles—some simple, others complex and difficult. Then, we seek workable solutions. Problem solving is purposeful thinking focused on a particular topic.

The ability to solve problems is a prized commodity in the workplace and invaluable in our personal and family lives. Without it, our options in life are indeed limited.

---

* Note to the reader: Your child may be confused by "problem solving" appearing sometimes with a hyphen and sometimes without. Help him/her learn the general rules of hyphenating: No hyphen when the two words are used as a noun; a hyphen when they are used as an adjective, as in "problem-solving skills."

Problem Solving from a Brain Research Perspective

Howard Gardner, professor of psychology at Harvard University, considers problem solving a key element in defining intelligence. For him, intelligence is not a number from an IQ test but something far more powerful and practical—"a problem-solving and/or product-producing capability . . . that is valued across cultures."* Gardner identifies eight intelligences: logical-mathematical, linguistic, spatial, musical, bodily-kinesthetic, naturalist, interpersonal, and intra-personal. Very importantly, each of these intelligences operates from a different part of the brain. However, they are typically used in varying combinations. Problem-solving or product-producing thinking from only one intelligence is rare; most real-life problems require a mix of intelligences.

While we are born with all eight intelligences, we develop some more than others due to personal preference and the encouragement and practice afforded by family and culture. This, along with the fact that no two brains are the same, results in very different problem-solving performances in our homes as well as in classrooms. We should provide our children opportunities both to hone their strengths as well as improve their weaknesses. Life isn't choosy; there are no guarantees that where it drops us will be a good fit with our learning and performance strengths. Thus, each child should be encouraged to develop his/her capacities in all eight areas to the fullest extent possible. The challenge for both parents and teachers, therefore, is to provide many problem-solving opportunities which call on a rich, integrated mix of intelligences.

I strongly recommend that you acquaint yourself with Gardner's explanation of multiple intelligences. User-friendly sources include *Seven Kinds of Smarts* by Thomas Armstrong and the ITI book for your grade level. (See Appendix A)**

What Problem Solving Is Not

The human brain does not have to be taught to solve problems—it's a built-in, automatic function as natural as breathing. It seeks patterns in a powerful, meaning-making process that is propelled by both survival instinct and curiosity. Schemes to teach children critical thinking through contrived, step-by-step approaches to solve particular kinds of problems are not supported by brain research about how the brain works. What parents and teachers can and should do, however, is to provide children with lots of opportunities to solve problems—problems meaningful to them, not the dry, who-cares worksheet variety.

Practice in handling real problems is how we train ourselves to be effective problem solvers. Every area of home life and curriculum content at school should pose worthwhile problems for children to solve. Practice develops not only problem-solving capabilities but strengthens self-concept and increases the likelihood that learning will be stored in long-term memory.

---

* *Frames of Mind: Theory of Multiple Intelligences* by Howard Gardner. (New York: Basic Books, Inc., 1985), p. xi.
** *Seven Kinds of Smarts* by Thomas Armstrong. (New York: Penguin Books USA, Inc., 1993).

WHY PRACTICE PROBLEM SOLVING?

Since life is composed of one problem-solving experience after another, trying to avoid problem solving is futile and foolish. A baby wants a rattle, problem solving begins. When a toddler can't reach the cookie in the jar, problem solving continues. Want to ride a bike like the big kids? Solve the problem by learning how! Don't know what career you want? Research, become an intern, work for a temporary employment company. Daughter's sick but you can't miss work? Call grandma, a friend, a "sick kid" sitter, take a personal day off. Wonder what to do about dinner? Look in the freezer, run to the store, make reservations at a local restaurant. Need money? Drive to the cash machine, borrow from your kids, raid the home emergency fund, or figure out how to solve the problem without money. Problem solving isn't a choice; it's a survival imperative.

A Typical Day In The Life Of . . . (Insert Your Name Here)

Daily living, including what goes on at our home and workplace, provides an unending parade of opportunities to analyze situations, generate alternative solutions, choose the most feasible solution, and then implement it. And, since every solution raises more problems, the need to solve problems is as unavoidable as breathing. Think about what's happened in your life today and the many questions you faced. Have you solved them all? If you're like most people, probably not; some dilemmas take longer than others to solve. Do we always get to "like" our solutions? Not necessarily! If the old, overworked, over-repaired car breaks down again and our favorite choice is to buy a newer model but there's not enough money in the family budget, then we may have to settle for another quick fix until we can save enough cash or float a loan to cover the purchase price of a newer car. But, in the meantime, we must have a short-term solution.

HOW DO YOU PRACTICE PROBLEM SOLVING?

As mentioned earlier, problem solving is an innate capability that we have been perfecting since infancy. When we were hungry, we developed a distinct cry that our parents recognized as a "feed me" signal; when wet, we developed a variation on the food cry that communicated our need; when we wanted attention, we learned to be coy and charming. We've been solving problems all our lives.

However, to further enhance children's problem-solving capacities, we as parents and family members must provide them lots of practice and help them become more conscious of their problem-solving processes.

Practice problem solving? We can't live without it! But by consciously noticing the problems and their solutions, we can make future decisions faster and more confidently.

Give Your Child Lots of Practice

Give your child lots and lots of practice. Assign him/her chores that require thinking and problem solving not just rote grunt work. Without over burdening your child, invite him/her into aspects of family management that are understandable now and essential knowledge/skill as an adult. Problems in life are a reality. The better we become at handling them, the more successful and enjoyable our lives become.

Make Problem-Solving Processes More Conscious

There are many ways to make problem-solving processes more conscious. Here are but a few. Once your child gets started, he/she will create his/her own.

Teach Your Child How to Use the Generic Steps in Problem Solving. Sometimes simply bringing to mind the generic steps* in problem solving can help. When we feel lost, it helps to ask ourselves, "Where am I now? Am I still working to analyze the problem? Have I exhausted the possibilities; have I generated all the possible alternative solutions? Do I know enough to make an informed choice among the alternatives?" With these basic steps in mind, adults and children can travel around their mental landscape, exploring their problem, moving and sorting the pieces until the problem is solved.

Teach Your Child About Multiple Intelligences. Give your child practice solving problems using all eight intelligences. Teach your child to rewrite inquiries by substituting one intelligence for another so that he/she can tackle a problem using his/her strongest intelligence(s). In others words, help your child realize that there is more than one way to analyze a problem, more than one useful perspective, more than one possible solution.

Teach Your Child to Talk to Him/Herself. Teach your child to become conscious of his/her inner voice—how to direct it and keep it positive and accurate. Self-talk such as, "I don't know what I'm doing; I'll never be able to get this," is not helpful. On the other hand, "Man, this is easy; I'll blitz this one, no worries," may not be accurate either and may lead to overlooking valuable information. Encourage your child to consciously ask him/herself where he/she is in the generic problem-solving steps.

Useful self-talk might include: "Where have I seen this kind of thing before? What do I already know about this situation?" "I heard my dad talk about this once. Now, what did he say?" "Perhaps I'm not looking at the real issues here . . . just the most obvious ones. What else could be causing this problem?"

Teach Your Child How to Process the Process. Problem solving is a learned skill; thus, prior experience is invaluable. Learning to process the process significantly speeds up our learning curves. In the TRIBES program,* teachers are encouraged to have children analyze the process of working together after each group assignment; you can apply these same ideas at home. The analysis can be

---

* The generic steps in problem solving are: identify the problem, generate alternative solutions, select the most feasible alternative, implement the chosen alternative, assess how well the chosen solution is working, and repeat the cycle.

about household chores—the quality of the job and the smoothness of the process of working together, the way siblings and/or friends play together, and so forth. Was the problem solving the result of random guesswork, did they have a hunch or hypothesis that guided them, did prior experience help? Was it easy or difficult (if difficult, what did they learn from the process)? What Lifelong Guidelines and LIFESKILLs were most helpful? Was it helpful to repeat to themselves the generic steps in problem solving? And so forth.

Although "processing the process" with family members is similar to self-talk, it often produces greater feedback potential because it draws on the wider resources of two or more brains.

Allow Your Child to Make Mistakes and Experience the Consequences.
Often, trouble making decisions is due to lack of experience in making decisions. Parents and teachers too often wish for a mistake-free life for their children. Not possible! It wasn't and isn't for us, why should we expect it to be any different for our children? If the consequences aren't life threatening or likely to do long-term physical or psychological damage, allow your child to experience the unworkability or dissatisfying results of ineffective problem-solving decisions. Inconvenience, disappointment, and even a little pain are great teachers. Allow the experience—things, events, or other people—to teach your child. The more adept children become at learning from the circumstances around them—without lectures from the adults in their lives—the better off they'll be.

Make Sure Your Child Can "See" a Problem and Alternative Solutions.
If your child is hesitant to engage in problem solving because it is consistently unsettling or if he/she impulsively picks unworkable solutions, make sure your child has the mental wiring** that allows language (oral or written) to be processed in ways that allow him/her to "see" a problem and possible solutions for it. It's difficult to solve a problem if we can't "see" the alternatives. See the discussion of visualizing and verbalizing in Chapter 4.

Problem Solving and Preparation.
Many problems we face on a day-to-day basis could be solved to greater satisfaction with a little planning in advance because effective problem solving depends on the feasibility of the options available to us at the time. If all the alternatives available are unsatisfactory, then our solution will be unsatisfactory. Consequently, thinking ahead and making contingency plans for situations that are likely to occur will allow us to come up with better solutions. For example, if we live in earthquake country, where most west coast residents do, plan ahead. Having a full emergency pack on hand, at home and in each car, is bound to improve our problem solving in the event of an earthquake. Likewise, the daily problem of what to wear to work or school can be solved more to our satisfaction if we wash, dry, fold, and return items to their proper place in the closet and drawers as soon as they get dirty.

---

* See *TRIBES: A New Way of Learning and Being Together* by Jeanne Gibbs (Sausalito, California: CenterSource Systems, 1995).

** Learning is the result of real, physiological changes in the brain. Dendrites grow, axons mylinate, and neurons enlarge, thus allowing neurons to connect to more and more other neurons. Such connections are often referred to as "mental wiring."

WHAT DOES PROBLEM SOLVING LOOK LIKE IN THE REAL WORLD?

We

- Look for misplaced and lost belongings
- Call a plumber to fix leaky pipes
- Phone 911 in an emergency
- Find the doctor best for us
- Save money until there's enough to buy what we want without going into debt
- Apply for a mortgage before buying a house
- Develop a sales strategy to sell our old house
- Open the "Help" section on the computer program when something isn't working right
- Brainstorm solutions with family, friends, and coworkers
- Ask advice from someone who has had a similar problem

WHAT DOES PROBLEM SOLVING LOOK LIKE AT HOME?

Adults

- Evaluate the family budget and decide what to cut in order to stay within the family income
- Develop a retirement plan
- Teach our child skills that will enable him/her to make minor repairs around the house
- Discuss behavior concerns and decide on logical, natural consequences for misdeeds
- Organize car pools to get children to and from sports events, medical/dental appointments, and after-school care in a timely way
- Exchange babysitting duties with other families in the neighborhood in order to "buy" time alone to plan/carry out family plans
- Confer with school officials and teacher(s) concerning our child's lack of progress or disinterest in learning; create a plan to help solve the problem and stick to it

Children

- Resolve differences with siblings, friends, and neighbors in an amicable way

- Brainstorm ways to share family belongings such as sports equipment, bikes, ice skates, basketballs, and so forth

- Ask for advice from other family members when facing difficult decisions rather than expect others to fix the problem for them

- Come up with alternative solutions to help solve problems the family is facing

- Find/create substitutes for needed items, for example, a piece of string for a broken shoelace

- Find ways to care for pets, toys, and other belongings in ways that exhibit care and concern while avoiding creating problems for others

- Learn to live within their allowance and to develop long-term saving plans which enable them to buy purchase "big ticket" items such as a bicycle, baseball mit, etc.

- Report any unusual e-mail or contacts via the Web to an adult in the home

OPPORTUNITIES TO PRACTICE PROBLEM SOLVING

AGES 4-8

- Listen to the story *Jumanji*. Describe two or more problems that happen to the two children in the story. Share how you would solve each of those problems in the book and, if applicable, in your own life. Discuss your ideas with the person reading you the book. Ask for his/her solutions to the same problems.

- Listen to a family member read *The Story of the Five Chinese Brothers*. Divide a piece of paper into six equal sections. In the first section, draw an elephant. In each of the other sections, illustrate what each of the five brothers thought an elephant was like. Explain, to the family member who read you the story, two or more reasons why the brothers' problem-solving strategies weren't working.

- Read one of the books in the Arthur Series (books by Marc Brown). Divide a piece of drawing paper in half. On the first half, draw a picture showing Arthur's problem. Write words to explain the problem. On the other half of the paper, draw Arthur's solution to the problem. Decide if you agree with Arthur's solution. Share your ideas and feelings about the solution with someone in your family. Offer one or more other choices Arthur could have tried.

- Create a plan that allows you to share a toy or bike with a brother/sister in a fair way. Explain your idea and ask him/her to offer other ideas to help solve the problem. Try both solutions and discuss which one works best for the two of you. Explain the solution to an adult in your family.

- Create a plan to solve the problem of nightly mess (toys and other items that don't belong) in the family room every night. Organize your toys and other personal belongings in your area or room. Give each item its own special spot. Return it to this spot when you are finished using it. Ask other family members to return each borrowed item back where they found it.

- Make a plan to care for a family pet when you are home from school. Include exercise, feeding, and playing time. Try your plan for one week and discuss the results with a parent or another adult in your house. Share your pet's reactions to your care and attention. Make any changes that will improve your time with this pet.

- Plan to pack your backpack or school bag at night before you go to bed. Draw/list materials, clothing, or objects you will need to bring for class each day of the week. Post this near the door of your bedroom. Place all of these regular items in the bag first. Add any other items that the teacher wants you to have for special events or projects. Recheck your bag in the morning to make sure that everything you need is carefully packed in the backpack. Discuss your plan with a parent or an older brother/sister after two weeks. Make any changes that will help so that you always have the right school materials when you need them.

- Create a plan to solve the "great unmatched socks mystery." Implement your plan for one month. Share with a parent how well your solution is working.

- Identify two problems that most concern you at home. Use your LIFESKILL of Problem Solving to analyze the problem, generate alternatives, and select a solution. Share your thoughts with a parent. Ask him/her for additional ideas.

AGES 9-12

- Choose a picture book to read to a younger brother/sister; select one with many opportunities for problem solving. Practice reading the story with emotion and expression. Arrange to read it to a younger brother/sister and some of his/her friends. Stop reading the story each time a problem has been introduced by the author. Ask your audience to predict what will happen next. Gather at least four ideas about how to solve the problem. Continue reading to reveal the author's solution. Invite the children to compare their predictions to what actually happened in the book. Which solutions do they like best? Continue reading, pausing, predicting, brainstorming, and comparing throughout the story. Share with a parent what you learned about the LIFESKILL of Problem Solving by reading and discussing this story.

- Identify a pressing problem in your community. Collect information: newspaper articles addressing this issue, news clips, radio broadcasts, and/or attend a public meeting on the subject. Identify the opposing points of view about the problem and how to solve it. Determine which side represents your feelings on this issue. Add your own solutions for the problem. Share your solutions with an adult family member.

- Find out how to solve the following: Turning in a stray animal, licensing a pet, locating the owner of a nearby open lot, obtaining emergency medical care, helping someone who is choking. Explain to a parent how to solve each problem and ask them to provide feedback on how well you used the LIFESKILL of Problem Solving.

Chapter 21—Problem Solving

- Brainstorm five or more problems that the adults in your family have had to deal with in the past month. List each problem and beside it write the solution your family chose. Brainstorm two or more solutions for each problem. Confer with an adult to determine if any of these ideas had been seriously considered as a solution for the problem. Discuss why or why not.

- Locate five or more "brain teaser" puzzles and/or logic puzzles that require problem-solving skills to find a solution. Determine three or more LIFESKILLS that will help you to find the answers. Keep a log noting how many minutes you spend before you find a solution for each puzzle. Write/draw the solution(s) on a piece of paper. Rank the puzzles from easiest to hardest and decide how each LIFESKILL provided support for your efforts. Try each puzzle a second, third, and fourth time to see if you can increase the speed with which you find the solution. Share these results with another puzzle fan in your house. Also share with him/her what you have learned about the LIFESKILL of Problem Solving.

- Create a long-term savings plan to buy something special for yourself or another family member. Research the cost of the item (include any sales tax), the amount you can save weekly, and determine an approximate date when you will have saved the amount of money needed to purchase the product. Brainstorm two or more ways you can earn extra money to add to your savings, shortening the amount of time necessary to save the needed amount. Identify two or more LIFESKILLS that will help you to reach your goal. Every week share with a parent your progress and what you're learning about the LIFESKILLS you are using during this project.

- Brainstorm five typical problems that children your age face every day, such as lost homework, tardiness, fights, being offered drugs/alcohol, finding money, losing a pet. With a friend, choose three of the problems to dramatize. Create two different endings for each problem. Present your skits to your family during dinner time and ask them to vote for the best solution.

- Learn the following computer skills and create a step-by-step procedure chart for each process: Emptying the cache, deleting and restoring a file, copying and booting up a restored hard drive, downloading and opening a file, and defragmenting the hard drive to create more space. Share with a parent how well you used the LIFESKILL of Problem Solving as you were learning to do these procedures. Practice each procedure until you can teach it with ease to another person.

- Learn to solve the following problems: shut off the water main to the house, turn off the electricity to the house, shut off the gas/butane line, change a flat tire, contact the poison control center, perform the Heimlich maneuver, or apply CPR. Practice until you can perform each with confidence and in a safe, calm way. Ask for feedback from a friend or adult whose opinion you respect.

AGES 13+

- Discuss the following topics with your parents/guardians:
    - ~ Drug use and abuse
    - ~ Curfews
    - ~ Under-age drinking of alcoholic beverages
    - ~ Peer pressure to be sexually active

    Together, brainstorm strategies and write procedures to solve each problem in ways that work for you and your family. Keep the completed list in a wallet or purse.

- Create an action plan that will provide for the safe use of the Internet by a younger brother or sister. Discuss this plan with an adult. Include a way to block unwanted mail. Write safety procedures with the child and insist that he/she follow them. If he/she encounters unwanted e-mail or any sexual comments or content, insist that he/she tell or a parent immediately. Help him/her learn to access the web with an eye on safety first. Check with this child daily to determine if further precautions are necessary for personal safety.

- Invite your parents to read the adult book *Protecting the Gift: Keeping Children and Teenagers Safe (And Parents Sane)* by Gavin De Becker. Ask them to discuss a variety of situations and problem-solving procedures to follow. Volunteer to take classes in the art of self-defense (e.g., Judo, Karate, Tae-Kwan-Do). Practice until you reach some degree of proficiency at self-protection. Discuss under which situations and settings you will feel justified in using your newly developed skills.

- Find out what to do, whom to call, which switch to push/pull, and/or which handle to turn to solve each of the following problems: The furnace won't start, the hot water heater has no hot water, the toilet is clogged, gas is leaking into the kitchen or another part of the house, the smoke detector or security system won't turn off after the emergency has ended, or water is dripping through the ceiling from an upstairs bathroom. Record your problem-solving procedures for each emergency on a 5"x 8" card and place it in a prominent position near the location of the potential problem. Teach another family member how to do each of the safety procedures. Practice them once a month.

- In your journal, record each problem-solving situation you experienced within the previous 24 hours. Classify the problems in categories that work for you, such as family, friends, schoolwork, and situations. Create a second list with the following columns: "Problem Not Solved" and "Problem Solved." Now place the same problems into these new categories. Share the list of Problems Not Solved with a family member and ask him/her for additional solutions. After trying some of the solutions, share the results with him/her.

- Research all sides of a community problem that catches your interest. Interview one or two key people who represent different sides of the issue. Then write a brief summary of the problem; present your information to family members at dinner time. Share your problem-solving process and the solution(s) that seems most practical to you.

- Create a self-evaluation feedback sheet. List all of the Lifelong Guidelines and LIFESKILLS at the top. Provide room to write the problem and the solution you tried. Create a "Reflection" section. For this part, choose two or more Lifelong Guidelines/LIFESKILLS that you used to determine the best solution. If your solution didn't work, identify two or more Lifelong Guidelines/LIFESKILLS that you should consider using the next time you need to solve a problem.

- Research a referendum on the ballot of an upcoming local election. Identify the main issues the referendum is designed to solve. Determine what problems the referendum, as written, will cause. Share with a parent how you would have written the referendum in order to best solve the original problem and avoid creating new ones. Share your ideas with your family during dinner time.

SIGNS OF SUCCESS

Congratulations! Children are showing signs of Problem Solving when they

- Think of many solutions for a problem, rate the choices, and then determine which is best
- Persevere until they find answers
- Share their thinking and reasoning with family and friends
- Ask another person for their perspective and opinion
- Clearly understand the problem
- Accept advice from someone who has solved the same problem
- Discuss misunderstandings in a calm, reasonable manner; persist until the problem gets solved
- Enjoy a puzzle or a challenge

Keep Trying! Children need more practice when they

- Don't like to make decisions
- Whine or cry when they have to solve a problem
- Refuse to listen to advice from people with more experience
- Ignore problems and hope they will disappear
- Brainstorm one answer and stop thinking
- Let others think for them and ignore their "gut feelings"
- Consistently make "bad" choices or provide "off-the-wall" responses

Literature Link ~ Problem Solving

Ages 4-8

Flat Stanley	Jeff Brown (New York: HarperTrophy, 1996)
Jumanji (TE)	Chris Van Allsburg (Boston: Houghton Mifflin, 1981)
Math Curse	Jon Scieszka (New York: Viking Childrens Books, 1995)
When Bluebell Sang	Lisa Campbell Ernst (New York: Aladdin Paperbacks, 1992)

Ages 9-12

Dragonwings (ASA)	Lawrence Yep (New York: HarperTrophy, 1989)
Journey to Jo'berg (AFA)	Beverly Naidoo (New York: HarperTrophy, 1988)
Just Juice (HA)	Rosa Guy (New York: Scholastic Books, 1998)
Kid's Guide to Dealing With Daily Dilemmas, A	Linda Schwartz (Santa Barbara, CA: Learning Works, 1993)

Ages 13+

Endurance, The: Shackleton's Legendary Antarctic Expedition	Caroline Alexander New York: Knopf, 1998)
Kids' Guide to Social Action: How to Solve the Social Problems You Choose and Turn Creative Thinking into Positive Action	Barbara A. Lewis, Pamela Espeland, Caryn Pernu (Minneapolis MN: Free Spirit Publishing, 1998)
Stones in Water	Donna Jo Napoli (London: Puffin Books, 1999)
Stonewall's Gold	Judy Sheindlin (New York: St. Martins Press, 200)

Family Resources

Judge Judy Sheindlin's Win or Lose by How You Choose	Judy Sheindlin (New York: HarperCollins Juvenile Books, 2000)
Kids Can Cooperate: A Practical Guide to Teaching Problem Solving	Elizabeth Crary (Seattle, WA: Parenting Press, 1984)
"What Happened at School Today?": Helping Your Child Handle Everyday School Problems	Judi Craig, Ph.D. (New York: Hearst Books, 1994)

Multicultural books: **(AFA)**=African American, **(ASA)**=Asian American, **(HA)**=Hispanic American, **(ME)**=Multi-Ethnic, **(NA)**=Native American, **(TE)**=listed in the teacher edition of this book, *Tools for Citizenship and Life: Using the ITI Lifelong Guidelines and LIFESKILLS in the Classroom*, **(BFE)**=available through Books for Educators

Resourcefulness

Chapter 22

"THERE IS A WAY!"

resourceful *adj* able to meet situations: capable of devising ways and means
ways and means *n pl* 1: methods and resources for accomplishing something and especially for defraying expenses

Resourcefulness: To respond to challenges and opportunities in innovative and creative ways

WHAT IS RESOURCEFULNESS?

Remember Apollo 13, maroned in space with dwindling oxygen and no heat? The ground crew was urgently assembled in a room and given the exact same items contained in the space capsule. Their assignment: Solve the oxygen problem before the astronauts die. Their solution is the epitome of resourcefulness in action. They applied innovative thinking skills to devise unusually imaginative and creative solutions through the ingenious use of ideas and materials. In a billion dollar space exploration program, they saved the mission and the lives of three astronauts with a $3.00 role of duct tape!

We all know family members, co-workers, and friends who are renouned for recognizing and taking on uncommon opportunities, applying unusual strategies, and landing on their feet! They are the people we go to when we have an unusual problem to solve or when all the tried and true answers aren't working. Resourcefulness is highly valued in any society.

Resourceful people stand out from the crowd. They tend to be multi-talented, multi-track thinkers with optimistic, "can do" attitudes. They are masters at making do with limited resources; in fact, they excel at going beyond "making do." When the going gets tough, they thrive.

Multi-Talented. As author Leslie Hart points out, creativity is the result of flexible use of known patterns and mental programs.* Resourcefulness isn't the result of wishful thinking; you have to

---

* See *Human Brain and Human Learning* by Leslie Hart (Kent, Washington: Books For Educators, Inc., 1999), pp. 166-167.

know a lot about many things to be resourceful. MacGyver, the non-gun-packing TV character of the 1970s, couldn't pull off his escape and capture schemes without a formidable knowledge of science, especially chemistry. Similarly, it should come as no surprise that most of the early astronauts were mid-Western farm boys who had grown up on farms where resourcefulness was practiced daily and spelled the difference between economic success or failure. They grew up as Jack-of-all-trades and masters of many. Whether on the ground or in space, they were well-equipped to be resourceful.

Multi-Track Thinking. Resourceful people have multi-track minds. While exploring what seems to be the most feasible solution, they continue to mull over additional alternatives. At the same time, they keep testing whether the question is really worth asking and if their analysis of the problem is accurate. Often a different perspective is all that's needed.

Optimism. Resourceful people are visionaries who exercise perception and imagination. They are optimists with a "can-do" attitude; they are certain they will find a workable solution. They trust that there is no simple or right answer and that there is more than one workable solution. They expect to use a wide variety of techniques to accomplish their task. They know they may well be surprised by the options that become available as they proceed.

For the resourceful person, no idea is considered too foolish or unworkable to consider. The solution may emerge out of logical, deductive reasoning or pure happenstance. Resourceful people are not afraid of failure arising from trial and error experimentation. They enjoy exploring the possibilities as they reach into their bag of tricks, find a previous idea or solution, twist it, turn it, sometimes even totally reinvent it, or abandon it completely. They are pragmatists and they keep moving forward.

WHY PRACTICE RESOURCEFULNESS?

In the real world, few problems come with instructions about how to solve them. If we aren't resourceful, our problem-solving capabilities will be anemic and underpowered. In our fast-paced, ever-changing world, what worked before may not work now or ever again. Resourcefulness is a necessity, not a luxury.

Resourcefulness Is Needed for Everyday Living

From the number of problems we encounter each day, we might think that humans are problem magnets. No money for supplies? Tooth just cracked but the checkbook is empty? Nothing in the refrigerator for dinner? Two meetings scheduled at the same time? The forward on the basketball team has the chickenpox and no on else on the team has had them? All of these circumstances call for innovative problem solving and creative thinking. The more serious the problem, the greater the need for resourcefulness.

Resourcefulness Is Respected Everywhere. Resourceful people are often called upon to deal with problems and situations that have been mishandled or ignored, where problems have remained unsolved.

People who can find solutions within the current circumstances and resources—without requiring an influx of money—are highly respected and carefully listened to.

Resourcefulness and Citizenship

Effective citizenship in a democratic society requires high levels of resourcefulness. We must be resourceful to ferret out information needed to identify and analyze problems. For example, today's expensive Superfund sites could have been avoided early on at minimal expense but we didn't see the potential problems at the time. Rachel Carson used the LIFESKILL of Resourcefulness to create environmental theories and criteria to help us recognize environment problems much earlier than anyone else. Her book, *Silent Spring*, is a landmark contribution to environmental research and activist citizenship.*

Solving problems once identified requires even more resourcefulness. From my perspective, the challenges we face far outstrip available resources to solve them using conventional solutions. More of the same, reinvoking solutions that worked before but are ineffective now, ignoring a problem in hopes that it will resolve itself, are dead ends. If we are to thrive as a society, we must be resourceful enough to come up with new solutions.

To grow such a citizenry, we must give our children lots of practice solving problems that require resourcefulness. In the ITI model, this is done through various social/political action projects. Here's an example.

A True Story from Co-Author Sue Pearson. It wasn't too long after my first ITI training that I realized my children's desks (old, big, slant-top lecture type with chair attached and an opening for books on the left side) were not conducive to learning clubs or grouping of any kind. If I tried to group them in rectangles, half of the students couldn't get into their desk storage areas. When I tried circles, they bumped their heads on others' desks while bending over to get materials. In addition, everything left on top of the desks, such as baskets of materials to be shared or plants, slid right off.

My school couldn't afford new furniture and wouldn't for years. A few of us went to the principal and shared our dream of having flat-top desks with separate chairs and storage access from the top.

Shortly afterward, our principal found an offer of 700 desks, free for the asking, on the Internet. We suggested she take them sight unseen. A few months later we received a local address where the desks were being stored. On the third floor of a dusty old warehouse, our dreams were answered—enough "new" desks to outfit about seven classrooms.

The resourcefulness of our parent group was immediate and overwhelming. They borrowed trucks and recruited people to help move the desks to our school. Our resourceful students arrived at school wearing bathing suits beneath their clothes. The fourth graders hosed down the desks and chairs, the fifth graders scrubbed them clean and the sixth graders buffed them dry and carried them up to our classrooms. Our old desks were sold as "homework stations" for a few dollars each.

* See *Silent Spring* by Rachel Carlson (New York: Houghton Mifflin Company, 1962).

Not only did we get the desks free, but we made money in the process. A wonderful example of the LIFESKILL of Resourcefulness in action.

HOW DO YOU PRACTICE IT?

There is no patented formula or set of directions for becoming more resourceful. But, there are some tips. Some of the suggestions below are for you as a parent/family member; others are for children.

Be Open to Challenges

We can't sit home and play it safe if we want to practice resourcefulness. This doesn't mean that we should endanger ourselves but we must be willing to court uncertainty. By accepting more challenges, by opening our souls to new adventures, by taking chances, our brains develop new capabilities for future use. We learn more and become increasingly resourceful—more of the person we want to be.

Volunteer for Projects

To stretch your "resourcefulness index," volunteer for a new committee or accept a new position. Start a new club or organization, such as Grandparents As Parents Club, Cancer Support Group, and so forth. Share a hobby or skill. Offer suggestions and don't give up if at first your ideas aren't embraced with enthusiasm. Think of Benjamin Franklin, Thomas Edison, Marie Curie, George Washington Carver, George Pullman, W. E. B. DuBois, and Steve Wozniak; also think of a single mother stretching a dollar ten ways, a father working two jobs to provide for his family, or a grandparent learning to cope with increased mobility. The LIFESKILL of Resourcefulness has to start somewhere. Why not with you?

Lessons from a Jedi Warrior

Resourcefulness is an attitude—one well illustrated by the Jedi warriors*: Stay in the present, use a new point of view to overcome obstacles, go back to the source, and don't accept failure as an option—try, try, and try again.

Stay in the Present. One of the key skills of a Jedi warrior is his mental capacity to stay in the present and ignore negative thoughts and anger. Stay focused on the task at hand. Ignore negative feedback from family, friends, peers, and co-workers who offer comments such as: "We tried that already. Been there, done that. It won't work!" "That's a crazy idea. Where'd you get that one?" "Don't tell that one to the boss."

Such negative responses turn off creative juices and stifle independent, innovative thinking. They also make us feel insignificant, unintelligent, and incapable of performing tasks. Worse,

---

* The Jedi warriors are the "good guys" of George Lucas' *Star Wars* movies. Their ability to focus their thoughts, stay in the present, and control their emotions gives them access to the Force.

they focus our attention on ourselves instead of on the problem to be solved or the product to be created. They erect barriers where none existed before. They create restrictions and restraints in thinking that once flowed freely.

Overcome Obstacles by Changing Point of View. Resourceful people often surmount obstacles in their path merely by changing their point of view. What we are may identify as a mountain, they see as a molehill. What we see as permanent, they see as temporary. What we see as a dead-end barrier, they see as a hurdle to be jumped, a delightful challenge to enliven the day.

Go Back to the Source (And May the Force Be with You). When stumped, go back to the source of the problem. Retry an idea that may have first seemed unrelated or unworkable. Rework an alternative solution, or replay a solution. If it doesn't work, why doesn't it? Is it the concept that's unworkable or its execution? Can you adjust something? Try a different material? Use another source? Find a less expensive way to do it? If still stumped, go to someone you trust, someone who will listen to your ideas and dream with you. Then, go back to the source.

Don't Accept Failure As an Option—Try, Try, and Try Again. To be resourceful, we must persevere. Remember, if the problem we face were an easy one, it would already have been solved. Persistence opens doors. Don't accept failure as an option. Keep trying.

WHAT DOES RESOURCEFULNESS LOOK LIKE IN THE REAL WORLD?

We

- Recycle aluminum cans, plastic bottles, and cardboard
- Find new ways to use technology in medicine, education, government, and business
- Pass on wearable clothing and usable items to charitable organizations for redistribution
- Invent a tool, machine, or product to meet a need
- Create new, innovative ways to accomplish tasks
- Think "outside the box" and sometimes even build a new box

WHAT DOES RESOURCEFULNESS LOOK LIKE AT HOME?

Adults

- Stay open to new and different ways to share information
- Brainstorm a variety of ways to solve a problem

- Provide a variety of inexpensive but worthwhile recreational and educational experiences for children

- Work two or three jobs to take care of our family's basic needs

- Use hand-me-down clothing/toys and shop at garage sales and second-hand stores

- Stretch a paycheck to meet many bills; budget money in ways that support each family member's growth and happiness

Children

- Appreciate different ideas and new ways of thinking

- Delve for the unknown and be innovative and imaginative when creating projects

- Show creativity in thinking, brainstorming original ideas, and conceiving unusual projects

- Use toys and materials in new and creative ways

- Wear hand-me-down clothing, play with second-hand or self-made toys, and ride used bicycles and make the most of these resources

- Work for neighbors to earn money for special purchases

- Search for needed information through the internet, interviews with family elders, the library, and other relevant resources

OPPORTUNITIES TO DEVELOP RESOURCEFULNESS

AGES 4-8

- Listen to/read *The Super Camper Caper* by John Himmelman. List two or more ways the family tries to use the LIFESKILL of Resourcefulness and the results. Then share one idea of your own to help the family.

- Make a list (words or drawings) of five or more activities or games that will give you an idea of something you can do the next time you say, "I'm bored!" or "I have nothing to do!" Make sure these activities or games are things you can do by yourself. Post the list on the refrigerator door. Invite your family to add other ideas to the list. During the next three weeks when you feel bored and feel you've nothing to do, choose an activity off the list and do it until you don't feel bored or at loose ends.

- Take an old single sock, stuff it with one or two other old socks. Make a knot as far up the leg as possible. Use this new toy to entertain your dog by playing tug of war.

Chapter 22—Resourcefulness

- Sort through the toys that you and your brothers and your sisters don't play with any more. Sort them into two piles: GIVE AWAY and NEW USE. Judge each toy. If it is still usable or needs just minor repairs, place it in the GIVE AWAY pile. Find an organization in your community that provides free toys for children and daycare centers. Take your GIVE AWAY pile to them. If the toy is broken beyond repair or too dirty to be cleaned up, place it in the NEW USE pile. Go through each item; look for parts or pieces that might combine to make a new toy or be useful somewhere else. Keep those pieces and use them within one week only. At the end of that week, put the rest of the old, broken toys in a trash bag and put it out for trash pick up; keep your house/ garage/yard as neat and tidy as possible during this project. Share with a parent what you have learned about the LIFESKILL of Resourcefulness during this project.

- Choose a toy from the "New Use" pile. Imagine another life or purpose for this toy. Work to change its appearance and purpose. Draw a picture of the new toy and demonstrate its use.

- Think of some object (perhaps a toy, item of clothing, computer equipment, or sports equipment) that you would like to own. Choose something that costs more than $30. Research legal ways that you could acquire it for less than $10. Narrow your search to three ways. On a chart illustrate the object you want, the three ways you could obtain it for less than $10, and which choice you feel is most creative and workable.

- Look over the "new" hand-me-down clothing that you are going to be wearing. Change the look of each piece to make it "new." Choose one of the following techniques: dye the cloth to make it a new color, change the buttons, add an iron-on design, turn long pants into shorts, cut off long sleeves to make them short, or other such changes. Share with a parent what you learned about the LIFESKILL of Resourcefulness by making these alterations to the clothing.

- Organize the deposit beverage containers. Rinse out each can and bottle. Toss the cans and plastic bottles into a plastic bag and place it inside a 20-30 gallon container. Place each glass bottle back into cardboard holder or box it came in. When the bag or containers are full, take them to your nearest recycle center. Use the deposit money for something special. (*Note:* Some states do not have deposit money on beverage containers.)

AGES 9-12

- Define "boredom." Describe your emotions/attitudes when you are bored. Identify five or more ways you can use the LIFESKILL of Resourcefulness to wipe out boredom. Post the list in your room and add to it as you think of clever activities to keep yourself busy.

- Choose a toy that you no longer care about. Imagine another life for this toy. Create a new use for it. Illustrate the toy and its new purpose. Share this with a family member or friend.

- Create a game that uses three different items from your home recycle bin. Write down the objective(s) of the game. Choose a name for your game; establish at least three rules and a simple scoring system. Invite your family members to play the game with you. Ask for feedback and make any changes that will help others understand the goals, the rules, and how to score it. Invite some some friends to play the final version of the game.

- Determine two or more ways to share family resources (e.g., paper, crayons, markers, pencils, books, scissors, glue). Organize these materials in a neat and orderly way in baskets. Create "Borrowing procedures" that will provide guidelines for using the materials.

- Discuss fair ways to share expensive, one-of-a-kind technology devices (e.g., computer, TV, DVD, camcorder, boom box, VCR, Music Maker) in your home. Write procedures and create a schedule to help organize the plan. Try it for two or more weeks. Brainstorm any changes that will enhance the plan's effectiveness.

- Invent a new game consisting of materials from your home recycle bin. Write one objective (goal) of the game. Choose a name and establish three or more simple rules. Play the game with your family. Ask for feedback and make changes that will improve the game. Invite some neighborhood children to play the new game.

- Discuss ways to share, in fair and orderly ways, two of the most popular items at home that now generate friction between your and sibling and/or friends. Identify the most practical and efficient ways. Write "Procedures for Using _____"; list three to five steps. Phrase them positively and in sentences; include graphics for easy reference. Write the steps in alternating colors. Post the procedures on the refrigerator door (or other location that is easily visible) for two weeks or until the procedures work smoothly.

- Take care of your own clothes for at least three weeks. This includes putting them in a dirty clothes hamper as soon as you take them off, spot removal, washing, drying, ironing, and putting them away. Learn to do two simple repairs, such as sewing on a button or mending a seam. Choose one outfit and redesign a part of it to look fashionable and new (ask for permission before you make any permanent changes). Show the outfit to your family and notice any reactions. Take a photo of the outfit and share it with a neighborhood friend who has similar interests. Share with a parent who is primarily responsible for doing the laundry for your family what you learned about the LIFESKILL of Resourcefulness by doing your own laundry and doing repairs and about how this parent uses the LIFESKILL of Resourcefulness in order to do so many tasks simultaneously.

- Create a business to earn extra money. Choose from one of the following or develop one of your own ideas: pet sitting, dog walking, babysitting, plant sitting, and yard care. Choose a name for the business, prepare flyers (including your name, the business name, phone number, price) and hand them out to your neighbors. Operate your business for at least three months. Share with a parent what you learned about the LIFESKILL of Resourcefulness.

- Brainstorm three emergency situations that might happen to someone your age. For each situation, identify at least two plans of action for each situation. Discuss your ideas with your family and ask if they have any others to suggest as solutions.

- Identify a place in your community that needs some tender, loving care. Consider an empty lot or yard with trash scattered around that needs cleaning or a local statue or monument that needs repairs. Write a plan that includes the goal, obtaining the owner's permission, a list of free or inexpensive materials that will be needed, a time schedule, the skills needed, a sign-up sheet, and an evaluation sheet to determine the effectiveness of your plans.

Chapter 22—Resourcefulness

AGES 13+

- Define "boredom." Describe your emotions/attitudes when you are bored. Identify five or more ways you can use the LIFESKILL of Resourcefulness to wipe out boredom. Post the list in your room and add to it as you think of clever activities to keep yourself busy.

- Think of some object (e.g., toy, item of clothing, computer game, sports equipment) that you need or want. Choose something that costs more than $30. Research legal ways that you could acquire this item for $10 or less. Narrow your search to the three most practical ways. On a chart, list the item, the three ways you can get it for $10 or less and which choice you feel is most workable. Explain this to your family.

- Create a neighborhood business to earn extra money. Choose from one of the following or develop one of your own ideas: pet sitting, dog walking, baby-sitting, plant sitting, and yard care. Choose a name for the business, prepare flyers (including your name, the business name, phone number, price) and hand them out to your neighbors.

- Take care of your own clothes for at least three weeks. This includes putting them in a dirty, clothes hamper as soon as you take them off, spot removal, washing, drying, ironing, and putting them away. Learn to do two simple repairs, such as sewing on a button or mending a seam. Choose one outfit and redesign a part of it to look fashionable and new (ask for permission before you make any permanent changes). Show the outfit to your family and notice any reactions. Take a photo of the outfit and share it with a neighborhood friend who has similar interests. Share with a parent who is primarily responsible for doing the laundry for your family what you learned about the LIFESKILL of Resourcefulness by doing your own laundry and doing repairs and about how this parent uses the LIFESKILL of Resourcefulness in order to do so many tasks simultaneously.

- Earn credits or money towards attending Girls Scout or Boy Scout Camp by participating in fund-raising activities (cookie, firewood, gift-wrapping sales). Leave an itinerary with your parents, go with a partner, bring some change, wear identification and your uniform, and greet people in a friendly way as you go door-to-door with your wares. Note accurate records of sales, keep an eye on your inventory, and compute the amount of money you should have at the end of the day. Give your scout leader the money, your records, and any remaining inventory. Ask for a receipt for any camp credits.

- Design your own greeting cards, wrapping paper, and note cards. Use colored paper, photos, and/or personal drawings to make them attractive. Make a mock up set and share this product with neighbors. Offer to make some personalized stationary for a fair price. Create a special mark (e.g., Hallmark's crown) that represents you to place on the back, center, bottom of each piece. Turn this enterprise into a business and operate it for at least six weeks prior to a holiday such as Valentine's Day or Christmas.

- Plan a food garden for a family of four that would provide enough food for at least three nights a week. Choose three or more different-colored vegetables/plants from the following groups—yellow, green, purple, and orange/red. Determine the size of the garden, the kinds and numbers of plants you will need, a planting schedule, maintenance tasks, and a recipe for each of the vegetables. Share this information with your family. Ask them if you can use your plans to create a real garden in your yard.

- Read local newspaper advertisements and visit a favorite supermarket. Plan a shopping list for a family of four for one week. Include food items for three healthy, nutritious meals (including one brown bag lunch) a day per person, paper products, and cleaning supplies. Create one list that keeps within a weekly budget of $70 or less. Then create a second list with items that cost more than $70 but less than $100.

- Organize a "Second Chance" program for your neighborhood or community. Design a plan for collecting supermarket and restaurant food that would otherwise be disposed of and distributing it to the food banks, soup kitchens, and senior citizens of need in your area. Discuss with health department officials any guidelines that need to be adhered to or strictly followed. Invite a local reporter to share the success of your vision with the entire community.

- Design a disaster kit for your region of the country. Decide which disaster is most likely—tornado, earthquake, blizzard, flood, or hurricane. Discuss with your family six or more items that will help sustain life for you and your family for three days. Choose a sturdy, easy-to-carry container that would hold up during a disaster and place all of the chosen items inside. In addition, choose one personal item that you would like to include. Label the container and share it with your family. Place it in a safe, easy-to-reach location. Check the supplies monthly and replace those that aren't good any more.

SIGNS OF SUCCESS

Congratulations! Children are showing signs of Resourcefulness when they

- Think of new plans for old materials
- Brainstorm many ideas before choosing one
- Use skills and techniques in a new way
- Offer creative and innovative ideas that are out of the ordinary
- Share materials with family members and friends
- Overcome obstacles that stand in the way of solutions
- Create a new product
- Determine the least expensive way to accomplish a goal
- Observe problems in their neighborhoods and search for answers
- Strive to protect the natural environment

Keep trying! Children need more practice when they

- Waste materials and money
- Show no respect or concern for the home and natural environment
- Repeat the same solution even though it hasn't worked the first few times
- Laugh and make fun of other children's imaginative and creative answers
- Try the first solution that comes to mind
- Are impulsive
- Have a limited choice of skills and techniques to use for problem solving
- Give up on a project

Literature Link ~ Resourcefulness

AGES 4-8

Chicken Sunday (AFA)	Patricia Polacco (New York: Putnam & Grosset Group, 1992)
Fly Away Home	Eve Bunting (Boston, MA: Houghton Mifflin, 1991)
Harry, the Dirty Dog	Gene Zion (New York: HarperTrophy, 1976)
Table Where Rich People Sit, The	Byrd Baylor (New York: Simon & Schuster, 1994)

AGES 9-12

Dawn Rider (NA)	Jan Hudson (New York: Puffin Books, 2000)
Homecoming, The	Cynthia Voigt (New York: Athenium, 1981)
Pinballs, The	Betsy Cromer Byars (New York: HarperCollins Juvenile Books, 1993)
Secret of the Seal, The (NA)	Deborah Davis (New York: Random House Children Publisher, 1994)

AGES 13+

Burning Up (AFA)	Caroline B. Cooney (New York: Delacorte Press, a division of Seymour Lawrence, 1999)
But I'll Be Back Again	Cynthia Rylant (New York: Beech Tree Books, 1993)
Girls and Young Women Leading the Way: 20 True Stories About Leadership	Frances A. Karnes, Suzanne M. Bean, Rosemary Wellner (ed.) (Minneapolis, MN: Free Spirit Press, 1993)

Family Resources

A Penny Saved: Teaching Your Children the Values and Life Skills They Will Need to Live in the Real World	Neale S. Godfrey (New York: Fireside Books, Simon & Schuster, 1996)
Money Doesn't Grow on Trees: A Parent's Guide to Raising Financially Responsible Children	Neale S. Godfrey (New York: Fireside Books, Simon & Schuster, 1994)
101 Activities for Kids in Tight Spaces	Carol Stock Kranowitz (New York: St. Martin's/Griffin, 1995)
Teaching Values: An Idea Book for Teachers (and Parents) (B4E)	Gary A. Davis (Los Angeles: Westwood Publishing, 1996)

Multicultural books: **(AFA)**=African American, **(ASA)**=Asian American, **(HA)**=Hispanic American, **(ME)**=Multi-Ethnic, **(NA)**=Native American, **(TE)**=listed in the teacher edition of this book, *Tools for Citizenship and Life: Using the ITI Lifelong Guidelines and LIFESKILLS in the Classroom*, **(BFE)**=available through Books for Educators

Responsibility

Chapter 23

"Privilege demands responsibility."

responsibility *n* **1**: the quality or state of being responsible: as in
a: moral, legal, or mental accountability   **b:** reliability, trustworthiness
2: something for which one is responsible; able to answer for one's conduct and obligations

Responsibility: To respond when appropriate, to be accountable for your actions

WHAT IS RESPONSIBILITY?

The root of the word responsibility is "to respond"—to respond to people, animals, things, and circumstances, moment by moment, with integrity and caring—with a sense of what's right. Being responsible means speaking up and/or taking action when the moment calls for it even if it's inconvenient, unpopular, or there's no reward for doing so.

We hear much about irresponsibility these days. Most irresponsibility results not from doing the wrong thing but from doing nothing—failing to act when circumstances warrant a response from us. For example:

- Failing to speak up when someone has been put down or treated unfairly or when someone has broken the law, such as stealing time, services, or materials at work or school

- Withholding information or expertise that is important to successfully complete a team assignment

- Failing to pay child support or bills as agreed

- Failing to arrive on time for appointments

- Leaving tools, equipment, toys, and such out in the weather without adequate protection

- Ignoring a leak rather than fixing it immediately

Do any of these sound familiar? Although any one event may seem insignificant, added up over a lifetime, they form a pattern of irresponsibility.

We demonstrate the LIFESKILL of Responsibility when we say and do the right thing at the right time; we also demonstrate the LIFESKILL of Responsibility when, after the fact, we own up to our words, actions, and deeds or to our failure to respond.

Acting Responsibly Is a Choice

It's the rare individual who is responsible at all times in all areas. Even as adults, our performance is a like a roller coaster ride with noble highs and ignoble lows. Some of us excel with responsibilities at work but at home are irresponsible as spouse, parent, and/or family member. Conversely, if we possess a strong sense of familial responsibility, it may clash with what's expected of us at work. And then come our responsibilities to our community and country.

Being responsible is not for the faint-hearted. It demands strength, endurance, competence, a well-integrated sense of values, and an accurate sense of what our time, energy, and available resources can accomplish. Above all, the desire and commitment to be a responsible person must be lit and nurtured from within. Consequently, teaching about responsibility needs to be clear, pervasive, non-coercive, and supportive of the long-term rather than an issue of control or power at the moment. Adults must model and expect it, but can't force or coerce it.

Being responsible can sometimes exact a terrible personal price. For example, consider the consequences and travails of many corporate whistle blowers or the anguish we feel when we must tell a loved friend hurtful news. But being responsible is also a source of a "deep sense of personal satisfaction."*

WHY PRACTICE RESPONSIBILITY?

What would life be like without responsibility? Drivers would neglect to observe traffic laws. Lawyers would overlook material supporting their client's legal problems. Doctors would disregard current research. Teachers would refuse to plan lessons. Store managers would forget to reorder popular products. Mothers and fathers would ignore babies' cries. Bosses wouldn't have sufficient cash flow to pay their workers at the end of the month. The staff at your favorite fast food restaurant would abandon their posts. Sound a bit chaotic and unpredictable? Yes.

Having things work—be it within the family, among friends and neighbors, or between citizens and their federal government or anything in between—can only occur if both sides keep their agreements with each other. When we're responsible, others can count on us and we can count on them. Without agreement to be responsible, there can be no social structures or sense of family. Schools could not exist. Even government cannot exist without agreement to adhere to societal agreements which, in our system, are called laws.

Responsibility is the glue that holds our lives together. Without it, our lives would spin apart and sink into chaos.

---

* "A deep sense of personal satisfaction" is a phrase coined by Brenda Wyckoff, fourth grade teacher in Sedona, Arizona. Her ability to enable students to experience who they could be is an extraordinary gift to her students.

HOW DO YOU PRACTICE IT?

How do we practice being responsible? How do we teach it? Typically, we admonish children to be responsible but offer little guidance about how to do so. The core of our messages is often "Just go out and do what's right"—somewhat like telling children to "Just say no to drugs" without helping them discover what to say yes to.

Although good advice, it is freighted with assumptions. It assumes that each child, especially a young child, is well equipped with essential prerequisites such as:

- A well-developed sense of what is right and what is wrong, a "moral compass" to help them analyze what's going on at the moment and make a choice

- A belief that they can make a difference, that they know enough to speak out and act, that they can positively impact what is going on (rather than merely exposing themselves to ridicule and abuse)

- A belief that they are resilient and resourceful and that, no matter what happens, they will land on their feet and can move on

- A deep and abiding commitment to live "above the line"—living their lives in ways that contribute to society rather than become burdensome, giving back to the community because it's the right thing to do, being the kind of person others like to be around, doing their share

With such prerequisites in hand, one can tune into one's intuition—that inner voice or conscience—and then act accordingly.

Tips from Brain Research

As with all the Lifelong Guidelines and LIFESKILLS, the attributes of responsibility are many and rich. Children need numerous examples of responsibility and lack of responsibility and ample opportunity to discuss the fallout from each. As author Leslie Hart points out, we can't know what something is until we also understands what it isn't.* For good discussion prompts, use good literature (such as the books recommended in the Literature Links in this book), key turning points in history, or favorite quotes. Historical examples include the horror wrought by Nazis soldiers who were "only following orders" and the brutality of Columbus when dealing with the natives. Attention-grabbing quotes include:

- "Never doubt that a small group can change the world. Indeed that is the only way it happens." Margaret Mead

- "All that is necessary for the forces of evil to win in the world is for enough good men to do nothing." Edmund Burke (1729-1997), Irish-born British politician and author

---

* See Leslie Hart's discussion of making meaning through pattern detection and identification in *Human Brain and Human Learning* (Kent, Washington: Books For Educators, Inc., 1998), Chapter 7, pp. 115-132.

- "When Hitler attacked the Jews, I was not a Jew; therefore, I was not concerned. When Hitler attacked the Catholics, I was not a Catholic; therefore, I was not concerned. When Hitler attacked the unions and the industrialists, I was not a member of the unions and I was not concerned. Then, Hitler attacked me and the Protestant church—and there was nobody left to be concerned."*

Practical Applications. Set aside at least two weeks to introduce and focus on the LIFESKILL of Responsibility. Begin by defining responsibility using the T-chart format shown in Appendix B. Apply it to current issues in the family or neighborhood (behavior and events), and/or to school, community, nation, and world. Ask how the situation would have been different if the LIFESKILL of Responsibility had been use. Be sure to include examples of failure to act or speak up and stress that omission is as serious as commission. Also, read at least two books/passages a day from the literature list or from books of your choice. Allow ample time to discuss the issues and how they affect the characters.

Practice Makes Perfect. To be responsible in all areas of our life requires great focus and lots of practice. Be patient with yourself as a model. Although, in hindsight you'll realize that you weren't always perfect, each of us is a work in progress when it comes to the LIFESKILLS and Lifelong Guidelines. Being responsible is a bodybrain effort. More than "knowing" what's right, children must often juggle intense emotions as they consider the consequences of their actions or lack of action. A home environment marked by absence of threat (real or perceived) and one in which reflective thinking is nurtured is an absolute must for children practicing the LIFESKILL of Responsibility.

WHAT DOES RESPONSIBILITY LOOK LIKE IN THE REAL WORLD?

We

- Pay bills in a timely fashion
- Complete a project to specifications
- Research issues and vote in local, state, and national elections
- Acknowledge when we have made a mistake or been wrong at work or at home
- Care for elderly family members as needed
- Abide by traffic laws
- Ignore gossip and instead search for the truth
- Provide for our own care by holding down a job, maintaining a healthy lifestyle, and contributing to society

* Martin Niemoller, quoted in the *Congressional Record*, 14 October 1968.

WHAT DOES RESPONSIBILITY LOOK LIKE AT HOME

Adults

- Model the Lifelong Guidelines and LIFESKILLS for all family members
- Create a safe and caring environment for children and spouse
- Provide supervision for children at all times
- Provide for their family's health by offering nutritious meals and snacks
- Keep accurate records of children's physical exams, immunizations, illnesses and medicines
- Arrive on time for school conferences, PTA meetings, and children's performances (school and neighborhood events)
- Meet financial requirements in a timely way
- Stretch a paycheck to meet family bills; live within the family budget while saving for retirement and important future events such as college tuition, special family vacations, and so forth
- Create and stick with a plan for maintaining auto, household, and yard; repair items promptly
- Participate in workshops, course, classes and conferences that support the concepts of "adult as a lifelong learner"
- Comply with laws or work to change them
- Learn about child growth and development—especially how the brain develops—and plan for experiences that will enhance our child's progress as learner and future citizen

Children

- Practice the Lifelong Guidelines and the LIFESKILLS
- Accept responsibility for their negative actions and stand up for others who have been rudely or unfairly treated
- Protect brothers and sisters from abuse and put-downs
- Commit to improving their skill, knowledge, and behavior
- Seek lifelong interests and hobbies by studying hard at school and participating in extracurricular and community activities
- Return borrowed materials to people or to their places as agreed

- Work for neighbors to earn money for special purchases

- Wear hand-me-down clothing, play with second-hand toys, and ride used bicycles without complaint in order to help the family stay within its budget

- Find and organize for use the supplies necessary for projects, at home and at school

- Bring home and return school items promptly and reliably

OPPORTUNITIES TO PRACTICE RESPONSIBILITY

AGES 4-8

- Read/listen to *The Berenstain Bears* and the *Messy Room* by Jan and Stan Berenstain. List two responsibilities that bear children did not do. Explain what happened in the story because they were not acting in a responsible way. Share one time when you did not use the LIFESKILL of Responsibility. Describe two or more choices you could try next time so that you can act in a responsible way.

- Discuss with your family which two chores a week can be your responsibility. Draw pictures of the correct way to complete the chore. Invite someone to guide you through the correct steps the first few times you do the chore to make sure that you follow the correct pattern. Perform these chores for one month and then learn two new household jobs. Explain to a parent how it feels to know that your family is counting on you to get the job done.

- Write/draw morning procedures that will get your day off to an organized and smooth start without relying on others to help you. Include ways to greet your family, preparing clothing, book bag packing, and any other tasks that need to be considered. Try the procedures for two weeks and make any changes you feel would help to improve them.

- Find three activities (e.g., read a book, play peek-a-boo, build with blocks) that you can use to amuse your baby brother or sister while Mom/Dad are preparing dinner. Check with your parents to make sure the activities are safe for the baby. Volunteer to do this whenever the family needs your help. Change activities when the old ones know longer keep the baby's attention.

- Brainstorm three or more peaceful actions you and your family can follow when you disagree about something. Assign a "signal" or "sign" for each action that can be used to remind a family member of the agreement. Add other ideas for helping remind family members to be responsible for their behavior that you hear in stories, see on TV/video, or observe at a friend's house.

Chapter 23—Responsibility

AGES 9-12

- Create a yearlong celebration calendar for your family. Design one sheet for each month. Illustrate with appropriate drawings. Mark each important day (e.g., birthdays, anniversaries, holidays, weddings, reunions) with a special symbol and words. Share the completed calendar with your family. Hang it in a prominent place so all can can be reminded of important family events.

- Observe your family "manager" as the checks are written, bills are paid, and records are kept. Volunteer to help in this process by using the calculator to compute the amount remaining in the family checkbook. Investigate how many family bills remain the same each month and how many accounts have varying amounts due. Determine why there might be a difference in the way companies compute their bills. Brainstorm one way that your family can add more money each month to a family savings account. Volunteer to organize and follow through with this plan. Report monthly account growth to your family.

- Take on the responsibility of coordinating chores for the family for two months. Brainstorm a "real-life" name for each job/responsibility. Some examples might be botanist (plant care specialist), maintenance engineer (sweeper), switchboard operator (telephone messenger), and landscaper (mowing lawn, planting seasonal flowers). Create enough meaningful jobs so that there is one for each sibling. Develop procedures for each task, print them up, place in plastic sleeves, and put them into a procedure binder called "Family Chores" so that each worker will understand his/her responsibilities. Teach the procedures to the person who is to take on each of those responsibilities. Interview each "worker" once a week to see how well your procedures are working. Revise them as needed.

- Practice three or more ways to receive and send messages (such as telephone, voice mail, e-mail, snail mail, beeper). Research the proper manners for each method of communication. Ask a family member to check all messages for accuracy. Learn how to make a "911" call (BUT, do not practice on a real phone). Also compose a "safety" message that you can repeat if there is no adult in the house. Write it on a large index card and place a copy of it next to each phone.

- Draft an agreement for proper use of the Internet and World Wide Web that is appropriate for someone your age. Investigate three or more websites that provide safety tips or features that protect children from wandering into sites that contain inappropriate information for them. Discuss the names (if any) of chat rooms you may enter. Create a computer journal. Record the following on a daily basis: date, time you started surfing, time you ended surfing, chat rooms entered, and names of the sites visited. Inform your parents when you receive any e-mail that is inappropriate or makes you feel uncomfortable. Share your journal with a parent at least once a week. Share with him/her what you are learning about the LIFESKILL of Responsibility and the Lifelong Guideline of Trustworthiness.

- Research how many gallons of gas your family car(s) holds. Compute how much a tank full of gas will cost for each vehicle if you buy the regular octane., the "extra octane," and the "supreme." Refer to an area map and plot a route that uses the least amount of gasoline to get to your favorite supermarket, movie, and mall. Also plot routes that will take you to the nearest (vs. your favorite) supermarket, movie, and mall. Predict which routes require less gasoline and explain why it might be responsible to make some different choices.

- Design a first aid kit for use in your house in case of an emergency. Use a watertight container. Include a source of light, important phone numbers, and coins to make a call from a pay phone. Put in five or more other items that you feel are important in times of trouble. Share this kit with your family and explain why you chose the items you did. Put the kit in a place all family members will remember in an emergency.

- Compile an annotated list of at least five "friends of animals"—individuals or groups — that help wild animals that are lost, sick, or in trouble. Include the name of the responsible party to contact, two or more phone numbers, and any areas (e.g., towns, cities, counties) or specialties they cover (e.g., small vs. large animals, sick vs. well). Design a handout using a program such as PrintShop that uses attractive graphics. Present the information from your annotated list in an appealing way. Also offer important safety tips. Obtain permission to post this information on library bulletin boards, supermarket shopper boards, and community center information boards.

- Research a Native American tribe in your state or region. Discover why Native Americans are considered to be the "original conservationists" of our country. List three or more responsibilities they carried out to conserve the "gifts from Mother Earth." Identify two lessons we can learn from them and use today in regard to natural resources.

AGES 13+

- Ask your family for feedback on how responsible a person you they think you are. Ask them to identify three strengths and two areas you need to work on. Make a plan to become responsible in these two areas. Identify what Lifelong Guidelines and/or LIFESKILLS you you are not using when you are acting irresponsibly and what behaviors you need to do to be responsible in these two areas. Implement your plan for six weeks. Share with a parent what you have learned about using the LIFESKILL of Responsibility and how others have responded to your change in behavior.

- Learn how to manage a checking account and be responsible for your own money. Open an account with your first paycheck. Carefully read any information you are given, ask questions to clarify your understandings, and choose your checks. Balance your checkbook after each withdrawal (after you write a check). Check your mental math using a calculator. Repeat if the amounts do not agree. Wait for your monthly statement and determine if you and the bank agree on the balance. Determine if the difference is because of a mistake in your calculations and records or mistakes by the bank. Take appropriate actions to remedy the matter. Ask an adult for help when you are confused or unsure as to what procedures to follow. With a parent, brainstorm all the behaviors for handling money that represent using the LIFESKILL of Responsibility and those that illustrate not using the LIFESKILL of Responsibility. Make an agreement with yourself to handle money responsibly.

Chapter 23—Responsibility

- Keep a calendar or personal organizer that will help you meet your responsibilities on time. Record (in pencil so you can erase and make changes) the dates and times of your appointments, practices, long-term homework assignments, and work schedule. Also note special family days and obligations that are important. Include an emergency card with your name, address, phone number, medical information (e.g., illnesses, allergies to medicines), and the person to contact should you be hurt or injured in an accident. Update the information as needed. Remember, not knowing is not a reason for not using the LIFESKILL of Responsibility; use your calendar/organizer to enable you to respond as appropriate.

- Develop a flexible plan that provides adequate time for doing homework. Use your calendar or personal organizer to schedule study time in blocks of fifteen minutes or longer in between sports practices, work assignments, and appointments. Learn to use the time wisely by concentrating and focusing on the task. Use the shorter times for easier assignments while saving longer time blocks for those assignments that require intense concentration. Review your grades and homework report card comments with your parents to determine if the current plan is encouraging or discouraging learning. If your schoolwork is showing signs of distress, revise the plan or make some serious choices regarding sports participation and employment .

- Take responsibility for teaching yourself the Lifelong Guidelines and LIFESKILLS. Develop T-charts with your family for each of the Lifelong Guidelines or LIFESKILLS that as a family you have not yet worked on together or that need more work. See Appendix A for an example of a T-chart for describing a Lifelong Guideline or LIFESKILL. Use the following organizers: Looks Like, Sounds Like, and Feels Like *and* Does Not Look Like, Does Not Sound Like, and Does Not Feel Like. Add additional notes throughout the rest of the year that will enhance developing understanding of each area. Take on the responsibility of modeling these behaviors for younger siblings. At least once a month share with a parent what you are learning about the LIFESKILL of Responsibility by taking on this assignment.

- Interview a local politician about his/her responsibilities. Ask if there are any unwritten responsibilities, too. Write a job description for his/her position specifying the duties that you feel are important.

- Read your school's handbook with an adult in your family. Ask questions about any parts that you don't understand. Then in your own words, explain the responsibilities that you feel students are expected to follow.

- Create an EDITH (Emergency Drill In The House) plan for your family to use in case of fire or other emergencies. Post a sign in each room that lists emergency evacuation procedures, alternate routes, a specified place away from the house where everyone will come together for a safety check, and a phone number outside the area to be used as a message center. Ask your family to practice the drill at least twice. Make any adjustments necessary for safety reasons. Post the plan with a location easy to find during an emergency. Review the place with your family at the dinner table.

- Create a personal plan to use the family computer responsibly. Include how much time you will spend on the computer each day (one hour or less) and the programs you'll use. Keep a computer log noting when you sign on and off, how much time you spent using each program and any products you created. Share this plan and journal with your family.

SIGNS OF SUCCESS

Congratulations! Children are showing signs of Responsibility when they

- Consistently use the Lifelong Guidelines and LIFESKILLS
- Offer to help a friend understand something new
- Locate the rightful owner of a "found" object
- Return borrowed items (from library and friends) on time and in good condition
- Do something that is expected of them without being told to do it
- Can be counted on to perform their jobs as agreed
- Practice a musical instrument for an upcoming lesson or concert
- Follow family procedures and guidelines

Keep trying! Children need more practice when they

- Are frequently late for family events and offer no reason or apology
- "Forget" to do chores or complete them with disregard for the Lifelong Guidelines of Person Best
- Show no concern for the home and natural environment
- Cheat on work and tests
- Neglect their duties
- Misuse/abuse free time
- Ignore requests for assistance
- Use put-downs
- Refuse to become and stay organized; use ignorance as an excuse for not responding when they should

Literature Link ~ Responsibility

Ages 4-8

Arthur Lost and Found	Marc Brown (New York: Little, Brown & Company, 1998)
Lights on the River (HA)	Jane Resk (New York: Hyperion Press, 1996)
Paperboy, The	Dav Pilkey (New York: Orchard Books, 1996)
Rueben and the Blizzard (AM)	Merle Good (Intercourse, PA: Good Books, 1995)

Ages 9-12

Arilla Sun Down (NA) (AFA)	Virginia Hamilton (New York: Point Signature, Scholastic Books, 1995)
Jeremy Thatcher Dragon Hatcher	Bruce Coville (New York: Harcourt Brace, 1991)
On the Far Side of the Mountain	Jean Craighead George (Burnsville, MN: Econoclad, Sagebrush Corporation, 1999)
Young Landlords, The (AFA)	Walter Dean Myers (New York: Viking Press, 1989)

Ages 13+

Armageddon Summer	Jane Yolen (New York: Voyager Picture Book, Harcourt Brace, 1999)
Kid's Guide to Service Projects, The: Over 500 Service Ideas for Young People Who Want to Make a Difference	Barbara A. Lewis, Pamela Espeland (Minneapolis, MN: Free Spirit Publishers, 1995)
Man Who Was Poe, The	Avi (New York: Orchard Books, 1989)
Pigman, The	Paul Zindel (New York: Harcourt Brace, 1991)

Multicultural books: **(AFA)**=African American, **(ASA)**=Asian American, **(HA)**=Hispanic American, **(ME)**=Multi-Ethnic, **(NA)**=Native American, **(TE)**=listed in the teacher edition of this book, *Tools for Citizenship and Life: Using the ITI Lifelong Guidelines and LIFESKILLS in the Classroom*, **(BFE)**=available through Books for Educators

Family Resources

Children: The Challenge — Rudolph Dreikurs *(New York: Plume, 1991)*

How to Help Your Child With Homework: Every Caring Parent's Guide to Encouraging Good Study Habits and Ending the Homework Wars— For Parents and Children Ages 6-13 — Marguerite Cogorno Radencich, Jeanne Shay, Schumm and Pamela Espeland (Ed.) (Minneapolis, MN: Free Spirit Publishing, 1997)

Parenting With Love and Logic: Teaching Children Responsibility — Foster W. Cline, MD., Jim Fay (Contributor), (Colorado Springs, CO: Nav Press, 1990)

Sense of Humor

Chapter 24

"Laughter feels good."

sense *n* **1: a:** meaning conveyed or intended **b:** discerning awareness and appreciation
humor *n* **1:** a quality which appeals to the sense of the ludicrous or absurdly incongruous
2: something that is designed to be comical or amusing

Sense of Humor: To laugh and be playful without harming others

WHAT IS SENSE OF HUMOR?

A sense of humor enables us to experience joy and laughter even when faced with misfortune. It is a state of mind and a spirit that we carry through life. It flows through our lives and relationships, enhancing them daily.

A sense of humor allows us to find and experience joy and delight. It removes feelings of stress and tension. And, it just happens to be our all-time favorite LIFESKILL! How could anyone survive without it? Especially a parent! Humor is one of the healthiest and most powerful methods of maintaining perspective about life's difficult experiences.

Two Kinds of Humor

There are various kinds or genre of humor. One is teller based. We tell stories about ourselves and our mishaps or we tell stories reflecting our perspective of life's situations (a funny thing happened on the way to the forum). This kind of humor is usually not perceived to be threatening; it is safe and is enjoyed by the widest audiences. Comedians Jack Benny, Bob Hope, and Bill Cosby are famous for this kind of humor. Humor isn't generated at the expense of other people; the audience and the people in the joke all laugh together. This is the model for the LIFESKILL of Sense of Humor.

Another kind of humor, however, is aimed at other individuals (mother-in-law and spouse jokes) or groups (racial, ethnic, blondes, and liberals). This humor may be, and often is, harmful and mean-spirited. It is often used to build up the teller at the expense of others. Sitcoms specialize in this brand of humor. It is the realm of put-downs and should be eliminated from homes and classrooms. See Chapter 7 for a discussion of the Lifelong Guideline of No Put-Downs.

WHY PRACTICE A SENSE OF HUMOR?

A sense of humor generates laughter. Laughter, in turn, is very beneficial for everything from your imagination to your physical health to your relationships with others. By cultivating laughter, you not only make life more enjoyable, you make it longer, healthier, and happier.*

The Many Benefits of Humor

A sense of humor allows us to discern and value the incongruities in life and provides moments of joy and pleasure. Quite simply, laughter makes us feel better. Our problems and worries are temporarily suspended. We experience a flood of "feel good" molecules of emotion** after which the day looks brighter and our hurdles less formidable. Such natural chemicals jump-start emotions that promote more active learning and a healthy level of self-esteem.

There is a social benefit as well. Our sense of humor helps people see us as fun to be with, likeable, and interesting, making us feel confident, self-assured, and relaxed. In addition, when we make others laugh, we help them to feel better, too.

Physical Benefits. Laughter benefits us physically, from reducing tension to boosting the immune system to curing life-threatening illnesses.*** It releases natural substances (such as endorphins) which help relieve pain, block substances which suppress the immune system (such as epinephrine and cortisol), and speed up the production of immune enhancers (such as beta-endorphins).

Since the diaphragm is being used when we laugh, our respiration increases and so does the amount of oxygen in the blood. This movement of the diaphragm also provides an "internal massage" to other organs including the stomach, kidneys, and liver. Studies also show a direct correlation between blood pressure and laughter; high blood pressure decreases as laughter increases.

In summary, recent research emphasizes the importance of the bodybrain connection in relation to good health. Humor is a well-known antidote to stress and a strong force in building family ties.

---

* Two classic works in this area are *Molecules of Emotion: Why We Feel the Way We Feel* by Candace Pert and the popular press books of physician Norman Cousins, *Anatomy of an Illness As Perceived by the Patient: Reflections on Healing and Regeneration* (New York: W. W. Norton & Company, 1995).

** *Molecules of Emotion: Why We Feel the Way We Feel* by Candace Pert, research scientist, is a "must read" book for teachers and administrators (New York: Simon & Schuster, 1997).

*** See *Love, Medicine, and Miracles: Lessons Learned About Self-Healing from a Surgeon's Experiences with Exceptional Patients* and *Peace, Love, and Healing: Bodymind Communication and the Path of Self-Healing* both by Bernie Siegel, M.D. (New York: HarperCollins, Publishing, 1990).

Sense of Humor Is a Choice

We all know people who have a great sense of humor. They are fun to be with and make time pass more quickly with less energy expended, especially with difficult tasks. They brighten up the room.

We also know people who never seem to crack a smile or offer so much as a twinkle in the eye over a funny comment. For whatever reason, a sense of humor isn't a priority for them. It's too bad because their brains and bodies—and the brains and bodies of those around them—are losing out on healthy jolts of natural chemicals that enhance well-being.

Responding to others' sense of humor and developing our own is a choice. Through our modeling of the LIFESKILL of Sense of Humor, students can see the choice clearly and make a life-enhancing decision.

Humor and Leadership

Make no mistake: Displaying a sense of humor is a critical quality of those who lead and gain the support of others.* From George Rogers Clark** to John F. Kennedy to the beloved neighbor down the street, humor and laughter are a powerful attractor, spirit lifter, and relationship glue. Commit yourself to developing the LIFESKILL of Sense of Humor. It is a professional and personal imperative.

HOW DO YOU PRACTICE IT?

How do we go about laughing if it's not easy for us? How can we develop that humorous perspective which can influence our spirit, body, and mind so positively? One of the best ways is to stay in touch with our "inner child" or "playful clown." We all have it but many times we conceal it due to the seriousness of work and life. We must allow ourselves to be playful and childlike (which is very different from being child*ish*). Watch babies play peek-a-boo. They laugh and giggle with glee. Glee is definitely something adults need more of in their lives.

Begin to enjoy life more and note the humorous situations that occur daily. Avoid dwelling on the negative, the "ain't it awful" game, the perpetual tales of woe. Learn to relax and to see the "funny" side of predicaments. Study how other people, known for their sense of humor, react to circumstances. Watch their signals and body language; listen to the words they use. Then use these as models for improving your own ability to recognize, appreciate, and use humor.

---

* See "Theory and Implications Regarding the utilization of Strategic Humor by Leaders" by C. B. Crawford, Department of Communication, Fort Hays State University. http://www.fhsu.edu/htmlpages/faculty/cocc/lead03.htm

** George Rogers Clark, older brother of William Clark of Lewis and Clark fame, taught William his formula for leadership—give your followers jokes, songs, and a vision of glory. Not bad advice for the classroom. See *From Sea to Shining Sea* by James Alexander Thom (New York: Ballantine Books, December 1986). It is also a thoroughly read aloud researched and beautifully written historical novel, terrific book for ages nine and up.

Remember, humor is infectious if you allow it to be. Join in the fun!

Humor Is Developmental

Our sense of humor goes through stages.* Babies laugh and coo at our funny faces and sounds. Young children adore nonsense jokes that may have no meaning to anyone except themselves. The primary age child likes simple jokes and riddles, and often finds "bathroom" humor hilarious (much to the embarrassment of his/her parents). Students in intermediate grades begin to understand word plays and puns, often trying some of their own, although they may have to explain the punch line to you.**

Understanding verbal humor also depends heavily on one's ability to turn words into images, a mental wiring that can be developed (see Chapter 6, Active Listening).

Experience Is the Best Teacher

Experiment with humor. Come up with your own jokes, puns, riddles, and situations. When doing so, always be mindful of your audience. Are they laughing out of genuine enjoyment or out of embarrassment and nervousness? If the latter, re-read Chapter 7 about the Lifelong Guideline of No Put-Downs.

The Best Humor Is Spontaneous and Circumstantial

Some people seem to dedicate their lives to collecting and telling jokes. Consider the family get-together that can't begin without the latest joke from Uncle Joe. Often, however, such canned jokes can have a put-down edge to them; at a minimum they often derail the conversation at hand. In contrast, the most beneficial humor is spontaneous and circumstantial— teller-based humor arising from the moment, the task at hand, the circumstances.

As you hone the LIFESKILL of Sense of Humor, focus on developing teller-based humor whose content is of the moment—spontaneous, circumstantial, welcoming, and inclusive.

WHAT DOES SENSE OF HUMOR LOOK LIKE IN THE REAL WORLD?

We

- Laugh at jokes, riddles, limericks, puns, and skits
- Enjoy comedians
- Read comic books, humorous stories, and watch funny movies

---

* See *Thinking and Learning: Matching Developmental Stages with Curriculum and Instruction* by Lawrence Lowery. (Kent, WA: Books For Educators, Inc., 1989).

** Co-author Sue Pearson's personal favorite came from a second grade boy, David, who said that his mom was coming home from the hospital. When she inquired about health, David replied, "Oh, she's okay. We just had her spayed." Talk about humor being circumstantial!

- Laugh at ourselves in funny situations
- Use humor to alleviate stress and tension
- Play games that make us laugh ("Twister," "Trivial Pursuit")
- See the bright side of difficult experiences
- Laugh when a baby does something cute
- Enjoy listening to funny experiences shared by friends and relatives
- Chuckle when toddlers try to make sense of language (such as calling every man "daddy" or every four-legged creature "doggy")

WHAT DOES SENSE OF HUMOR LOOK LIKE AT HOME?

Adults

- Enjoy the company of other family members
- Smile and chuckle a lot
- Laugh at jokes and riddles
- "Play with words" to create puns
- Use humor to alleviate a child's fears and make him/her feel more comfortable
- Inject humorous comments during family discussions and throughout the day
- Do silly things to lighten the moment for those we care about
- Delight in unusual comments that come "out of the mouths of babes"
- Show a bright, positive attitude to family, neighbors, and co-workers

Children

- Share jokes and riddles from books they are reading
- Write jokes, riddles, and puns that are age-appropriate
- Laugh at themselves when they do or say something funny
- Can laugh at themselves when they make a simple mistake that doesn't hurt anyone
- Understand what is considered appropriate humor to use with family, friends, neighbors, and and fellow participants in clubs/organizations
- Chuckle and enjoy small jokes while working with a family member

OPPORTUNITIES TO PRACTICE SENSE OF HUMOR

AGES 4-8

- Read three or more books written by Dr. Seuss. Share one part in each book that you think is really funny. Share one part in each book that you "don't get" or don't find funny. Study the illustrations to see if they make you laugh. Share two or more drawings that "tickle" your sense of humor. Draw your own "Dr. Seuss" type character and hang it in your room.

- Listen to three or more of the Arthur series (Marc Brown). Determine if there is a joke or something funny that weaves through all three stories (we call that a running joke). Predict if you think this joke is in all of the Arthur stories. Check through the at least three more Arthur books at the library to see if your prediction is correct.

- Create your own book of favorite jokes and riddles. Keep a school composition tablet handy. When you hear a funny joke or riddle, write it on a page in the book. Illustrate the funny part. Read your book before going to bed so that your dreams will be funny ones.

- Practice saying silly tongue twisters three times in a row. Here are some examples:
    ~ Bobby bought Billy Bear some bright blue blocks.
    ~ Six silly sheep share some slimy, slippery slushes.
    ~ Thistles, thorns and thumbtacks stick thirty thumbs.
    ~ Four fat foxes flee Florence's Friday fish feast.

Create two tongue twisters of your own and ask family members to try saying them more than once and very fast.

- Learn to sing a silly song with motions. Teach it to your family. Some choices include:
    ~ On Top of Spaghetti
    ~ In a Cabin in the Woods
    ~ Barnyard Boogie
    ~ Found a Peanut

Watch your family to see if they laugh as they sing the words and make the motions.

- Learn three or more "Knock, Knock" jokes. Share them with some of your friends. Ask if they have any to tell you. Add these new ones to your collection.

- Read Animal Trunk: Silly Poems to Read Aloud by Charles Ghigna. Choose which poem is your favorite one and explain why you like it so much. Identify the poem you like least and share why it doesn't seem funny to you with someone in your house.

Chapter 24—Sense of Humor

AGES 9-12

- Divide a sheet of paper in half the long way. Label one side "HUMOR" and the other side "PUT-DOWNS." Watch one of the Peanut's Gang videos. Identify each humorous part as being truly funny or being used in a way that put one of the characters down. Make a tally in the matching column every time something funny happens. Compute the totals the video is done. Discuss with your parents the two kinds of humor. Express your feelings about people who use "put-down" humor.

- Read a silly story like Sideways Stories from Wayside School by Louis Sachar. Decide which chapter was the funniest for you; explain why. Interview an adult in your family as to the funniest book he/she ever read and share your favorite back with him/her.

- Start a collection of jokes and riddles focused on one topic or category (e.g., dogs, cats, space). Write each one in a black composition notebook and create an illustration that adds to the humor. Share this collection with your best friend.

- Make a list of silly or humorous songs that your family can sing at their next reunion or celebration. Invite Grandpa/Grandma to add some old favorites to the list. Compile a collection of CD's or tapes that include these songs so that the family members can sing along.

- Invent a cartoon character of your own. Name him/her and write three or more four-frame strips highlighting your character in funny situations. Fit the name of your cartoon in the first frame, upper left-hand corner. Sign your name beneath the title. Add dialog in the "balloons" in each frame. Show these pieces of art to a friend and observe his/her reactions.

- Say the following tongue-twisters*; try to synchronize your brain and tongue to work together.
    - ~ Double bubble gum bubbles double.
    - ~ Sixty-six sick chicks
    - ~ A bloke's back brake block broke.
    - ~ You know New York. You need New York. You know you need unique New York.

  Identify a strategy that writers use to create tongue twisters. Write three of your own using any strategy that will help you complete the task.

- Read the Sunday or daily funnies. Decide which cartoon character is most like you and why. Explain your choice to someone in your family.

AGES 13+

- Identify 3 or more sit-coms that appear on TV and that your parents have given you permission to watch. Tally the jokes in the following categories: put-downs, sexual innuendoes, non-hurtful humor. Watch one program for each show and mark the matching category each time there is laughter. Compare and contrast the totals for each category and each show. Determine which program is least hurtful to people and sets the best example of true humor for youthful viewers. Share your opinion with a family member.

- Say the following tongue-twisters; try to synchronize your brain and tongue to work together.

    ~ Strange strategic statistic

    ~ Shy Sarah saw six Swiss wristwatches

    ~ Sinful Caesar sipped his snifter, seized his knees, and sneezed

   Write three or more easy ones for younger children to say.

- Read the following quotation and decide if you agree or disagree with the writer's assessment of humor:

    ~ "Humor is by far the most significant activity of the Brain."

    ~ Edward De Bono

    ~ Discuss your feelings with a friend who likes to laugh.

- Teach your younger siblings and some neighborhood children to play Charades. Explain the rules and motions that are acceptable for use. Write some book titles, movies, songs and quotations on individual pieces of paper to help jump-start the action. Divide into teams. Ask each participant to share what they enjoyed about the game when everyone has had a t least one turn.

- Observe a mime artist (e.g., Marcel Marseau, Cirque de Soliel) in action either on TV, in a movie or in person. Look at the motions he/she uses to make the action real and humorous. Develop your own mime routine. Design a costume that adds to your characterization. Perform this act for your family or in an amateur show.

- Study 3 different cartoonist's styles (e.g., Charles Schultz, Bill Watterson, Gary Larsen). Determine why each one is appealing to a certain kind of audience, or following and offer your explanation for this attraction. Identify your most favorite cartoon, as well as your least favorite, and explain your reasons to a friend.

- Reflect on the teachers you have had since kindergarten. Identify two or more that used humor in a non-hurtful way. Analyze your feelings about the learning that took place in those two classrooms. Write a personal "humor recommendation" proposal for a first-time teacher. Offer suggestions for providing fun and humor in the classroom so no one's feeling are hurt. Present this to a new teacher in your family or neighborhood.

Chapter 24—Sense of Humor

- Watch a segment of a Charlie Brown video together. Analyze the humor and divide it into two kinds: "Humor That Hurts People" and "Humor That Doesn't Hurt People." As you watch the video segment, make a tally mark in the appropriate column. Total the columns. Compare your analysis with your family. Which kind of humor was used more in the video? Discuss how hurtful humor relates to the Lifelong Guideline of No Put-downs. In your journal, describe your feelings about the humor used in the Charlie Brown segment you watched.

- Design a humorous birthday card for a friend or relative. Use humor that doesn't hurt or offend. Illustrate your card and make an envelope for it. Sign the card and present it on his/her special day.

- Read some one-frame cartoons (such as "All in the Family") and study the words and illustrations for examples of humor. Create a one-frame cartoon based on something funny you did or said as a young child (ask your family for help if you can't remember any). Using marker or watercolors, fill in the drawing with bright colors. Sign your name in the lower right-hand corner. Show it to your family.

- Study some longer cartoon strips or collections (e.g., "Calvin and Hobbes"). Observe how the story develops and how the cartoonist uses art to expand the reader's understanding. Experiment with a joke or riddle and turn it into a three- or four-frame cartoon. Design your own drawings and use special print for the words. Show it to three or more people.

- Read a fairy tale. Rewrite it through the eyes of a different character (such as Cinderella as seen through her step-sister's eyes or "The Emperor's New Clothes" through his wife's eyes). Read the new story to a friend and ask for his/her opinion.

- Research the history of clowns and create a poster with some of the following information: clowns through the ages, various clown faces, clothes that clowns wear, and clown actions. Organize a "Clown School" and practice making audiences laugh through the use of mime, pantomime, and funny skits. Interview a local clown; ask for tips about performing and make-up. Volunteer to perform at a local children's hospital or for a younger group of students in your neighborhood.

- Watch a video/movie of a famous pantomime artist such as Marcel Marceau, Charlie Chaplin, or the Cirque de Soleil performers. Observe how they develop humor through movement. Create a routine for you to perform. Practice until you feel comfortable then perform it for your family after dinner. Observe any reactions to your act. Ask how you can improve your performance next time.

- Study a book such as *CDC* or *CDB!* (see "Literature Link" on page 27.8) Notice how puns and alphabet letters are used to convey fun and humor. Write four or more alphabet puns of your own. Illustrate each one and staple them together in book form. Present these to your family at dinner time and display it in the family room for two weeks.

- Research humor in another culture and the part that humor plays in that culture. Determine two or more ways that humor is the same and two or more ways it is different. Chart the information on a Venn diagram. Explain what you learned to your family.

- Dramatize three or more different ways you can show concern or displeasure when someone tells offensive jokes attacking a person's looks, race, religion, or culture. Practice your skit until you can remember your part without any prompting. Share your ideas with a family member.

SIGNS OF SUCCESS

Congratulations! Children are showing signs of a Sense of Humor when they

- Laugh with family members over funny incidents
- Use humor that doesn't hurt or offend individuals or put-down ethnic, racial, and religious groups; ask others *not* to tell such jokes
- Share comments that are optimistic and up-beat
- Understand political cartoons
- Write, direct, or act in a skit that pokes fun at a situation
- Laugh spontaneously because they feel great and life is wonderful
- Giggle with a friend over something silly
- Create their own jokes, riddles, and puns that other people understand and enjoy
- Laugh at humorous songs

Keep trying! Children need more practice when they

- Offend people with racial, ethnic, or religious jokes and other put-downs
- Don't realize that no one else appreciates their attempts at humor
- Often have to ask others to explain the meaning of a joke or humorous play on words
- Are the only one not laughing during a humorous incident
- Haven't laughed once in an hour or two
- Forget to "play" for part of each day
- Can't write simple jokes and riddles

Literature Link ~ Sense of Humor

Ages 4-8

Are You My Mother?	P. D. Eastman (New York: Random House, 1988)
Dogzilla	Dav Pilkey (New York: Harcourt Brace, 1993)
Jack and the Beanstalk	Richard Walker (Kingswood, Bristol, UK Barefoot Books, 1999)
Old Man and His Door, The (HA)	Gary Soto (New York: GP Putnam's & Sons, 1996)
Zelda and Ivy	Laura McGee Kvasnosky (Cambridge, MA: Candlewick Press, 1998)

Ages 9-12

Barrel of Laughs, A Vail of Tears, A	Jules Feiffer (New York: HarperCollins Publishers, 1995)
Ben and Me: A New and Astonishing Life of Benjamin Franklin As Written by His Good Mouse Amos	Robert Lawson (Illustrator) (New York: Little, Brown & Company, 1988)
Bud, Not Buddy (AFA)	Christopher Paul Curtis (New York: Delacorte Press, 1999)
Chicken Doesn't Skate, The	Gordon Korman (New York: Scholastic Books, 1998)
Sideways Stories from Wayside School	Louis Sachar (New York: Avon Books, 1985)

Ages 13+

Dinky Hocker Shoots Smack	M. E. Kerr (New York: HarperTrophy, 1989)
Drawing on the Funny Side of the Brain: How to Come Up With Jokes for Cartoons and Comic Strips	Christopher Hart (New York: Watson-Guptill Publishing, 1998)
Rules of the Road	Joan Bauer (London: Puffin Books, 2000)

Multicultural books: **(AFA)**=African American, **(ASA)**=Asian American, **(HA)**=Hispanic American, **(ME)**=Multi-Ethnic, **(NA)**=Native American, **(TE)**=listed in the teacher edition of this book, *Tools for Citizenship and Life: Using the ITI Lifelong Guidelines and LIFESKILLS in the Classroom*, **(BFE)**=available through Books for Educators

Family Resources

Family: The Ties That Bind and Gag — Erma Bombeck (New York: Fawcett Books, 1991)

Grin and Share It: Raising a Family With a Sense of Humor — Janene Wolsey Baadsgaard (Salt Lake City, UT: Deseret Books, 1999)

Simplify Your Life With Kids: 100 Ways to Make Family Life Easier and More Fun — Elaine St. James (Kansas City, MO: Andrews McMeel, 1997)

Parents As Teachers: Tips of the Trade

Chapter 25

There are several important tools or teaching strategies to help you help your child to learn the Lifelong Guidelines and LIFESKILLS. None requires special training, just practice; you have already used some of them intuitively. The powerful on-going teaching strategies are:

- Modeling
- Target talk
- Literature
- Song
- Written procedures
- Clear criteria to clarify expectations

While the description of these methods may seem new and terrifyingly complex to learn, take heart. Remember, you're already using parts of them. This chapter will help you fine-tune your teaching and parenting skills. Take time to master each of these ways of teaching your child. Used daily, they will significantly increase your effectiveness as a parent and your joy of being with your child.

To add power and focus to a lesson now and then, consider using video clips, journal writing, and celebrations. These are described in Chapter 26 along with advice on how to get started.

DAILY TEACHING STRATEGIES

As our own lapses in applying the Lifelong Guidelines and LIFESKILLS will attest, habits of mind for social and personal behaviors are not the result of a one-time multiple choice test. When it comes to these guidelines for behavior, we must model them always, reinforce them daily, and provide formal lessons weekly. Acquiring mental programs for identifying and choosing the best solution in social interactions and during personal dilemmas requires PRACTICE! PRACTICE! PRACTICE! Start with intention and intensity. You can't make an impact on old behaviors or extinguish undesirable ones unless you provide plenty of daily experiences to the contrary.

The following teaching strategies should be used daily. Make them your own.

Modeling

The single most powerful strategy for teaching the Lifelong Guidelines and LIFESKILLS is modeling. As you have already discovered with your child, family members, and other children and adults, "Do what I do" is always more powerful than "Do what I say."

As we all know, however, consistent modeling of our values and beliefs is more easily said than done. Be prepared for some self-evaluation. Be willing to reflect on your own conduct and to be open to fine-tuning any "less than perfect" manners, attitudes, and conduct. Muster the courage to make appropriate changes as needed. Model for your child how to make changes in long-standing patterns of behavior. Remember, modeling isn't about being perfect; it's about showing others how to be the best human being possible—imperfect perhaps but always improving and always willing to make amends for mistakes.

Do As I Do. As a parent and your child's first teacher, you are his/her main role model. Children watch to see if we are offering up only "token" lessons about the Lifelong Guidelines and LIFESKILLS or if we truly believe that they are important social and behavioral guidelines for all to follow—at home and elsewhere. Take time to visualize exactly the kind of person you want to be and what you want mirrored in your child's behaviors. Then, define and write down strategies that will achieve these personal goals. Remember, you're on stage and actions always speak louder than words.

Learn to "walk your talk."* Also learn how to discuss with your child those times when you or they fall short.

Target Talk

The second most powerful strategy for teaching children the Lifelong Guidelines and LIFESKILLS is to acknowledge their use as they occur. Take advantage of the "teachable moment" when the demonstration of, or need for, the appropriate behaviors occurs naturally. Target talk provides an opportunity for your child to understand what the Lifelong Guidelines and LIFESKILLS look like, sound like, and feel like, and do *not* look like, do *not* sound like, or do *not* feel like, in varying situations. Common language, pictures, and actions begin to emerge as family members experience supportive responses to their use of the Lifelong Guidelines and LIFESKILLS. You'll be surprised how quickly your child will make target talk comments about the behavior of others . . . and you. Be prepared!

The Goal of Target Talk. As parent- and teacher-trainer Pat Belvel points out, misbehavior is a teaching opportunity. It is a symptom that children do not know enough of the appropriate behaviors and/or know too many of the wrong behaviors. She developed "target talk"** as a teaching tool to provide clear pictures of expected behaviors.

Additional pictures of what the Lifelong Guidelines and LIFESKILLS do and don't look like, sound like, and feel like are essential because each Lifelong Guideline is conceptually rich and its application to real life is always complex. Mastering the Lifelong Guidelines and LIFESKILLS

---

* "Walk your talk" means to make congruent what we say and what we do.
** Target talk as used in the ITI model is adapted from Pat Belvel's classroom management work, Training and Consulting Institute, Inc., San Jose, California. http://www.trngedu.com/

is a lifelong pursuit. Be patient. For example, the attributes of truthfulness are not only complex but often subtle and frequently circumstance-dependent. To illustrate this point, a group of teachers attending a class at the University of California, Davis,* took on the challenge to define the Lifelong Guideline of Truthfulness. Their definition appears in Chapter 3, page 1.

If we were honest with ourselves, we would have to admit that, even as adults, we also experience difficulty applying the Lifelong Guidelines of Truthfulness in our lives. So it shouldn't come as a surprise that children need lots of opportunities for guided practice and heaps of patience—many subtleties come with maturity. Learning to apply the Lifelong Guidelines and LIFESKILLS is a lifetime endeavor, a work in progress. Have patience, knowing that social and self awareness are developmental in children, but continue the dialogue on a daily basis.

How to Use Target Talk. Target talk is simple to use but you may need to leave behind a habit of providing rewards for behavior (ice cream, tickets to the circus) or methods that place the responsibility for standards of behavior on someone else. For example, statements from an adult such as, "I like the way [Sue] is using her time," are bondage statements that may control behavior for the moment but keep the focus on pleasing others rather than on the child developing his/her own sense of what's right or wrong, appropriate or inappropriate. In contrast, target talk helps children develop responsibility for their behavior by helping them recognize, and value for themselves, the behaviors that are appropriate.

The three steps of target talk should be short and to the point. For example:

- First, use the child's name. "Mike, . . ."

- Second, label the Lifelong Guideline/LIFESKILL that the child is using. "Mike, you are using the Lifelong Guideline of Active Listening. . ."

- Third, identify the action. "Mike, you are using the Lifelong Guideline of Active Listening when you face your sister, look interested, and are able to tell in your own words what your sister meant."

Verbal feedback is quick and easy. Short, written messages are also important because they provide a long-lasting communication, one that can be referred to again and again by the child. An easy device for capturing written comments from all members of the family is the Acknowledgements Box. Comments should be brief, using the three-step format described above, and nonjudgmental: "I want to acknowledge Jack for using the Lifelong Guideline of No Put-Downs when he helped me with grammar and spelling for my thank-you letter to Grandma." Remember, the purpose of the acknowledgements** is to get your child to reflect on his/her own behavior and build his/her own internal dialogue about it. He/she will soon begin to "feel" the acknowledgement inside because he/she said so; the child's own perspective then becomes the motivator and guide for behavior. This decreases the power of peer pressure later on.

At dinner and/or breakfast each day, simply pull a couple of acknowledgements from the box and read them. Children are always eager to hear positive things others have to say about them.

---

* The extension course in brain-compatible learning was taught by Karen Olsen, associate of Susan Kovalik & Associates, in 1993.
** Acknowledgements differ from compliments in subtle but powerful ways. Compliments arise from the speaker having applied his/her criteria for what's good or commendable. Acknowledgements are a way of applying generally accepted criteria to actions. The goal is to redirect children from relying on external standards to internal ones.

Target talk is best done without value judgment. As the Sergeant in the TV series *Dragnet* would say, "Just the facts, ma'am." The facts are: **who**, **what** Lifelong Guideline or LIFESKILL was demonstrated, and **how** it was used. Such clear statements provide immediate feedback about use of the desired behaviors. Children see the Lifelong Guidelines and LIFESKILLS in action and make their own judgments about how useful they are. This independent valuing process is critical to building values, behaviors, and character that will last a lifetime.

Using Target Talk to Correct Misbehavior. Target talk is a very powerful—and easy to use—teaching tool for dealing with misbehavior. First ask "What happened here?" Then, "What Lifelong Guidelines and/or LIFESKILLS didn't you use?" Lastly, "What Lifelong Guidelines and/or LIFESKILLS could you have used to avoid this happening?" Remember to stay neutral in tone. This is the teaching phase of correcting misbehavior. And always make sure the child understands how his/her misbehavior made the other person feel. Strengthening your child's awareness of how his/her behavior affects others is a critical step in the process to assist him/her to internalize standards of behavior.

The consequences phase—sometimes thought of as the punishment phase—should always be in proportion to the gravity of the act. If the child has been rude or unfair, ask how he/she could rectify the action or make amends with the wounded party. If the result of the child's actions are grave, such as hitting someone, damaging their property, playing with matches, then the consequences should be grave, appropriate to the infraction. In addition to the consequences you may set, ask your child what consequences/punishment would help him/her to remember not to do such things again. Often children are harder on themselves than adults would be and the connection between cause and effect is usually more direct in the child's mind (despite the apparent lack of adult logic).

If such conversations between you and your child fail to curb the behavior, add an audience—the person injured plus whoever else was present and, if necessary, other family members. In our experience, the only children that continue to misbehave are those who feel no connection to others and therefore feel they have nothing to lose by misbehaving. Children want to belong, they want to matter, they want to be loved and respected.

Literature

There is nothing better than a great story to pique children's interest and curiosity and, in the process, to teach a meaningful lesson. For your daily focus and/or nightly story time with your child, select a story rich with examples of the Lifelong Guideline or LIFESKILL you are currently focusing on or that addresses an important incident/situation from the day. Which stories offer strong examples of Trustworthiness? Truthfulness? Active Listening? Integrity? Which teach the destructiveness of Put-Downs? Which support development of Personal Best or Resourcefulness? There are stories that immediately come to mind because they teach about all of the Lifelong Guidelines and many of the LIFESKILLS; for example, *Charlotte's Web* by E. B. White, *Stone Fox* by John Reynolds Gardiner, *Shiloh* by Phyllis Reynolds Naylor, *My Side of the Mountain* by Jean Craighead George, and *Red Fern* by Wilson Rawls. The strong characterizations created by the various authors grab youth (and often adults) emotionally and make a child's participation with the characters seem more real than imaginary; this goes far to reducing the need to make the same mistakes in his/her own life.

At appropriate points during the story (end of the chapters or after a key event), discuss the use and/or non-use of the Lifelong Guidelines and LIFESKILLS. Invite your child to make connections between situations and actions of the characters and the Lifelong Guideline and LIFESKILL that you want to focus on. Provide time for him/her to locate and share situations in the book when the characters were using that Lifelong Guideline or LIFESKILL. Conversely, ask for examples when the characters are not using them or even deliberately ignoring them. Is your child able to identify the consequences? It is always easier to see the behavior of others than our own. Then, ask your child to transfer examples of both use and non-use of the Lifelong Guidelines and LIFESKILLS from the book into his/her own real-life experiences. You'll discover that such discussions strengthen family bonds and help to keep the lines of communication open.

Literature Lists. The book lists provided at the end of each chapter suggest titles that enrich "togetherness time" for parent or caregiver and child and provide a forum for discussing the Lifelong Guideline or LIFESKILL examined in that chapter. Use these books as a beginning point and then make your own selections from there. Use your personal experiences and judgment to determine which stories are appropriate, both in content and age/maturity for your own child.

The "Literature Links" provided in each chapter are organized by age: 4-8, 9-12, and 13+. Among them, you will find a few that are also recommended in the teacher edition of this book, *Tools for Citizenship and Life: Using the ITI Lifelong Guidelines and LIFESKILLS in Your Classroom*. These cross-over titles are marked by the initials "TE." If your child is in an ITI classroom, you may want to ask the teacher if he/she plans to use these books. If your child is not in an ITI classroom/school, you might want to use the teacher's edition, which has over 300 suggested titles, for additional recommendations.

These cross-over books are favorites that are just too hard to omit. Besides, most of us reread favorite books all of the time. Co-author Sue Pearson remembers when her son Michael was about three years old and simply *had* to hear *Curious George* by Margaret Ray every night before bedtime for what seemed like a year! You know as well as we do that you cannot change *one* single word in the story or try to turn two pages at once. They'll catch you at it; they know! Children find comfort in hearing a story over and over again and knowing the ending.

Recommended Family Resources. Following the book lists are resources to help you teach your child more about the Lifelong Guidelines and LIFESKILLS. They range from philosophical to "how-to," from serious to light hearted. You can pick and choose according to your interests and needs.

Symbols to Help Choose Books for Your Family. Because many different types of families will be reading this book, we are including some identification symbols after the book's description to help you determine if the title is one that will meet your needs. (See the explanation of symbols on the next page.)

Prereading Children's Books Is Important. Prereading a story before you read it aloud to your child is important for several reasons. First, you need to determine if the story content and language are consistent with what you want your child to experience. Such previews allow you to sidestep any objectionable language or skip parts that might upset your child and to select books that support your family's belief/value system.

Previewing guarantees there will be no hidden surprises. Co-author Sue Pearson once pre-read a book that she was going to use with her fourth graders and decided that the language was acceptable and created no problems. She promptly bought additional copies for a class set. Imagine her surprise later in the year as she began reading Chapter 8 and found the word "bastard"! She inwardly choked, quickly altered the syllable break to "ba-stard" and slapped a heavy accent on

Character Begins at Home: Family Tools for Teaching Character and Values

> ### Symbols Used on Literature Lists
>
> **(AFA)**=African American, **(AM)**=Amish, **(ASA)**=Asian American, **(HA)**=Hispanic American, **(ME)**=Multi-Ethnic, and **(NA)**=Native American
>
> **(TE)**=title is also listed in *Tools for Citizenship and Life: Using the Lifelong Guidelines and LIFESKILLS in the Classroom* by Sue Pearson and Karen D. Olsen, contributing editor (Kent, Washington: Books for Educators, 2000). This book is designed for public and private school teachers implementing the Kovalik ITI model in their classroom/school. It is also a valuable resource for parents.
>
> **(B4E)**=book is available from Books for Educators, Inc., 17051 SE 272nd Street, Suite 18, Kent, Washington 98042; phone: 888-777-9827; fax: 253-630-7215, www.books4educ.com. For more information, see the back of this book.

the last syllable. When she checked later, the original copy was indeed okay; the newer copies for the class set came from a different publisher. To this day, she doesn't believe any of the children caught on but it does show that different versions of a book may exist. Always preread!

Second, is there any content and language that is not age-appropriate? While our lists are grouped by age levels, 4-8, 9-12, and 13+, we all understand that children grow and mature at different rates; what is right for your four-year old may not be the best choice for your neighbor's four-year old. Likewise, your fifteen-year-old son may be ready for books that your fifteen-year old nephew would not understand. Consider a child's life experiences before suggesting, or helping to choose a book.

A third reason for prereading is to familiarize yourself with the story so you can add drama and spice to your reading and have some fun yourself. Prereading also gives you the opportunity to look for appropriate "discussion" spots—those places in the plot that provide a natural focus for sharing ideas, values, and the importance of the Lifelong Guidelines and LIFESKILLS, especially as to how they've been used in your family. Looking ahead helps you to determine the most effective places to make connections with your child's experiences.

Using Literature to Introduce and Reinforce a Lifelong Guideline or LIFESKILL. Although many "Opportunities to Practice" provide specific instructions for using a particular book, there are innumerable ways to use literature to introduce or reinforce a Lifelong Guideline or LIFESKILL when reading a book listed in the "Literature Links" or any other book of your choice. Here are but a few. As you read these, think of ways you could use them as is and ways you could better adapt them for your own child and your own sources of literature.

- *Character Web:* Read a book that exemplifies one of the Lifelong Guidelines or LIFESKILLS. Write the name of one main character in the center of a large piece of paper (2' x 3' or bigger). Draw a circle around the name. Add rays coming out from the circle, similar to a child's drawing of the sun. (For very young children, consider using a felt story board.) Have your child identify a Lifelong Guideline or LIFESKILL that this story character used to solve problems and reach his/her goals. Write the target word on the ray and the action below the ray. For example, based on *Charlotte's Web*, put the name Wilbur in the center circle. Add a ray; above it write perseverance; under the ray write the descriptors of action from the text, e.g., "He thought and thought until he created a plan to help save his friend Charlotte, the spider." (See an example of a character web on page 25.7.)

Chapter 25—Parents As Teachers: Tips of the Trade

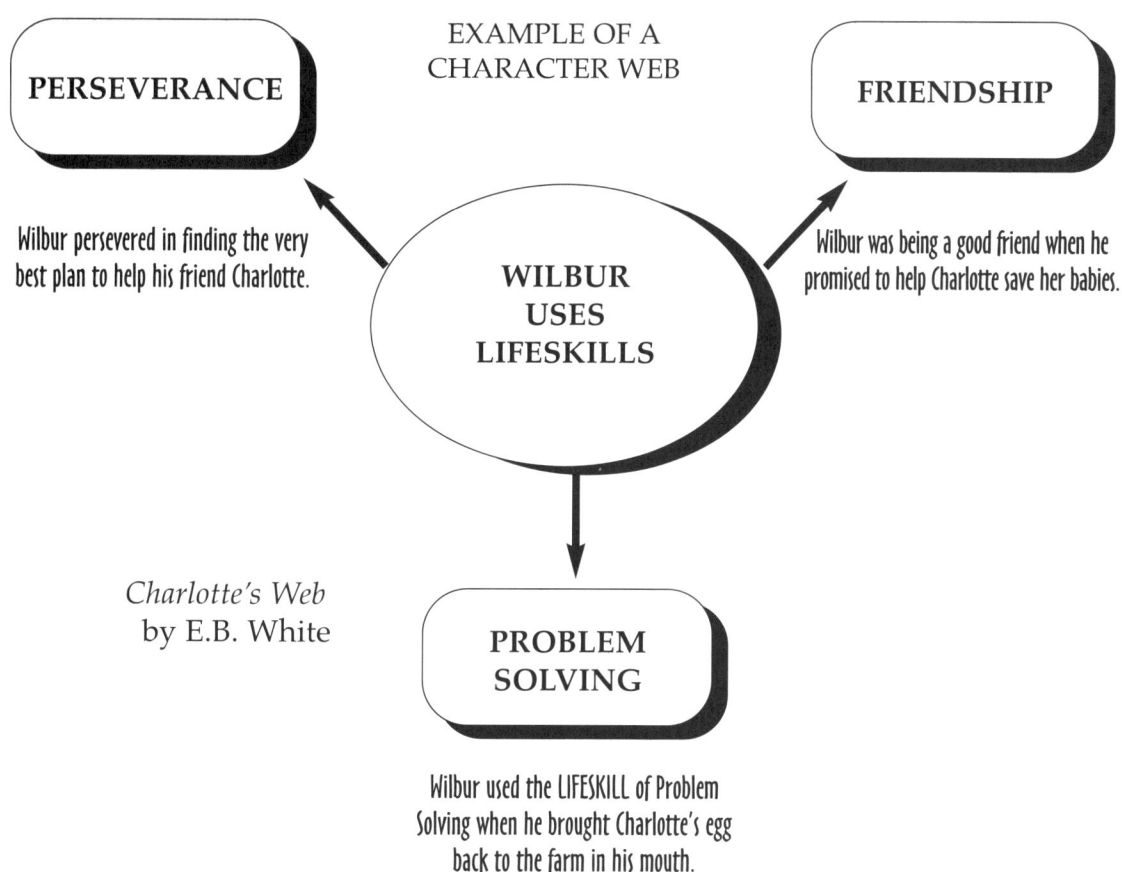

- *Solve a Problem:* Identify three Lifelong Guidelines or LIFESKILLS that were used to solve a problem in the story. Identify two Lifelong Guidelines or LIFESKILLS that were not used and thus resulted in problems.

- *Rewrite the Ending:* After reading a traditional story such as *The Three Little Pigs,* rewrite the ending as if the characters had used the Lifelong Guidelines/LIFESKILLS to solve their problem.

- *Play "Who Am I?":* After completing several stories, play "Who Am I?" Choose a character from a book you have read. Share the Lifelong Guidelines/LIFESKILLS used along with one or two behaviors illustrating use or non-use of those particular Lifelong Guidelines/LIFE-SKILLS. Invite other children or family members that have read the book to guess who the character is.

- *Share Experiences:* After reading a biography or autobiography, label three or more Lifelong Guidelines or LIFESKILLS which made the person who he/she was, what he/she became famous for. Next, invite family members to share their experiences in developing these same Lifelong Guidelines or LIFESKILLS. Discuss as a family how these "famous" characteristics are lived on a day-to-day basis in your lives.

- *Lifelong Guidelines/LIFESKILLS in History:* Compare the lives and character traits (Lifelong Guidelines/ LIFESKILLS) of two well-known people. Select people from different time periods and settings (e.g., Rosa Parks and Princess Diana). Use a Venn diagram,* to identify character strengths and weaknesses they have in common and strengths and weaknesses unique to each. Discuss whether or not the Lifelong Guidelines/LIFESKILLS are unique to the time period/setting of the story.

- *Local Newspaper:* Find local newspaper articles that reflect the Lifelong Guidelines/LIFESKILLS being used or problems that occurred because they weren't used. Read the articles with your child and have him/her determine which Lifelong Guideline/LIFESKILL was or wasn't used. Ask your child to share his/her thinking with you.

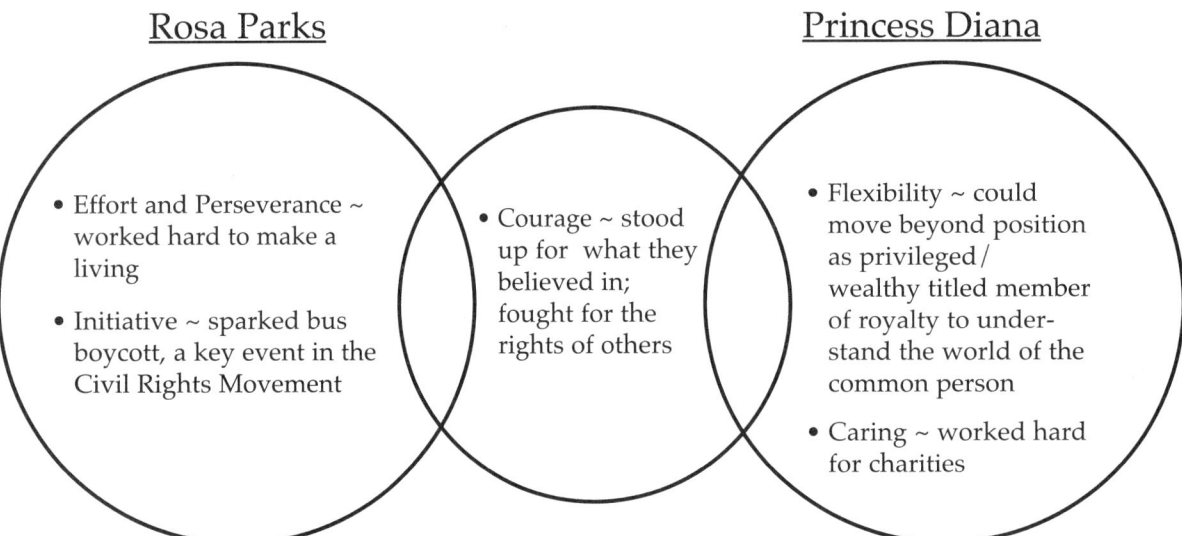

Hopefully these few ideas will have you thinking in many different directions. Perhaps you remember a favorite biography and think, "Of course, why didn't I ever mention perseverance when we read about Thomas Edison or Rosa Parks?" Or, perhaps you recall a link to humor using *Charlotte's Web*. How about the courage shown in *The True Story of Ruby Bridges?* Eventually, you'll wonder why you ever thought it would be hard to make connections. They'll be popping up everywhere!

If, however, you think your child isn't picking up on important aspects of the story or missing the moral dilemmas of the characters, here are some questions—in no particular order—that you can ask to help you child focus on relevant pieces of the story as it unfolds:

- What is. . . ?
- Who was. . . ? What kind of person do you think he/she is?
- Where is. . . ?
- What is happening? What do you think will happen next?
- How did it happen?
- Why do you think he/she did that?
- Do you agree with _____'s actions?
- What would you have done? Why?

- What other way could you have. . . ?
- Can you predict the ending of the story?
- Can you suggest another way for the story to end?
- What would happen if. . . ?
- If you were the author, what would you have changed about the story? Why?
- What is your opinion of _____?
- What choice would you have made?
- How would you. . . ?

---

* A Venn diagram is a useful and understandable way to compare similarities and differences. It consists of three overlapping circles. As illustrated above, the left and right circles contain what is true about each of two elements but not true of both. The middle circle that overlaps the other two circles contains characteristics true.

Using Literature: A Cautionary Note. As you use literature to open doors to discussing character and values with your child, do remember the Golden Rule of reading great literature: *Enjoy the story! First should come the pleasure of discovery and love for a good story well told.* Second comes the value of that story to teach us lessons about life.

The corollary to this rule is: "Don't kill the golden goose." If we want children to read throughout the lives, don't kill their joy of reading by over analyzing everything. Co-author Karen Olsen vividly recalls gagging and choking over *Silas Marner,* a piece of "great" British literature, as a high school sophomore. Day after day, every line was dissected for meaning and metaphor, nuance and nonsense. By the end of the story, few in class could assemble the plot (who cares!) and there wasn't a single character anyone identified with or cared about. Next came *Great Expectations,* similarly taught. Karen didn't read a piece of "great" literature for fun until after graduating from college. And she was an English major!

So, first, enjoy the story for it adventure and characters. Once your child is hooked on the book—and that may take two or three readings, especially with younger children—then dig a little deeper.

Song

Songs are a wonderful teaching device. They combine the power of memorable melody and the rhyme of poetry. Both significantly increase the likelihood that what is learned will be stored in long-term memory. Best of all, singing is fun and something that all can do; musical talent and training are not required. Also, rather than giving your child a stern lecture about behavior, try breaking into a song to remind him/her of the Lifelong Guideline/LIFESKILL needed at the moment. What a delight!

Resources available to help you launch your musical career together include *Spread Your Wings: The Lifelong Guidelines* by Jeff Pedersen (available in video, CD, and audio cassette), *Lifelines* by Jeff Pedersen (CD), and *LIFESKILLS* by Russ and Judy Eacker (CD or audio cassette; songbook is also available).* Or, log on to *http://www.scottsdale.org/schools/elem/DesertCanyon/iti.htm*, internet home of Jean Spanko, a gifted ITI teacher using the ITI model with middle school students. The lyrics, written to favorite oldies, are delightful and very singable. Students will pick up the melody and lyrics in a flash. (Two samples of Jean's work appear on the next page.)

Once you have started using songs as a teaching device, encourage your child to develop lyrics to his/her favorite tunes. Children delight in writing such songs. Plus, it extends and deepens their ownership of each Lifelong Guideline and LIFESKILL. Also, writing lyrics is a painless invitation to writing and reading.

---

* Both are available from Books for Educators, Inc.—888/777-9827; e mail: books4@oz.net; www.books4educ.com See order form at the back of this book.

Pride, Great Pride
(to the tune of *Ain't She Sweet?*)

Pride, great pride
Feel it way down deep inside.
When you just can't rest
Until you do your best,
Feel that PRIDE.

Mastery,
Just remember "CCC."
When it's correct, complete,
And comprehensive
How proud you'll be.

When you've got pride
You'll aim much higher.
That little spark
Becomes a fire.

Pride, great pride
Feel it way down deep inside.
When you just can't rest
Until you do your best,
Feel that pride!

Resourcefulness
(to the tune of *This Old Man*)

When you face problems tough,
Resourcefulness will be enough.
Look around for answers,
Change your point of view.
Great ideas will come to you.

Keep your mind focused well;
Stay away from folks that tell you
"This won't work,
We tried it once before."
Show those people out the door.

If you fail, don't give in
Try your first ideas again.
The solution may be
Just a step away.
Be resourceful every day.

When you're stumped, you can ask
Trusted friends to share your task.
They can listen well
And dream along with you . . .
Give a different point of view.

Think in ways new and strange.
There's a world that you can change.
Be resourceful and you'll
See the answer clear.
All the world will stand and cheer.

Written Procedures

Perhaps the most common cause of "misbehavior" is lack of agreement about what behaviors are expected. The parent expects "x" and that's news to the child! The result is lots of frustration for both parent and child.

Written procedures help you plan ahead for frequently occurring events (going to grandma's house or the grocery store), social interactions (such as going to a birthday party), and tasks (cleaning one's room or doing homework). By describing what social and personal behaviors are expected, procedures allow children to be successful.

Think of answers to the following questions. What does my child need to know and be able to do in order to do what's appropriate? How is he/she expected to behave? What is he/she expected to bring?

Written procedures are an important leadership strategy in the ITI model—in both classroom and in the home. Examples from the classroom include entering and leaving the room, what students should do when they've finished an assignment, and going to and coming from assemblies. Likewise at home, written procedures describe the personal and social behaviors/actions expected when a child is getting ready for school, coming home, doing homework, playing with toys, inviting/having friends over, doing regular chores, carrying out emergency safety procedures, and the like. Written procedures for coming home might include removing shoes, hanging up his/her coat, greeting politely and cheerfully whomever is there, taking belongings to his/her room before setting them down, and so forth. (See examples of written procedures on the previous page.)

By writing procedures on paper and posting them on the refrigerator, the family bulletin board, or a homework binder, your child can refer to them whenever necessary. Procedures help prevent confusion, frustration, and misbehavior. They also eliminate the need for stating expectations over and over again (otherwise known as nagging!). As a bonus, babysitters find such procedures extremely helpful as well.

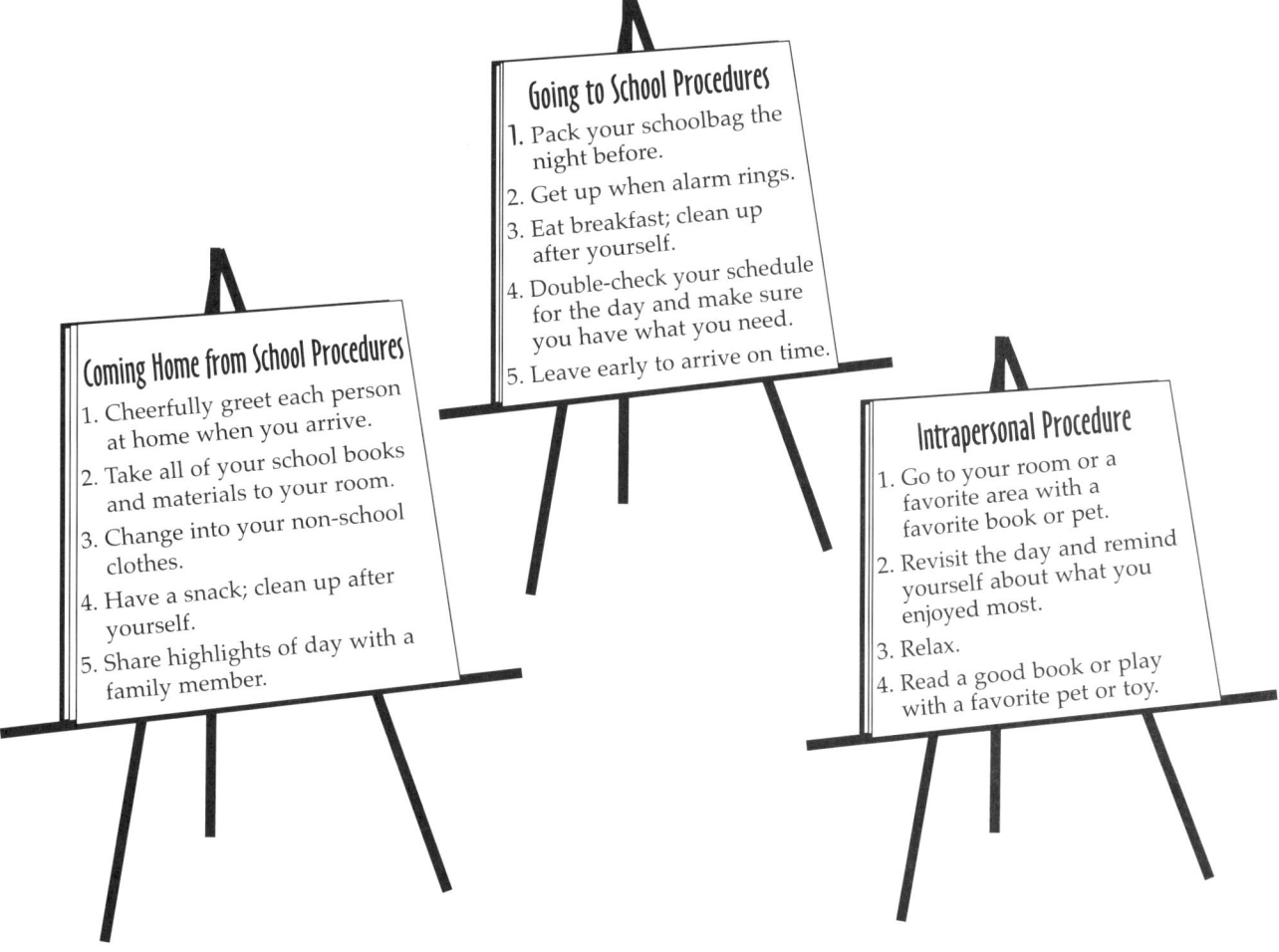

Clear Expectations

It's difficult to do our personal best and meet other people's expectations if the criteria for the task are not clear. Often, what is perceived as misbehavior is merely the result of not knowing what is expected, in behavior and/or performance. Written procedures describe expectations for personal and social behaviors but criteria for performing tasks or jobs are also needed. In the real world, such criteria are often called specifications. Call them what you wish, they are critical.

"Is It Done?" How to Avoid the Arguments. A common source of argument is whether or not a task was done according to expectations of the "boss"—the person who assigned the job to be done—whether written or not. "I'm finished!" says the child. "No you're not," says the adult. The problem: uncommunicated or misunderstood criteria for completion. As in the classroom, the child ought not to have to ask, "Teacher, is this right?" "Mom . . . Mom . . . Mom, is this what you wanted me to do?" The criteria should be clear so that the child can assess his/her own performance. Your ultimate goal is criteria that meet real-world standards for acceptability and excellence.

What kinds of assessment do you plan to use? The ITI model applies the 3C's of assessment to "opportunities to practice" or other activities:

- **Is it complete?** Was the job completed as stated in the "Opportunities to Practice"? Does it reflect real-world standards for work performed in the work place while remaining age-appropriate? Does it reflect pride in workmanship and personal best?

- **Is it correct?** Is the information/action correct?

- **Is it comprehensive?** Has the child addressed the task as thoroughly as possible given his/her capabilities at this age? Did the child just follow the specific directions given to him/her or did he/she handle closely related tasks that, if left undone, would adversely affect the outcome of the assigned job? For example, if asked to clean the sink in the bathroom, did the child also wipe up the toothpaste dripped on the nearby countertop?

Keep in mind that criteria should "grow" as the child's capabilities grow. What was personal best at six years of age is unacceptable at age nine.

THE HOME AS CLASSROOM

In your role as first teachers, use the physical environment to help provide a continuous message to your child. Don't be afraid to use the refrigerator door as a bulletin board (it already is anyway!) and/or a wall in the family eating area. Post the current Lifelong Guideline or LIFESKILL with its definition where it can be easily referred to.

Daily visual reminders help in recognizing and identifying expectations. With the words posted, it's easier to remember to capture the teachable moment using target talk to provide feedback about the use and non-use of a particular Lifelong Guideline or LIFESKILL.

Sometime during the sixth century B.C., Lao-Tzu (a name meaning "old sage") wrote,

"The journey of a thousand miles begins with one step."

Enjoy the journey!

Chapter 26
Getting Started

There are innumerable ways to begin using the Lifelong Guidelines and LIFESKILLS. Our advice to you is to:

- Start with the Lifelong Guidelines
- Create a schedule for the first four to five weeks; know what you want to do each day
- Make your "lessons" memorable
- Capture the "teachable moment"

The following plans are recommended by parents and teachers using the ITI Lifelong Guidelines and LIFESKILLS in their home and classroom. The first plan recommends introducing and teaching a Lifelong Guideline for a week. This allows clear focus and lots of practice. Rote memory is ineffective for this kind of learning. Use the recommended teaching strategies in Chapters 25 and 26 to give your child different ways of looking at the behavior guideline and thus avoid boredom.

START WITH THE LIFELONG GUIDELINES

Introduce all five Lifelong Guidelines at once as a collection of behaviors to enhance living and growing together for everyone everywhere at every age. Then, go back and teach each one in-depth using the ideas here or others that you know will work for your family.

When to Teach the LIFESKILLS

Remember that the LIFESKILLS are not separate from the Lifelong Guidelines; the LIFESKILLS define the Lifelong Guideline of Personal Best. Begin teaching the LIFESKILLS only when you are ready to teach the Lifelong Guideline of Personal Best. Again, the LIFESKILLS are *not* separate from the Lifelong Guidelines; they are the working definition of doing our personal best.

To teach your child the LIFESKILLS, follow what worked for you when teaching the Lifelong Guidelines. Just remember that developing habits of mind and heart take time. Use modeling, target talk, literature, song, written procedures, and clear expectations daily. Add other ways of teaching and practicing a LIFESKILL or Lifelong Guideline that you think will best support your child. Above all, have fun with your child. Learning values and appropriate behaviors may be serious business but it need not be grim! Enjoy watching your child grow.

CREATE A SCHEDULE

Some parents question why they even have to have a plan to introduce and teach the Lifelong Guidelines. After all, isn't the best way to teach them naturally, whenever the circumstances are appropriate? The answer is yes and no. The best way to teach the Lifelong Guidelines and LIFESKILLS is to teach them in the most natural way possible during the "teachable moments" of life. But, we also know that busy personal and family schedules have a way of pushing the best of intentions aside. The result, all too often, is that focus is lost, days slip by with no or only minimal teaching. Character development is too important to parents and children to be left to happenstance.

Good teaching is not an accident. For one month, set aside a small portion of each day to teach your child a deeper understanding of the Lifelong Guidelines. The time of day isn't important, although some parents prefer to have a set schedule so the day doesn't slip past them. What is important is that you sit down with your child with purpose and a clear plan for what you are to teach during the month and day by day.

The "one a week" plan below is popular and widely used. Its strength is that it allows you to focus in depth on one Lifelong Guideline (and later on, one LIFESKILL) at a time. This is particularly important with younger students.

The "one a day" plan* is also workable. Its strength is that it allows students to see where they are going by the end of the first week. This is useful for older students from upper elementary through high school. You decide, based on your own child's needs, learning patterns, and temperament.

---

* The "one a day" schedule was created by Joy Raboli, classroom teacher in Albany, Oregon, and former associate, Susan Kovalik & Associates, Inc.

Plan One: One a Week for Five Weeks

Plan number one focuses on teaching one Lifelong Guideline per week. The following chart offers suggestions for teaching and providing practice for the Lifelong Guideline each day during each of the five weeks. During the second week, while focusing on the Lifelong Guideline of Truthfulness, you can use the same combination of teaching strategies or change them as you see fit. Likewise, during the third, fourth, and fifth weeks, while focusing on the Lifelong Guidelines of Active Listening, No Put-Downs, and Personal Best, follow the suggestions on the next page or change them according to your intuition. For descriptions of each of these teaching strategies, see pages 26.5-26.9 and 25.2-25.10. For example, for the first week focus on the Lifelong Guideline of Trustworthiness:

LIFELONG GUIDELINES
TRUSTWORTHINESS   TRUTHFULNESS
ACTIVE LISTENING   NO PUT-DOWNS
PERSONAL BEST

WEEK		Mon	Tue	Wed	Thu	Fri
	ONE	**TRUSTWORTHINESS** Define~Story~Song	**TRUSTWORTHINESS** Video~Discuss~Role Play	**TRUSTWORTHINESS** T-chart~Literature	**TRUSTWORTHINESS** Role Play~Literature	**TRUSTWORTHINESS** Song~Role Play~Journal
	TWO	**TRUTHFULNESS** Define~Story~Song	**TRUTHFULNESS** Video~Discuss~Role Play	**TRUTHFULNESS** T-chart~Literature	**TRUTHFULNESS** Role Play~Literature	**TRUTHFULNESS** Song~Role Play~Journal
	THREE	**ACTIVE LISTENING** Define~Story~Song	**ACTIVE LISTENING** Video~Discuss~Role Play	**ACTIVE LISTENING** T-chart~Literature	**ACTIVE LISTENING** Role Play~Literature	**ACTIVE LISTENING** Song~Role Play~Journal
	FOUR	**NO PUT-DOWNS** Define~Story~Song	**NO PUT-DOWNS** Video~Discuss~Role Play	**NO PUT-DOWNS** T-chart~Literature	**NO PUT-DOWNS** Role Play~Literature	**NO PUT-DOWNS** Song~Role Play~Journal
	FIVE	**PERSONAL BEST** Define~Story~Song	**PERSONAL BEST** Video~Discuss~Role Play	**PERSONAL BEST** T-chart~Literature	**PERSONAL BEST** Role Play~Literature	**PERSONAL BEST** Song~Role Play~Journal

Plan Two: Five Per Week for a Month

This plan focuses on a particular Lifelong Guideline each day of the week and repeats the same schedule throughout the month. Monday is devoted to the Lifelong Guideline of Trustworthiness; Tuesday focuses on Truthfulness; Wednesday is for Active Listening; Thursday is for No Put-Downs; and Friday explores Personal Best.

LIFELONG GUIDELINES
TRUSTWORTHINESS   TRUTHFULNESS
ACTIVE LISTENING   NO PUT-DOWNS
PERSONAL BEST

WEEK		Mon	Tue	Wed	Thu	Fri
		TRUSTWORTHINESS	TRUTHFULNESS	ACTIVE LISTENING	NO PUT-DOWNS	PERSONAL BEST
	ONE	TRUSTWORTHINESS Define~Story~Discuss	TRUTHFULNESS Define~Story~Discuss	ACTIVE LISTENING Define~Story~Discuss	NO PUT-DOWNS Define~Story~Discuss	PERSONAL BEST Define~Story~Discuss
	TWO	TRUSTWORTHINESS Video~Tally~Graph	TRUTHFULNESS Video~Tally~Graph	ACTIVE LISTENING Video~Tally~Graph	NO PUT-DOWNS Video~Tally~Graph	PERSONAL BEST Video~Tally~Graph
	THREE	TRUSTWORTHINESS T-chart~Role Play~Real Life	TRUTHFULNESS T-chart~Role Play~Real Life	ACTIVE LISTENING T-chart~Role Play~Real Life	NO PUT-DOWNS T-chart~Role Play~Real Life	PERSONAL BEST T-chart~Role Play~Real Life
	FOUR	TRUSTWORTHINESS Creative Writing~Journal	TRUTHFULNESS Creative Writing~Journal	ACTIVE LISTENING Creative Writing~Journal	NO PUT-DOWNS Creative Writing~Journal	PERSONAL BEST Creative Writing~Journal
	LITERATURE	*The Bears on Hemlock Mountain*, *The Velveteen Rabbit*, *The Secret Garden*	*Berenstein Bears Tell the Truth*, *Sam, Bangs and Moonshine*, *Pinocchio*	*3 Little Pigs-Wolf's Point of View*, *Charlotte's Web*, *Horton Hears a Who*	*Ugly Duckling*, *Ira Sleeps Over*, *Crow Boy*, *Whipping Boy*, *Charlie Brown* books	*Amazing Grace*, *Stone Fox*, *The Giving Tree*, *The Three Little Pigs*, *Brave Irene*

Plan Three: Your Choice

Your choice is your choice but take a few tips from brain research. Plan for a minimum of 20-30 minutes a day, five days a week, plus taking advantage of the teachable moments in family life.

MAKE YOUR "LESSONS" MEMORABLE

In addition to the teaching strategies that should be used daily, as described in Chapter 25, there are numerous teaching strategies that can give real punch and enthusiasm to your teaching. Use these strategies to introduce or reteach a Lifelong Guideline or LIFESKILL. They may be used as often as you wish but usually not every day. They include:

- Video clips
- T-charts
- Discussion
- Role playing
- Journal writing
- Social/political action
- Celebrations

Video Clips

Good videos, like good literature, are a terrific teaching resource. But not the entire movie; children typically spend more time than they should watching movies and TV. Think video segments. Even movies that may seem objectionable in their entirety have short segments with powerful messages for youth (and adults). Usually a 5-8 minute clip is sufficient. Whether it models the values and behaviors you are trying to teach or whether it shows a lack of such values and behaviors, both are needed to help children get a clear picture of what they are targeting. To really know what something is, we must also know what it isn't. This is particularly important when applying values and morals to everyday life. For example, when is telling the truth being rude and uncaring? When does being trustworthy become being taken advantage of? When does doing your personal best become dangerous to your health?

Video clips are often a good lead-in to be followed by T-charts and discussion. Charlie Brown movies, for example, contain wonderful examples of put-downs usually understandable to five-year olds (as well as adults!). Ask the children to keep a tally of the number of put-downs they hear during a brief segment. Then relate the put-downs to real-life situations, behaviors, and personal experiences. Co-author Sue Pearson, after the class learned the basics of "No Put-Downs," had her students watch a section of one of the Charlie Brown videos. Students were appalled by the number of nasty comments, offered in the guise of humor. The "humor" didn't seem so funny anymore.

Harriet the Spy by Louise Fitzhugh is an appropriate story that focuses on trust, or the lack of it. Seeing a video scene with new eyes is a beginning step in seeing behaviors with new eyes, the eyes of the Lifelong Guidelines.

To extend the video experiences, make up topics for discussion, such as name calling, disparaging remarks about physical attributes, or references to family circumstances.

One last reminder: Make sure that the video clip you select is age-appropriate, i.e., comprehensible to children of your child's age group.

Picture Making—T-Charts

An excellent way to introduce a Lifelong Guideline or LIFESKILL, and to do an in-depth refresher course if needed, is to brainstorm pictures of what a particular Lifelong Guideline or LIFESKILL looks like, sounds like, and feels like *and* what it does *not* look like, sound like, or feel like.

How to Use T-Charts. Using a large piece of paper (2'x 3'), write the name of the Lifelong Guideline or LIFESKILL across the top of the page and create three columns. Label the first column "Looks Like," the second "Sounds Like," and the third "Feels Like" (see below). Allow your child sufficient time so that he or she can fill in the spaces with only minimal prompting. Children's intuitive understanding of the Lifelong Guidelines and LIFESKILLS is often surprising. Let your child fill in the chart with his/her own words or volunteer to write down your child's ideas. (For younger children, draw simple pictures to illustrate the meaning.)

TRUSTWORTHINESS

Looks Like	Sounds Like	Feels Like
kids sharing ideas	"I've got a secret!"	safe
people working together	"Will you teach me how to do that?"	comfortable
child running an errand	"Please take this to Mrs. X down the street"	I'm trusted
children helping one another	"Would you help me?" "Yes."	friendliness
child turning in found object	"I found this. It belongs to someone else."	honesty

To introduce the T-chart and the topic, ask your child to think of personal experiences at home, school, or neighborhood or situations from stories that will fit into each category. The example on the following page is for the Lifelong Guideline of Trustworthiness.

Create a second chart that illustrates what the Lifelong Guideline or LIFESKILL does *not* look like, does *not* sound like, or does *not* feel like. This contrast of what something is and what is isn't significantly sharpens the learner's understanding of what he/she is trying to learn.

Lifelong Guideline/LIFESKILL OF _____

LOOKS LIKE	SOUNDS LIKE	FEELS LIKE	DOES NOT LOOK LIKE	DOES NOT SOUND LIKE	DOES NOT FEEL LIKE

Save both charts and add to the columns daily throughout the first week of study and at least monthly thereafter as your child identifies more attributes. Post both charts side by side in an easily-seen location; after a month, collect them in a binder that can be easily referred to. The more pictures your child has for each of the Lifelong Guidelines and LIFESKILLS, the more adept he/she will become at applying them in personal and social settings.

Discussion

The more you and your child use the Lifelong Guidelines and LIFESKILLS, the more at ease you and your child will be with them. Think through in advance ways to:

- Identify the need to use the Lifelong Guidelines and LIFESKILLS in daily family life, especially uses you know to be important to your child—behaviors that he/she can use to make his/her life work, to make happen those things he/she wants to have happen

- Give succinct and memorable descriptors of what those behaviors might be

- Avoid value judgment; allow your child to make the judgments of value for him/herself, thus internalizing the behaviors

- Identify other ways people use the Lifelong Guidelines and LIFESKILLS, both in and out of the home

Discussion should be part of your introduction to and on-going teaching of each Lifelong Guideline and LIFESKILL. It can occur during your "lesson" and carry over to family conversation at the dinner table; it should also pop up during the day as part of child-parent interactions to solve a problem or correct behavior. Give considerable thought to discussion as a way to capture the "teachable moment." For example, "Wait until your father gets home" doesn't have the teaching value that stopping at the moment and helping your child think though his/her behavior does. Key questions to ask include:s

- What Lifelong Guidelines or LIFESKILLS didn't he/she use (that caused the problem)

- Which Lifelong Guidelines and LIFESKILLS he/she could have used to have avoided the problem

- Which Lifelong Guideline and LIFESKILLS are needed to "clean up" the problem (to correct the mistake, fix/replace what's broken, and or make amends for hurt feelings, and so forth)

An excellent resource for structuring discussions is *TRIBES: A New Way of Learning and Being Together* by Jeanne Gibbs.*

Sharing Our Childhood Memories. Since children love hearing their parents and relatives share stories of their childhood experiences, don't forget to share some of your own childhood experiences with family and friends at home and in school that relate to the Lifelong Guideline or LIFESKILL being

---

* *TRIBES: A New Way of Learning and Being Together* by Jeanne Gibbs is not generally carried by most book stores but is available through Books for Educators, Inc. www.books4educ@aol.com

discussed. Avoid becoming preachy. Let children know that adult lives are also works in progress and that the Lifelong Guidelines and LIFESKILLS are lifelong pursuits.

Role Playing

Role playing is highly appealing to children; there is action to watch, dialogue to hear, and a story line to follow. Often because of the emotional impact, the moral or lesson just pops out and it's easier for students to make connections to real life.

Role playing can be formal—with time to invent and rehearse an assigned scenario—or spontaneous with no preparation time. Both methods are powerful and especially effective for teaching children alternative responses. For example, set up a simple situation: "Instead of _____ [the offending action such as hitting Jack], role play what Lifelong Guideline or LIFESKILL you could have used to have prevented the problem."

Conversely, if a story or incident worked out well, ask the question, "What if Kenny had not used the Lifelong Guideline or LIFESKILL of _____? Role play what would have happened then."

Have your family act out the options. Be playful. Know that for many children, hearing about something is seldom as powerful as doing it and seeing it.

Journal Writing

Journal writing is an excellent device to help children process what *they* think about something. With no one looking over their shoulder or judging what they say, they can be reflective about what they truly think. And, because writing is thinking on paper, the act of writing requires children to sort through their thoughts to the bottom line.

Encourage your child to keep a journal and reflect on experiences that relate to the Lifelong Guidelines and LIFESKILLS. Remember, a journal differs from a diary which primarily records what occurs from day to day.

Social and Political Action Projects

Social and/or political action projects put learning to the test: Can children apply what they have been learning to personal use in the real world? What we know from brain research is that locking knowledge and skill into long-term memory requires using that knowledge or skill— lots of opportunities to use them in varying situations (rather than in rote repetition). While test-taking is usually performed from short-term memory, use of knowledge and skill in real world settings over time requires that such knowledge and skill be stored in long-term memory.

For example, if studying the LIFESKILL of Caring, encourage your child to act upon it—to assist at a home for the elderly (sing, help with a Christmas party, and so forth), volunteer at a soup kitchen, offer to help a neighbor just home from the hospital by taking care of his/her yard for two weeks. If studying the LIFESKILL of Resourcefulness, have your child start a business (walking pets for neighbors, mowing lawns, washing windows, teaching others how to use the internet or make a web page, delivering newspapers. The projects don't have to last a lifetime. Two to four weeks is enough to make the learning memorable. If studying the LIFESKILL of Initiative, look around the neighborhood. What political action is needed? A crosswalk light needed at a dangerous intersection, pollution to be cleaned up, an empty lot to be made safe, drug pushing outside the school to be stopped, low voter registration and turn out to be improved?

Young citizens of a democratic society should start learning the gears and levers of democracy from infancy. Several good resources for helping you guide your child through planning and carrying out social/political projects include: *The Kid's Guide to Social Action: How to Solve the Social Problems You Choose—and Turn Creative Thinking into Positive Action* by Barbara Lewis (Minneapolis, MN: Free Spirit Publishing, 1998), *The Kid's Guide to Service Projects: Over 500 Service Ideas for Young People Who Want to Make a Difference* by Barbara Lewis (Minneapolis, MN: Free Spirit Publishing, 1995), *What Do You Stand For?: A Kid's Guide to Building Character* by Barbara Lewis (Minneapolis, MN: Free Spirit Publishing, 1998), and *Enriching the Curriculum Through Service Learning* edited by Carol W. Kinsley and Kate McPherson (Alexandria, VA: ASCD, 1995). All of these books are available through Books for Educators.

Celebrations

How will you celebrate your accomplishments as a family? As the saying goes, "All work and no play makes Jack a dull boy." It is important to take time to acknowledge our growth and development as people, regardless of our age. Pride in our accomplishments—a deep sense of personal satisfaction in a job well done—is an important source of motivation to do one's personal best the next time. Do create a family culture and spirit in which each person acknowledges others on a daily basis and all celebrate their joy and pride in fun ways all can share in. In families, accomplishment by any one member should be considered a gain for the group.

Do note, however, that celebration of accomplishments is vastly different from receiving a reward. While rewards, such as ice cream treats, a trip to McDonald's, and so forth, work in the short run, they are extremely detrimental in the long run.* Your goal is to instill in your child the desire to do what is needed because it needs to be done and to feel a sense of personal satisfaction from doing his/her part. Surprisingly enough, external rewards work against us; they extinguish the behavior that is rewarded. The key to development of character and values in the long run is teaching children to internalize a sense of satisfaction from a job well done because it's the right thing to do and they say so, not because they received an external reward. Reliance on other's opinions of behavior and choices corrupts character at its core and overly strengthens the power of peer pressure.

Celebration, on the other hand, is taking time to acknowledge your child's success in implementing the Lifelong Guidelines and LIFESKILLS and to experience that deep sense of personal satisfaction that comes with doing so. The feedback is thus internal, not external; the sense of pride is thus internally generated—and earned. Thus, the celebration is outward with others but the pride and satisfaction is felt within.

---

* For a hair-raising discussion of the dangers of rewards, see Alfie Kohn's book, *Punished by Rewards: The Trouble with Gold Stars, Incentive Plans, A's, Praise, and Other Bribes* (New York: Houghton Mifflin, 1993).

Celebrate the day-by-day triumphs. Learn to appreciate them as everyday miracles in the life of your child. And celebrate, celebrate, celebrate. Let your love and joy in your child grow as he/she grows.

Life Is Our Best Teacher

This book provides hundreds of opportunities to practice the Lifelong Guidelines and LIFESKILLS. Life provides thousands more. The purpose of this book is to offer some beginning points and strategies. Go back to your own roots and experiences for "hooks" that will help you make the Lifelong Guidelines and LIFESKILLS memorable and part of the fabric of family life in your home . . . where character begins.

Appendix A ~ ITI Resources

See last page for ordering instructions.

Integrated Thematic Instruction: The Model
Third Edition, Updated 1997
by Susan Kovalik with Karen D. Olsen $27.50

ITI: The Model is the most comprehensive book available on how to apply brain research to curriculum, instruction, and learning for grades K-6. The brain research base is clearly and succinctly described; implementation strategies are practical and provide step-by-step explanations of how to create a bodybrain-compatible learning environment and develop a yearlong theme as a structure for integrating all basic skills and content areas. Loaded with curriculum examples, implementation tips, starting points, and timelines. Practical, insightful.

The Way We Were . . . The Way We Can Be:
A Vision for the Middle School
Third Edition, by Ann Ross and K. Olsen . . $27.50

This book in the ITI series applies brain research and the ITI model to the middle school setting. The brain research base is clear, succinct, and readily understandable. Application strategies are practical and doable yet very powerful. The book also describes how to develop a yearlong theme to integrate all content and skills regardless of the structure of the school—from departmentalized classrooms to block schedules to self-contained.

Synergy: The Transformation of America's High Schools Through Integrated Thematic Instruction
by Karen D. Olsen $27.50

America's high schools have survived waves of reform efforts unchanged. This book makes the case for achieving true transformation rather than merely tinkering with the present system. It challenges the very roots of high school and calls for radical change and a defined purpose. It describes how to use brain research and the ITI model as a vehicle for classroom and schoolwide restructuring.

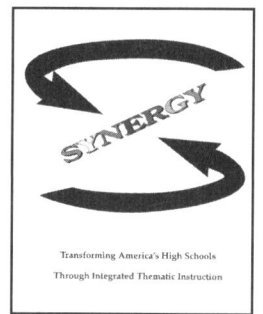

Kid's Eye View of Science:
A Teacher's Handbook for Implementing an Integrated Thematic Approach to Teaching Science, K-6
Second Edition, by Susan Kovalik and Karen D. Olsen $27.50

Kid's Eye View of Science will change forever how you think about teaching science. Starting with brain research as a basis for creating a brain-compatible environment using the ITI model, the book provides the tools needed to throw open the doors of natural curiosity and high levels of thinking and problem solving. Includes step-by-step descriptions of how to implement the ITI model and how to make your science curriculum brain-compatible. Join our mascot, "Mary Froggins," in her campaign to make science the core of your integrated curriculum.

Character Begins at Home: Family Tools for Teaching Character and Values

Getting Started Video Set
Stage 1 of the ITI Stages of Implementation and *LIFESKILLS: Creating a Class Family*
(2 video set, 45 total minutes) $149.95

Stage 1 of the ITI Stages of Implementation: First Things First

In this video, Joy Raboli takes you through the first steps of setting up an ITI classroom, illustrating each aspect of Stage 1 of the *ITI Stages of Implementation.* Included are the physical layout of the room, beginning curriculum and instructional strategies, how to invite parents into the program, and what you can expect students to accomplish. This is a video that will answer your practical questions.

Can be purchased separately. (28 min. video $79.00)

LIFESKILLS: Creating a Class Family

Research conclusively shows that learning is accelerated when the issues of inclusion, mutual respect, and being in communication with each other are resolved and the classroom promotes a sense of community. Join Joy Raboli and Karen Janik and their 60 fifth and sixth graders for a look at what a multi-age class family looks like and how to create one in your own classroom.

Can be purchased separately. (17 min. video $79.00)

Spread Your Wings:
The Lifelong Guidelines
(19 min. video) $19.95

With original lyrics, music, and vocals, Jeff Pedersen illustrates the ITI Lifelong Guidelines as he takes us on a walk with students through a zoo. He introduces each song with heartfelt comments about what it means to apply the Lifelong Guidelines in every aspect of one's life. Thse five guidelines are the cornerstone of interpersonal skills and are based upon respect for others and self.

Spread Your Wings: The Lifelong Guidelines
(audio tape) $11.95
(compact disc) $12.50

Original lyrics, music, and vocals weave a vivid tapestry of images; provides a cheerful reference point for each of the Lifelong Guidelines: Truthfulness, Trustworthiness, Active Listening, No Put-Downs, and Active Learning.

LIFESKILLS (audio tape) $12.50
LIFESKILLS (compact disc) $16.50
LIFESKILLS (songbook) .... $ 6.50
by Judy and Russ Eacker

Music is a wonderful way to introduce the LIFESKILLS which can become a partner in creating a trusting environment that enhances learning. These original tunes and lyrics are whimsical and memorable. Cassette and CD each contain 17 songs. Lyrics booklet includes words for all 17 songs; the large print is ideal for making sing-along copies. Singable and fun. Created by R&J Productions. Each sold separately.

Lifelines:
Songs of Character
(45 min. CD) $12.00

Jeff Pedersen's original songs add vitality to one's day while reinforcing the LIFESKILLS of Perseverance, Caring, Initiative, Curiosity, Friendship, Sense of Humor, and Effort. Use the joy and power of music to bring deeper meaning to these LIFESKILLS for your family. Lyrics for each song are included.

Appendix A ~ ITI Resources

Lifelong Guidelines and LIFESKILLS

A wall poster set $39.95

The ITI Lifelong Guidelines call for trustworthiness, truthfulness, active listening, no put-downs, and personal best. What is personal best? The LIFESKILLS poster set provides colorful definitions and examples. The set includes a Lifelong Guidelines poster, a Personal Best Clubhouse poster (18" x 22 1/2"), and posters for each of the 18 LIFESKILLS (8 1/2" x 11"). The LIFESKILLS include such traits as cooperation, caring, integrity, initiative, perseverance, responsibility, and problem-solving. Artwork by Gwen Pribble is whimsical, action-oriented, and multi-ethnic. An ideal resource for any character education program—at home or school.

Example of 3 of the 18 small posters included

LIFESKILLS Notecards

Susan Kovalik & Associates $15.95

These lovely notecards with a garden motif each feature a separate LIFESKILL on a cream background. Use them to write to friends or family or to thank a student or co-worker for their use of a LIFESKILL! Set of seventeen on high quality paper with matching envelopes; suitable for framing or using to make a table centerpiece.

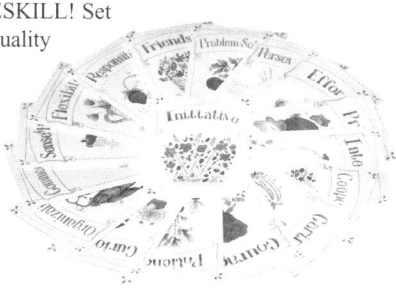

Lifelong Guidelines Mugs

Susan Kovalik & Associates . . . $6.00

Like the popular posters you have in your classroom, these mugs offer a daily reminder of the Lifelong Guidelines. An added bonus, you can fill them up with sixteen ounces of your favorite beverage! They're insulated, and come in an oatmeal shade with green top. Hidden key or coin compartment under the bottom.

Lifelong Guidelines & LIFESKILLS T-Shirts & Sweatshirts

T-Shirts $17.00*
Sweatshirts $26.00*

Send the message that you care about how we treat each other—wear a LIFESKILLS T-Shirt! Two designs are available: garden theme and LIFESKILLS Live It!. Garden theme: The Lifelong Guidelines are printed over the heart and the LIFESKILLS, which help you do your personal best, are on the back. On the LIFESKILLS LIVE IT! T-shirt, the design appears only on the front.

<u>T-Shirt (LIFESKILLS LIVE IT!):</u> white with multi-color design (50/50 Cotton & Poly.)
<u>T-Shirts (Garden Design):</u> yellow haze, mint green & ash gray (Preshrunk 100% Cotton)
<u>Sweatshirts Colors:</u> ash gray only (50/50, crew neck)
<u>Sizes:</u> L, XL, XXL *(please add $1.00 for XXL)*

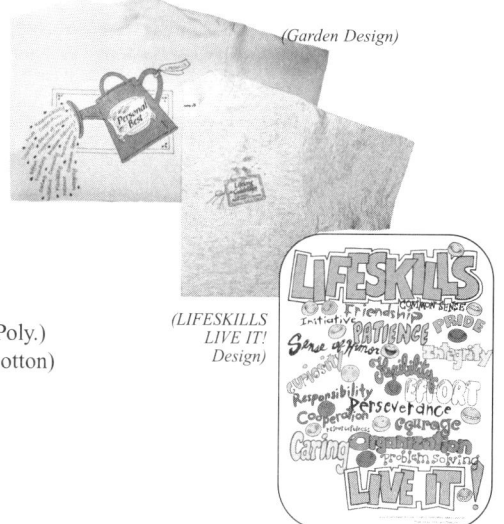

A.3

Appendix B ~ Ways to Organize Information

At the heart of good study skills is finding structures for organizing and remembering information that work for us. And, because every brain is unique, different things work for different learners. The following are examples of three very effective organizers that work well for learners of all ages—kindergarten to adult.

T-Charts —

An effective way to compare information and/or make it easily readable and memorable

Example 1: Simple

HOW TO MAKE AND KEEP FRIENDS

HELPS	HURTS
Sharing toys	Grabbing toys
Saying kind words	Using put-downs

Example 2: Complex

Lifelong Guideline/LIFESKILL OF _____

LOOKS LIKE	SOUNDS LIKE	FEELS LIKE	DOES NOT LOOK LIKE	DOES NOT SOUND LIKE	DOES NOT FEEL LIKE

Venn Diagrams

An efficient way to compare similarities and differences between two items.

Example 1: Simple

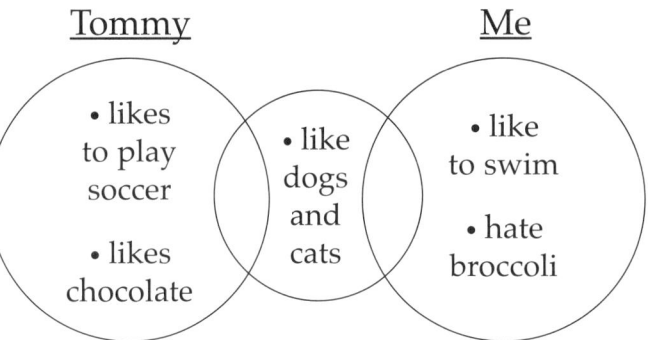

Example 2: Complex

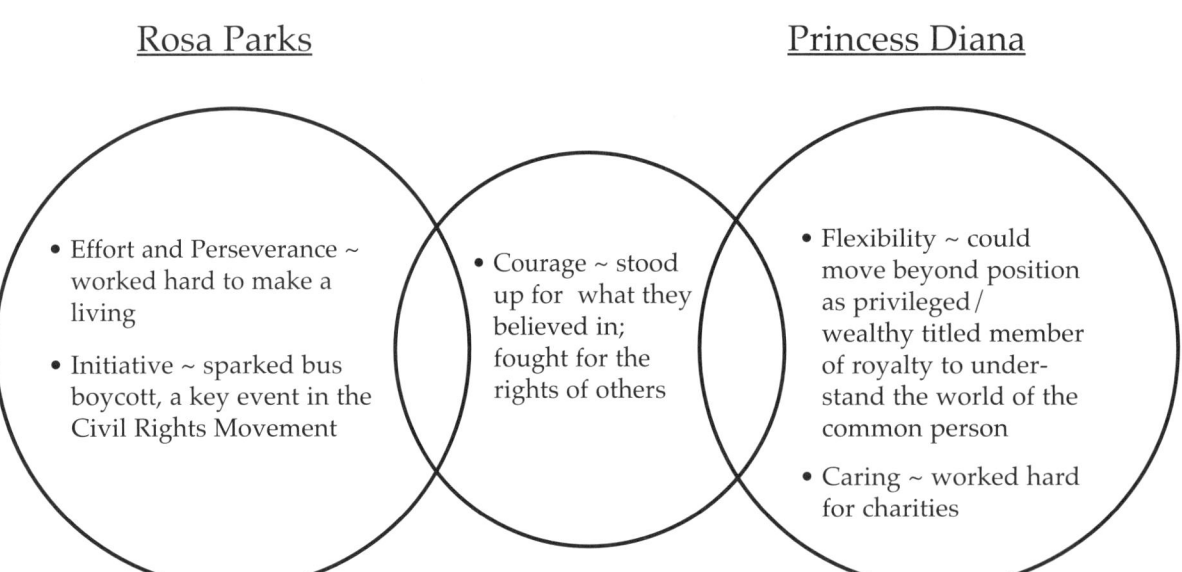

Appendix B ~ Ways to Organize Information

Mindmaps

An effective way to organize information and show interrelationships among ideas/things

Example 1: Simple

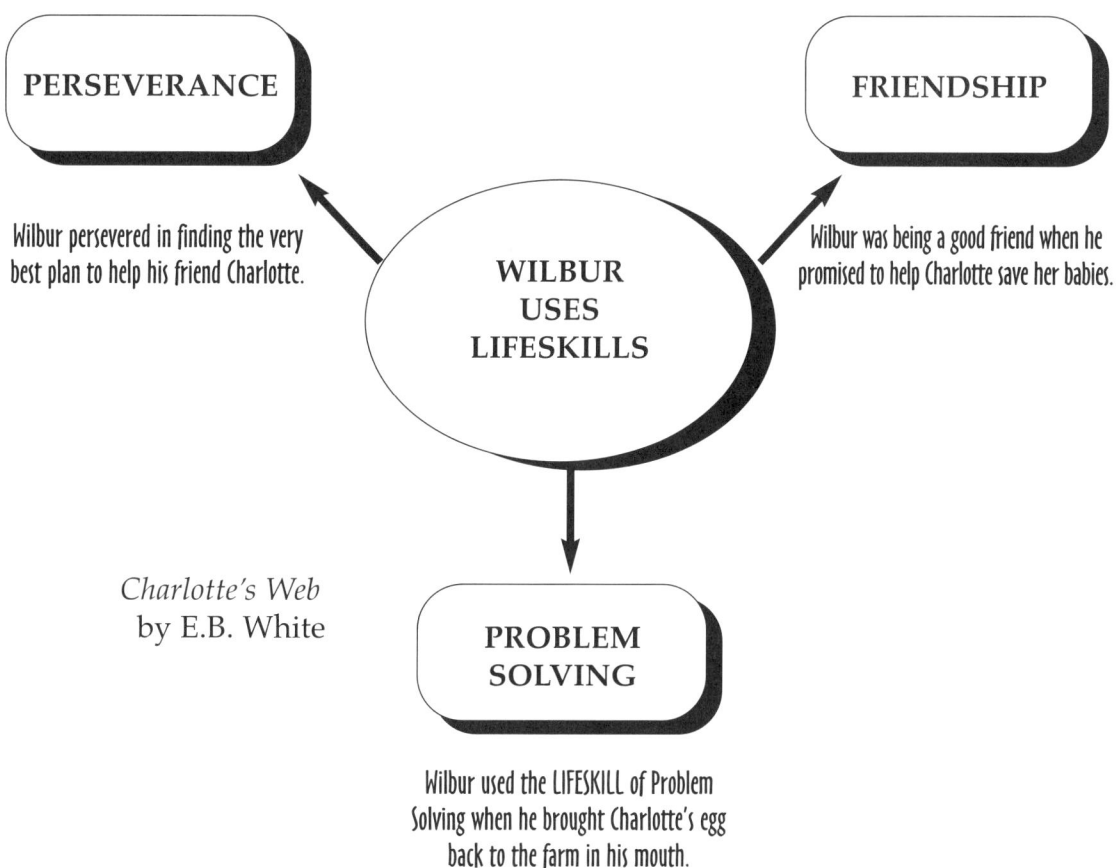

Charlotte's Web
by E.B. White

Example 2: Complex

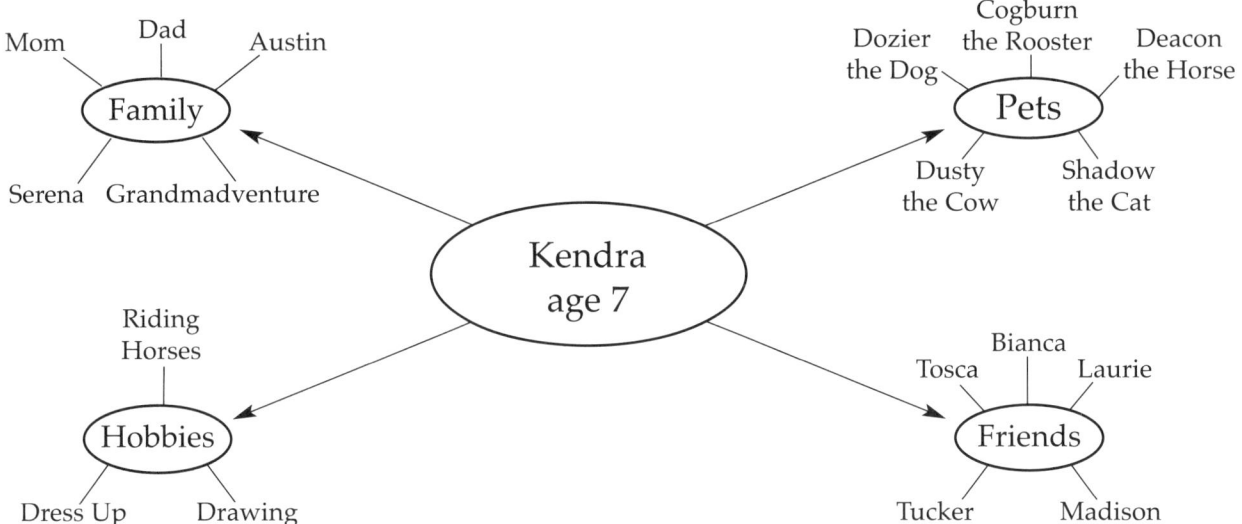

Book List

Multicultural books: **(AFA)**=African American, **(AM)**= Amish, **(ASA)**=Asian American, **(HA)**=Hispanic American, **(ME)**=Multi-Ethnic, **(NA)**=Native American, **(TE)**=listed in the teacher edition of this book, *Tools for Citizenship and Life: Using the ITI Lifelong Guidelines and LIFESKILLS in the Classroom*, **(BFE)**=available through Books for Educators

AGES 4-8

100th Day Worries (Chapter 12) . . . . Margery Cuyler (New York: Simon & Schuster, 2000)
Aani and the Tree Huggers (ASA) (Chapter 9) . . . . Jeannine Atkins (New York: Lee & Low Books, 2000)
Abuela (HA) (TE) (Chapter 11). . . . . Arthur Dorros (New York: E.P. Dutton, 1991)
Akiak: A Tale from the Iditarod (Chapter 19) . . . . Robert Blake (New York: Philomel Books, a Division of Putnam Grosset, 1997)
Alejandro's Gift (HA) (Chapter 12). Richard E. Albert (San Francisco: Chronicle Books, 1994)
Alexander and the Terrible, Horrible, No Good, ... Judith Viorst (New York: Aladdin Books, 1987)
  Very Bad Day (TE) (Chapter 13)
Amelia Bedelia (TE) (Chapter 8) . . . . Peggy Parrish (New York: HarperCollins, 1992)
Amelia's Road (Chapter 13). . . . . Linda Jacobs Altman (New York: Lee & Low, 1993)
Anthony Reynoso: Born to Rope (HA) (Chapter 13) . . . . Martha Cooper (New York: Clarion Books, 1996)
Araminta's Paint Box (Chapter 9) . . . . Karen Ackerman (New York: Aladdin Paperbacks, a Division of Simon & Schuster, 1998)
Are You My Mother? (Chapter 24) . . . . P. D. Eastman (New York: Random House, 1988)
Armadillo from Amarillo, The (HA) (Chapter 11) . . . . Lynne Cherry (New York: Harcourt Brace, 1994)
Arthur Lost and Found (Chapter 23). . . . . Marc Brown (New York: Little, Brown & Company, 1998)
Arthur's Really Helpful Bedtime Stories (Chapter 15) . . . . Marc Tolon Brown (New York: Random House, 1998)
Bat Boy and His Violin, The (AFA) (Chapter 6) . . . . Gavin Curtis (New York: Simon & Schuster, 1998)
Benny's Had Enough (Chapter 8) . . . . Barbro Lindgren (Stockholm, Sweden: R&S, 1999)
Buford, the Little Bighorn (Chapter 9) . . . . Bill Peet (New York: Houghton Mifflin, 1991)
Butterfly Boy (HA) (Chapter 18). . . . . Virginia Kroll (Honesdale, PA: Boyd Mills, 1997)
Butterfly House (Chapter 7). . . . . Eve Bunting (New York: Scholastic Press, 1999)
Chester's Way (Chapter 13) . . . . Kevin Henkes (New York: Mulberry Books/Simon & Schuster, 1997)
Circle of Thanks (NA) (Chapter 15). Susi Gregg Fowler (New York: Scholastic Books, 1998)
Chicken Sunday (AFA) (Chapter 22). . . . . Patricia Polacco (New York: Putnam & Grosset Group, 1992)
Dancing Man, The (Chapter 10) . . . . Ruth Lercher Bornstein (New York: Clarion Books, 1998)
Dogzilla (Chapter 24) . . . . Dav Pilkey (New York: Harcourt Brace, 1993)
Elizabeth and Larry (Chapter 14). . . . . Marilyn Sadler (New York: Simon & Schuster, 1990)
Fanny's Dream (Chapter 5) . . . . Carolyn and Mark Buehne (New York: Dial Books, Simon & Schuster, 1996)
Flat Stanley (Chapter 21). . . . . Jeff Brown (New York: HarperTrophy, 1996)
Fly Away Home (Chapter 22) . . . . Eve Bunting (Boston, MA: Houghton Mifflin, 1991)
Fly, Eagle, Fly: An African Tale (AFA) (Chapter 12). . . . . Retold by Christopher Gregorowski (New York: Simon & Schuster Publishing, 2000)
Franklin Is Messy (Chapter 17). . . . . Paulette Bourgeois (New York: Scholastic Trade Books, 1995)
Frog Girl (NA) (Chapter 8). . . . . Paul Owen Lewis (Berkeley, CA: Tricycle Press, 1999)
From Father to Son (HA) (Chapter 17) . . . . Patricia Almada (Crystal Liake, IL: Rigby Press, 1997)
Garden of Happiness, The (HA) (Chapter 15) . . . . Erika Tamar (New York: Harcourt Brace Publishing Co., 1996)

L.1

Gardener, The (Chapter 16) . . . . Sarah Stewar (New York: Farrar, Straus & Giroux, 1997)
George and Martha: The Complete Stories . . . . James Marshall (Boston: Houghton Mifflin Company, 1997)
   of Two Best Friends (Chapter 14)
Golden Tales: Myths and Legends from . . . . Lulu Delacre (New York: Scholastic Trade, 1996)
   Latin America (HA) (Chapter 20)
Harry, the Dirty Dog (Chapter 22) . . . . Gene Zion (New York: HarperTrophy, 1976)
Hawk, I'm Your Brother (NA) (Chapter 12) . . . . Byrd Baylor (New York: Athenium, 1976)
I Lost My Bear (Chapter 17) . . . . Jules Feiffer (New York: William Morrow & Co, 1998)
Jack and the Beanstalk (Chapter 24) . . . . Richard Walker (Kingswood, Bristol, UK Barefoot
                                                                                                                                  Books, 1999)
Jumanji (TE) (Chapter 21) . . . . Chris Van Allsburg (Boston: Houghton Mifflin, 1981)
Lights on the River (HA) (Chapter 23) . . . . Jane Resk (New York: Hyperion Press, 1996)
Little Polar Bear and the Husky Pup (Chapter 10) . . . . Hans de Beer (New York: North-South Books, 1999)
Little Scarecrow Boy, The (Chapter 6) . . . . Margaret Wise Brown (New York: HarperCollins
                                                                                                                                  Juvenile Books, 1998)
Lulie the Iceberg: Her Imperial Highness . . . . Miya Hisako (New York: Kodansha International, 1998)
   Princess Takamado No (Chapter 9)
Marguerite Makes a Book (Chapter 18) . . . . Bruce Robertson (Los Angeles: J. P. Getty Museum, 1999)
Marshmallow (Chapter 14) . . . . Clare Turlay Newberry (New York: Smithmark
                                                                                                                                   Publishing, 1999)
Math Curse (Chapter 21) . . . . Jon Scieszka (New York: Viking Childrens Books, 1995)
Mightiest Heart, The (AFA) (Chapter 14) . . . . Lynn Cullen (New York: Dial Books, 1998)
Mirandy and Brother Wind (AFA) (Chapter 19) . . . . Pat McKissack (New York: Dragonfly, a Division of
                                                                                                                                  Random House, 1997)
Mitten, The (Chapter 17) . . . . Jan Brett (New York: Putnam Books, 1989)
My Rows and Piles of Coins (AFA) (Chapter 19) . . . . Tololwa M. Mollel (Boston: Houghton Mifflin, 1999)
Not Yet, Yvette (AFA) (Chapter 18) . . . . Helen Ketteman (Morton Grove, IL: Albert Whitman
                                                                                                                                  & Co, 1995)
Old Man and His Door, The (HA) (Chapter 24) . . . . Gary Soto (New York: GP Putnam's & Sons, 1996)
Painted Dreams (HA) (Chapter 6) . . . . Karen Lynn Williams (New York: William Morrow
                                                                                                                                  & Company, 1998)
Paperboy, The (Chapter 23) . . . . Dav Pilkey (New York: Orchard Books, 1996)
Passage to Freedom: . . . . Ken Mochizuki (New York: Lee & Low, 1997)
   The Sugihara Story (ASA) (Chapter 16)
Patchwork Quilt, The (AFA) (TE) (Chapter 7) . . . . Valerie Flourney (New York: Dial Books, A Division
                                                                                                                                 of Penguin Books, 1985)
Penny's Worth of Character, A (Chapter 20) . . . . Jesse Stuart, Jim Wayne Miller, Jerry A. Herndon, James
                                                                                                                    McGifford (Ashland, KY: Jesse Stuart Foundation, 1993)
People Could Fly, The: American Black . . . . Virginia Hamilton (New York: Knopf, a division of
   Folktales (AFA) (Chapter 20)   Random House, 1993)
Polar the Titanic Bear (Chapter 11) . . . . Laurie McGaw (New York: Little, Brown & Co, 1994)
Quiltmaker's Gift, The (Chapter 7) . . . . Jeff Brumbeau (Duluth, MN: Pfeiffer-Hamilton
                                                                                                                                  Publishers, 2000)
Rag Coat, The (Chapter 5) . . . . Lauren Mills (New York: Little, Brown and Co, 1991)
Red Flower Goes West (Chapter 10) . . . . Ann Warren Turner (New York: Hyperion Books, 1999)
Rueben and the Blizzard (AM) (Chapter 23) . . . . Merle Good (Intercourse, PA: Good Books, 1995)
Reuben and the Quilt (AM) (Chapter 16) . . . . Merle Good (Intercourse, PA: Good Books, 1999)
Sam and the Lucky Money (ASA) (Chapter 7) . . . . Karin Chinn (New York: Lee & Low, 1995)
Seven Blind Mice (Chapter 8) . . . . Ed Young (New York: Philomel Books, 1992)
Sitting Ducks (Chapter 10) . . . . Michael Bedard (New York: Grosset and Dunlap, 1998)
Shaman's Apprentice, The (Chapter 19) . . . . Lynne Cherry and Mark Plotkin (New York: Harcourt
                                                                                                                                  Brace Publishing Company, 1998)
Something Beautiful (AFA) (Chapter 15) . . . . Sharon Dennis Wyeth (New York: Bantam Doubleday Dell
                                                                                                                                 Publishers, 1998)
Squids Will Be Squids: . . . . Jon Scieszka (New York: Viking Childrens Books, 1998)
   Fresh Morals, Beastly Fable (Chapter 5)
Sr. Anne's Hands (AFA) (Chapter 16) . . . . Marybeth Lorbiecki (New York: Dial Books, 1998)
Story of Ferdinand, The (TE) (Chapter 18) . . . . Munro Leaf (New York: Viking Press, 1987)

Book List

Story of the Jumping Mouse, The (NA) (Chapter 6) . . . . John Steptoe (New York: Mulberry Books, William Morrow & Company, 1989)
Stranger in the Mirror (ASA) (Chapter 5) . . . . Allen Say (Boston: Houghton Mifflin Publishing Co, 1995)
Table Where Rich People Sit, The (Chapter 22) . . . . Byrd Baylor (New York: Simon & Schuster, 1994)
Tar Beach (AFA) (Chapter 11) . . . . Faith Ringgold (New York: Crown Publishers, 1991)
Verdi (Chapter 20) . . . . Janell Cannon (New York: Harcourt Brace, 1997)
Very Busy Spider, The (Chapter 18) . . . . Eric Carle (New York: Philomel Books, 1984)
When Bluebell Sang (Chapter 21) . . . . Lisa Campbell Ernst (New York: Aladdin Paperbacks, 1992)
Zelda And Ivy (Chapter 24) . . . . Laura McGee Kvasnosky (Cambridge, MA: Candlewick Press, 1998)

AGES 9-12

Active Citizenship Today: Field Guide (Chapter 9) . . . . Charles Degelman (California: Close-Up Foundation, 1994)
All for the Better: . . . . Nicholas Mohr (Austin, TX: Raintree Books, Steck-Vaughn
    A Story of El Barrio (HA) (Chapter 13)   Publishing Company, 1996)
Angela Weaves a Dream (HA) (Chapter 17) . . . . Michele Sola (New York: Hyperion, 1997)
Arilla Sun Down (NA) (AFA) (Chapter 23) . . . . Virginia Hamilton (New York: Point Signature, Scholastic Books, 1995)
Aunt Harriet's Underground Railway . . . . Faith Ringgold (New York: Crown Publications, 1992)
    in the Sky (AFA) (Chapter 17)
Autumn Journey (Chapter 13) . . . . Priscilla Cummings (Toronto, Canada: Cobblehill Press, 1997)
Barn, The (Chapter 13) . . . . Avi (London: Orchard Books, 1994)
Barrel of Laughs, A Vail of Tears, A (Chapter 24) . . . . Jules Feiffer (New York: HarperCollins Publishers, 1995)
Baseball Saved Us (ASA) (Chapter 6) . . . . Ken Mochizuki (New York: Lee & Low Books, 1995)
Be A Perfect Person in Just Three Days (TE) (Chapter 17) . . . Stephen Manes (New York: Clarion Press, 1982)
Ben and Me: A New and Astonishing Life of Benjamin . . . . . . Robert Lawson (Illustrator) (New York: Little, Brown &
    Franklin As Written by His Good Mouse Amos (Ch.24) .   Company, 1988)
Blubber (TE) (Chapter 5) . . . . Judy Blume (New York: Simon & Schuster, 1983)
Boy of Tache, A (NA) (Chapter 6) . . . . Ann Blades (Burnsville, MN: Econo-clad Books, Sagebrush Corporation, 1999)
Bridge to Terabithia (TE) (Chapter 18) . . . . Katherine Patterson (New York: HarperCollins Childrens Books, 1978)
Bud, Not Buddy (AFA) (Chapter 24) . . . . Christopher Paul Curtis (New York: Delacorte Press, 1999)
Cat Ate My Gymsuit, The (TE) (Chapter 16) . . . . Paula Danziger (Chicago, IL: Econo-clad Books, 1999)
Catherine Called Birdy (Chapter 16) . . . . Karen Cushman (London: Clarion Press, 1994)
Chasing Redbird (NA) (Chapter 11) . . . . Sharon Creech (New York: HarperCollins, 1998)
Chicken Doesn't Skate, The (Chapter 24) . . . . Gordon Korman (New York: Scholastic Books, 1998)
Chicken Soup for the Kid's Soul: 101 Health Stories . . . . Jack Canfield, Ed. (Deerfield Beach, FL: Communications,
    of Courage, Hope and Laughter (Chapter 10)   1998)
Cliques, Phonies and Other Baloney (TE) (Chapter 14) . . . . . Trevor Romain (Minneapolis, MN: Free Spirit Press, 1998)
Crow Boy (ASA) (TE) (Chapter 5) . . . . Taro Yashima (New York: Viking Press, 1976)
Eighteenth Emergency, The (Chapter 8) . . . . Betsy Cromar Byars (New York: Viking Press, 1996)
El Chino (ASA) (Chapter 19) . . . . Allen Say (Boston: Houghton Mifflin and Co., 1990)
Everywhere (ASA) (Chapter 7) . . . . Bruce Brooks (New York: HarperCollins, 1990)
Danger Zone (AFA) (Chapter 18) . . . . David Klass (New York: Scholastic Books, 1996)
Dawn Rider (NA) (Chapter 22) . . . . Jan Hudson (New York: Puffin Books, 2000)
Devil's Arithmetic, The (Chapter 20) . . . . Jane Yolen (New York: Puffin Books, 1990)
Diego (HA) (Chapter 15) . . . . Jeanette and Jonah Winter (New York: Alfred A. Knopf, 1991)
Dragonwings (ASA) (Chapter 21) . . . . Lawrence Yep (New York: HarperTrophy, 1989)
Friends, The (ASA) (Chapter 11) . . . . Kazumi Yumoto (New York: Farrar, Straus & Giroux, 1996)
Frightful's Mountain (Chapter 9) . . . . Jean Craighead George (New York: E. P. Dutton, 1999)
Girls and Young Women Inventing: 20 True Stories . . . . Frances A. Karnes, Suzanne M. Bean, and Rosemary
    About Inventors Plus How You Can Be One   Wallner (Minneapolis, MN: Free Spirit Publishing, 1995)
    Yourself (ME) (Chapter 11)
Goodnight Mr. Tom (Chapter 7) . . . . Michelle Magorian (New York: HarperTrophy, 1986)
Homecoming, The (Chapter 22) . . . . Cynthia Voigt (New York: Athenium, 1981)
Hostage To War (Chapter 12) . . . . Tatiana Vasileva (Greenville, SC: Polaris, 1999)

Island of the Blue Dolphins (NA) (Chapter 19) . . . . Scott O'Dell (New York: Yearling Books, a division of Random House, 1987)
It's Our World Too! Stories of Young People Who Are Making a Difference (ME) (Chapter 10) . . . . Philip Hoose (New York: Little, Brown & Company, 1993)
Jeremy Thatcher Dragon Hatcher (Chapter 23) . . . . Bruce Coville (New York: Harcourt Brace, 1991)
Johnny Tremain (Chapter 10). . . . . Esther Forbes (New York: Yearling Book, Random House, 1987)
Journey to Jo'berg (AFA) (Chapter 21) . . . . Beverly Naidoo (New York: HarperTrophy, 1988)
Julie of the Wolves (TE) (Chapter 10). . . . . Jean Craighead George (New York: HarperTrophy, 1974)
Just Juice (HA) (Chapter 21). . . . . Rosa Guy (New York: Scholastic Books, 1998)
Kid's Guide to Dealing With Daily Dilemmas, A (Ch. 21) . . . . Linda Schwartz (Santa Barbara, CA: Learring Works, 1993)
La Mariposa (HA) (Chapter 13) . . . . Francisco Jimenez (Boston: Houghton Mifflin, 1998)
Legend of Luke, The (Chapter 15) . . . . Brian Jacques (New York: Philomel Books, 2000)
Letter to Mrs. Roosevelt, A (Chapter 19) . . . . C. Coco De Young (New York: Delacorte Press, 1999)
Lily's Crossing (Chapter 14) . . . . Patricia Reilly Giff (New York: Yearling Books, 1999)
Maniac McGee (Chapter 16) . . . . Jerry Spinelli (New York: HarperCollins, 1992)
Mayeros: A Yucatec Maya Family (HA) (Chapter 17). . . . . . . George Ancona (New York: Wm. Morrow & Co, 1997)
Me and My Little Brain (Chapter 12) . . . . John D. Fitzgerald (New York: Yearling Books, A Division of Random House, 1972)
Mouse of Amherst, The (Chapter 14) . . . . Elizabeth Spires (New York: Frances Foster Books, A Division of Farrar, Strauss & Giroux, 1999)
My Name Is Maria Isabel (HA) (Chapter 20) . . . . Alma Flor Ada (London: Athenium, 1993)
Night the Bells Rang,The (Chapter 14) . . . . Natalie Kinsey-Warnock (New York: Cobblehill, Dutton, 1991)
Not-Just-Anybody Family, The (TE) (Chapter 9). . . . . Betsy Cromer Byars (New York: Yearling Books, A Division of RandomHouse, 1987)
Number the Stars (TE) (Chapter 7) . . . . Lois Lowry (Boston, MA: Houghton Mifflin, 1989)
People Shall Continue, The (NA) (Chapter 19) . . . . Simon Ortiz (Chicago Econo-clad Books, 1999)
Pinballs, The (Chapter 22). . . . . Betsy Cromer Byars (New York: HarperCollins Juvenile Books, 1993)
Pink and Say (AFA) (TE) (Chapter 7). . . . . Patricia Polacco (New York: Philomel Books, 1994)
Planet of Junior Brown, The (AFA) (Chapter 15) . . . . Virginia Hamilton (New York: Aladdin Paperbacks, 1984)
Richard Wright and the Library Card (AFA) (Chapter 6) . . . . William Miller (New York: Lee & Low, 1997)
Roll of Thunder, Hear My Cry (AFA) (TE) (Chapter 20) . . . . Mildred D. Taylor (New York: Dial Books, 1976.)
Sachiko Means Happiness (ASA) (Chapter 18) . . . . Kimiko Sakai (San Francisco: Children's Book Press, 1990)
Secret of the Seal, The (NA) (Chapter 22) . . . . Deborah Davis (New York: Random House Children Publisher, 1994)
Sideways Stories from Wayside School (Chapter 24) . . . . Louis Sachar (New York: Avon Books, 1985)
Sign of the Beaver, The (NA) (TE) (Chapter 12) . . . . Elizabeth George Speare (New York: Yearling Books, A Division of Random House, 1994)
Skin I'm In, The (Chapter 6) . . . . Sharon G. Flake (Boston, MA: Jump at the Sun, A Division of Hyperion Books, 2000)
Sounder (AFA) (Chapter 13). . . . . William H. Armstrong (New York: HarperCollins, 1989)
Stone Fox (NA) (TE) (Chapter 8) . . . . John Reynolds Gardiner (New York: HarperTrophy Books, 1988)
Story of Thomas Alva Edison, The (Chapter 11) . . . . Margaret Cousins (New York: Random House, 1997)
Sweet Clara and the Freedom Quilt (AFA) (TE) (Ch. 15). . . . . Deborah Hopkinson (New York: Knopf, 1993)
Tales of a Fourth Grade Nothing (TE) (Chapter 8). . . . . Judy Blume (New York: E.P. Dutton Childrens Books, 1972)
Trumpet of the Swan, The (TE) (Chapter 20) . . . . E.B. White. (New York: HarperTrophy Books, 1973)
Ultimate Lego Book (Chapter 11). . . . . Kjeld Kirk Kristiansen (New York: DK Publishing, 1999)
View from Saturday, The (Chapter 9). . . . . E. L. Konigsberg (London: Athenium, 1996)
Walk Two Moons (NA) (Chapter 18). . . . . Sharon Creech (New York: HarperTrophy Publishers, 1996)
Where the Red Fern Grows (TE) (Chapter 12). . . . . Wilson Rawls (New York: Bantam Books, 1984)
Wringer (Chapter 16) . . . . Jerry Spinelli (New York: HarperTrophy, 1998)
Young Landlords, The (AFA) (Chapter 23) . . . . Walter Dean Myers (New York: Viking Press, 1989)

Book List

AGES 13+

Absolutely Normal Chaos (Chapter 17) . . . . Sharon Creech (New York: HarperCollins Juvenile Books, 1997)

Anne Frank, the Diary of a Young Girl (TE) (Chapter 10) . . . . Anne Frank (New York: Bantam Books, Division of Random House, 1993)

Autobiography of a Face (Chapter 5) . . . . Lucy Grealy (New York: HarperPerennial, 1995)

Armageddon Summer (Chapter 23) . . . . Jane Yolen (New York: Voyager Picture Book, Harcourt Brace, 1999)

Backwater (Chapter 15) . . . . Joan Bauer (New York: Putnam Publishing Group, 1999)

Ballad of Lucy Whipple (Chapter 8) . . . . Karen Cushman (New York: HarperCollins Juvenile Books, 1998)

Black Hands, White Sails (AFA) (Chapter 17) . . . . Patricia McKissack and Frederick L. McKissack (New York: Scholastic, 1999)

Boy and the Otter, The (Chapter 15) . . . . A. R. Lloyd (New York: Holt, Rinehart and Winston, 1984)

Buried Onions (HA) (Chapter 17) . . . . Gary Soto (New York: Harcourt Brace, 1997)

Burning Up (AFA) (Chapter 22) . . . . Caroline B. Cooney (New York: Delacorte Press, a division of Seymour Lawrence, 1999)

But I'll Be Back Again (Chapter 22) . . . . Cynthia Rylant (New York: Beech Tree Books, 1993)

California Blues (Chapter 7 & 18) . . . . David Klass (New York: Point, Scholastic Books, 1996)

California Blue (Chapter 18) . . . . David Klass (New York: Scholastic Point, 1996)

Call of the Wild (Chapter 16) . . . . Jack London (New York: Tom Doherty, Inc., 1986)

Canyons (Chapter 8) . . . . Gary Paulsen (New York: Bantam Doubleday Dell Publishing, 1990)

Cay, The (AFA) (Chapter 14) . . . . Theodore Taylor (New York: Camelot Books, 1995)

Chicken Soup for the Teenage Soul: 101 Stories of Life, Love and Learning (Chapter 7) . . . . Jack Canfield (Ed.), Mark Victor Hansen (Ed.), and Kimberly Kirberger (Ed.) (Deerfield Beach, FL: Health Communications, 1997)

Chinese Cinderella: The True Story of an Unwanted Daughter (ASA) (Chapter 19) . . . . Adeline Yen Mah (New York, NY: Delacorte Press, 1999)

Chocolate War, The (Chapter 16) . . . . Robert Cormier (New York: Laureleaf Books, a division of Random House, 1991)

Contender, The (Chapter 20) . . . . Robert Lipsyte (New York: HarperCollins Books, 1967)

Crazy Horse Electric Game, The (Chapter 13) . . . . Chris Crutcher (New York: Dell Publishing Co, 1991)

Daily Reflections for Highly Effective Teens (Chapter 12) . . . . Sean Covey (New York: Simon & Schuster, 1999)

Day No Pigs Would Die, A (Chapter 8) . . . . Robert Newton Peck (New York: Random House Childrens Publishing, 1994)

Dinky Hocker Shoots Smack (Chapter 24) . . . . M. E. Kerr (New York: HarperTrophy, 1989)

Door Near Here, A (Chapter 7) . . . . Heather Quarles (New York: Laureleaf Books, A Division of Random House, 2000)

Drawing on the Funny Side of the Brain: How to Come Up With Jokes for Cartoons and Comic Strips (Chapter 24) . . . Christopher Hart (New York: Watson-Guptill Publishing, 1998)

Endurance, The: Shackleton's Legendary Antarctic Expedition (Chapter 9 & 21) . . . . Caroline Alexander (New York: Knopf, 1998)

Fahrenheit 451 (Chapter 11) . . . . Ray Bradbury (New York: Simon & Schuster, 1993)

Finding My Voice (Chapter 16) . . . . Marie G. Lee (Boston, MA: Houghton Mifflin and Company, 1992)

Girls and Young Women Leading the Way: 20 True Stories About Leadership (Chapter 22) . . . . Frances A. Karnes, Suzanne M. Bean, Rosemary Wellner (ed.) (Minneapolis, MN: Free Spirit Press, 1993)

Girls Who Rocked the World: Heroines from Sacajawea to Sheryl Swoopes (ME) (Chapter 15) . . . . Amelie Weldon (Hillsboro, OR: Beyond Words Publishing Co., 1998)

Her Story: Women Who Changed the World (ME) (Chapter 12) . . . . Ruth Ashby, Ed. and Deborah Gore Ohrn, Ed. (New York: Viking Childrens Books, 1995)

Hold Fast to Dreams (Chapter 10) . . . . Andrea Davis Pinkney (New York: William Morrow & Company, 1995)

Holes (Chapter 14) . . . . Louis Sachar (New York: Farrar, Strauss & Giroux, 1998)

How the Garcia Girls Lost Their Accents (HA) (Ch. 13) . . . . . Julia Alvarez (New York: Plume Press, 1991)

Hug a Thousand Trees With Ribbons: The Story of Phyllis Wheatley (AFA) (Chapter 6) ... Ann Rinaldi (New York: Gulliver Books, A Division of Harcourt Brace, 1996)
I Know Why the Caged Bird Sings (AFA) (Chapter 10) ..... Maya Angelou (New York: Random House, 1969)
Into the Wild (Chapter 8) .... Jon Krakauer (New York: Bantam Doubleday Dell Publishing, 1997)
Jemmy (NA) (Chapter 10) .... Jon Hassler (New York: Fawcett Books, 1991)
Joyride (Chapter 8) .... Gretchen Olson (Honesdale, PA: Boyds Mill Press, 1999)
Juan Gonzalez (HA) (Chapter 19) .... Dennis Tuttle (New York: Chelsea House Publications, 1994)
Kidstories: Biographies of 20 Young People You'd Like to Know (ME) (Chapter 12) ..... James R. Delisle and Pamela Espeland (Minneapolis, MN: Free Spirit Publishers, 1991)
Kid's Guide to Service Projects, The: Over 500 Service Ideas for Young People Who Want to Make a Difference (Chapter 23) .... Barbara A. Lewis, Pamela Espeland (Minneapolis, MN: Free Spirit Publishers, 1995)
Kids' Guide to Social Action: How to Solve the Social Problems YouChoose and Turn Creative Thinking into Positive Action (Chapter 21) .... Barbara A. Lewis, Pamela Espeland, Caryn Pernu (Minneapolis MN: Free Spirit Publishing, 1998)
Kids With Courage: True Stories About Young People Making a Difference (ME) (Chapter 10) .... Barbara A. Lewis (Minneapolis, MN: Free Spirit Publishing, 1992)
Last Days of Summer (Chapter 14) .... Steve Kluger (Austin, TX: Bard Books, 1999)
Legend of Jesse Owens, The (AFA) (Chapter 16) ..... Hank Nuwer (New York: Franklin Watts, Inc., 1998)
Lesson Before Dying, A (Chapter 20) .... Ernest J. Gaines (New York: Vintage Books, 1997)
Light in the Forest, The (NA) (Chapter 5) .... Conrad Richter (New York: Fawcett Juniper Press, 1995)
Lord of the Flies (Chapter 9) .... William Gerald Golding (New York: Perigree Books, Putnam House, 1959)
Lyddie (Chapter 6) .... Katherine Patterson (London: Puffin Books, 1995)
Man Who Was Poe, The (Chapter 23) .... Avi (New York: Orchard Books, 1989)
M. C. Higgins, the Great (AFA) (Chapter 20) .... Virginia Hamilton (New York: Simon & Schuster, 1999)
Midnight Hour Encores (Chapter 11) .... Bruce Brooks (New York: HarperTrophy, 1988)
Nightjohn (AFA) (Chapter 6) .... Gary Paulsen (New York: Doubleday Books, 1995)
100 Men Who Shaped the World (ME) (Chapter 13) .... Bill Yenne (Blue Wood Book, 1994)
100 Women Who Shaped the World (ME) (Chapter 13) ..... Gail Meyer Rolka (Blue Wood Book, 1994)
160 Ways to Help the World: Community Service Projects for Young People (Chapter 18) .... Linda Leeb Duper (New York: Checkmark Books, 1996)
Pigman, The (Chapter 23) .... Paul Zindel (New York: Harcourt Brace, 1991)
Puppies, Dogs, and Blue Northers: Reflections on Being Raised by a Pack of Sled Dogs (Chapter 7) .... Gary Paulsen (New York: Bantam Doubleday Dell Publishers, 1998)
Outsiders, The (Chapter 14) .... S.E. Hinton (London: Puffin Books, 1997)
Quilted Landscapes: Conversations with Young Immigrants (ME) (Chapter 19) .... Yale Strom (New York: Simon and Schuster, 1996)
Rules of the Road (Chapter 24) .... Joan Bauer (London: Puffin Books, 2000)
Runner, The (Chapter 20) .... Cynthia Voigt (New York: Athenium, a division of MacMillan, 1985)
Snow Bound (Chapter 9) .... Harry Mazer (New York: Dell Publishing Company, 1975)
Steal Away Home (AFA) (Chapter 9) .... Lois Ruby (New York: Simon & Schuster, 1999)
Stones in Water (Chapter 21) .... Donna Jo Napoli (London: Puffin Books, 1999)
Stonewall's Gold (Chapter 21) .... Judy Sheindlin (New York: St. Martins Press, 200)
Summer of My German Soldier (Chapter 18) .... Bette Greene (New York: Puffin Books, 1999)
Tall Mexican: The Life of Hank Aguirre, All-Star Pitcher, Businessman, Humanitarian (HA) (Chapter 15) ..... Robert E. Copley (Houston, TX: Arte Publico Press, 1998)
To Be a Slave (AFA) (Chapter 11) .... Julius Lester (New York: Scholastic, Inc., 1988)
Warriors Don't Cry: A Searing Memoir of the Battle to Integrate Little Rock's Central High School (AFA) (Ch. 5) ...... Melba Patillo Beals (New York: Archway Paperbacks, Simon & Schuster, 1995)
When Zachary Beaver Comes to Town (Chapter 5) ..... Kimberly Willis Holt (New York: Henry Holt & Co, 1999)
Within Reach: My Everest Story (Chapter 12) .... Mark Pfetzer and Jack Galvin (New York: E.P. Dutton, 1998)
Yolanda's Genius (AFA) (Chapter 5) .... Carol Fenner (New York: Aladdin Books, Simon & Schuster, 1995)
Zach (AFA) (Chapter 6) .... William Bel (New York: Simon & Schuster, 1999)

Book List

Family Resources

Another Sip of Chicken Soup for the Soul: Heartwarming Stories of the Love Between Parents and Child (Ch. 6) — Andrews McMeel (Kansas City, MO: Health Communications, 1998)

A Penny Saved: Teaching Your Children the Values and Life Skills They Will Need to Live in the Real World (Chapter 22) — Neale S. Godfrey (New York: Fireside Books, Simon & Schuster, 1996)

Awakening Your Child's Natural Genius: Enhancing Curiosity, Creativity, and Learning Ability (B4E) (Ch. 11) — Thomas Armstrong (New York: J. P. Tarcher, 1991)

Beyond Sibling Rivalry: How to Help Your Children Become Cooperative, Caring and Compassionate (Chapter 7) — Peter Goldenthal (New York: Henry Holt and Company, Inc., 1999)

Bringing Kids Up Without Tearing Them Down: How to Raise Confident, Successful Children (Chapter 5) — Dr. Kevin Leman (Nashville, TN: Thomas Nelson, Inc., 1995)

Children: The Challenge (Chapter 23) — Rudolph Dreikurs (New York: Plume, 1991)

Common Sense Parenting: A Proven Step-by-Step Guide for Raising Responsible Kids and Creating Happy Families (Chapter 8) — Ray Burke, Ph.D. and Ron Herar (Boys Town, NE: Boys Town Press, 1996)

Cooperative Sports and Games Book: Challenge Without Competition, The (Chapter 12) — Terry Orlick (New York: Random House, 1978)

Don't Sweat the Small Stuff With Your Family: Simple Ways to Keep Daily Responsibilities and Household Chaos from Taking Over Your Life (Chapter 17) — Richard Carlson (Boston, MA: Hyperion Press, 1998)

Easy to Love, Difficult to Discipline: The 7 Basic Skills for Turning Conflict into Cooperation (Chapter 9) — Becky A. Bailey (New York: William Morrow Company, 2000)

Emotional Intelligence: Why It Can Matter More Than IQ (B4E) (Chapter 6) — Daniel Goleman (New York: Bantam Books, 1997)

Endangered Minds: Why Children Don't Think and What We Can Do About It (Chapter 10) — Jane Healy, Ph.D. (New York: Simon & Schuster, 1990)

Explosive Child, The: A New Approach for Understanding and Parenting Easily Frustrated, "Chronically Inflexible" Children (Chapter 13) — Ross W. Greene (New York: HarperCollins, 1998)

Family Manager, The (Chapter 13 & 17) — Kathy Peel (Westport, CN: Word Books, Greenwood Publishing Group, 1996)

Family: The Ties That Bind and Gag (Chapter 24) — Erma Bombeck (New York: Fawcett Books, 1991)

Five Love Languages of Children, The (Chapter 7) — Gary D. Chapman and Ross Campbell (Chicago: Northfield Publishers, a Division of Moody Press, 1997)

Get A Clue!: A Parents' Guide to Understanding and Communicating with Your Preteen (Chapter 7) — Ellen Rosenburg (New York: Owl Book, Henry Holt and Company, 1999)

Good Friends Are Hard to Find: Help Your Child Find, Make and Keep Friends (Chapter 14) — Fred Frankel (Pasadena, CA: Perspective Publishing, 1996)

Grin and Share It: Raising a Family With a Sense of Humor (Chapter 24) — Janene Wolsey Baadsgaard (Salt Lake City, UT: Deseret Books, 1999)

Growing Good Kids: 28 Activities to Enhance Self-Awareness, Compassion and Leadership (Chapter 15) — Deb Delisle, Jim Delisle (Minneapolis, MN: Free Spirit Publishing Inc., 1996)

How to Help Your Child With Homework: Every Caring Parent's Guide to Encouraging Good Study Habits and Ending the Homework Wars—For Parents and Children Ages 6-13 (Chapter 23) — Marguerite Cogorno Radencich, Jeanne Shay Schumm and Pamela Espeland (Ed.) (Minneapolis, MN: Free Spirit Publishing, 1997)

Hurried Child, The: Growing Up Too Fast Too Soon (Chapter 18) — David Elkind (Reading, MA: Perseus Books, 1988)

Judge Judy Sheindlin's Win or Lose by How You Choose (Chapter 21) — Judy Sheindlin (New York: HarperCollins Juvenile Books, 2000)

Kid Cooperation: How to Stop Yelling, Nagging and Pleading and Get Kids to Cooperate (Chapter 9) — Elizabeth Pantley (Oakland, CA: New Harbinger Publications, 1996)

Kids Can Cooperate: A Practical Guide to Teaching Problem Solving (Chapter 21) — Elizabeth Crary (Seattle, WA: Parenting Press, 1984)

Let's Make a Memory: Great Ideas for Building Family Traditions and Togetherness (Chapter 14) — Gloria Gaither, et al (Westport, CN: Word Books, Greenwood Publishing Group, 1994)

Lotions, Potions, and Slime: Mudpies and More (Ch. 19) . . . . . Nancy Blakey (Berkeley, CA: Tricycle Press, 1996)

Loving Your Child Is Not Enough: . . . . Nancy Samalin and Martha Moraghan Jablow
  Positive Discipline That Works (Chapter 19)   (New York: Penguin Press, 1998)

Meeting the Needs of Children: Creating Trust . . . . Louis Edward Raths (College Park, PA: Educator's
  and Security (Chapter 16)   International Press, 1999)

Money Doesn't Grow on Trees: A Parent's Guide to . . . . Neale S. Godfrey (New York: Fireside Books,
  Raising Financially Responsible Children (Chapter 22)   Simon & Schuster, 1994)

101 Activities for Kids in Tight Spaces (Chapter 22) . . . . Carol Stock Kranowitz (New York: St. Martin's/Griffin, 1995)

Parenting With Love and Logic: Teaching Children . . . . Jim Fay (Contributor), Foster W. Cline, MD.
  Responsibility (Chapter 23)   (Colorado Springs, CO: Nav Press, 1990)

Playground Politics: Understanding the Emotional . . . . Stanley I. Greenspan, M.D. (Reading, MA: Perseus
  Life of Your School-Age Child (Chapter 14)   Books, 1994)

Playing Smart: A Parent's Guide to Enriching, Offbeat . . . . Susan K. Perry (Minneapolis, MN: Free Spirit
  Learning Activities for Ages 4 to 14 (Chapter 11)   Publishing, 1990)

Playwise: 365 Fun-Filled Activities for Building Character, . . . Denise Chapman et. al. (New York: Putnam
  Conscience, and Emotional Intelligence   Publishing Group, 1996)
  in Children (Chapter 18)

Positive Discipline from A-Z: From Toddlers to Teens, ... Jane Nelson, Lynn Lott, H. Stephen Glenn (Rocklin, CA:
  1001 Solutions to Everyday Parenting Problems,   (Prima Publishing, 1999)
  Revised and Expanded 2nd Edition (Chapter 5)

Punished By Rewards: The Trouble With Gold Stars, ... Alfie Kohn (Boston, MA: Houghton Mifflin and
  Incentive Plans, A's, Praise, and Other   Company, 1993)
  Bribes (B4E) (Chapter 16)

Raising Children With Character: Parents, Trust and . . . . Elizabeth Berger, MD (Northvale, NJ: Jason Aranson, 1999)
  the Development of Personal Integrity (Chapter 16)

Raising Self-Reliant Children in a Self-Indulgent . . . . H. Stephen Glenn and Jane Nelson (Rocklin, CA: Prime
  World: Seven Building Blocks for Developing   Publishing, 1989)
  Capable Young People (B4E) (Chapter 15)

Raising Your Spirited Child: A Guide for Parents . . . . Mary Sheedy Kurcinka (New York: HarperTrade, 1991)
  Whose Child Is More Intense, Sensitive, Perceptive,
  Persistent and Energetic (Chapter 19)

Secret of Parenting: How to Be in Charge of Today's . . . . Anthony Wolf (New York: Farrar Strauss & Giroux, 2000)
  Kids—From Toddlers to Preteens—Without
  Threats or Punishment (Chapter 8)

7 Habits of Highly Effective Families, The: Building a . . . . Stephen R. Covey and Sandra Merrill Covey (Trumbill,
  Beautiful Family Culture in a Turbulent World (Ch. 20)   CT: Golden Books Publishing Company, 1998)

Simple Fun for Busy People: 333 Ways to Enjoy Your . . . . Gary Krane and John Bradshaw (Berkeley, CA: Conari
  Loved Ones More in the Time You Have (Chapter 12) . . .   Press, 1998)

Simplify Your Life With Kids: 100 Ways to Make . . . . Elaine St. James (Kansas City, MO: Andrews McMeel, 1997)
  Family Life Easier and More Fun (Chapter 24)

Sharing Nature With Children (Chapter 11) . . . . Joseph Cornell (Watertown, NY: Dawn Publishing, 1998)

Simplify Your Life With Kids: 100 Ways to Make . . . . Elaine Saint-James (Kansas City, MO: Andrews
  Family Life Easier and More Fun (Chapter 11)   McMeel Universal, 1997)

Teaching Children Patience Without Losing Yours (Ch. 18) . . . Jerry Wilde and Polly Wilde (LGR Publishers, 1999)

Teaching Values: An Idea Book for Teachers . . . . Gary A. Davis (Los Angeles: Westwood Publishing, 1996)
  (and Parents) (B4E) (Chapter 22)

Uncommon Sense for Parents with Teenagers (Chapter 8) . . . . Michael Riera (Berkeley, CA: Celestial Arts Publishing, 1995)

"What Happened at School Today?": Helping Your . . . . Judi Craig, Ph.D. (New York: Hearst Books, 1994)
  Child Handle Everyday School Problems (Chapter 21)

What Kids Need to Succeed: Proven, Practical Ways . . . . Peter Benson, PH.D., Judy Galbraith, M.A., and Pamela
  to Raise Good Kids (B4E) (Chapter 20)   Espeland (Minneapolis, MN: Free Spirit Publishing, 1998)

Why Johnny Hates Sports (Chapter 10)   Fred Engh (East Rutherford, NJ: Avery Publishing
      Group, 1999)

Bibliography

"The Importance of Effective Communication," Northeastern University, College of Business Administration, October, 1999. http://www.cba.neu.edu/~ewertheim/inter/commun.htm

Bell, Nanci. *Visualizing and Verbalizing for Improved Language Comprehension.* Palo Alto, CA: Gander Publishing, Inc., 1991.

Belvel, Pat. See training manuals by Pat Belvel, Training and Consulting Institute, Inc., San Jose, California. http://www.trngedu.com/

Burke, Edmund. *Letter to Sheriffs of Bristol, April 3, 1777.*

Calvin Coolidge Memorial Foundation. http://www.calvin-coolidge.org/

Canfield, Jack and Mark Victor. *A 2nd Helping of Chicken Soup for the Soul: 101 More Stories to Open the Heart and Rekindle the Spirit.* Deerfield Beach, FL: Communications, Inc., 1995.

Carlson, Rachel. *Silent Spring.* New York: Houghton Mifflin Company, 1962.

Cohen, Elizabeth. *Designing Groupwork: Strategies for the Heterogeneous Classroom, Second Edition.* New York: Teachers College Press, 1994.

Cole, Robert W., Editor, *Educating Everybody's Children.* Alexandria, VA: ASCD, 1995.

Coontz, Stephanie. *Phi Delta Kappan,* March, 1995, p. 16.

Cousins, Norman. *Anatomy of an Illness As Perceived by the Patient: Reflections on Healing and Regeneration.* New York: W. W. Norton & Company, 1995.

Crawford, C. B. *Theory and Implications Regarding the Utilization of Strategic Humor by Leaders.* Department of Communication, Fort Hays State University. http://www.fhsu.edu/html-pages/faculty/cocc/lead03.htm

Dietal, J. Edwin. *Exceptional Leadership: Leading Through Patience and Persistence.* Practice Development Website. http://www.abenet.org/lpm/newsletters/skills/w98Dietel.html

Donne, John, *Devotions Upon Emergent Occasions. Meditation XVII, 1624.* John Donne Society Home Page http://www.csus.edu/org/

Edison, Thomas Alva. Hope Page http://www.thomasediso n.com. October, 1999. (Chapter 8.3)

Garbarino, James. *Raising Children in a Socially Toxic Environment.* San Francisco: Jossey-Bass Publishers, 1995.

Gardner, Howard. *Frames of Mind: Theory of Multiple Intelligences.* New York: Basic Books, Inc., 1985.

Gibbs, Jeanne. *TRIBES: A New Way of Learning and Being Together.* Sausalito, CA: CenterSource Systems, LLC, 1995.

Glasser, William. *Choice Theory: A New Psychology of Personal Freedom.* New York: Harper Perrenial, 1998.

Glickman, Carl. *Renewing America's Schools: A Guide to School-Based Action.* San Francisco: Jossey-Bass Publishers, 1993.

Gurian, Michael. *The Wonder of Boys.* New York: G. P. Putnam's & Sons, 1996.

Hannaford, Carla. *Smart Moves: Why Learning Is Not All in Your Head.* Arlington, VA: Great Ocean Publishers, 1995.

Hart, Leslie A. *Human Brain and Human Learning, Revised Edition.* Kent, WA: Books for Educators, Inc., 1999.

Healy, Jane. *Failure to Connect: How Computers Affect Our Children's Minds—For Better and Worse.* New York: Simon & Schuster, 1998.

Keirsey, David. *Please Understand Me II: Temperament, Character, and Intelligence.* Del Mar, CA: Prometheus Nemesis Book Company, 1998.

Kohn, Alfie. *Punished by Rewards: The Trouble with Gold Stars, Incentive Plans, A's, Praise, and Other Bribes.* New York: Houghton Mifflin, 1993.

Kouzes, James M. & Barry Z. Posner. *The Leadership Challenge.* San Francisco: Jossey-Bass, Inc., 1996.

Kovalik, Susan J. with Karen D. Olsen. *ITI: The Model.* Kent, WA: Susan Kovalik & Associates, 1997.

Kryger, Abraham. "Benefits of Telling the Truth." http//www.wellnessmd.com/tellingtruth.html

Lindamood-Bell Learning Processes Center, 800/233-1819.

Lowery, Larry. *Thinking And Learning: Matching Developmental Stages with Curriculum and Instruction.* Kent, Washington: Books for Educators, Inc., 1989.

Mayer, Jeffrey J. *If You Haven't Got the Time to Do It Right, When Will You Find the Time to Do It Over?* New York: Simon & Schuster, 1990.

McGeehan, Jane, et al. *Transformations: Leadership for Brain-Compatible Learning.* Kent, WA: Susan Kovalik & Associates, 1999.

Olsen, Karen D. & Susan J. Kovalik. *ITI Classroom Stages of Implementation.* Kent, WA: Susan Kovalik & Associates, 1999.

Olsen, Karen D. & Susan J. Kovalik. *ITI Schoolwide Stages of Implementation.* Kent, WA: Susan Kovalik & Associates, 1998.

Olsen, Karen D. *Making Bodybrain-Compatible Education a Reality: Coaching for the ITI Model.* Kent, WA: Books for Educators, Inc., 1999.

Olsen, Karen D. *Synergy: Transforming America's High Schools Through Integrated Thematic Instruction.* Kent, Washington: Books for Educators, Inc., 1995.

"The Orman Health Letter," published monthly by TRO Productions, Inc., Baltimore, MD, and http://www.wellnessmd.com/tellingtruth.html

Pert, Candace. *Molecules of Emotion: Why You Feel the Way You Feel.* New York: Scribner, 1997.

Rich, Dorothy. *MegaSkills: How Families Can Help Children Succeed in School and Beyond.* Boston: Houghton-Mifflin, 1992

Roosevelt, Eleanor. *You Learn by Living.* New York: Harper & Brothers, 1960.

Ross, Anne & Karen D. Olsen. *The Way We Were . . . The Way We CAN Be: A Vision for the Middle School.* Kent, WA: Susan Kovalik & Associates, 1995.

Ross, W. D., translator, *Nicomachean Ethics by Aristotle, 350 BC.* The Internet Classics Archives/Works by Aristotle, http://classics.mit.edu/Browse/browse-Aristotle.html

Siegel, Bernie. *Love, Medicine, and Miracles: Lessons Learned About Self-Healing from a Surgeon's Experiences with Exceptional Patients.* New York: HarperCollins, 1990.

Siegel, Bernie. *Peace, Love, and Healing: Bodymind Communication and the Path of Self-Healing.* New York: HarperCollins, 1990.

Smith, Charles A. *The Peaceful Classroom: 162 Activities to Teach Preschoolers Compassion and Cooperation.* Beltsville, MD: Gryphon House, 1993.

Thomas, James Alexander. *Sea to Shining Sea.* New York: Ballantine Books, 1986.

Twain, Mark, *Notebook, 1984.*

Index

3 C's of Assessment, 15.8
Active Listening, Lifelong Guideline of, Chapter 4
Aesop's Fables, 5.2, 16.6
Bell, Nanci, 6.3, 6.4
brain, 1.2, 4.2, 6.1, 6.3, 9.4, 10.1, 13.5, 14.4, 16.3, 24.2
Brain Gym, 18.9, 21.6, 21.7, 21.9
C.U.E., 1.3, 17.10
Caring, LIFESKILL of, Chapter 7
choice, 24.4, 24.8, 25.6, 25.7, 26.2, 26.3, 27.3, 27.6
citizenship, 10.1, 10.2, 12.2, 12.8, 14.3, 18.2, 21.2, 21.3, 25.3
class meetings, 19.4, 19.7, 21.5, 22.12
clutter, 20.3—20.7, 22.6
Common Sense, LIFESKILL of, Chapter 8
community circle, 1.3, 1.4, 2.1, 4.5, 6.6, 7.4, 8.5, 10.3, 10.5, 12.4, 15.6, 17.14, 21.5
community service, 10.4
Cooperation, LIFESKILL of, Chapter 9
Courage, LIFESKILL of, Chapter 10
Curiosity, LIFESKILL of, Chapter 11
Effort, LIFESKILL of, Chapter 12
emotions, 1.3, 4.4, 4.5, 5.3, 5.6, 6.2, 6.5, 10.2, 10.4, 13.7, 17.7, 20.3, 22.4, 26.4, 27.2
emotions and learning, 1.2
environment, 1.2, 2.1, 1.4, 1.5, 1.6, 1.8, 1.9, 3.2, 4.2, 4.10, 6.10, 7.2, 10.3, 11.1, 11.5, 12.2, 12.3, 14.1, 14.3, 14.4, 16.2, 17.11
Flexibility, LIFESKILL of, Chapter 13
Friendship, LIFESKILL of, Chapter 14
full spectrum lighting, 20.3
Gardner, Howard, 8.7, 16.6, 24.2
Gibbs, Jeanne, 2.4, 4.9, 12.1, 12.3, 12.4, 12.7, 17.9, 25.9
Glasser, William, 7.2
Hart, Leslie, 20.2, 25.1, 26.3
ITI model developed by Susan Kovalik, 1.1, 1.2, 8.1, 9.3, 14.2, 15.4, 17.4, 20.3, 25.3
Initiative, LIFESKILL of, Chapter 15
Integrity, LIFESKILL of, Chapter 16
Kovalik, Susan, 1.2, 1.3, 19.2
leadership, 5.2, 10.6, 13.2, 13.3, 16.3
Lifelong Guidelines, list of, 1.3
LIFESKILLS, list of, 1.3, 9.2

Lindamood-Bell Learning Processes, 6.1
mentor, 12.4, 15.5, 20.5
modeling, 2.6, 3.2, 6.10, 7.2, 10.2, 10.3, 11.3, 12.3, 13.2, 14.3, 14.6
multiple intelligences, 16.6, 24.2, 24.4
No Put-Downs, Lifelong Guideline of, Chapter 5
Olsen, Karen D., 11.2, 17.4
Organization, LIFESKILL of, Chapter 17
parent involvement, 2.8, 9.4
Patience, LIFESKILL of, Chapter 18
Pedersen, Jeff, 3.5, 4.6, 6.7, 7.5
peer pressure, 16.1, 16.4
Perseverance, LIFESKILL of, Chapter 19
Personal Best, Lifelong Guideline of, Chapter 6
personality inventory, 16.2
personality preferences, 20.3
Pride, LIFESKILL of, Chapter 20
Problem Solving, LIFESKILL of, Chapter 21
procedures, 4.5, 4.6, 6.6, 11.6, 12.3, 12.5, 12.8, 15.7, 17.9, 25.6, 25.7, 26.6, 26.8
Resourcefulness, LIFESKILL of, Chapter 22
Responsibility, LIFESKILL of, Chapter 23
role model, 2.1, 7.2, 21.10
self-evaluation, 2.1, 4.6, 6.8, 8.2, 8.5, 8.4, 24.7
Sense of Humor, LIFESKILL of, Chapter 24
social/political action, 4.4, 11.6, 17.1, 24.8, 25.3
stress, 5.2, 5.3, 7.1, 10.3, 10.4, 13.1, 17.7, 21.2, 22.4, 27.1, 27.2, 27.5
Susan Kovalik & Associates, 1.2, 3.1
target talk, 2.6, 2.7, 2.8, 9.4, 10.3
T-chart, 3.3, 3.5, 5.5, 9.4, 9.5, 17.8
teachable moment, 3.6, 10.3, 19.3
technology, 12.2, 16.5, 21.1, 25.5
temperament, 20.3
time management, 20.5
TRIBES, 2.4, 12.1, 12.3, 12.4, 12.7, 24.4
Trustworthiness, Lifelong Guideline of, Chapter 2
Truthfulness, Lifelong Guideline of, Chapter 3

Order Form

Books For Educators, Inc.

17051 SE 272nd Street, Suite 18 • Kent, WA 98042-4959
Call toll free! 888-777-9827   Fax: 253-630-7215
E-mail: books4@oz.net
Internet: www.books4educ.com

Hours: M-Th, 6:00 a.m.-4:30 p.m., Pacific Time • Closed Fridays

---

Payment Method

☐ VISA or Master Card   ☐ Check Enclosed Ck #_____

Card # _____   Exp. Date _____

Qty	Title	Price	Total

Please Fax or Mail Authorized Purchase Orders	AZ Residents Only (.05) State Sales Tax	
	WA Residents Only (.082) State Sales Tax	
	Shipping	
PRICES SUBJECT TO CHANGE WITHOUT NOTICE	Total	

25+ of Same Title=Free Shipping
DOES NOT APPLY TO RUSH SERVICE

Name _____

Street Address _____

City _____   State ____   Zip Code _____

Phone (____) _____

Shipping via UPS. Please specify which shipping you prefer.
Add the correct amount above.

Regular Service

☐ Regular Ground UPS Service *(prices listed below)*
- 0-$34.99 = $5.00
- $35-$59.99 = $6.00
- $60-$499.99 = 10% of order
- $500 + = 5% of order

Rush Service Options

☐ 3-Day Service
☐ 2-Day Service
☐ 1-Day Service

} *Please call for rush shipping costs*

Books For Educators, Inc.

17051 SE 272nd Street, Suite 18 • Kent, WA 98042
Call toll free: 888-777-9827 Fax: 253-630-7215
www.books4educ.com   E-mail books4@oz.net
Hours: M-Th, 6:00 a.m.-4:30 p.m. • Pacific Time • Closed Fridays

Ordering Instructions

- VISA or Master Card Accepted
- Authorized Purchase Orders must be Faxed or Mailed

Shipping Information

- Shipping via UPS — Street addresses only (no P.O. box numbers, please)
- Shipping costs listed below

Shipping Costs

Regular Ground UPS Service *(prices listed below)*

0-$34.99 = $5.00
$35-$59.99 = $6.00
$60-$499.99 = 10% of order
$500 + = 5% of order

Rush Service   3-Day Service
                2-Day Service   } *Please call for rush shipping costs*
                1-Day Service

* *Prices subject to change without notice*

Order Form

Books For Educators, Inc.

17051 SE 272nd Street, Suite 18 • Kent, WA 98042-4959
Call toll free! 888-777-9827   Fax: 253-630-7215
E-mail: books4@oz.net
Internet: www.books4educ.com

Hours: M-Th, 6:00 a.m.-4:30 p.m., Pacific Time • Closed Fridays

---

Payment Method

☐ VISA or Master Card   ☐ Check Enclosed Ck #_____

Card #_____   Exp. Date _____

Qty	Title	Price	Total

Please Fax or Mail Authorized Purchase Orders

AZ Residents Only (.05) State Sales Tax _____
WA Residents Only (.082) State Sales Tax _____
Shipping _____
Total _____

PRICES SUBJECT TO CHANGE WITHOUT NOTICE

25+ of Same Title=Free Shipping
DOES NOT APPLY TO RUSH SERVICE

Name _____

Street Address _____

City _____ State _____ Zip Code _____

Phone (   ) _____

Shipping via UPS. Please specify which shipping you prefer.
Add the correct amount above.

Regular Service
☐ Regular Ground UPS Service *(prices listed below)*
   0-$34.99 = $5.00
   $35-$59.99 = $6.00
   $60-$499.99 = 10% of order
   $500 + = 5% of order

Rush Service Options
☐ 3-Day Service
☐ 2-Day Service
☐ 1-Day Service

Please call for rush shipping costs

Books For Educators, Inc.

17051 SE 272nd Street, Suite 18 • Kent, WA 98042
Call toll free: **888-777-9827** Fax: 253-630-7215
www.books4educ.com   E-mail books4@oz.net
Hours: M-Th, 6:00 a.m.-4:30 p.m. • Pacific Time • Closed Fridays

Ordering Instructions

- VISA or Master Card Accepted
- Authorized Purchase Orders must be Faxed or Mailed

Shipping Information

- • Shipping via UPS — Street addresses only (no P.O. box numbers, please)
- Shipping costs listed below

Shipping Costs

Regular Ground UPS Service *(prices listed below)*

0-$34.99 = $5.00
$35-$59.99 = $6.00
$60-$499.99 = 10% of order
$500 + = 5% of order

Rush Service   3-Day Service
2-Day Service   } *Please call for rush shipping costs*
1-Day Service

* *Prices subject to change without notice*